NEW PLAYWRIGHTS

The Best Plays of 2001

SMITH AND KRAUS PUBLISHERS
Contemporary Playwrights / Full-Length Play Anthologies

Humana Festival 1993: The Complete Plays

Humana Festival 1994: The Complete Plays

Humana Festival 1995: The Complete Plays

Humana Festival 1996: The Complete Plays

Humana Festival 1997: The Complete Plays

Humana Festival 1998: The Complete Plays

Humana Festival 1999: The Complete Plays

Humana Festival 2000: The Complete Plays

Humana Festival 2001: The Complete Plays

Humana Festival 2002: The Complete Plays

Humana Festival: 20 One-Act Plays 1976–1996

New Dramatists 2000: The Best Plays by the Graduating Class

New Dramatists 2001: The Best Plays by the Graduating Class

New Playwrights: The Best Plays of 1998

New Playwrights: The Best Plays of 1999

New Playwrights: The Best Plays of 2000

Women Playwrights: The Best Plays of 1992

Women Playwrights: The Best Plays of 1993

Women Playwrights: The Best Plays of 1994

Women Playwrights: The Best Plays of 1995

Women Playwrights: The Best Plays of 1996

Women Playwrights: The Best Plays of 1997

Women Playwrights: The Best Plays of 1998

Women Playwrights: The Best Plays of 1999

Women Playwrights: The Best Plays of 2000

Women Playwrights: The Best Plays of 2001

If you require prepublication information about forthcoming Smith and Kraus books, you may receive our semiannual catalogue, free of charge, by sending your name and address to *Smith and Kraus Catalogue, PO Box 127, Lyme, NH 03768*. Or call us at (800) 895-4331, fax (603) 643-1831. www.SmithKraus.com.

NEW PLAYWRIGHTS

The Best Plays
of 2001

CONTEMPORARY PLAYWRIGHTS
SERIES

SK
A Smith and Kraus Book

A Smith and Kraus Book
Published by Smith and Kraus, Inc.
177 Lyme Road, Hanover, NH 03755
www.SmithKraus.com

Copyright © 2003 by Smith and Kraus, Inc.
All rights reserved
Manufactured in the United States of America
Cover and text design by Julia Gignoux, Freedom Hill Design, Reading, Vermont

First Edition: June 2003
10 9 8 7 6 5 4 3 2 1

The Library of Congress Cataloging-In-Publication Data

New Playwrights: the best plays of 2001. —1st ed.
    p. cm. — (Contemporary playwrights series)

ISBN 1-57525-297-X
1. American drama—20th century. I. Series.
PS634.N416 2000
812'.5408—dc21   00-029707

CONTENTS

FOREWORD

Each year I go to the theater over two hundred times and read several hundred plays I wasn't able to see, for one reason or another. The following pages contain some of my faves from all the plays I saw or read that had a production in 2001. I had to make some really hard decisions, because I saw or read many fine plays. There's this myth, caused largely by the paucity of new plays on Broadway (aka the 700-pound gorilla on the back of the American drama), that our time is a slim-pickins for new plays. In fact, there is an abundance of terrific new plays written and produced each year — you just have to know where to look for them. Fortunately, I do.

I will admit that the choices herein reflect my prejudices as to what "good" playwriting is. I am not a fan of the dominant style favored by many professional theaters, which I can only describe as Anything But Realism. I like good stories, developed in a more or less linear way, about our world, populated by characters I think pretty much anyone could care about. I believe that American drama went astray when it tried to imitate European styles such as surrealism and its culmination, the Theatre of the Absurd. I also believe that it went astray when it focused on putting down its characters rather than illuminating their complexity with compassion and, yes, humor. If you are one of those who wish that American playwrights would write more like Beckett or Genet or their successors, such as Muller and Kroetz, you probably will dislike these plays about as much as most American theatergoers dislike siting through a play by Muller and Kroetz . . .

Some of the playwrights whose work I have included are not exactly new voices. Evan Smith and Douglas Carter Beane have had previous work produced Off Broadway. Two of Mr. Beane's plays, *Advice from a Caterpillar* and *As Bees in Honey Drown,* have actually had commercial Off Broadway productions. Evan Smith's *The Uneasy Chair* was produced by Playwrights Horizons, the same invaluable institution that produced *Psych.* I would venture to say, though, that these writers are not exactly household names (in households which care about drama). The other playwrights whose work I have included are less known than the above two. Mia McCullough I had never heard of until her play *Chagrin Falls* won the American Theatre Critics Association's prestigious Osborn Award, given annually to a truly new playwright. Ms. McCullough is a Chicago playwright, working with a small theater there called Stage Left. If I edit these anthologies every year, I plan to include each year's Osborn Award–winner, so *Chagrin Falls* begins this tradition. Annie Weisman is a California-based playwright, and *Be Aggressive* premiered at the La Jolla Playhouse. At this writing, nobody in New York has plans to produce either of these fine new plays, which doesn't surprise me because women playwrights generally have a harder time getting produced than men.

Nevertheless, these two plays are no less worthy of your attention than the work by their better known male contemporaries. Howard M. Gould's *Diva* has also not had a New York production, which surprises me as it's a brilliant and very funny satire that makes vicious fun of television — you'd think it would appeal to New York theaters and producers.

These six plays represent the best that American drama has to offer. They're wonderful reads; but more important, they are plays audiences will love.

D. L. Lepidus

INTRODUCTION

Do not underestimate the value of an anthology of new American plays tied to a specific calendar year, especially, and, perhaps, conspicuously 2001. After all, a collection of plays gives us a multifaceted impression of people, events, and ideas that captured the imaginations of playwrights, readers, and audiences during the year in question. Moreover, plays are highly compressed renderings of the world — not so much the physical world as a social one. Consequently, a collection of plays is a barometer of culture. It measures our beliefs — and it reflects our aspirations. In some cases, it reveals our deepest desires, our darkest secrets, even our fears and obsessions. It chronicles our condition.

In as much as six plays can encompass seven separate subjects, tell six different stories, unveil six disparate themes, this collection gives us six individual styles of doing those things — and there's value in that. Since the spoken word — predominantly dialogue — is the playwright's palette, we naturally associate the language playwrights use with the human voice. By a weird kind of extrapolation, however, when theater artists talk about a play's voice, they usually mean the sum total of the play's effects — language, theatricality, story, spectacle, and so on. With that conceit in mind, each of these plays offers a distinct voice — one that can be appreciated when read and one that is clearly amplified when experienced in the theater — and there's value in that. Obviously, more people read fiction than read plays; nonetheless, an anthology of plays prompts the reader to explore these voices in a way that invites imagining production — and there's value in that.

It's worth the reminder that this anthology is not a "greatest hits" of 2001, which is not to say that these plays are unpopular. On the contrary, the plays contained in this collection have had distinguished productions during the calendar year, but neither the plays nor their writers are household names. Rather, these are among the next wave of plays to emerge from the fertile ground of American regional, resident, and alternative theater, premiering in

La Jolla and Chicago as well as New York, prompting subsequent productions in such disparate cities as Williamstown, Palo Alto, Pittsburgh, and Coral Gables. That these are not Tony Award or Pulitzer Prize–winning plays is only further proof that the breadth and depth of American playwriting has grown beyond awards just as surely as it has grown beyond Broadway and New York City. Certainly, the quality and scope and diversity of American playwriting today is second to none in the English-speaking world; the exuberance and eclecticism represented in this volume is evidence of it — and there is a value in that too.

One last thought: In a year that will be remembered for a single set of events that changed our national self-perception overnight — literally — and has dominated our national discourse ever since, there is value in knowing what was happening in our culture, what was on people's minds apart from September 11. This volume of plays gives us a glimpse of American preoccupations, behavior, humor — American life — pre-9/11, and yes, there is value in reading that, knowing that, witnessing that life on stage.

Michael Kinghorn
Senior Dramaturg
Arena Stage
Washington, DC

36 VIEWS

By Naomi Iizuka

Only a part of what is perceived comes through the senses
from the object; the remainder always comes from within.

— Matthew Luckiesh, *Visual Illusions*

PLAYWRIGHT'S BIOGRAPHY

Naomi Iizuka's most recent play, *36 Views,* was produced at the Berkeley Repertory Theatre and the Joseph Papp Public Theatre/New York Shakespeare Festival this past season. Her other plays include *Polaroid Stories; Language of Angels; War of the World* (written in collaboration with Anne Bogart and SITI Company); *Aloha, Say the Pretty Girls; Tattoo Girl;* and *Skin.* Ms. Iizuka's plays have been produced by Actors Theatre of Louisville; Campo Santo Theater Company and Intersection for the Arts in San Francisco; Dallas Theatre Center and Undermain Theatre in Dallas; Cobalt Theatre in Chicago; Frontera at Hyde Park in Austin; Printer's Devil and Annex in Seattle; Brooklyn Academy of Music, Soho Rep, and Tectonic Theatre in New York; San Diego's Sledgehammer Theatre; and the Edinburgh Festival. Her plays have been workshopped by San Jose Rep, Geva Theatre in Rochester, Breadloaf, Sundance Theatre Lab, A.S.K. Theater Projects, Public Theatre, McCarter Theatre, Seattle's A Contemporary Theatre, the Bay Area Playwrights' Festival, Midwest PlayLabs, En Garde Arts/P.S. 122, and the New York Theatre Workshop.

Language of Angels is published in *Theatre Forum; War of the Worlds* and *Aloha, Say the Pretty Girls* are published by Smith and Kraus; *Polaroid Stories* is published by Dramatic Publishing; *Tattoo Girl* is included in *From the Other Side of the Century,* published by Sun and Moon; and *Skin* is included in *Out of the Fringe,* published by TCG. *36 Views* is published by Overlook Press.

Ms. Iizuka is currently working on commissions from the Actors Theatre of Louisville, the Kennedy Center, the Children's Theatre of Minneapolis, and the Mark Taper Forum. She is a member of New Dramatists and the recipient of a Whiting Award, a Gerbode Foundation Fellowship, an NEA/TCG Artist-in-Residence grant, a McKnight Fellowship, a PEN Center USA West Award for Drama, Princeton University's Hodder Fellowship, and a Jerome Playwriting Fellowship.

Ms. Iizuka received her BA from Yale University and her MFA from the University of California/San Diego. She has taught playwriting at the University of Iowa and at the University of Texas, Austin.

ORIGINAL PRODUCTION

36 Views was originally produced by the Public Theatre/New York Shakespeare Festival (George C. Wolfe, producer) and by Berkeley Repertory Company (Tony Taccone, artistic director and Susan Medak, managing director).

36 Views was commissioned by A.S.K. Theater Projects in Los Angeles. The play was written under the auspices of Princeton University's Hodder Fellowship and workshopped at the McCarter Theatre, A.S.K. Theater Project's Common Ground Festival, the Public Theatre's New Works Now, Sundance Theatre Lab, and Breadloaf.

CHARACTERS

DARIUS WHEELER: a dealer of Asian arts and antiquities

SETSUKO HEARN: an assistant professor of East Asian literature

JOHN BELL: Darius Wheeler's assistant

CLAIRE TSONG: a restorer of Asian artifacts

ELIZABETH NEWMAN-ORR: a free agent

OWEN MATTIASSEN: the chair of the East Asian Studies Department

36 VIEWS

ACT I
Scene One

Darkness. Suspended in the darkness is a hanging scroll. On the scroll is a painting of a Japanese woman in formal pose, Kamakura era, gilt background, a portrait of a lady. In the shadows is Darius Wheeler. As he speaks, he becomes more and more visible.

DARIUS WHEELER: True story. This is a true story.

I'm in the middle of the Doi Larng mountain range, no-man's land between Thailand and Myanmar — Burma, end of what they call the old Elephant Trail — Kipling country, used to be Now — Well now it's something else.

I'm talking early eighties, opium in every little village east of Mae Hong Son, opium not even the half of it — sapphires, ivory, pigeon-blood rubies from the Mogok Valley — black market all of it, and you could get a bullet in your brain trying to do business with these people. Some hophead Palang with an M-16, he just blows you away on the spot, 'cause he thinks you're a white devil —

Or a ghost —

(The sound of the shakuhachi flute. Setsuko Hearn is revealed in Heian-era kimono, wig, and white face paint. She begins to remove her makeup and her wig.)

DARIUS WHEELER: 'Cause these tribal people, they hate ghosts — Or maybe, maybe he just doesn't like the look in your eye. Human nature, a little cultural miscommunication —

And what are you going to do about it, you're in the middle of what they call the Shan state. There are no maps for this part of the world. You disappear and that's it, you're shit out of luck, head on a pole, tiger meat —

Then again, you go in there, and you meet the right people, and maybe, say, you do some business with these people, and maybe, just maybe you come away with something so beautiful, something so incredibly beautiful, something you'd never find, not in a million years on the outside, and if you're lucky, if you're smart, you get yourself out of there in one piece. So I'm there with my Lahu guide, feeling lucky, tiny Shan village, waiting for my contact, friend of a friend . . .

(Darius Wheeler continues to speak. His voice grows fainter, a distant echo.)

. . . And it's a miracle we even get there, driving through these insane mountain passes, and the whole time I'm thinking: I'm going to die, just wing it into oblivion on one of these switchbacks, one wrong move and that's it, that's all she wrote, my whole life is passing before my eyes, 'cause these Lahu guys, they're driving way too fast, wasted out of their minds on maekong whisky and Jack, and at the time, I, too, am wasted out of my mind, too wasted to see this place for what it is —

Because the thing is, all right, it's beautiful country, indescribably beautiful, and maybe ten white guys have ever seen it before, like no place else in the world, rows and rows of emerald green paddy fields, Pai river coming down from way up north, the water this dark green, deep, the color of tea —

It's nightfall when we get to where we're going, tiny Shan village, tattooed Shan guys standing around with AK-47s, smell of fire and jhoss sticks burning, I pay my guides a few thousand baht for their trouble, light up a smoke, wait for my contact, friend of a friend, hooked up with him in Bangkok, crazy Australian guy — "I hear you have an interest in Asian antiquities" is how it all began, I didn't know this guy from Adam, dumb, in retrospect, very, very dumb, and it's getting darker and darker, and it's dawning on me my situation, when finally I see him in the distance, driving up with his men and I see in the flatbed of his truck he's got all these crates and his men start unloading the crates, prying them open, and I get a look at what he has . . .

(The sound of the shakuhachi flute is joined by the sound of drums. Setsuko Hearn is turning. With each turn, a layer of kimono is removed. The music grows louder, the pace grows faster. The sound of wooden clappers. Silence. The sound of the shakuhachi flute, alone and unadorned.)

DARIUS WHEELER: Unbelievable what I saw that night: Song Dynasty temple paintings, Kushan Period Buddhas almost two thousand years old. He had stuff from Angkor Wat, museum quality, objects there's no way he should've had, and I'm thinking, who are you? Who are you? Because the thing was, this was the thing, I knew, as soon I saw it, as soon as I touched it and held it in my hands, I knew it was real. No question in my mind, it was real, and if I had enough money, it was mine.

(The sound of the shakuhachi flute ends. Setsuko Hearn performs hikinuki *— a Kabuki costume change in which threads are pulled and the outer*

kimono falls away, revealing a new costume underneath. Setsuko Hearn is transformed into an urban, late twentieth-century Western woman. The sound of wooden clappers.)

Scene Two

Evening. Setsuko Hearn and Darius Wheeler in Wheeler's loft space. The space is divided by translucent shoji screens. The Kamakura-era painting, the portrait of the woman in formal pose, is prominently featured. Somewhere else in the space, a party is in progress. Voices, music.

DARIUS WHEELER: Beautiful, isn't it. Everything else I bought that night, I sold, made out like a bandit. This one I never had the heart to sell.

SETSUKO HEARN: Why is that, do you suppose?

DARIUS WHEELER: I don't know, call it an appetite for beauty.

SETSUKO HEARN: I see.

DARIUS WHEELER: Is that such a terrible thing to be? Don't we all gravitate towards beauty? Don't we all crave beautiful things? It's second nature, don't you think. I don't know that we can help ourselves.

SETSUKO HEARN: A philosopher and also quite the renegade.

DARIUS WHEELER: Oh, I don't know about that.

SETSUKO HEARN: I think you're being modest, Mr. Wheeler. I'm guessing you've had more than your share of adventures in the Orient.

DARIUS WHEELER: I have some tales to tell.

SETSUKO HEARN: I'm sure you do, all kinds of wild and woolly tales.

DARIUS WHEELER: Very wild, very woolly, yes.

SETSUKO HEARN: Let me guess: rickshaws and opium dens. A rendezvous with some shady characters on the back streets of Hong Kong, Chinese Triad types, practitioners of Kung Fu. Or perhaps it was on the South China Sea, a foggy night, a sampan full of Malay pirates, inscrutable, ninjalike.

DARIUS WHEELER: Is it my imagination or are you making fun of me?

SETSUKO HEARN: Am I?

DARIUS WHEELER: You know, I think you are.

SETSUKO HEARN: I'm afraid that tales from the Orient, there's this sort of wilted quality to them.

DARIUS WHEELER: Ah.

SETSUKO HEARN: I've offended you.

DARIUS WHEELER: No, on the contrary. The ridicule, the skepticism, I find it kinda bracing. So tell me, I'm curious: am I the biggest idiot you've ever met?

SETSUKO HEARN: Let's just say, you seem to be a man with a weakness for stereotype.

DARIUS WHEELER: You know, you look very familiar to me. I can't say from where. Maybe you look like someone else.

SETSUKO HEARN: Possibly.

DARIUS WHEELER: Jakarta? Sidney?

SETSUKO HEARN: I've never been.

DARIUS WHEELER: Are you sure?

SETSUKO HEARN: Very.

DARIUS WHEELER: Maybe you have an evil twin.

SETSUKO HEARN: Maybe I am an evil twin. People make mistakes, Mr. Wheeler. They misapprehend.

DARIUS WHEELER: I don't know why, but I feel as if I know you.

SETSUKO HEARN: You don't. Trust me. We're perfect strangers.

(The sound of wooden clappers.)

DARIUS WHEELER: Darius Wheeler.

SETSUKO HEARN: Setsuko Hearn.

DARIUS WHEELER: Please forgive me. I'm being a terrible host. Here I let you just stand there without any kind of refreshment, parched, no doubt. What are you drinking? I have this wonderful plum wine in honor of Utagawa. Very light, very seasonal. The guy probably prefers single malt scotch, but what the hell. Plum wine? Good stuff.

SETSUKO HEARN: All right.

DARIUS WHEELER: Plum wine it is.

(Darius Wheeler prepares drinks, cracking ice with a pick.)

DARIUS WHEELER: Somehow I feel like you know a lot more about me than I know about you.

SETSUKO HEARN: Funny, I feel that way, too.

DARIUS WHEELER: So fill me in, Setsuko. Tell me something about yourself.

SETSUKO HEARN: There's nothing really to tell, I'm afraid. My life is very humdrum compared to yours. Very uneventful, very tame.

(Darius Wheeler's hand slips. A cut.)

SETSUKO HEARN: Are you all right?

DARIUS WHEELER: A little cut. It's nothing.

SETSUKO HEARN: Are you sure?

DARIUS WHEELER: Yeah, no, it's fine.

SETSUKO HEARN: You know, I actually found your story very entertaining, Mr. Wheeler.

DARIUS WHEELER: Darius, please, and don't be kind. I'll just think you're feeling sorry for me.

SETSUKO HEARN: No, but I did. Truly. It was very, I don't know, very sort of Hunter S. Thompson meets *Apocalypse Now.* I mean that in the best possible sense.

DARIUS WHEELER: Say no more, please. I think I get the picture. *(Handing Setsuko Hearn her drink.)* Dozo.

SETSUKO HEARN: Thank you.

(The sound of wooden clappers.)

SETSUKO HEARN: *(Approaching the portrait again.)* This really is, it's exquisite. I'm guessing what? Kamakura period?

DARIUS WHEELER: Very good. Takanobu.

SETSUKO HEARN: Rings a bell.

DARIUS WHEELER: Portrait painter. Late twelfth century. Painted on silk. Japanese painting, up to that point, the human face, you know, it was just a mask. A line here, a line there, two dots. Takanobu, he was after this thing, to make something lifelike. To create this thing that was real. Their eyes, everything that was going on in their eyes. The way the light hits the skin. The shape of the mouth. Kampai.

(Darius Wheeler and Setsuko Hearn drink. Light shift. The objects in Wheeler's loft space are revealed. Objects that look like works of art.)

SETSUKO HEARN: It's good. Umeshu.

DARIUS WHEELER: Yes.

SETSUKO HEARN: Ume, it means summer plums. By themselves, they're bitter, but once they've aged in the shochu, the spirits, they become very sweet. It's really, it's lovely. Please, I don't want to keep you from all your other guests.

DARIUS WHEELER: Don't worry. I don't know half the people out there. Trust me, I won't be missed. So what did you think of the show tonight? What do you think of Utagawa's work?

SETSUKO HEARN: I like it. I like the sensibility. I like the way he mixes Asian and Western forms, the way he deploys classical techniques, and yet his vision is so unconventional, so contemporary in a way — I'm curious: how do you know Utagawa?

DARIUS WHEELER: I don't. I've never met the man. I'm hosting this little get-together as a favor for an old friend.

SETSUKO HEARN: That's nice of you.

DARIUS WHEELER: I have my moments. He, like you, is quite a fan.

SETSUKO HEARN: And you are not.

DARIUS WHEELER: No.

SETSUKO HEARN: Not Oriental enough for you?

DARIUS WHEELER: It's just one white man's humble opinion.

SETSUKO HEARN: You're a traditionalist.

DARIUS WHEELER: Let's just say I have high standards.

(The sound of wooden clappers.)

SETSUKO HEARN: *(Approaching an art object.)* Chinese?

DARIUS WHEELER: Liao Dynasty. The goddess Guanyin. That's an Undayana Buddha, eighth century Korean, Silla Dynasty, gilt bronze. That's a, that's a Muromachi ink painting. Sixteenth century, Unkoku school, you can see what they call *suiboku,* or splashed ink technique, very unusual, very abstract. I got it at a private auction in Kyoto. No catalogue, no pre-viewing, some of the stuff is in really bad shape, but every so often, you find a gem. I got it for a song. Do you like it?

SETSUKO HEARN: Very much.

DARIUS WHEELER: Here, wait, let me show you, I want to show you something else.

(Darius Wheeler retrieves a jade figure from its case. The sound of the shakuhachi flute begins.)

DARIUS WHEELER: Jade. Sung Dynasty era, over nine hundred years old. Very rare. Because the thing about jade, it's meant to be held, you see, and what it does, it warms to your skin, human touch, it alters the stone, there's a kind of chemical reaction, it actually changes the color of the stone. With each touch it changes over time, almost imperceptible, impossible to replicate. Very old jade like this, it comes in these translucent colors I can't describe, beautiful, unimaginably beautiful.

(Darius holds out the jade figure.)

DARIUS WHEELER: Here. Feel.

(Setsuko Hearn touches the jade. Their hands touch. Darius Wheeler and Setsuko Hearn begin to recede from view.)

Scene Three

Light on John Bell. The sound of the shakuhachi flute continues. As John Bell speaks, Claire Tsong is revealed. She's reading from a transcript. John Bell is the voice behind the words she reads.

JOHN BELL: A list of beautiful things:
   The curve of a lover's neck, delicate, white.
   The touch of a lover's fingertips.
   The weight of a lover's hair, the scent, clove and sandalwood.
   The rustle of silk undone,
   Warm breath against one's skin —
   (The sound of the shakuhachi flute ends.)

Scene Four

A desk is revealed. The desk is covered with papers, catalogues, slides, pens, paints, paint brushes, books. John Bell starts sifting through papers on the desk. Claire Tsong approaches him. The sound of wooden clappers.

CLAIRE TSONG: John?

JOHN BELL: Claire? What are you doing here? You're not supposed to be here.

CLAIRE TSONG: Where's Utagawa?

JOHN BELL: I don't know, I don't know, I don't know where he is.

CLAIRE TSONG: Did you see him at the show?

JOHN BELL: No, he was running late. I got a message from his assistant. He was supposed to come directly here.

CLAIRE TSONG: Looking for something?

JOHN BELL: I wrote his assistant's number on this little piece of paper. I thought I left it here. Goddamnit.

CLAIRE TSONG: *(Holding up the transcript.)* What's this?

JOHN BELL: Nothing.

CLAIRE TSONG: Where's it from?

JOHN BELL: Nowhere. *(Taking the transcript.)* Can you please not touch my stuff, please, Claire, thank you.

CLAIRE TSONG: John —

JOHN BELL: I have to go.

CLAIRE TSONG: Oh come on, John. John —

(John Bell exits. Elizabeth Newman-Orr enters.)

CLAIRE TSONG: Cheers.

ELIZABETH NEWMAN-ORR: It's so crowded out there. I needed some air. I was feeling a little flushed. Do you happen to know where Mr. Wheeler is by any chance?

CLAIRE TSONG: No clue.

ELIZABETH NEWMAN-ORR: I'm an old friend of his.

CLAIRE TSONG: He's got a lot of old friends. He's a very friendly guy. Make yourself at home. I'm sure he wouldn't mind.

ELIZABETH NEWMAN-ORR: Thanks.

(Elizabeth Newman-Orr scans the works of art.)

ELIZABETH NEWMAN-ORR: So what do you like?

(Claire Tsong studies the art objects and then picks one.)

CLAIRE TSONG: I like this. It's nice. A little showy, but nice.

ELIZABETH NEWMAN-ORR: Is it real?

CLAIRE TSONG: I guess it all depends on how you define real.

ELIZABETH NEWMAN-ORR: That's being a little coy, don't you think?

CLAIRE TSONG: It's old. It's painted by the guy it's supposed to be painted by. I guess that makes it real. Most of the time with a fake, it's pretty obvious. There's something really stupid going on, something that doesn't make sense. Wrong materials, shoddy workmanship.

ELIZABETH NEWMAN-ORR: And what is it you do? I don't think you said.

CLAIRE TSONG: I'm an artist actually. Mixed media.

ELIZABETH NEWMAN-ORR: That's a big, broad category. It could mean all kinds of things.

CLAIRE TSONG: Yes.

ELIZABETH NEWMAN-ORR: *(Referring to another art object.)* Real?

CLAIRE TSONG: Iffy.

ELIZABETH NEWMAN-ORR: It looks real.

CLAIRE TSONG: Lots of things look real. You go to a museum, it all looks real. And don't get me started on auction houses. What a shell game those guys are running. You wouldn't believe the crap that cycles through, third-rate counterfeits somebody paid a lot of money for, and now they gotta pawn off on somebody else, or else end up eating the loss.

ELIZABETH NEWMAN-ORR: You sound like an expert.

CLAIRE TSONG: It's not about expertise. It's all about the eye.

ELIZABETH NEWMAN-ORR: The eye? That sounds so hoodoo.

(The sound of the shakuhachi flute begins. In the foreground, Setsuko Hearn

and Darius Wheeler begin to come into view. They reconstruct the pose that they were last in. The pose becomes real, fleshed out.)

CLAIRE TSONG: It's like it's physical, you know, I'm talking about a physical sensation, an instinct. It's like there's an invisible thread between you and this thing — I don't know. It's hard to explain, it's not objective, it's irrational, it's completely irrational. You can't quantify or predict it. You just know, all of a sudden you know.

(The sound of wooden clappers.)

Scene Five

The sound of the shakuhachi flute continues. John Bell and Owen Matthiassen appear. John Bell, Owen Matthiassen, Claire Tsong, Elizabeth Newman-Orr, Darius Wheeler, and Setsuko Hearn are figures in a woodblock print, flesh figures in a floating world. The sound of wooden clappers. Darius Wheeler and Claire Tsong see each other. It's a moment of nagashime, a sideways glance as seen in old woodblock prints of Kabuki actors. The sound of wooden clappers. The sound of the shakuhachi flute ends.

Scene Six

The woodblock print instantly dissolves into movement. Claire Tsong, Elizabeth Newman-Orr, and John Bell exit in different directions. The sound of a party in progress.

OWEN MATTHIASSEN: Darius —

DARIUS WHEELER: Owen —

SETSUKO HEARN: Dr. Matthiassen —

OWEN MATTHIASSEN: Setsuko, my dear, I'm so glad you made it. Utagawa should be here any minute now. Darius, what are you drinking?

DARIUS WHEELER: Plum wine.

OWEN MATTHIASSEN: Umeshu, how delightful.

DARIUS WHEELER: You're in fine spirits, Owen.

OWEN MATTHIASSEN: I am, I am. I'll have a drop, if it's not too much of a bother.

DARIUS WHEELER: Not at all.

(Darius Wheeler prepares a drink.)

OWEN MATTHIASSEN: Darius, you've outdone yourself. I just ran into an old friend of mine from Waseda I haven't seen in ages, and some woman from the consulate, turns out I knew her father. I see you've met my brilliant young colleague.

DARIUS WHEELER: I have. I had no idea.

SETSUKO HEARN: Dr. Matthiassen is too kind.

OWEN MATTHIASSEN: Dr. Hearn is a shining star in our department. We're incredibly lucky to have her join our ranks. Almost lost her to Stanford, you know.

SETSUKO HEARN: You are really, really too kind.

(Darius Wheeler gives Owen Matthiassen his drink.)

OWEN MATTHIASSEN: What happened to your hand?

DARIUS WHEELER: Nothing.

OWEN MATTHIASSEN: Darius, you're hemorrhaging.

DARIUS WHEELER: I'm fine, Owen, I'm fine. *(To Setsuko Hearn.)* So what are you working on exactly?

OWEN MATTHIASSEN: Dr. Hearn's field of expertise is writing from the eleventh century, diaries, memoirs, pillow books written by women of the Heian era. How the writer speaks in her most private moments, depictions of her interior life, the private self.

DARIUS WHEELER: That doesn't sound humdrum at all.

(Setsuko Hearn turns away, approaching an art object.)

OWEN MATTHIASSEN: Humdrum? Hardly. Where did you get that idea? On the contrary, it's fascinating, the feminine vernacular in the golden age of Japanese literature. Some wonderful women writing back then: Sei Shonagon, Izumi Shikibu —

DARIUS WHEELER: Lady Murasaki.

SETSUKO HEARN: Very good.

OWEN MATTHIASSEN: *The Tale of Genji.* Darius, I'm impressed. Have you read it?

DARIUS WHEELER: I have not.

OWEN MATTHIASSEN: Oh, but you must.

SETSUKO HEARN: You'd like it.

DARIUS WHEELER: Would I?

OWEN MATTHIASSEN: It's very engaging. Romance, intrigue. Some fine translations out there, Waley's always good, accessible, surprisingly modern, I find.

DARIUS WHEELER: Owen, I haven't read a book in over a decade.

OWEN MATTHIASSEN: Nonsense.

DARIUS WHEELER: Sad, but true. I'm a philistine, Owen. You've just always been too polite to notice. I had no idea I was conversing with such a shining star. I have to say, I feel a little out of my depth in such learned company.

OWEN MATTHIASSEN: Oh you do not. Don't listen to a word he says. *(Joining Setsuko Hearn.)* Breathtaking, isn't it? Nobody has this kind of stuff anymore. I don't know how he does it. Fantastic pieces, uncanny really. Good eye. I have to say, I take a little pride in my contribution to all of it. I've known Darius for ages, you know.

SETSUKO HEARN: You studied with Dr. Matthiassen?

OWEN MATTHIASSEN: Oh no no no. Darius has never been much for the academic life, I'm afraid.

DARIUS WHEELER: I was a lazy bum, dropped out of school, never made it through my second year.

SETSUKO HEARN: It doesn't seem to have held you back.

OWEN MATTHIASSEN: An understatement, my dear, you have no idea. He's done fabulously well. I always knew he would.

DARIUS WHEELER: Owen is an eternal optimist.

OWEN MATTHIASSEN: I'm a fantastic judge of human nature. The man leads a charmed life. I envy you, Darius, I do, surrounded by things most of us only see in picture books. A nice life. I could think of a lot worse. You have an eye for beautiful things.

DARIUS WHEELER: I like to think so.

SETSUKO HEARN: You don't care for Utagawa's work, however.

OWEN MATTHIASSEN: Darius despises contemporary art. He's very contrary, willfully anachronistic.

DARIUS WHEELER: I like his *shunga.*

OWEN MATTHIASSEN: Ah, yes, his erotic prints.

SETSUKO HEARN: And why is that?

OWEN MATTHIASSEN: They're very, very vulgar.

DARIUS WHEELER: Exactly. They're honest. They're getting at something basic and real.

OWEN MATTHIASSEN: The more graphic, the less beautiful, I find.

DARIUS WHEELER: I don't think Utagawa's about beauty, Owen. I think that's precisely the problem. I think he's about making a point. He's about ideas, his art is all about ideas, ideas about ideas.

(Enter John Bell.)

OWEN MATTHIASSEN: I disagree entirely.

JOHN BELL: Mr. Wheeler —

DARIUS WHEELER: It's just a series of abstractions tarted up to look like art.

OWEN MATTHIASSEN: I disagree, I have to disagree.

JOHN BELL: Mr. Wheeler —

DARIUS WHEELER: I mean the guy's got craft, I'll give him that. Technically, he's great, but what he has to say — I wonder why it is that he can't just make a beautiful thing and leave it at that.

SETSUKO HEARN: I wonder what you mean when you say beautiful.

DARIUS WHEELER: Beautiful means beautiful.

SETSUKO HEARN: That's something of a dead end, don't you think?

DARIUS WHEELER: No, no I don't.

SETSUKO HEARN: It's so absolute.

DARIUS WHEELER: Of course, it is. It has to be. What are you left with otherwise?

(The sound of wooden clappers.)

JOHN BELL: Mr. Wheeler —

DARIUS WHEELER: I'm sorry — John, what is it?

JOHN BELL: I just spoke with Utagawa-san's assistant just now, and it seems — well, it seems that he won't be able to make it this evening.

OWEN MATTHIASSEN: What do you mean? I spoke to his assistant on the phone just this afternoon.

JOHN BELL: Something came up apparently, some sudden obligation he couldn't get out of. He sends his sincere regrets.

OWEN MATTHIASSEN: I see. How disappointing. I was so looking forward to meeting the man in person. Although I guess I shouldn't be surprised. I hear he's somewhat of a recluse, you know. Poor Darius, putting this whole evening together, loathing his work as you do. We should tell the other guests.

DARIUS WHEELER: I'll take care of it.

OWEN MATTHIASSEN: Well, there's nothing to be done. Another time perhaps. Life is full of the unexpected, best to be flexible, I find. At any rate, what a delight, my dear, to find you here. Here, let's go this way. I want you to see this, mandala painting, Nepalese, thirteenth century, when I first saw the thing, I was completely stupefied.

(Owen Matthiassen and Setsuko Hearn exit. Darius Wheeler and John Bell remain. The sound of wooden clappers.)

Scene Seven

The party begins to dissolve. Guests begin to exit into the night. Darius Wheeler begins to exit after Owen Matthiassen and Setsuko Hearn. Enter Elizabeth Newman-Orr.

DARIUS WHEELER: All right let's wind this up, shall we. John, can you make an announcement. The guest of honor is a no show. Everybody just go home.

JOHN BELL: Mr. Wheeler, one more thing.

DARIUS WHEELER: Yeah, John, what? What is it?

ELIZABETH NEWMAN-ORR: Mr. Wheeler, Elizabeth Newman-Orr. It's a pleasure. You have a beautiful space here, so many beautiful things.

DARIUS WHEELER: Thank you. Do I know you?

ELIZABETH NEWMAN-ORR: I'm a friend of Utagawa's. I'm actually, I'm more of a friend of a friend, really an acquaintance, I'm more of an acquaintance.

DARIUS WHEELER: I see.

ELIZABETH NEWMAN-ORR: I lie.

DARIUS WHEELER: I see.

ELIZABETH NEWMAN-ORR: I'm uninvited. I know no one. You've found me out, I'm afraid.

DARIUS WHEELER: I won't tell. Now if you'll excuse me.

ELIZABETH NEWMAN-ORR: Mr. Wheeler, if I could, I was speaking just now with your assistant. I was hoping you and I could find a time to meet, tomorrow perhaps. I have a small matter I was hoping to discuss with you.

DARIUS WHEELER: Tomorrow's kinda tight for me.

ELIZABETH NEWMAN-ORR: I believe you'll find it worth your while.

DARIUS WHEELER: And should I trust your judgment?

ELIZABETH NEWMAN-ORR: I'm a woman of unerring judgment.

DARIUS WHEELER: I'm intrigued. Should I be intrigued?

ELIZABETH NEWMAN-ORR: I think so. I'll be glad to explain everything at length. Tomorrow perhaps?

DARIUS WHEELER: So eager. All right, look, why don't you set something up with John. Now if you'll excuse me.

ELIZABETH NEWMAN-ORR: Of course. Good night, Mr. Wheeler.

(Elizabeth Newman-Orr and John Bell exit. The sound of a party breaking up. Kurogo, stage assistants in black overcostumes, remove props and scenery. The sound of wooden clappers. Owen Matthiassen appears holding a portfolio.)

OWEN MATTHIASSEN: Darius, a word with you.

Scene Eight

Light shift. Late evening. Owen Matthiassen and Darius Wheeler occupy a sliver of light.

DARIUS WHEELER: Where did Dr. Hearn go?

OWEN MATTHIASSEN: She had to leave, the lateness of the hour.

DARIUS WHEELER: What a pity.

OWEN MATTHIASSEN: She said to tell you that she had a lovely time. Marvelous girl, isn't she. Very smart, humbling really, and so young. My God, I remember being that young. I remember it vividly. How did I get to be so old?

DARIUS WHEELER: You're not that old.

OWEN MATTHIASSEN: I'm ancient. It's ridiculous.

DARIUS WHEELER: You're young at heart.

OWEN MATTHIASSEN: Don't condescend, Darius. It's not nice.

DARIUS WHEELER: What do you have there, Owen? One of Utagawa's sly little "masterpieces."

OWEN MATTHIASSEN: Out of my price range, I'm afraid. No no, something else. Very exciting. More to your taste, I assure you. Here take a look. Stumbled upon it today, private gallery, little hole in the wall, one of those things, at the right place, at the right time.

(A woodblock print is revealed. A reproduction of a woodblock print. Larger than life. Owen Matthiassen and Darius Wheeler appear as tiny human figures in the foreground of Hokusai's landscape.)

OWEN MATTHIASSEN: Hokusai, for Chrissakes. When I first saw it, I couldn't believe my eyes. Fuji from Kajikazawa. First edition, not cheap, but fair, more than fair, and all things considered, in pretty good shape, some water damage, it's true, and the color's faded a bit, but other than that — I mean, good Lord, almost two hundred years old. Paper. Can you imagine. It's a miracle it hasn't sustained worse damage. Survival is a kind of beautiful thing, isn't it. After all these years. Look at the mountain through the mist. Gorgeous, just gorgeous.

DARIUS WHEELER: Owen, this is a fake.

OWEN MATTHIASSEN: What are you talking about?

DARIUS WHEELER: It's good. I mean, whoever did this is pretty good.

OWEN MATTHIASSEN: Well, I know you're the expert, but I like to think I know a thing or two. For God's sakes, I've been collecting prints for years. Look at the watermarks, the publisher's seal. The artist's hand is proof enough, the vigor and delicacy of the lines, the weight of detail. I'm telling you, I've examined this print. I've studied it. I know what it looks like. I know what it should look like.

DARIUS WHEELER: It's nice, Owen.

OWEN MATTHIASSEN: Nice? It's not just nice. It's spot on.

DARIUS WHEELER: Whoever the artist is, he knows what he's doing. The only problem is: whoever he is, he's not Hokusai. Look at the color. Look at it, really look.

(The colors of the woodblock print slowly transform, becoming unnaturally bright and lurid.)

DARIUS WHEELER: The color is a dead giveaway. It's all wrong. I don't care how much you distress it, underneath the stain, whatever this is, tea, coffee grounds, ash, it's way too bright, way too brassy. Look at these blues. Aniline pigment, artificial, inorganic, imported to Japan from Germany. This print dates — or should date — from the 1830s. This kind of pigment wasn't introduced into Japan until the mid-1850s. We're talking twenty years after the fact. The print's nice, Owen. It just happens to be fake.

(Owen Matthiassen fades away. The sound of wooden clappers. Light on Claire Tsong in a distant corner of the space.)

Scene Nine

A disclaimer in fine print.

CLAIRE TSONG: The vendor will not be responsible for the correctness of description, authenticity, or any defect or fault in or concerning any article, and makes no warranty whatever, but will sell each object exactly as is, without recourse.

(The sound of wooden clappers.)

CLAIRE TSONG: Always read the fine print. There is always fine print.

(The sound of the shakuhachi flute. Claire Tsong and the woodblock print fade away. Darius Wheeler remains.)

Scene Ten

Pre-dawn light. The sound of the shakuhachi flute continues. A kurogo, a stage assistant, enters. His face is wrapped in black fabric. He carries a large rectangular panel covered by a drop cloth. He removes the cloth, revealing an Edo-period screen. On the screen is a painting of a garden in autumn. The sound of wooden clappers.

The kurogo *begins removing his black overcostume. Darius Wheeler goes to the desk and notices the transcript Claire Tsong was looking through earlier. He picks it up and reads. Setsuko Hearn is revealed in a sliver of light.*

SETSUKO HEARN: A list of beautiful things:
>The curve of a lover's neck,
>The touch of a lover's fingertips,
>The weight of a lover's hair, the scent,
>The rustle of silk undone,
>Your tongue, your lips,
>The taste, salt and wet,
>Warm breath against one's skin.
>*(The* kurogo *removes the last piece of fabric covering his face. The* kurogo *is revealed to be John Bell. The sound of wooden clappers. The sound of the shakuhachi flute ends. Setsuko Hearn vanishes. Darius Wheeler exits.)*

Scene Eleven

The day after the party. Midmorning. Wheeler's loft space. John Bell is examining the screen that he unwrapped in the previous scene. Claire Tsong is packing up, putting away the dropcloth along with various paints and tools.

CLAIRE TSONG: All right, you're not listening, or maybe I'm not making myself clear. All this is, at the end of the day, is fine furnishing, bric-a-brac for the leisure class.

JOHN BELL: Last I looked, Claire, it was called art.

CLAIRE TSONG: I'm telling you, pal, it's all just capital.

JOHN BELL: Spare me, please.

CLAIRE TSONG: OK, you know what your problem is? You romanticize this stuff. You spend all your time surrounded by all this "art," and it's affecting your brain. Strip it all away, and all you have is money jazzed up to make you think it's something more than money — which it's not. That it has some kind of deep, spiritual aura because it's art — which it doesn't.

JOHN BELL: I know you don't believe that.

CLAIRE TSONG: I believe all kinds of things.

(The sound of wooden clappers.)

CLAIRE TSONG: So? What do you think? How does it look?

JOHN BELL: It's nice, Claire. This is really nice work.

CLAIRE TSONG: Is this a surprise?

JOHN BELL: What do you want me to say?

CLAIRE TSONG: That I'm brilliant, a genius, the best.

JOHN BELL: You're brilliant, a genius, the best.

CLAIRE TSONG: Fuck you.

JOHN BELL: You are, Claire. The restorations are really, they're great. I know what this looked like before.

CLAIRE TSONG: Trashed. A lost cause.

JOHN BELL: Pretty much.

(John Bell writes Claire a check.)

JOHN BELL: Listen, Wheeler has some other screens he'd like you to take a look at. Minor stuff: mildew damage, fading, standard wear and tear.

CLAIRE TSONG: Wheeler can kiss my ass. Like I sit around waiting for him to kick down some crap for me to tinker with. Like I don't have better things to do.

JOHN BELL: Claire, it's way too early in the day.

CLAIRE TSONG: I don't even know why you still work for that guy. He's like the evil empire.

JOHN BELL: You work for him, too.

CLAIRE TSONG: I'm an independent contractor. There's a difference. I'm my own little business of which I am the boss. I do the work because I choose to.

JOHN BELL: Why? I mean, why do you choose to work for Wheeler?

CLAIRE TSONG: *(Taking the check.)* Imp of the perverse. I don't know. Who knows. I'm a masochist, I guess. Besides I'm subsidizing my own art — look, don't change the subject. I'm trying to educate you. Somebody has to. This is about your future. These are economic realities I'm talking about.

(Claire Tsong retrieves a can of spray paint. She begins to shake it.)

CLAIRE TSONG: How much does Wheeler pay you, if you don't mind me asking.

JOHN BELL: I don't like talking about money, Claire.

CLAIRE TSONG: Why?

JOHN BELL: It makes me feel awkward.

CLAIRE TSONG: Guilty?

JOHN BELL: No. I don't know. Maybe a little. I don't know.

CLAIRE TSONG: You act like it's a dirty word, and it's not. It's just a thing like any other thing. Don't mystify it. Don't do that to yourself. You should've quit a long time ago. It's so stupid. It doesn't make any sense.

(Claire Tsong aims the spray paint can at the screen she just restored.)

JOHN BELL: Claire —

CLAIRE TSONG: Would I be destroying it?

JOHN BELL: Claire –

CLAIRE TSONG: Or restoring it? How would I be affecting its market value? But now here's the thing: what if I happened to make it a better painting? Or better yet, what if you couldn't tell the difference?

JOHN BELL: Claire, please —

CLAIRE TSONG: Do you really want to spend the rest of your life worrying about market value? Because frankly, I think you're a lot more interesting than that.

JOHN BELL: Wait —

(Claire Tsong sprays. John Bell blocks the screen with his body. A flower of paint blooms on his shirt.)

CLAIRE TSONG: You're brilliant, for one thing. It's like your brain is a very big thing, and it's filled with all this knowledge. You try to hide it, but I'm so onto your game. You know all this stuff, you don't even let on the half of it.

JOHN BELL: Yeah? What stuff do I know?

CLAIRE TSONG: Art, for one. Literature. Languages, you're like fluent in all these languages. What do you speak? No, wait, let me guess: Japanese. Uh huh. Korean? Right. Chinese — how many dialects? No, wait, let me: Mandarin, Hunan, Cantonese —

JOHN BELL: My Cantonese is really, really basic.

CLAIRE TSONG: Oh my God, John, stop it. You're learned. Step to it, buddy, you're really learned.

JOHN BELL: I have a master's in East Asian studies and an unfinished thesis that's never going to get finished. I happen to know a few languages. I also happen to have a drawerful of unfinished novels, and once upon a time, a long time ago, I played the French horn.

CLAIRE TSONG: You're a Renaissance man.

JOHN BELL: Jack of all trades, master of none.

CLAIRE TSONG: John, honey, you gotta work on your self-esteem. You're withering on the vine here. Wheeler's using you. Cheap, overeducated labor. What are you anyway?

JOHN BELL: What am I? I don't know, Claire. That's so existential.

CLAIRE TSONG: What's your title?

JOHN BELL: I'm an assistant.

CLAIRE TSONG: And what does that mean exactly?

JOHN BELL: Uh, that I assist. Look, Claire, I like my job. And I like Wheeler.

(Enter Darius Wheeler.)

JOHN BELL: The guy's like a legend, broke all the rules, and I guess I kinda respect that.

CLAIRE TSONG: Please. Dealers are the scum of the earth, and Wheeler's in a
class all his own.

JOHN BELL: He's complex.

CLAIRE TSONG: He's a prick.

JOHN BELL: He's a complicated guy.

CLAIRE TSONG: He's a self-absorbed, narcissistic prick. He's also a liar, a con
artist, and a thief.

(Enter Elizabeth Newman-Orr. The sound of wooden clappers.)

DARIUS WHEELER: I was at this party once in Boston, and this attractive Asian
woman comes up to me from out of nowhere, and she just starts in on
me — calls me a liar, a con artist, and a few other choice names I'm not
going to share in mixed company, and people, you know, they're starting to turn around and look, and before I know it, right, she's hurling
her drink at me, hard, you know, in my face, and I hear the glass shatter, and the room goes silent, and I feel a heat and a kind of stinging,
and I reach up and touch my face, and I look at my hand, and I see there's
this red liquid all over my fingers, and I'm thinking to myself, Jesus Christ,
I'm bleeding. Turned out to be tomato juice. But for a second or two, I
thought it was blood.

(The sound of wooden clappers. John Bell and Claire Tsong exit.)

Scene Twelve

Late morning. Darius Wheeler and Elizabeth Newman-Orr remain.

DARIUS WHEELER: The world is full of crackpots. Most of them are harmless,
but then again you never know.

ELIZABETH NEWMAN-ORR: So what was the story? Who was she?

DARIUS WHEELER: Who knows. A kook.

ELIZABETH NEWMAN-ORR: Your reputation, I have to say, precedes you.

DARIUS WHEELER: And what exactly have you heard?

ELIZABETH NEWMAN-ORR: Nothing but praise.

DARIUS WHEELER: Is that right?

ELIZABETH NEWMAN-ORR: Praise tempered by maybe just a little bit of envy.

DARIUS WHEELER: Look, I don't need to tell you, this business is full of thwarted souls with nothing good to say about anyone. I'm a lucky man. Some people have a problem with that. Don't get me wrong, I'm good at what I do, but I'm also very lucky. That's all it really is, you know. Dumb luck.

ELIZABETH NEWMAN-ORR: That's very modest of you.

DARIUS WHEELER: It's the God's honest truth.

ELIZABETH NEWMAN-ORR: How homespun.

(Elizabeth Newman-Orr moves toward the screen from the previous scene, the screen that Claire Tsong restored.)

ELIZABETH NEWMAN-ORR: This is new.

DARIUS WHEELER: It's a beauty, isn't it? Just came in this morning. Edo era. Museum quality, in mint condition.

ELIZABETH NEWMAN-ORR: What kind of restorations?

DARIUS WHEELER: Hardly any at all.

(The sound of wooden clappers.)

DARIUS WHEELER: Interested?

ELIZABETH NEWMAN-ORR: Another time perhaps.

DARIUS WHEELER: By then it'll be gone. It never pays to wait. It's the nature of the business. Things move, they get traded, they circulate.

ELIZABETH NEWMAN-ORR: I guess I'll just have to take my chances. I'm curious: do you ever find yourself getting attached to a particular object, something very special?

DARIUS WHEELER: Rarely.

ELIZABETH NEWMAN-ORR: I would find that hard, I think.

DARIUS WHEELER: Things come and go in this life. It's best not to get too attached.

ELIZABETH NEWMAN-ORR: That's very Zen of you.

DARIUS WHEELER: What can I say? I'm a Zen kinda guy. Now what can I do for you today?

ELIZABETH NEWMAN-ORR: Suppose there were a painting, very ancient, very rare, part of a large, private collection in Hong Kong. A Taiwanese banker and his Austrian wife.

DARIUS WHEELER: Villa on Lugard Road. A smallish collection, some nice lacquerware, Imari, tasteful, very tasteful.

ELIZABETH NEWMAN-ORR: Keeping track of the bodies?

DARIUS WHEELER: I'm a dealer, Ms. Orr. You never know when someone's going to want to sell.

ELIZABETH NEWMAN-ORR: You know the painting I'm talking about.

DARIUS WHEELER: I might.

ELIZABETH NEWMAN-ORR: Suppose my clients purchased this painting in a private sale, and it turned out, unbeknownst to either seller or purchaser, that the painting was a national treasure.

DARIUS WHEELER: Ah.

ELIZABETH NEWMAN-ORR: If authorities were to get wind of the transaction, which they would, if we were to go through more traditional channels of sale and transfer, the painting would need to be returned to its country of origin.

DARIUS WHEELER: It's tricky these days.

ELIZABETH NEWMAN-ORR: I was given your name.

DARIUS WHEELER: Given my name by whom?

ELIZABETH NEWMAN-ORR: I'd rather not say.

DARIUS WHEELER: Ever mysterious. I like that quality in a woman. In a business associate, I like it less so. Now if you'll excuse me.

ELIZABETH NEWMAN-ORR: Can't we be candid with one another, Mr. Wheeler? I'd like that so much. It would make everything so much easier.

DARIUS WHEELER: What are we talking about?

ELIZABETH NEWMAN-ORR: I think you have an idea.

DARIUS WHEELER: Why don't you spell it out for me.

ELIZABETH NEWMAN-ORR: The discreet transport of an object from one place to another.

(The sound of wooden clappers.)

DARIUS WHEELER: Ah. I see. Well, now OK this is the thing, Ms. Orr, about the part of the world we're dealing with here, because it's all a little cowboys and Indians, and that can go a lot of ways. You're talking tariffs and tea money, never mind some government type getting a bug up his ass, and throwing a wrench in the works. Now it used to be, you could go in, pick up almost anything. Nowadays, it's a different story. These people, they've gotten very touchy about their culture. They see us raiding their temples, pilfering their Buddhas, and they get a little pissed off, understandably perhaps, and they confiscate our property, and more than that, they throw people like myself in jail for long and indeterminate prison sentences — have you ever spent time in a third world jail, Ms. Orr?

ELIZABETH NEWMAN-ORR: Ten percent of the purchase price placed in an offshore account.

DARIUS WHEELER: You have got to be kidding me.

ELIZABETH NEWMAN-ORR: Fifteen percent.

DARIUS WHEELER: Twenty percent. Half up front, half upon the object's arrival.

ELIZABETH NEWMAN-ORR: I think — I think that can be arranged.

(Elizabeth Newman-Orr exits.)

Scene Thirteen

The sound of the shakuhachi flute begins. Darius Wheeler returns to his desk and picks up the transcript he was reading earlier. He scans the pages. Setsuko Hearn appears in a sliver of light. As she speaks, she becomes more visible, more real.

SETSUKO HEARN: No rain tonight, no moon, the air is perfectly still
Not even the faintest breeze stirs the leaves.
In the pool in the garden below, carp swim beneath the surface —
Flashes of white in the murky green
Their bellies slick and wet —
The tickle of waterweed
The soft wet moss —
The curve of your neck, your fingertips
The rustle of silk undone —
Your mouth, your tongue
Your lips, the taste of your lips, salt, wet
The warmth of your breath against my skin
And I am seized with sudden longing.
(The sound of wooden clappers. The sound of the shakuhachi flute ends. Setsuko Hearn vanishes.)

Scene Fourteen

Enter John Bell carrying files.

DARIUS WHEELER: John?

JOHN BELL: Yes?

DARIUS WHEELER: What's this?

JOHN BELL: What's what?

DARIUS WHEELER: *(Holding up the transcript.)* This. What's this?

JOHN BELL: Oh. That. It's a, it's a —
(The sound of wooden clappers.)

Scene Fifteen

A history of origins.

JOHN BELL: It's a transcription — Of a manuscript. It turned up in a private library, and was sent to us for appraisal just the other day. I've been meaning to tell you — I've been translating it, looking into its provenance. Japanese, eleventh century Heian era — A memoir or pillow book. The author remains nameless, hard biographical data are, as is often the case, scant.

The earliest known owner of the document appears to have been a Dutch trader and sometime scholar by the name of Van Rijn, stationed on the island of Dejima in the seventeenth century. There's an oblique mention of it in a letter he wrote to his wife. (I have it on file.) How or why he disposed of it remains unclear. Regardless of the disposition, the document disappears for almost a century, resurfacing again in the first decade of the eighteenth century, when it was transferred along with various other scrolls —

To a money lender in Edo — whose eldest son lost it one night in a single game of chance to an affluent sake maker by the name of Sato. (I found a reference in an article on the redistribution of capital in the Edo period by a French Marxist in the sixties, his name escapes me.) Sato presented the document shortly thereafter to the celebrated courtesan Hanaogi, who kept it until her death, when it was appropriated by the proprietor of a local teahouse in satisfaction of outstanding and unspecified debts.

Next we hear of it, it's in the possession of one Constance Hooley, the daughter of Methodist missionaries from Buffalo, New York, transplanted to Japan in the 1880s to spread the word of the Lord — she makes passing mention of it in a small, self-published anthology of Japanese literature compiled by her on behalf of her ladies' church group.

Upon the Reverend Hooley's death, Constance Hooley sells the document along with various other Asian antiquities to a Chinese shipping magnate by the name of Liu, who sells it shortly thereafter to a wealthy Englishman and amateur poet, one Thaddeus Biddle, who happened to be touring the Orient on holiday in search of souvenirs. Biddle pays an astronomical price by the standards of the day — he was, he writes, "utterly enchanted by the work, besotted by its curious and ineffable beauty" (I'm quoting directly from his journal here). He took the document along with the rest of his acquisitions back to Europe, where it eventually ended up in the hands of an antiquarian in Lyon who bought it in the years preceding World War One, and sold it to a Scotsman in the spring of 1952, who bequeathed it to his nephew along with the rest of his private library in the fall of 1979. There is a bill of sale. The original's in pretty bad shape.

    That's about the long and the short of it. I don't know the whole story. I just translated it, that's all.

DARIUS WHEELER: Heian era?

JOHN BELL: Yes. A memoir of sorts. It actually partakes more of the *zuihitsu* genre, loosely translated: books of miscellany. A hybrid form consisting of lists, poems, memoir fragments, and observations. A pillow book, if you will.

DARIUS WHEELER: What do you make of it? Is it authentic?

JOHN BELL: From what I can tell, it appears to be, yes.

    (Darius Wheeler exits with the transcript.)

JOHN BELL: Mr. Wheeler, wait —

    (The sound of wooden clappers. Claire Tsong appears.)

CLAIRE TSONG: So what exactly did you tell him?

    (The sound of wooden clappers.)

Scene Sixteen

Late afternoon of the same day. Wheeler's loft.

JOHN BELL: I lied. Claire, I lied. I can't believe this. What have I done? What was I thinking? I don't know what came over me. I was totally caught up in something else. I wasn't thinking. He caught me completely off guard. I panicked. I made up this stupid story right on the spot. It was like a reflex. It was like it wasn't even me doing the talking.

CLAIRE TSONG: And Wheeler?

JOHN BELL: He believed me. He believed every word out of my mouth.

CLAIRE TSONG: Wow. That is so — great.

JOHN BELL: What are you? Nuts? Don't you get it? I lied not just once or twice, but over and over and over again, and the thing is, I didn't even mean to do it, even as I was looking this guy right in the eye, this guy I look up to, this guy I like — I know you don't like him, but I do, I like the guy, Claire — and I'm telling him all these facts, except they're not facts, because I'm lying through my teeth, I just happen to be lying with this incredible degree of specificity. I don't know what came over me. This is so unethical. Not to mention illegal.

CLAIRE TSONG: Fraud.

JOHN BELL: Jesus Christ.

CLAIRE TSONG: Look, it's only illegal if he tries to sell it.

JOHN BELL: Oh my God, what have I done? Claire, what have I done? I can't believe this.

CLAIRE TSONG: How was it written?

(The sound of wooden clappers.)

CLAIRE TSONG: I mean I know it's a "translation," but your original, was it written in *kanji* or *kana* or what?

JOHN BELL: *Kana*, it was written in *kana*. Or more accurately speaking, *onna moji*, which is a kind of, it's a kind of, it's a kind of precursor to *hiragana*. Syllabic, purely syllabic.

CLAIRE TSONG: How close to contemporary Japanese?

JOHN BELL: There are, you know, there are echoes. I mean, the meanings of individual words have changed over time, and the usages, how the language sounds, the spoken language, and the syntax, the syntax is different, archaic, it's archaic, but the strokes, the strokes are pretty much the same, I mean the basic shape is identical, I mean virtually identical, I mean I guess it depends on how you define identical.

CLAIRE TSONG: *(Handing John Bell a paintbrush.)* Here.

(The sound of wooden clappers.)

CLAIRE TSONG: Show me.

(The sound of the shakuhachi flute. John Bell draws Japanese kana, *or letters, with the paintbrush on a panel of the shoji screen. He writes* kirei. *He returns the paintbrush to Claire Tsong. She mimics his strokes and picks up where he left off. She continues to write. She creates the artifact. Darkness.)*

Scene Seventeen

A translation. Japanese lettering etches itself into the void, strokes of ink on blank pages. The sound of the shakuhachi flute. Setsuko Hearn appears in a sliver of light dressed as the Heian-era lady. As he speaks, Darius Wheeler emerges from the darkness. John Bell and Claire Tsong create the pillow book.

SETSUKO HEARN: In the evening, I hear a tapping at my screen, like the sound of rain on the eaves, and yet there is no rain tonight. There is no moon. The air is perfectly still. Within my chambers, the air is dark as ink. I cannot see your face. In the pool in the garden below, carp swim beneath the water, their bellies brush against the cool wet mud. I hear them breathing in the dark.

JOHN BELL: A list of beautiful things:

The touch of a lover's fingertips.

The rustle of silk undone —

SETSUKO HEARN: Your mouth, your tongue,

The hollow of my neck,

The inside of my thigh,

The taste, salt and wet,

Warm breath against one's skin —

(The sound of the shakuhachi flute changes tone. Light on the screen that Claire Tsong restored. A painting of a garden. It is an autumn scene: bare branches shrouded in mist. The painting of the garden in autumn begins to transform into a painting of a garden in summer: branches in bloom, ripe fruit. Fireflies. A summer night.)

DARIUS WHEELER: I hear the ladies whispering of late. So many tongues fluttering all at once. It's as though I live in a nest of starlings. If I could, I would snip each wagging tongue, chop it into little bits, and feed the bits to the carp.

CLAIRE TSONG: A secret no longer secret is like an oyster pried open. How clumsy the blade, how strange the pearl.

SETSUKO HEARN: I have taken a new lover who is not without charms. Lord S wonders why I am otherwise engaged this evening. I tell him I am busy chanting sutras.

JOHN BELL: A list of unsuitable things: Gossip, slander, accusation.

DARIUS WHEELER: I hear things, Lord S says. Do you? Rumors, he says. Do not take me for a fool.

JOHN BELL: Do not tramp filth into my chambers. Lord S asks if I am seeing another. Bad enough that he suspects and that I lie. Worse that I do not care.

SETSUKO HEARN: At night, my new lover whispers monstrous things to me, too terrifying to imagine. I feel a tingling through my belly, a chill more pleasurable than words.

DARIUS WHEELER: Who is this new lover?

CLAIRE TSONG: She is a lady of the fifth rank, new to court. I spied her at the moon-viewing, her sleeve spilled over the edge of her vessel, and trailed across the water — crimson, vermilion, a sliver of white.

SETSUKO HEARN: Her skill with silk, I have found, is surpassed only by her skill in love. She is very skillful in love.

DARIUS WHEELER: Why do you tell me these things.

SETSUKO HEARN: Why? I do not know. Faithless, I am a faithless creature. I received the letter in the morning on violet paper bound with plumeria. So exquisite I could not bear to open it.

(The sound of shakuhachi flute changes tone. Owen Matthiassen and Elizabeth Newman-Orr become visible in slivers of light.)

ELIZABETH NEWMAN-ORR: On the fifteenth day of the eighth month, we catch fireflies in the sleeves of our robes. They glitter through the summer silk. Later, we play games of chance.

OWEN MATTHIASSEN: A visiting sage entertains us with his parrot, a strange green bird who utters bits of wisdom. Lord S drinks too much rice wine and comports himself poorly. His wife sends a reproachful note the following morning. Her handwriting, I notice, is very poor.

SETSUKO HEARN: Some women are wives and mothers, I tell him. Some women choose different, less familiar paths. He calls on me several times afterwards. His letters moulder at my door.

DARIUS WHEELER: A list of unsuitable things:

ELIZABETH NEWMAN-ORR: A certain powerful man whose nose turns pink when he drinks. His wife, a well-born woman with the handwriting of a small, slow-witted child.

DARIUS WHEELER: You are unreasonable and unkind.

SETSUKO HEARN: Am I? And why is it you may have as many lovers as you wish? Why am I wrong that I would wish to enjoy the same? Foolish to even ask. I wish I had been born a man.

CLAIRE TSONG: But you are not a man. I think sometimes that you forget.

SETSUKO HEARN: I do not forget.

(The sound of the shakuhachi flute changes tone. Owen Matthiassen, Eliz-

abeth Newman-Orr, and Claire Tsong recede from view. Setsuko Hearn, Dar-
ius Wheeler, and John Bell remain.)

JOHN BELL: This morning I hear the servants smashing snails with wooden
cudgels. There is something very satisfying in the sound.

SETSUKO HEARN: An inauspicious wind. My mood grows worse with each passing day. I am a terrible person, I think.

JOHN BELL: The sound of footsteps on nightingale floors
The echo of the temple bell
All the words I have not spoken —
(John recedes from view.)

SETSUKO HEARN: One night passes. And then a second, and then a third. No
word from Lord S. Another night and not a word.

How like an autumn leaf my passion, brittle and unlovely in its passing.

DARIUS WHEELER: A list of unsuitable things:

SETSUKO HEARN: A new lover who is no longer new.

DARIUS WHEELER: Hasty action followed by regret.
*(The sound of the shakuhachi flute changes tone. Darius Wheeler recedes from
view. John Bell appears at his desk.)*

SETSUKO HEARN: We pass each other in the garden.
The blossoms have long been swept away.
The taste of your lips, now bitter as unripe plums.

You are my one heart's truth. Did I ever tell you this? Did I ever speak
this out loud? Would you have ever guessed?
*(The sound of the shakuhachi flute changes tone. Setsuko Hearn transforms
from Heian-era lady to contemporary, western woman.)*

SETSUKO HEARN: It was summer when I went to sleep last night, yet when I
awoke this morning, it was all of a sudden fall. The smell of foxfires at
daybreak, ice drops on the branches of the trees. In the hills near Hi-
gashiyama, I heard a deer cry. I looked for you by the lake. There was a
thick mist, I remember I could not see, and when I emerged from it at
last, the leaves had all turned crimson in the night. Strange. Nothing is
how it used to be.
*(The screen returns to its original image. A painting of a garden in autumn:
bare branches shrouded in mist. The sound of wooden clappers. The screen
vanishes. The sound of the shakuhachi flute ends.)*

Scene Eighteen

Light shift. Late afternoon of the same day. A corridor in the university. Set-suko Hearn is looking through the transcript of the pillow book. Darius Wheeler looks on.

SETSUKO HEARN: Where did you get this?

DARIUS WHEELER: It was found in a private library. It was sent to us for ap-praisal by the owner. People send us stuff. Most of the time, it's not worth the cost of shipping, but every so often, something comes your way. You never know.

SETSUKO HEARN: Who did the translation?

DARIUS WHEELER: My assistant.

SETSUKO HEARN: Working from the original?

DARIUS WHEELER: From photos. This whole thing, to be honest, is kinda out of my ken. My assistant gave me some background, smart guy, but he's a little naive in some ways. I thought I'd run it by you, see what you think.

SETSUKO HEARN: I don't know how to say this.

DARIUS WHEELER: Worthless, huh? You know, I gotta say I'm not surprised. I had a feeling. I thought I'd bring it by, what the hell. Look, to tell you the truth, what I really —

SETSUKO HEARN: No, wait. I don't think you understand.

(The sound of wooden clappers.)

SETSUKO HEARN: There's a quality, something in the voice, in the writing, it's uncanny. The batsubun, the epilogue, the interpolation of standard sea-sonal metaphors of transformation and loss, something in the syntax, the diction, even in translation — Utamakura, literally poem pillow, or pil-low book. Heian era, eleventh century. The number of extant examples in the genre is practically nil. I don't know how I can articulate this to you. For something like this to turn up in this way, it would change every-thing, everything we thought we knew, all the assumptions we've made — well, it would, it would be premature to speculate. I'd love to get my hands on the original, if I could. If I could just, if I could examine the original. In the meantime, if I could take a look at those photos. The sooner the better.

DARIUS WHEELER: I'll get right on it.

SETSUKO HEARN: Forgive me.

DARIUS WHEELER: No, it would be my pleasure. I mean that.

SETSUKO HEARN: Thank you.

DARIUS WHEELER: So what are you doing now?

SETSUKO HEARN: I was just, I was going to go back to my office, do a little bit of work.

DARIUS WHEELER: Are you free for dinner? I know this place. It's not far. Just a few blocks away from here. Nothing fancy. How does that sound?

SETSUKO HEARN: That sounds — nice. Listen, why don't you meet me out front. I need to stop by my office on the way out, make a quick call. I'll just be a minute.

(The sound of a tape rewinding.)

Scene Nineteen

Light on Elizabeth Newman-Orr removing hidden recording equipment taped to her skin. A fragment from a previous scene.

ELIZABETH NEWMAN-ORR: So what was the story? Who was she?

(The sound of a tape rewinding.)

DARIUS WHEELER: Hardly any at all.

(The sound of wooden clappers.)

DARIUS WHEELER: Interested?

ELIZABETH NEWMAN-ORR: Another time perhaps.

DARIUS WHEELER: By then it'll be gone.

(The sound of a tape rewinding.)

ELIZABETH NEWMAN-ORR: I was given your name.

DARIUS WHEELER: Given my name by whom?

ELIZABETH NEWMAN-ORR: I'd rather not say.

(The sound of a tape rewinding.)

ELIZABETH NEWMAN-ORR: Can't we be candid with one another, Mr. Wheeler? I'd like that so much. It would make everything so much easier.

DARIUS WHEELER: What are we talking about?

ELIZABETH NEWMAN-ORR: I think you have an idea.

DARIUS WHEELER: Why don't you spell it out for me.

(A phone begins to ring. Elizabeth Newman-Orr exits. Enter John Bell.)

Scene Twenty

John Bell answers the phone in Wheeler's loft. Light on Owen Matthiassen.

JOHN BELL: Hello?

OWEN MATTHIASSEN: John, it's Owen Matthiassen. Is Darius there, by any chance?

JOHN BELL: No, Dr. Matthiassen, I'm afraid he's left for the day.

OWEN MATTHIASSEN: I see. Well, John, maybe you can help me. I was on the phone just now with my colleague Dr. Hearn, and she mentioned the most fascinating thing. A manuscript that turned up. Japanese. Heian era. Apparently, Darius brought the translation around for her to take a look at. I'm curious how he got a hold of the thing, where it came from, how it came to light. Do you know anything about this? You understand it could be immensely valuable, priceless even. Although I suppose everything eventually has a price.

(The sound of wooden clappers. A dial tone.)

OWEN MATTHIASSEN: Hello? John, are you still there? John —? John —?

(The sound of a dial tone transforms into the sound of the shakuhachi flute. Light on the shoji panel where John Bell previously drew the word kirei. *The sound of the flute grows, a single note sustained. John Bell smashes his fist through the shoji panel, splitting the word apart. The sound of wooden clappers.)*

END OF ACT I

Act II
Scene Twenty-one

Darkness. Scattered pages of paper are suspended in the darkness. The paper is distressed, ancient-seeming. The pages are dyed vermilion, rose, dayflower blue. Some are covered with a sprinkling of gold leaf and tiny Japanese lettering or kana. *Light on Claire Tsong. She examines a page, takes a lighter out of her pocket, sets the page on fire, lets it burn, then blows it out. She retrieves a Polaroid camera. She takes a picture of the page. A flash. Darkness.*

Scene Twenty-two

A university lecture hall. Owen Matthiassen and Setsuko Hearn are backstage. The ambient sound of voices in the audience.

OWEN MATTHIASSEN: I spoke with the dean this morning. Needless to say, he's taken a personal interest in the matter. I have to say I've never seen anything like it. I've been getting calls from all over the States, Europe, Japan. The media interest is overwhelming. When is Darius getting a hold of the original?

SETSUKO HEARN: In the next day or so.

OWEN MATTHIASSEN: Good, good. I have to confess, this whole thing, I'm afraid it's a little beyond my scope of expertise. I'm more of a generalist, as you know. I guess that's what they call us now — rather euphemistically, I suspect. We're a dying breed. We used to call ourselves Orientalists, and we studied the Orient. That's how old I am. It was a different time, I suppose, a different way of doing things. It's exciting, this whole thing, it's all very exciting, and you should be, well, you should be pleased. So then I'll say a few words, and then you can give them a little bit of background, and then we'll take questions. Ready?

SETSUKO HEARN: Yes.

OWEN MATTHIASSEN: All right then —

(Owen Matthiassen goes on stage. The sound of the audience grows louder. Setsuko Hearn remains backstage.)

Scene Twenty-three

Light shift. Backstage of a press conference. Owen Matthiassen is speaking into a microphone. He is a distant figure. Setsuko Hearn remains in the foreground.

OWEN MATTHIASSEN: Ladies — gentlemen — please — if I could have your attention — I cannot stress enough the significance of this manuscript. Even in its fragmentary state, its impact on our field of scholarship is immeasurable —
(Owen Matthiassen continues to speak. His words grow faint. The sound of wooden clappers. Silence.)

Scene Twenty-four

A park near the university. Autumn. Crimson leaves, bare branches against the sky. Setsuko Hearn and Darius Wheeler are looking at Polaroids of the original manuscript. The middle of a conversation.

DARIUS WHEELER: There's some damage. You can see it, here and here. It's not the end of the world, but the sooner we can get a hold of it, get it in a climatized setting, the better.
SETSUKO HEARN: When do you think that will be?
DARIUS WHEELER: Tomorrow or the day after. Trust me. This part I know.
SETSUKO HEARN: Over a thousand years old — it's like a dream. You dream about this sort of thing, that lightning will strike, and maybe you'll be lucky enough to be there when it does. At least I do. I mean, I have. I guess everybody has at some point or another. Did you know —
DARIUS WHEELER: Tell me.
SETSUKO HEARN: Did you know that men of Heian-era Japan wrote in Chinese, a language not their own, and one in which most gained only, at best, a schoolboy proficiency —
DARIUS WHEELER: Is that right —
SETSUKO HEARN: But Heian-era women, by contrast, wrote almost exclusively in their native tongue, allowing them, I think, a kind of emotional clarity, an immediacy, a seamless correspondence between the inchoate thought and the written word. One might even go so far as to say that because they wrote in their native tongue, they were able to write with a candor and transparency virtually impossible for their male contemporaries.
DARIUS WHEELER: Now that seems very, very doctrinaire.

SETSUKO HEARN: Perhaps. Let's say instead that they wrote without artifice. They wrote about their innermost feelings — feelings of restlessness, uncertainty, desire, doubt. Modern, almost modern in their insights, oddly familiar, they wrote in a voice that was singular and unmistakably female —

(The sound of wooden clappers.)

SETSUKO HEARN: How is your hand?

(Darius Wheeler holds out his hand.)

SETSUKO HEARN: I can barely see where it was. What? What is it?

DARIUS WHEELER: Nothing. It's just you're so beautiful.

SETSUKO HEARN: I wonder how many women you've said that to. I'm guessing quite a few.

DARIUS WHEELER: What if I told you this was different?

SETSUKO HEARN: I don't think I'd believe you.

DARIUS WHEELER: You've got to be the most beautiful skeptic I've ever met.

SETSUKO HEARN: I'm afraid flattery needs to be a little more subtle than that.

DARIUS WHEELER: I know, I know how I sound. I know what you're thinking, and you know what, normally you'd be right.

SETSUKO HEARN: But not now.

DARIUS WHEELER: No, not now. You don't believe me.

SETSUKO HEARN: What I believe is that there are words —

DARIUS WHEELER: Yes —

SETSUKO HEARN: And then there are the feelings and thoughts behind the words, and that the relationship between the two is neither reliable nor precise, nor is it maybe meant to be —

DARIUS WHEELER: No?

SETSUKO HEARN: No, and that maybe the space between what we say and what we do, what we see and what we feel, that it's necessary, the space where anything can happen. Chaos, confusion, terrible, terrible confusion —

(Darius Wheeler and Setsuko Hearn kiss.)

SETSUKO HEARN: OK, you know what, this is really, this is not a good idea. I don't know you, and you don't know me, and whatever this is, it's based on nothing, a first impression.

DARIUS WHEELER: Love at first sight.

SETSUKO HEARN: Please.

DARIUS WHEELER: You don't believe in that.

SETSUKO HEARN: No. No, I don't.

DARIUS WHEELER: It's kinda old-fashioned.

SETSUKO HEARN: It's also very convenient.

DARIUS WHEELER: Look all I want — what I want — is for you to entertain, just for a second, the possibility that maybe what I'm saying to you, what I'm trying to say to you, that it's —

SETSUKO HEARN: What? The truth?

DARIUS WHEELER: Yes.

SETSUKO HEARN: Ah I see. What if we were truthful? What if we were good? What if desire were the same as love? What if it were all simple and clear?

DARIUS WHEELER: Maybe it is. Maybe sometimes it is.

SETSUKO HEARN: You know, I don't think so.

DARIUS WHEELER: How can you know that. How can you know for sure?

SETSUKO HEARN: Because nothing is that easy. In the world I live in, nothing is ever that easy.

(The sound of wooden clappers.)

DARIUS WHEELER: I like you so much.

(The sound of wooden clappers.)

DARIUS WHEELER: Everything I say sounds like a line. I know that. I know that. I'm blowing it, aren't I.

SETSUKO HEARN: It depends on what you're trying to do.

DARIUS WHEELER: Make you like me just a little. Something like that.

SETSUKO HEARN: I like you.

(The sound of wooden clappers.)

SETSUKO HEARN: It's that I look at you and I don't know what I'm seeing. What am I seeing?

DARIUS WHEELER: A deeply fucked-up individual.

SETSUKO HEARN: Is that right?

DARIUS WHEELER: The worst. And the funny thing is — this is the funny thing — he's fallen for this woman who happens to see through all his bull-shit, this beautiful, brilliant woman, and he can barely talk when he's around her, which I know is kinda hard to believe, but it's true, and I know, I know right now he sounds like an idiot and a jerk, probably because he is an idiot and a jerk, and she should probably tell him to just get lost, but I really — I hope she doesn't, I really hope she doesn't.

(Darius Wheeler and Setsuko Hearn are very close. The sound of a phone ringing.)

Scene Twenty-five

Claire Tsong's workspace. John Bell is studying the pages from the top of the act. They're pages from the "original" manuscript, distressed paper, ancient-seeming, with Japanese lettering, colored paper sprinkled with gold leaf. Claire Tsong is changing out of paint-spattered work clothes into dress clothes. She puts on makeup and fixes her hair, transforming herself. The phone continues to ring.

CLAIRE TSONG: Mulberry paper. Carbon-based ink. A little dirt, a little fire, a little tea — are you going to get that or what?
(The phone stops ringing.)
JOHN BELL: The calligraphy —
CLAIRE TSONG: Authentic. I know.
JOHN BELL: How did you do this?
CLAIRE TSONG: Honey, I'm just the midwife to your genius. Analyze the brushstroke. Hold it up to the light. I'm a very gifted girl. If you didn't know better, if you saw this under Plexiglas in some museum somewhere —
JOHN BELL: But it's not real.
CLAIRE TSONG: Isn't it? It looks pretty real to me.
JOHN BELL: It's not about what it looks like. It's about what it is. Eventually somebody's going to figure out the difference.
CLAIRE TSONG: And what if they don't?
(The sound of wooden clappers.)
CLAIRE TSONG: Provenance.
JOHN BELL: Claire —
CLAIRE TSONG: All you need to do is piece together a credible paper trail: a bill of sale, a catalogue reference, cut and paste, some signatures —
JOHN BELL: It's not that easy. Do you have any idea how many calls we've been getting? Everybody wants to see the original.
CLAIRE TSONG: Good thing we have it.
JOHN BELL: No, Claire, no. We have no original because there is no original, because even the so-called original is not an original.
CLAIRE TSONG: I guess it all depends on how you define "original."
JOHN BELL: You know, I define it the way I think most everybody else does. It's the thing that's real as opposed to the thing that's fake. I think it's pretty clearcut. Jesus Christ, what am I doing, what the hell am I doing? I feel like an impostor.
CLAIRE TSONG: That's because you are.

JOHN BELL: No, see, Claire, you're wrong. I'm not. This was not my idea. This was never my idea.

CLAIRE TSONG: No?

JOHN BELL: I didn't want this.

CLAIRE TSONG: You didn't want what? You didn't want to write what you wrote? You didn't want to get paid for doing what you do? You didn't want to take credit for something you did for once in your life? Can you maybe own up, John, can you maybe try?

JOHN BELL: We're different, OK, we see things differently. I'm not like you.

CLAIRE TSONG: You know, I think you are. I think you're exactly like me. I just don't think you realize it yet.

(The sound of wooden clappers.)

CLAIRE TSONG: Look just think of it as a little insurance policy. Somebody sniffs it out, you say you were duped, no harm, no foul.

JOHN BELL: I wish he'd never seen it. I don't know why I left it out in the first place. It was so stupid. I should've seen this coming, I should've known. What was I thinking?

CLAIRE TSONG: What were you thinking?

(The sound of wooden clappers.)

CLAIRE TSONG: All right, lookit, Wheeler needs to buy before he can sell. In order to sell the manuscript — the "original," that is — he needs to own it, and he doesn't own it.

JOHN BELL: Not yet. He wants me to talk to the guy, a guy who doesn't exist, get him to sell a thing, a thing that doesn't exist. This is insane, this whole thing is insane.

CLAIRE TSONG: Do it. If Wheeler wants to buy it, let him. You pick the price. Just remember, make it steep. The higher the price, the more desirable. We can split it, fifty-fifty.

JOHN BELL: I don't believe you, Claire. What kind of person thinks like this? It's like you planned this whole thing from the start.

CLAIRE TSONG: Doll, I couldn't have planned this if I wanted to. I just seized the day is all.

JOHN BELL: What about Wheeler?

CLAIRE TSONG: What about him?

JOHN BELL: I don't know, Claire — call me a nut, but I think he's maybe going to sue us, and then I think he's maybe going to have criminal charges brought against us, and then I think we're maybe going to go to jail.

CLAIRE TSONG: That's not going to happen.

JOHN BELL: How can you be so sure?

(The sound of wooden clappers.)

CLAIRE TSONG: Because I know him. I know his mind, I know how it works. I know him. He'd rather save face and eat the loss. Trust me. He's not going to say a word.

(The sound of wooden clappers. Claire Tsong performs bukkaeri — *a Kabuki costume change in which the upper half of the costume falls down over the lower half revealing a new pattern. Her appearance has completely transformed.)*

JOHN BELL: Claire —

CLAIRE TSONG: Look, just talk to him, set it up, call me when you're done. *(Picking up the pages of the "original" manuscript.)* Here, we don't want these lying around here, do we — What?

JOHN BELL: I don't know. Nothing. You just, I don't know, you look different.

CLAIRE TSONG: I just changed my clothes. That's all.

(Claire Tsong exits in a version of the kitsune roppo *exit — a Kabuki exit marked by leaps and bounds. John Bell vanishes. The sound of the shakuhachi flute begins.)*

Scene Twenty-six

A shunga. *An erotic woodblock print. The sound of the shakuhachi flute continues. Light shift. Two lovers in the shadows. Glimpses of naked flesh. The sound of breathing. A disembodied voice, faint and faraway, a recorded echo of what came before.*

SETSUKO HEARN: No rain tonight, no moon, the air is perfectly still
Not even the faintest breeze stirs the leaves.
In the pool in the garden below, carp swim beneath the surface —
Flashes of white in the murky green
Their bellies slick and wet —
The tickle of waterweed
The soft wet moss —
The curve of your neck, your fingertips
The rustle of silk undone —
Your mouth, your tongue
Your lips, the taste of your lips, salt, wet
The warmth of your breath against my skin —

Scene Twenty-seven

The sound of the shakuhachi flute continues. Light on Owen Matthiassen. Visible behind him is the fake Hokusai print of Mount Fuji.

OWEN MATTHIASSEN: Footnote number 27: Ibid, op. cit. Prevalent throughout the text is a sensibility the Japanese call *mono no aware,* i.e., an awareness of imminent loss, a melancholic perspective one finds throughout the history of Japanese literature. Loosely translated, *mono no aware* is the phenomenon by which one perceives the beauty of a thing only in the moment of recognizing its essential impermanence. Seasons pass. Flowers wither and die. Indeed, it is precisely this delimited life span which lends an object its beauty, which endows it with value, and renders it precious — no, not precious, not precious — priceless — priceless in our eyes.
(The sound of wooden clappers. Owen Matthiassen and the fake print recede from view.)

Scene Twenty-eight

Light on Setsuko Hearn and Darius Wheeler. They dress.

DARIUS WHEELER: What was she like?
SETSUKO HEARN: We don't really know. The details of her life, the circumstances that brought her to court, her name even are all unknown. Which is often the case.
DARIUS WHEELER: I have this image of her in my mind.
SETSUKO HEARN: Do you? Well, we know — what do we know — we know her skin was very white, and that she whitened it further with a cream made from nightingale droppings. We know she plucked the entirety of her eyebrows and blackened her teeth, as was the fashion of the day, and that she wore multiple layers of kimono — colorful, complicated, coded in a language of symbols, hidden meanings, of which we have only inklings. The Heian-era court in which she lived was a highly literate, highly aestheticized society. Like her peers, she spent her days writing poetry and preparing for the many festivals that marked the passing of the seasons. We know she was unmarried and during her time at court, she engaged in multiple romantic liaisons with both men and women. This

alone is a remarkable revelation. As an articulation of transgressive sexuality and a revisioning of gender stereotypes prevalent in a patriarchal culture — you know, I'm talking an awful lot.

DARIUS WHEELER: You have a lot to say.

SETSUKO HEARN: Yes. Yes, I do.

DARIUS WHEELER: What do you think happened to her? Afterwards, I mean.

SETSUKO HEARN: Maybe she left the court and married a provincial lord. Maybe she lived her final years as a Buddhist nun, chanting sutras in a temple. The fragment ends abruptly. We won't ever know with any degree of certainty. We can only speculate.

DARIUS WHEELER: Do you think she was happy?

SETSUKO HEARN: I don't know. I'm not sure. Perhaps. I mean I'm not sure I know what happy means.

DARIUS WHEELER: Happy means happy.

SETSUKO HEARN: Happy means happy, beautiful means beautiful. Oh, to live in the world you live in. What a great world. Everything's so clearcut, so simple.

DARIUS WHEELER: Sometimes things just are what they are, they mean what they mean.

SETSUKO HEARN: So I've heard. What? What is it?

DARIUS WHEELER: I want very much, I want to make you happy.

(The sound of wooden clappers.)

SETSUKO HEARN: I need to go. I need to get back to work.

DARIUS WHEELER: What if I say, I don't want you to.

SETSUKO HEARN: Then I would say, but I have to.

DARIUS WHEELER: And I would say, but I won't let you.

SETSUKO HEARN: Would you really say that?

DARIUS WHEELER: I might.

SETSUKO HEARN: Then I would say, unhand me, sir.

DARIUS WHEELER: "Unhand me"?

SETSUKO HEARN: Yes.

DARIUS WHEELER: I like that. It's quaint.

SETSUKO HEARN: I'm quaint.

DARIUS WHEELER: Are you quaint?

SETSUKO HEARN: Very very quaint. You'd be surprised.

(Setsuko Hearn and Darius Wheeler kiss.)

SETSUKO HEARN: I have to get back to the office. I've got a stack of work waiting for me and about a million calls to return, and I need to proof the draft of the article, I'm almost done —

DARIUS WHEELER: Dinner later? What about drinks? How about dinner and drinks, how about a nightcap —

SETSUKO HEARN: I don't know —

DARIUS WHEELER: Say yes.

SETSUKO HEARN: I don't know I don't know —

DARIUS WHEELER: I won't let you go until you say yes. Say yes, please say yes.

SETSUKO HEARN: Yes.

(The sound of wooden clappers. Setsuko Hearn exits. Darius Wheeler remains. Enter Elizabeth Newman-Orr.)

Scene Twenty-nine

The hanging scroll from the top of the play appears. Portrait of a lady, Kamakura era, gilt background. Wheeler's loft space, later that day.

ELIZABETH NEWMAN-ORR: Mr. Wheeler, you seem distracted.

DARIUS WHEELER: I'm sorry, what were you saying?

ELIZABETH NEWMAN-ORR: Just that I was running a little late. I called, but there was no answer. I got here as fast as I could. I take it there were no problems.

DARIUS WHEELER: No. None.

(Enter John Bell pushing a dolly on which rests a large box. He parks the dolly, and begins prying the front lid of the box open with a crowbar. It's a noisy and violent opening up.)

DARIUS WHEELER: Everything went smoothly. It arrived early this morning.

ELIZABETH NEWMAN-ORR: I'm impressed. So efficient. I have to hand it to you. You have a knack, but I wonder if you ever have any qualms.

DARIUS WHEELER: Qualms about what?

ELIZABETH NEWMAN-ORR: Breaking the law.

DARIUS WHEELER: I don't think about it that way.

ELIZABETH NEWMAN-ORR: How do you think about it?

DARIUS WHEELER: I don't, Ms. Orr. I think your question is a philosophical one, and I'm not much of a philosopher, I'm afraid.

ELIZABETH NEWMAN-ORR: It's such an interesting business, the business you're in. It's fascinating. You know, I read an item in the paper just this morning. About an ancient manuscript that was sent to you for appraisal. I understand it could be quite valuable.

DARIUS WHEELER: Yes.

ELIZABETH NEWMAN-ORR: But now you don't own it, do you — the original, that is?

DARIUS WHEELER: No.

ELIZABETH NEWMAN-ORR: You're just a representative.

DARIUS WHEELER: An interested party, yes.

ELIZABETH NEWMAN-ORR: I wonder how much that manuscript would fetch on the open market — the original, I mean?

DARIUS WHEELER: It's an interesting question.

ELIZABETH NEWMAN-ORR: I think so.

DARIUS WHEELER: You're full of interesting questions.

ELIZABETH NEWMAN-ORR: I try.

DARIUS WHEELER: I have a few interesting questions of my own.

ELIZABETH NEWMAN-ORR: Oh?

DARIUS WHEELER: For starters, I wonder who you are and why you're here. I have to say, I have an idea.

(John Bell pries the last nail loose. The front lid of the box crashes open. Revealed inside the box is a painting on silk — a portrait of a lady seemingly identical to the portrait of a lady already hanging in Darius Wheeler's loft.)

ELIZABETH NEWMAN-ORR: She has a twin.

DARIUS WHEELER: Not exactly.

ELIZABETH NEWMAN-ORR: I'm afraid I don't follow.

DARIUS WHEELER: This is a fake. I saw it once at a party at that villa on Lugard Road, had a chance to look at it up close. I didn't need to. I could tell it was a fake from a mile away. All you need to do is look at it a while. You'll see what I mean. I hope you like it, I really do, because you and whoever you work for just paid an awful lot of money for it. Is your mike picking me up — this is key — in order for this little exposé of yours to work — and I think that's what this was, I may be wrong, it's just a hunch — this painting needs to be authentic, an actual antiquity a country of origin would hate to see go. Because it's not, you have no crime, you barely have an impropriety, all you have is the purchase and transport of a second-rate fake for a large, some might say, absurdly large sum of money. But who am I to judge. In art, as in life, there's no accounting for taste. Your line producer didn't do his homework, Ms. Orr. In the future, you and he — forgive me, he or she — are going to have to do better than that.

(The sound of wooden clappers.)

ELIZABETH NEWMAN-ORR: If it's a crime to transport a national treasure, surely it's a crime to own one.

(The sound of wooden clappers.)

ELIZABETH NEWMAN-ORR: Oh. I see. Yours is a fake, too.

DARIUS WHEELER: You know, there are fakes, and then there are fakes. Some fakes are obvious, and some are pretty good. Some are so good, in fact, it's hard to be sure one way or another without carbon dating, autoradiography, all kinds of tests you'd have to get my permission to run. She is after all my property, and last I checked, that still counted for something.

ELIZABETH NEWMAN-ORR: You're very pleased with yourself, aren't you?

DARIUS WHEELER: I'm actually wracked with self-loathing.

ELIZABETH NEWMAN-ORR: Somehow I find that hard to believe.

DARIUS WHEELER: I hide it well. I think you know the way out. If not —

ELIZABETH NEWMAN-ORR: That's quite all right. I think I can manage. Thank you for your time, Mr. Wheeler and Mr. —

JOHN BELL: Bell.

ELIZABETH NEWMAN-ORR: Mr. Bell. Good day, Mr. Wheeler. Mr. Bell.
(The sound of wooden clappers. Elizabeth Newman-Orr exits.)

Scene Thirty

John Bell and Darius Wheeler study each other from a distance.

JOHN BELL: It's not a fake.

DARIUS WHEELER: No.

JOHN BELL: I didn't think so. I mean I didn't think it was.

DARIUS WHEELER: I lied, John. People lie. Sometimes they get caught, sometimes they don't. It depends on who they're lying to.

JOHN BELL: No, I understand, I understand completely.

DARIUS WHEELER: So?

JOHN BELL: Yeah?

DARIUS WHEELER: What's the story?

JOHN BELL: Sorry?

DARIUS WHEELER: The manuscript. How's it looking?

JOHN BELL: It's looking good, it's looking really good.

DARIUS WHEELER: Good.

JOHN BELL: He wants to sell.

DARIUS WHEELER: Great. What's he asking?

JOHN BELL: One million.

DARIUS WHEELER: Dollars.

JOHN BELL: Pounds. Pounds sterling.
(The sound of wooden clappers.)

JOHN BELL: But I get the sense, from the little bit I know, that it's just an arbitrary figure, a stab in the dark, because frankly I'm not really sure, you know, I'm not really sure he knows what he's doing.

DARIUS WHEELER: Tell him we'll have a courier ready with a check before the close of business. Or we can do a direct money transfer, Channel Islands account. It's his call. The thing I wonder is why he'd go so low. He could get twice that much, if he wanted to, more.

JOHN BELL: Maybe he doesn't realize what he has. You know, I don't know. I don't really know him.

DARIUS WHEELER: People are mysterious, aren't they, why they do what they do.

JOHN BELL: I guess so, yeah.

DARIUS WHEELER: Well, whatever it is, I want you to make the call right away, nail it down, last thing I want is cold feet and a bidding war. Oh, and John —

(The sound of wooden clappers.)

DARIUS WHEELER: Don't think I'm not aware of everything you've done. I am. When this is all settled, I want us to sit down together and have a talk. I want to talk about your future.

(The sound of wooden clappers. Exit Darius Wheeler. John Bell picks up the phone and dials. He exits listening as the phone rings on the other end of the line.)

Scene Thirty-one

Light shift. Darius Wheeler's loft. An hour later. Enter Claire Tsong in the new clothes she changed into earlier. She carries a package containing the original manuscript. She studies the two paintings, the two portraits of a lady, one real, one fake. Re-enter Elizabeth Newman-Orr.

CLAIRE TSONG: Hey.

(The sound of wooden clappers.)

ELIZABETH NEWMAN-ORR: Hey.

CLAIRE TSONG: Looking for Wheeler?

ELIZABETH NEWMAN-ORR: No, I'm actually, I'm looking for Mr. Bell. Is he in, do you know?

CLAIRE TSONG: He should be. I was just looking for him myself.

ELIZABETH NEWMAN-ORR: I'd love to talk to him.

CLAIRE TSONG: He's a very interesting guy.

ELIZABETH NEWMAN-ORR: I sense that.

CLAIRE TSONG: He knows all kinds of things.

ELIZABETH NEWMAN-ORR: I sense that, too.

CLAIRE TSONG: More than he lets on.

ELIZABETH NEWMAN-ORR: Do I know you? I do, don't I? We met the other night, at the party for Utagawa. I didn't, I didn't recognize you. New outfit. And your hair, it's different.

CLAIRE TSONG: Yeah, it's — well, yeah it's different.

ELIZABETH NEWMAN-ORR: I like it.

CLAIRE TSONG: Yeah?

ELIZABETH NEWMAN-ORR: No, it's very, it's really, it's pretty.

CLAIRE TSONG: Thanks, thank you. Claire.

ELIZABETH NEWMAN-ORR: Beth.

CLAIRE TSONG: It's nice to see you again.

ELIZABETH NEWMAN-ORR: Yeah.

CLAIRE TSONG: Are you OK?

ELIZABETH NEWMAN-ORR: Yeah, no, I'm fine. It's just, it's been a really shitty day. You know how that goes. You're an artist. I remember. Mixed media.

CLAIRE TSONG: Very good. And you? What do you do? I don't think you ever said.

ELIZABETH NEWMAN-ORR: I'm a writer, a journalist actually. I was working on a piece. It didn't quite pan out the way I'd planned. I thought maybe Mr. Bell, I thought maybe he might — well, I don't know what I was thinking. How do you know Wheeler? You know — never mind. I don't even care anymore. He's a piece of work, that guy.

CLAIRE TSONG: He's a prick.

ELIZABETH NEWMAN-ORR: I'm so glad I'm not the only one who thinks so.

CLAIRE TSONG: You're not.

(The sound of wooden clappers.)

CLAIRE TSONG: So you're a journalist, huh?

ELIZABETH NEWMAN-ORR: Not a very good one and probably not for long — but, yes, in theory, yes.

CLAIRE TSONG: Listen, you want to maybe, you want to go for a drink? You look like you could use a drink.

ELIZABETH NEWMAN-ORR: What about Mr. Bell?

CLAIRE TSONG: John? We'll catch up with him later. After you.

(Claire Tsong and Elizabeth Newman-Orr exit. The sound of wooden clappers.)

Scene Thirty-two

Owen Matthiassen and Setsuko Hearn in Owen Matthiassen's office. The fake Hokusai print hangs on the wall. Owen Matthiassen is holding a photocopy of the transcript.

OWEN MATTHIASSEN: Have you ever seen Mount Fuji? In real life, I mean?

SETSUKO HEARN: Once. Through the window of a passing train.

OWEN MATTHIASSEN: You were lucky. Half the time it's covered in clouds, you can't see a thing. Hokusai was an old man when he made his study of the mountain. He came up with forty-six views, why they call the series thirty-six views — well, things are sometimes more than they seem to be, I suppose. Or less. If he'd lived longer, I suspect there would've been more. The permutations are infinite. How we look at the thing itself, which part we're able to see, if we're able to see it at all.

(The sound of wooden clappers.)

SETSUKO HEARN: Dr. Matthiassen —

OWEN MATTHIASSEN: *(Paging through the photocopy.)* In fairness, it wouldn't have even occurred to me if I hadn't gotten the call from that journalist — I've forgotten her name. She's apparently seen the actual forgery, interviewed the forger. The story will air sometime next week. The text was very convincing, I must say. And of course, the photos were a nice touch. The thing is, though, and this is the awkward thing, it was all right here in front of us the whole time. Anomalies, inconsistencies. "On the fifteenth day of the eighth month, we catch fireflies . . . A visiting sage entertains us with his parrot." The parrot — nonindigenous, virtually unheard of in Heian-era Japan. "I received your letter in the morning on violet paper bound with plumeria." Plumeria. Again another nonindigenous species, anomalous, completely anomalous. The list goes on. At first I ascribed it to flaws in transcription, a certain license taken in translation, but the sheer volume of discrepancies, it's overwhelming. When I look at the text now, all I see are anomalies. Once you begin to look, you see, it gives itself away.

(The sound of wooden clappers. Owen Matthiassen fades away. Setsuko Hearn remains in the foreground.)

Scene Thirty-three

Light shift. Wheeler's loft. Early evening of the same day. Setsuko Hearn is looking at two virtually identical paintings of the lady, one original, the other fake. Darius Wheeler is preparing drinks. He gives one to Setsuko Hearn. The middle of a conversation.

SETSUKO HEARN: Tell me something about yourself.

DARIUS WHEELER: What do you want to know?

SETSUKO HEARN: I don't know where to begin. Where do I begin?

DARIUS WHEELER: Who was your first true love?

SETSUKO HEARN: Who was your first true love?

DARIUS WHEELER: Suzanne Henig. I was fifteen. She broke my heart.

SETSUKO HEARN: You've had other loves since.

DARIUS WHEELER: One.

SETSUKO HEARN: Only one?

DARIUS WHEELER: I've had affections.

SETSUKO HEARN: Which is different?

DARIUS WHEELER: Which is different, yes.

SETSUKO HEARN: Were you ever married?

DARIUS WHEELER: No. And you?

SETSUKO HEARN: Once. A long time ago. It lasted less than a year. I think we were friends more than we were lovers. We're still friends. We talk on the phone every so often. He's married, a father. I think we wanted different things.

DARIUS WHEELER: What did you want?

SETSUKO HEARN: To be very good at what I do.

DARIUS WHEELER: Ambitious.

SETSUKO HEARN: I used to be embarrassed by that word, but then I stopped. It's pointless to pretend to be something you're not. We make certain choices, some without even realizing. Tell me something else. Where are you from? Where did you grow up?

DARIUS WHEELER: Bellingham, Washington.

SETSUKO HEARN: Iowa. Fairfield, Iowa.

DARIUS WHEELER: That's not what I would've guessed.

SETSUKO HEARN: What would you have guessed?

DARIUS WHEELER: Tokyo. Los Angeles. I don't know.

SETSUKO HEARN: My father was a missionary in Japan. When he came back, he wanted to go home. Iowa was home. Did you have brothers and sisters?

DARIUS WHEELER: A sister. She lives on Mercer Island. On a clear day, you can see Mount Rainier. It's like a picture. It's, it's beautiful. And you?

SETSUKO HEARN: Only child.

DARIUS WHEELER: Your mother was Japanese.

SETSUKO HEARN: I was adopted actually. From an orphanage in Hangzhou. I was there until I was almost two. I'm Chinese by birth. My mother, my adopted mother, her family is Japanese.

DARIUS WHEELER: And your father?

SETSUKO HEARN: Scotch-Irish, a little German, you know, mixed. When I was growing up, people saw me, and they just assumed I was my parents' daughter — which of course, in almost every way, I am.

DARIUS WHEELER: Do you remember China?

SETSUKO HEARN: No. If no one had told me, I would never have known, I would never have even guessed. My earliest memories are of cornfields and big sky and college football. My dad was a big college football fan.

DARIUS WHEELER: Hawkeyes?

SETSUKO HEARN: You bet. Huge. Help me.

DARIUS WHEELER: What were you like as a little girl?

SETSUKO HEARN: Very studious. Very idealistic. I wanted to find out things, all kinds of things. And I believed I could. I think I was, in retrospect, very sheltered.

DARIUS WHEELER: Were you happy?

SETSUKO HEARN: Yes. Yes, I was.

DARIUS WHEELER: Listen —

SETSUKO HEARN: — No, please. Tell me something, tell me something else.

DARIUS WHEELER: I don't know what to say. What can I say?

SETSUKO HEARN: Who do you look like, your mother or your father?

DARIUS WHEELER: My father.

SETSUKO HEARN: And are you like him?

DARIUS WHEELER: In a way, I guess. He was an amateur collector. Collected woodblock prints. Got hooked when he was in the navy, stationed in Tokyo right after the war. He'd keep his prints between sheets of transparent paper. It gave him great pleasure. When I was eight, he took us back to Japan. He bought this Hokusai print on that trip, found it in a little hole in the wall in Shinagawa. Mount Fuji at sunset, crimson sky, seen across the Bay of Kuroda. He paid a lot of money for it, more than he had to spend. Ten years later, I remember coming home, and looking at it and realizing it was a fake.

SETSUKO HEARN: Did you tell him?

DARIUS WHEELER: No.

SETSUKO HEARN: But you thought less of him.

DARIUS WHEELER: My father loved the print. He loved it with a big and undiscerning heart. It didn't matter if it wasn't what he thought it was.

SETSUKO HEARN: Love is blind. Is that the moral of the story?

DARIUS WHEELER: Listen to me —

SETSUKO HEARN: I should've known better. I should've seen this for what it was. Don't.

(The sound of wooden clappers.)

SETSUKO HEARN: I tendered my resignation today, I take full responsibility for this, I'm the one to blame, it was my mistake. The only question I'm left with is what you stood to gain. What did you stand to gain? Money, I suppose —

DARIUS WHEELER: You think I knew. You think I'd do that to you —

SETSUKO HEARN: I suppose you needed somebody to certify the authenticity of your property, to ensure its value prior to sale —

DARIUS WHEELER: That's not what this is about —

SETSUKO HEARN: What is this about? Why don't you tell me what this is all about.

DARIUS WHEELER: It's not what you think —

SETSUKO HEARN: What I think? How dare you. What do I think? Tell me, what do I think?

DARIUS WHEELER: That I somehow, that I used you. Listen to me —

SETSUKO HEARN: I was so stupid, I can't believe how stupid I was —

DARIUS WHEELER: You made a mistake —

SETSUKO HEARN: My mistake was having anything to do with someone like you —

DARIUS WHEELER: All right, look don't pretend to be some kind of innocent —

SETSUKO HEARN: What are you saying —

DARIUS WHEELER: You think you are above reproach, you think you're pure, that you're some kind of victim —

SETSUKO HEARN: What are you saying —

DARIUS WHEELER: You were the one who wanted this. I just picked up the tab, and you were happy to let me —

SETSUKO HEARN: You disgust me, everything about you disgusts me —

DARIUS WHEELER: I did this for you. This was all for you. Listen to me —

SETSUKO HEARN: Don't.

(Setsuko Hearn drops her glass. It shatters. The clear liquid pools on the floor. In the light, it looks red.)

SETSUKO HEARN: You actually seemed, for a moment, you seemed sincere. I believed you. I wanted to believe you.

(The sound of wooden clappers. Setsuko Hearn exits. Darius Wheeler disappears from view.)

Scene Thirty-four

A gallery. Thirty-six paintings are revealed hanging in the space. From a distance, each painting looks like a canvas filled with flecks of color. Claire Tsong is cleaning up a broken glass. She sweeps up the pieces. Enter Elizabeth Newman-Orr with two drinks.

CLAIRE TSONG: It slipped.

ELIZABETH NEWMAN-ORR: I got you another. Excited?

CLAIRE TSONG: Nervous.

ELIZABETH NEWMAN-ORR: Don't be. Everything looks perfect. *(Gives Claire Tsong her drink. Elizabeth and Claire drink. The sound of wooden clappers.)*

CLAIRE TSONG: So? How did the interview with Wheeler go? What did he say?

ELIZABETH NEWMAN-ORR: Lots of things. He claims he didn't know. He claims he didn't know a thing. He says he was fooled like everyone else.

CLAIRE TSONG: Don't tell me you believe him.

ELIZABETH NEWMAN-ORR: You know, I kinda do. When we were editing the tape, he seemed — I don't know — I hate to say it, but he seemed kinda truthful.

CLAIRE TSONG: Did he?

(The sound of wooden clappers.)

CLAIRE TSONG: When you were interviewing him, did he ever tell you about how he got started, in his business, I mean?

ELIZABETH NEWMAN-ORR: I don't know, he told me a story, he told me some story about his father.

CLAIRE TSONG: That's not the story I'm talking about. It takes money, you know. You need a little nut, some capital to start a business like Wheeler had. He met this girl — he didn't tell you about the girl? Maybe it slipped his mind. This was a while ago. She was very young. She had some stuff, some artwork she'd inherited when her parents died, some scrolls, a screen, what turned out to be a celadon vase. She knew he knew a thing or two about Asian art. She asked him what he thought. He said it was all pretty much worthless, but he'd buy it all from her, if she wanted, for a lump sum, a very modest sum. She was an art student at the time. There were debts. She needed the cash. A year later, she sees this painting that used to belong to her parents. It's in a Christies catalogue, along with some other stuff he bought from her. The whole lot ended up selling for just under two million. She saw him later at a party in Boston. He said that art and business were two different things. That he hoped she was better at art than she was at business. And that he'd give her a job, if she wanted, doing restoration. She could make good money.

ELIZABETH NEWMAN-ORR: And she threw her drink in his face.

(The sound of wooden clappers.)

CLAIRE TSONG: She may have.

ELIZABETH NEWMAN-ORR: She sounds like an unusual girl.

CLAIRE TSONG: I don't know. I think, at the end of the day, she's just your run-of-the-mill, girl-next-door kinda girl.

ELIZABETH NEWMAN-ORR: I don't know about that.

CLAIRE TSONG: I guess she's a lot of things. I guess she's kinda complicated.

ELIZABETH NEWMAN-ORR: I like complicated.

CLAIRE TSONG: Yeah? I'm glad.

(Claire Tsong and Elizabeth Newman-Orr kiss. The sound of wooden clappers. They disappear from view.)

Scene Thirty-five

A gallery. The thirty-six paintings remain. The ambient sound of voices, laughter from another room in the gallery. Enter John Bell in new clothes. Enter Owen Matthiassen.

OWEN MATTHIASSEN: John.

JOHN BELL: Dr. Matthiassen. How are you?

OWEN MATTHIASSEN: Well, I'm doing well. I didn't know you were a fan of Utagawa's work.

JOHN BELL: My friend — well, she, she helped put this all together.

OWEN MATTHIASSEN: I see. He's supposed to make an appearance tonight, Utagawa, that is. At least that's what they tell me. You know, I saw your book in the bookstore the other day. There was a big display. I bought a copy, couldn't resist. I should tell you, as a piece of fiction, I rather enjoyed it. I bet you never imagined it would go on and have such a life of its own.

JOHN BELL: No. No, I didn't.

(The sound of wooden clappers.)

JOHN BELL: I didn't mean for things to go the way they did. That wasn't my intent.

OWEN MATTHIASSEN: You know, some of my colleagues, they become very skeptical when the author begins talking about intent, what he intended to do. They suspect the author's a bit of a liar in the first place. Why should they listen to him after the fact?

JOHN BELL: I don't remember writing what I wrote. It's like it was written by another person.

OWEN MATTHIASSEN: I've heard people say that. A speculative leap. But now you see, one always hears that fiction is based on real life. Of course, that would mean you'd have to be a Japanese woman going on a thousand years old, give or take a few decades. As far as I can tell, you are not.

JOHN BELL: Maybe in a past life.

OWEN MATTHIASSEN: Come now. You can do better than that.

JOHN BELL: I just wrote what I wrote. I don't know where it came from. Maybe I was just inspired.

OWEN MATTHIASSEN: The muse descended from the ether, and whispered in your ear. And you, humble scribe, you just jotted it all down.

JOHN BELL: Something like that, yes.

OWEN MATTHIASSEN: It's fascinating, isn't it, how the human mind works, how it spins yarns, its infinite capacity for fabrication. Such literary talent, such business acumen. You surprise me, John, how far you've come. I never would have guessed you had it in you.

JOHN BELL: You don't really know me. You don't know me at all.

(The sound of wooden clappers)

OWEN MATTHIASSEN: No. No, I suppose I don't.

(The sound of wooden clappers.)

OWEN MATTHIASSEN: You know, there's something about his new work, I don't know what to make of it. There's something I don't quite understand. Perhaps, it's generational. Or perhaps it's just me. Just a different way of seeing things. Either way, it's late, it's been a long day, and I should, I should get going. You must tell me if Utagawa shows up this time around. I'll be curious to hear.

(Owen Matthiassen exits. The sound of wooden clappers. John Bell disappears from view.)

Scene Thirty-six

A stage. Darius Wheeler and Setsuko Hearn appear. They stand apart. The sound of wooden clappers.

DARIUS WHEELER: So what happened to Darius Wheeler?

SETSUKO HEARN: He lived happily ever after. They all did, more or less.

DARIUS WHEELER: The guy lost his shirt.

SETSUKO HEARN: Not quite. There was one last twist. The manuscript he bought, the original that is, it wasn't what he thought it was.

DARIUS WHEELER: I thought it was a fake.

SETSUKO HEARN: It was. It was a fake Heian-era manuscript. It was also an original work by a contemporary artist, a very popular, if somewhat reclusive painter.
(The sound of wooden clappers.)

DARIUS WHEELER: So did Utagawa, did he ever show up that night, in that last scene?

SETSUKO HEARN: Yes.

DARIUS WHEELER: What was he like?

SETSUKO HEARN: She. Utagawa turned out to be a she, a woman, a young woman. She'd been making her living restoring masterworks. She'd picked up quite a few techniques along the way. She'd actually, oddly enough, worked for Darius Wheeler at one point. They knew each other. In passing.
(The sound of wooden clappers.)

DARIUS WHEELER: And did he and that lady professor, did they ever — ?

SETSUKO HEARN: No.

DARIUS WHEELER: That's too bad.

SETSUKO HEARN: He did just fine. She did just fine, too.

DARIUS WHEELER: Were they happy?

SETSUKO HEARN: Happy enough.
(The sound of wooden clappers.)

DARIUS WHEELER: So if, if I were to ask you to go for a drink later, you would say —

SETSUKO HEARN: Some other time.

DARIUS WHEELER: Right. Right.
(Setsuko Hearn approaches Darius Wheeler, touches the side of his face.)

SETSUKO HEARN: Good night.
(The sound of wooden clappers. Setsuko Hearn turns and starts her exit. The sound of her footsteps across the stage.)

DARIUS WHEELER: She turns. A memory pieces itself together in his mind. Her eyes. The look in her eyes. A picture forming as she recedes from view. *(The thirty-six paintings shift their alignment to form a larger picture, like individual tiles of a larger mosaic. The picture they form is of a woman, a portrait of a lady, an echo of the lady from the top of the play, but different — part ancient, part contemporary, part Japanese woodblock print, part animé. Bright light on the portrait of the lady. The sound of wooden clappers. Darkness.)*

END OF PLAY

CHAGRIN FALLS

By Mia McCullough

PLAYWRIGHT'S BIOGRAPHY

Mia McCullough's play *Chagrin Falls* premiered at Stage Left Theater in Chicago in September 2001. The play garnered several national and local awards, including the M. Elizabeth Osborn Award for New Plays given by the American Theater Critics Association, first prize in the Julie Harris Playwriting Competition, the Joseph Jefferson Award for Best New Work, the John W. Schmid After Dark Award for Best New Play, and a Jeff nomination for Best Production. *Chagrin Falls* closed the 2001–2002 season at the Cincinnati Shakespeare Festival. That production garnered four awards, including best production, at the Cincinnati Entertainment Awards. Ms. McCullough's play *Taking Care* premiered at Steppenwolf Theatre Company in their 2002–2003 season. Her play *Cyber Serenade* has been performed at theaters in Oregon and California and received its Midwest premiere at Stage Left Theater in April 2003. Author of twelve stage plays, five screenplays, two teleplays, and several pieces of short fiction, Ms. McCullough is a resident of Evanston, Illinois and works part-time at a shelter for battered women. She is a member of The Playwright's Collective, The Dramatists Guild, and Stage Left Theater Company and is a resident playwright with Chicago Dramatists.

INTRODUCTION

When I wrote *Chagrin Falls,* I wanted to peel away the social and political ramifications of the issues I was dealing with and look at the emotional consequences. I didn't want to add to a theoretical debate; I wanted to draw the truth out of these characters. What does it do to you if you kill livestock for a living? What about keeping people in cages, spending forty hours a week in a prison? What about serving in the military killing strangers? *Chagrin Falls* is not a play about whether or not capital punishment or war or eating animal flesh is ethical. It's a story about an unfortunate minority performing the dirty work for the convenience and peace of mind of the rest of the nation. It's all fine and dandy if you think a convicted murderer deserves to die, but could you strap him down to a table? Put the needle in his or her arm? Could you kill a cow? If we don't have the stomach for it as individuals, we have no right to expect other people to do it for us.

ORIGINAL PRODUCTION

Chagrin Falls premiered September 25, 2001 at Stage Left Theater in Chicago, Illinois. It was directed by Kevin Heckman; the stage manager was Leigh Barrett. The cast was as follows:

IRENE DELFORD . . . . Morgan McCabe
RILEY MACDOUGAL . . . . Don Tieri
HENRY HARCOURT. . . . . Cory Krebsbach
PATRICE DOUGHERTY . . . . Jennifer Willison
THADDEUS NEWELL . . . . Harry Eddleman
REVEREND MAYCOMB. . . . . Jack Tippett

CHARACTERS

IRENE DELFORD: weather-worn woman, early forties

RILEY MACDOUGAL: a recent retiree from the local slaughterhouse, early fifties

THADDEUS NEWELL: a prison guard, twenty-one

PATRICE DOUGHERTY: half-Vietnamese, a graduate student in journalism, twenty-six

HENRY HARCOURT: a prison guard, twenty

REVEREND: man, mid- to late thirties

MAN'S VOICE: can be played by any of the men

TIME

1999

PLACE

Chagrin Falls, Oklahoma

SETTING

The bar of Irene's Motel

CHAGRIN FALLS

Act I
Scene One

> *The lights come up on a barroom: rustic and old, but clean and presentable*
> *enough. We see the back of the bar, as if the audience were serving the drinks.*
> *Beyond the bar is an elevated area with several tables. Riley sits at the bar*
> *facing the audience, staring into his beer. Irene, a pretty, but weather-worn*
> *woman in her early forties, stands behind the bar, wearing an apron and*
> *talking on the phone.*

IRENE: Well, are you a relation of the victim or of the accused? . . . We've already got family of the victim staying here. I don't like to mix, it makes people uncomfortable. No, I'm not saying you can't stay here, I'm saying you shouldn't . . .
(Henry Harcourt, a young man in a prison guard's uniform, enters. Henry beats his hands on the bar in an arrhythmic pattern, waiting for Irene to get off the phone.)

IRENE: Look, I don't play favorites. I book whoever calls first and I stick with it. This time the family of the victim beat you to it. The Chagrin Falls Motel is down the road about five miles. It's just as close to the penitentiary. You want the number? She hung up on me.

HENRY: Who's that?

IRENE: Kin of the accused.

HENRY: Anyone showed up yet?

IRENE: No, but it's a little early. What can I do for you, Henry?

HENRY: Two burgers?

IRENE: All right . . . Say, you seen Thaddeus today?

HENRY: Nope.

RILEY: Why don't you call over to the house instead of asking every damn person that walks through the door.

IRENE: What if I wake her up? You know she don't sleep more than a few hours a day. Anyhow, he's due at work, right about now. I was just wonderin' where he's been.

RILEY: Even if you knew she wasn't sleepin', you wouldn't call.

IRENE: There some point in upsettin' her, in her state?

RILEY: You ruined a good friendship, is all I'm saying.

IRENE: You know, I'm not going to let you hang around here twenty-four hours a day if you're going to give me a hard time. You wanna be a pain in the ass, you can go down to McNeally's and sit with the rest of them old bastards.

(Irene exits into to the kitchen. Henry continues to tap on the bar.)

RILEY: Will you knock that off.

(Henry stops. He is feeling slightly chastised.)

HENRY: What's the matter? Got a hangover?

RILEY: Why are you so fucking happy all the time?

HENRY: I don't know. What do I got to be sad about? I got my wife, my friends, a baby on the way, and everyday I get out of jail free.

(Riley shakes his head, bewildered and amused.)

RILEY: You still like it over there?

HENRY: It's all right, I guess. They got me on suicide watch for the new guy last week. He keeps it pretty interesting.

RILEY: What's his name?

HENRY: Jonas Caldwell.

RILEY: What'd he do?

HENRY: Murdered and raped an eight-year-old girl.

RILEY: Good riddance.

HENRY: I s'pose. So, what'd you do on your first day as a free man?

IRENE: *(From offstage.)* Hung around here, makin' me crazy.

HENRY: Is that right? What'd they get you, anyway?

IRENE: *(Offstage.)* They didn't get him anything. After thirty years. Nothing.

RILEY: They said they got me somethin'. It just wasn't ready yet.

HENRY: Rumor has it, they got you somethin' real good.

RILEY: By whose standards?

(Irene reenters.)

IRENE: Well, I'll believe it when I see it.

RILEY: What do I care? It'll just be something stupid to put on the mantle-piece or hang on the wall. Remind me that I'm a washed-up old man with no way to fill my days.

IRENE: Oh Lord. We're gonna have to find you a hobby right quick.

(Patrice, a petite Asian woman, enters. She has a carry-on bag slung over her shoulders.)

IRENE: Hi. Can I help you?

PATRICE: The sign said I should ask for Irene at the bar.

IRENE: That's me.

PATRICE: I have a reservation. The last name is Dougherty.

IRENE: Oh, yeah, right. Hang on a sec. I'll go get the key.

(Irene exits. Riley and Henry stare at Patrice.)

HENRY: Hi.

PATRICE: Hi.

HENRY: You in town for the execution?

PATRICE: Yes.

HENRY: Friend of the victim?

PATRICE: No. I'm a journalist.

HENRY: Oh. One of them.

PATRICE: Yes.

(Irene enters with a key in hand.)

IRENE: Here you go. It's room number four. You need help with your bags?

PATRICE: No. I got it. Do you serve dinner in here?

IRENE: And breakfast, and lunch.

PATRICE: Is it too early? Is the kitchen open?

IRENE: My kitchen is always open. Have a seat, I'll get you a menu. Unless, you'd like to freshen up first.

PATRICE: No, I'll eat first.

(Irene hands Patrice a menu.)

IRENE: Sit wherever you want.

(Patrice sits at a table near the bar. Irene exits into the kitchen.)

HENRY: *(To Patrice.)* You writin' a story on Jonas?

PATRICE: Not exactly. It's more about capital punishment. I wanted to get the perspective of all the individuals involved in the process, the execution, including the death row inmate.

HENRY: Why'd you pick Jonas Caldwell?

PATRICE: Well, . . . the date of his execution fits the time frame I'm working in, and this is the only prison that gave me permission to observe.

HENRY: You're gonna watch him die?

PATRICE: That's the plan.

RILEY: What newspaper you with?

PATRICE: I'm not with a newspaper. I'm a graduate student. This article will be my thesis. My final project. I'm hoping to sell it to a newspaper or national magazine when I'm done.

HENRY: Are you Chinese?

RILEY: Henry!

HENRY: What?

RILEY: She's not Chinese, you idiot, she's Vietnamese, and it's rude to ask questions like that.

HENRY: I'm sorry. I wasn't trying to be rude. I've just never met an Oriental person before.

PATRICE: That's all right. Anyway, I'm only half Vietnamese.

HENRY: What's your other half?

PATRICE: I'm not sure. American soldier, probably. Do you work at the prison?

HENRY: Yeah, I'm a day guard. I'm on Jonas' watch for his last week.

PATRICE: Really?

HENRY: Yep.

PATRICE: I've been trying to get his consent to be interviewed. You wouldn't happen to know if he's gotten my letters?

HENRY: I wouldn't know about that, but it wouldn't matter if he did get them.

PATRICE: Why is that?

HENRY: He can't read much more than his own name, and he doesn't ever want us read the letters to him anymore. He used to let us look at 'em. Just to pass the time. Now he rips 'em up into tiny little pieces. And he gets a fair bit of mail. It's a mess sometimes —

PATRICE: Who writes to him?

HENRY: Oh, I don't know, folks opposing the death penalty. Religious leaders. Crazy women who want to marry him. I don't get that. I mean, I guess he's good looking enough, but why would anyone want to marry a guy on death row? I mean, it's not like they could —

PATRICE: Would you ask him if he'd let me interview him?

HENRY: Well, sure, I guess I can ask. He doesn't much like me, though, so I wouldn't be too hopeful. Not a day goes by that he doesn't offer to wring my neck. Says they can't kill him twice so what does it matter how many more people he knocks off.

(The door opens again, and Thaddeus enters with a book in hand.)

HENRY: Hey, Thaddeus. How's it goin'?

THADDEUS: How do you think it's goin'?

HENRY: Now there's the man you should ask. Thaddeus gets on with him much better than I do.

THADDEUS: Who do I get on with?

HENRY: Jonas Caldwell.

THADDEUS: I don't "get on" with him. I put up with him and I do my job.

(Thaddeus sits at the farthest end of the bar and reads his book, not looking up to talk to Henry.)

HENRY: Well, he don't give you half the shit he gives us.

THADDEUS: I don't know what to tell you, Henry. Luck of the draw.

HENRY: Say, what's your name?

PATRICE: Patrice.

HENRY: *(To Thaddeus.)* This is Patrice. She's doin' a story on capital punishment.

(Thaddeus takes a brief second to process the fact that Henry has used the words "capital punishment" before he acknowledges Patrice.)

THADDEUS: Hi.

PATRICE: Hi.

(Irene enters with Henry's burgers in a bag. Irene is one of the few people Thaddeus will look in the eye.)

IRENE: There you are. Why aren'tcha at work?

THADDEUS: Roger asked me to switch with him. I'm doin' his graveyard shift tonight.

IRENE: Where you been all day?

THADDEUS: I had some things to do.

IRENE: Whatcha got on your hands?

THADDEUS: Just some wood stain.

IRENE: *(Coy.)* Whatcha makin'?

THADDEUS: You mind fixin' somethin' for me to take home?

IRENE: All right. Don't tell me. Here you go, Henry.

HENRY: Thanks. I'll see you later, Patrice. Say, how do you spell that anyway?

PATRICE: What? My name?

HENRY: Yeah.

PATRICE: Why do you want to know how to spell it?

HENRY: 'Cause if I can't spell it, I can't remember it. It's a thing I got.

RILEY: Yeah, it's called brain damage.

IRENE: Riley, don't pick on the boy.

PATRICE: It's spelled P-A-T-R-I-C-E. Like "Pat" and "rice," but one word.

HENRY: Like rice patty. That's how I'll remember it. I'll see you tomorrow.

IRENE: Bye, Henry.

(Henry exits.)

RILEY: He's not the sharpest tack in the box.

IRENE: He don't mean to offend you. He just don't know any better. You find anything on the menu that suits ya?

PATRICE: You wouldn't happen to have any fish, would you? I don't eat meat.

IRENE: Nothing fresh today. I could throw some frozen cod in the deep fryer or there's canned tuna.

PATRICE: Tuna, then. And a salad, please. But not tuna salad. Just tuna on the side, no mayo.

IRENE: All right. Thaddeus, would you be able to go fishin' tomorrow, sometime?

THADDEUS: Sure.

PATRICE: You don't have to go fishing on my account. I can make do.

THADDEUS: That's all right. I usually go out a couple times a week, anyhow.

(Irene exits to the kitchen. Thaddeus tries to read while Riley talks to him.)

RILEY: So you're babysittin' this one, eh?

THADDEUS: Unfortunately.

RILEY: Who'd you piss off?

THADDEUS: You know me, Riley. I piss off everyone.

RILEY: What's he like?

(Patrice eavesdrops.)

THADDEUS: Illiterate. Belligerent. Has nightmares pretty near every night.

RILEY: He talk to you much?

THADDEUS: Too much. I can't get through half a chapter on his watch.

(Riley does not get the hint.)

RILEY: Well, they're not paying you to read, are they?

THADDEUS: They're not paying me to be his counselor either. There's psychologists who get a pretty penny to listen to that wacked-out drivel.

(Irene enters with a plastic bag full of food and a tray with Patrice's meal. She serves Patrice while the men talk.)

RILEY: You workin' this one?

THADDEUS: Yep, I'm on tie-down.

IRENE: Thaddeus, you shouldn't have to —

THADDEUS: Why not?

IRENE: It's too much.

THADDEUS: You gonna write me a note?

(Irene sets the bag down next to Thaddeus.)

IRENE: I'm sure if you talked to the warden —

THADDEUS: I'm not talkin' to anybody. It's my job . . . You put all this together just now?

IRENE: I fixed it up earlier. I thought you'd be by.

THADDEUS: Sorry. I didn't mean to —

IRENE: 'S all right.

THADDEUS: I gotta go sit with her.

IRENE: I know. There's somethin' in there for you, too.

THADDEUS: Thanks.

IRENE: You'll come by in the mornin', after work?

(Thaddeus glances sidelong at Riley.)

THADDEUS: Probably.

IRENE: See ya later.

(Thaddeus exits.)

IRENE: Food OK?

PATRICE: It's fine, thanks.

IRENE: Well, holler if you need anything. I gotta get ready for the dinner rush.

(Irene exits to the kitchen. Patrice looks around at the empty bar.)

PATRICE: Are there actually enough people in this town to create a "dinner rush?"

RILEY: Oh, yeah. There'll be about thirty men in here once the second shift gets done over at the slaughterhouse.

PATRICE: The slaughterhouse?

RILEY: Didn't you see it, driving in? It's just west of town.

PATRICE: I came from the East.

RILEY: Oh, well, then I guess you wouldn't have seen it. It's got a pretty powerful smell, though.

PATRICE: That's what that stench is.

RILEY: I wouldn't call it a stench. It mostly smells like raw beef with a slight hint of manure mixed in. 'Course you don't notice it once you've worked there a while.

PATRICE: You worked there?

RILEY: Thirty years. Retired last Friday.

PATRICE: You killed cows for thirty years?

RILEY: Well, I wasn't always killin' 'em. Sometimes I was cuttin' 'em, skinnin' 'em, stunnin' 'em. Spent the last ten years supervising the different areas. It's quite an operation we got over there. Not one of the biggest in the country, but we got the highest production rate for a plant our size.

PATRICE: Any other gruesome industries in this town I should know about?

RILEY: Just the prison and the slaughterhouse. A few farmers and cattle ranchers, too, of course.

PATRICE: I see.

RILEY: So where are you from?

PATRICE: I live in Boston.

RILEY: There a lot of Vietnamese immigrants livin' there?

PATRICE: I don't know. I haven't taken a poll . . . How did you know I was Vietnamese?

RILEY: I've been to Vietnam. I remember what people look like.

PATRICE: You're a veteran.

RILEY: Yes, I am.

(Pause.)

PATRICE: I guess killing cows isn't so hard after you've killed people.

RILEY: Killin' cows has a purpose, and you shouldn't assume things about people you don't know.

PATRICE: You didn't kill anyone while you were in Vietnam?

(Silence. Riley will not let her bait him. He takes a sip of his beer.)

PATRICE: Do you think killing people has a purpose? In a war?

RILEY: Not that I can see. Not unless you're going to eat 'em.

(Irene enters from kitchen.)

IRENE: Did you want somethin' to drink? I completely forgot to ask you.

PATRICE: . . . No. I'm fine. Is it all right if I eat in my room?

IRENE: Yeah, that's fine. You want me to bring it in to ya?

PATRICE: No, I've got it. Can you put it on my tab or something? Do you do that?

IRENE: I'll put it on your bill.

PATRICE: All right. Thanks.

(Patrice exits with her plate and glass.)

IRENE: What'd you say to her?

RILEY: Nothin'.

(Lights fade.)

Scene Two

It's morning. Lights come up on Patrice sitting at a table, eating breakfast. After a moment, Irene emerges from the kitchen with some cutlery. She begins to set place settings and napkins on the bar as she talks to Patrice.

IRENE: Everything all right?

PATRICE: Yeah, it's great, thanks. I'm sorry I came in so early. I don't sleep well in strange places. New places.

IRENE: Lots of folks have trouble adjusting. Especially when they come from a different time zone.

(Patrice watches Irene for a moment.)

PATRICE: Have you ever been inside the prison?

IRENE: No . . . isn't that funny? Make my living off the place and I ain't never been in it.

PATRICE: I'm going on a tour today.

IRENE: Is that right? I hear it's quite an experience.

(Riley enters carrying a side of beef wrapped in paper on his shoulder.)

RILEY: Hey, Irene. Where'dya want this?

IRENE: Jesus Christ, why are you bringing that in through here? Put it on the butcher's table.

(Irene holds the door to the kitchen open for him. She looks at the path he's tracked across her floor.)

IRENE: Goddamnit, you got blood all over my floor. Now, I gotta mop again. What're you doin' bringin' it in anyway?

RILEY: I had to drop some papers off at the plant. I figured I'd do Enrique a favor and drop off your delivery myself. Since I was coming over, anyway. *(Patrice looks around at the blood on the floor. She turns back to her food, looking disgusted. Irene is wiping up the blood as Riley emerges from the kitchen. He's got a sizeable stain on his shirt. It is the pinkish, watery blood of fresh meat, not the red blood of fresh kill.)*

IRENE: Well, next time use the back door. You got it all over yourself.
(She wipes at the blood stain on Riley's shirt. Patrice has pushed her plate away from her.)

RILEY: Don't fuss with it. Just some coffee. Please.

IRENE: You go home last night?

RILEY: Where else would I go?
(Irene pours Riley a cup of coffee.)

IRENE: You don't look like you changed clothes, is all.

RILEY: All my clothes look the same.

IRENE: You want some breakfast?

RILEY: Not just yet.

IRENE: All right.
(Irene stares at him a moment, and then exits into the kitchen. Riley looks over at Patrice.)

RILEY: Mornin'.

PATRICE: Good morning.
(Pause.)

PATRICE: I'm sorry I spoke to you that way last night. You were right. I don't know you, and it was very inappropriate.

RILEY: It's a sensitive issue for you.

PATRICE: More than I realized . . . Anyway, I'm sorry.
(Pause.)

RILEY: You're up early.

PATRICE: I'm going on a tour of the prison this morning. I guess I'm a little nervous. I couldn't really sleep.

RILEY: I wouldn't get too worked up about the prison. They keep those bastards locked in tight up there. They only get someone breaking out a couple times a year.

PATRICE: I know. I think it's more that this story, . . . I don't want to screw it up.

RILEY: I see.
(There is an uncomfortable silence. The door opens and Henry enters. Irene returns simultaneously with a brown bag.)

HENRY: Mornin'.

IRENE: Mornin'.

HENRY: Hey, Rice Patty!

PATRICE: Hi.

HENRY: It's Henry.

PATRICE: I remember.

(Irene sets the bag in front of Henry.)

HENRY: What is it today?

IRENE: Don't you believe in surprises?

HENRY: I like to have something to look forward to.

IRENE: Well, then you can peek when you can't take the suspense anymore.

(Henry sticks his nose in the bag and takes a sniff.)

HENRY: Turkey on rye. That's what I'm guessin'.

IRENE: It's good you got a knack for something, Henry.

HENRY: Can I pay you when I come back to pick up dinner?

IRENE: Sure.

RILEY: Tracey forget how to cook?

HENRY: Naw, she just can't stand the smell of food cooking right now, first trimester and all. I'll see y'all later.

(The door opens and Thaddeus enters as Henry exits. Thaddeus is in his guard uniform.)

HENRY: Mornin', Thaddeus.

THADDEUS: *(Low and mumbled.)* Mornin'.

RILEY: *(To himself.)* Why is it stupid people never have trouble reproducing?

(Thaddeus sits at his spot at the far end of the bar and opens his book.)

IRENE: Hi.

THADDEUS: Hi.

IRENE: Work was all right?

THADDEUS: I guess.

IRENE: You stayin'?

THADDEUS: No. She was real bad last night when I left. I'm gonna go home for a while and then go fishin'.

PATRICE: Please don't feel like you have to go fishing for me.

THADDEUS: It's all right. I like fishin'.

PATRICE: Well, at least let me keep you company. Or help, or something.

THADDEUS: You don't have to do that.

PATRICE: I know. I've just never been fishing. And I could . . . ask you about your job. I'd be interested to hear about it . . . for my article.

(Thaddeus looks at Irene for a moment.)

THADDEUS: All right. I'll come by around two or so. That time OK for you?

PATRICE: That's fine.

IRENE: I'll get you somethin' to go, then.

(The door opens and Reverend Johnny enters. He is a young man, in his mid-thirties, handsome and cleancut. He wears layman's clothes.)

IRENE: Mornin', Reverend.

REVEREND: Irene. Riley. Thaddeus.

(Both Thaddeus and Riley react to the sound of the Reverend's voice, though in different ways. Irene exits into the kitchen.)

THADDEUS: She OK?

REVEREND: She got better through the night. Finally fell asleep right before I left.

(Thaddeus nods, but looks back down at his book. Pause. Reverend looks at Riley who is concentrating on not looking at the Reverend.)

REVEREND: I'm sorry we missed the chance to talk the other day, Riley.

RILEY: Yeah, I . . . had some things to do. Some last minute retirement forms to fill out.

REVEREND: I understand. You can always reschedule.

(Riley gets up.)

RILEY: Yeah, I will. Well, I better get this shirt in the wash. I'll see y'all later.

(Riley is exiting as Irene comes in with a bag for Thaddeus, and a Styrofoam cup, which she fills with coffee for the Reverend.)

REVEREND: My apologies for scaring off your best customer.

IRENE: I think he's havin' a real hard time, Johnny.

REVEREND: I think so, too.

IRENE: I don't think he's been goin' home at night. Looks like somebody's been sleepin' on the bare mattress in room seven where the lock only works from the inside. I don't want to say anything to him because I don't want to embarrass him, and I don't mind . . .

REVEREND: I'm not getting the feeling he wants to talk to me, Irene.

IRENE: He just doesn't know how, Johnny. He just . . . He's not a verbal person. And he's very private about . . . Alice was something he held very close to himself, so that no one else could see. So, don't take it personally that he won't talk to you.

REVEREND: No. I wouldn't.

IRENE: But don't stop tryin'.

REVEREND: Maybe I'm just not the right person, Irene. For Riley. I'd like to think I can help everybody, but it doesn't really work that way.

(Thaddeus drains his coffee cup, takes the bag and gets up.)

REVEREND: You headin' home, Thaddeus?

THADDEUS: Yeah. Thanks for sittin' with her, Reverend.

REVEREND: Anytime.

THADDEUS: I really appreciate it. 'Specially on such short notice.

REVEREND: It's my pleasure.

THADDEUS: I'll see you later, Irene. Thanks.

IRENE: Sure, darlin'.

(*Thaddeus leaves.*)

PATRICE: Excuse me, but are you Reverend Maycomb?

REVEREND: Yes.

PATRICE: Hi, I'm Patrice Dougherty. We spoke on the phone.

(*The Reverend goes over and shakes her hand.*)

REVEREND: The reporter. Yes. I see you found the place OK.

PATRICE: Yes, thanks for the recommendation.

REVEREND: Are we still on for tomorrow?

PATRICE: Ten o'clock.

REVEREND: Perfect.

PATRICE: Should I meet you at the rectory or the prison?

REVEREND: The rectory has more of a relaxed atmosphere. It's the church right
down the way.

PATRICE: I saw it.

REVEREND: Ten o'clock, then.

PATRICE: Great.

(*The Reverend grabs his coffee and exits.*)

IRENE: So, you'll be interviewin' lots of folks, I gather.

PATRICE: I'm going to try.

IRENE: Gettin' the prison guard's perspective?

PATRICE: Yeah. It doesn't seem like anyone asks them what they think about
it. I'd think most people living in a prison town would have an opinion
on the subject one way or the other.

IRENE: I suppose we do have our thoughts on it.

PATRICE: Anyone ever interview you?

IRENE: Me? No. You need anything else?

PATRICE: No, I'm done. Thanks . . . Could I interview you?

IRENE: You want to put me in a story?

PATRICE: Sure, why not? You live here. Run a business. Your opinion's just as
valid as anyone else's.

(*Patrice pulls out a tape recorder.*)

IRENE: You gonna record me?

PATRICE: If that's all right.

IRENE: I guess.

PATRICE: What's your last name?

IRENE: Delford.

PATRICE: Irene Delford. So, what do you think about the death penalty?

(*Irene looks at the tape recorder with discomfort.*)

IRENE: I don't know.

PATRICE: Do you think it's justified? Immoral? Cruel? Necessary?

IRENE: It's just illogical, that's my problem with it.

(*Pause.*)

PATRICE: Could you elaborate on that?

IRENE: Well, it doesn't make any sense to tell someone that murder is the ultimate sin and wrongdoing and then turn around and punish them by committing the same atrocity you condemn them for. Either murder's wrong or it's not. It can't be illegal for the citizens but legal for the government. "A system built on hypocrisy." That's what Thaddeus calls it. But that's neither here nor there. Don't see how my opinion affects what happens up the way.

PATRICE: How long have you run this motel and restaurant?

IRENE: Took over when my father died. 'Bout six years ago.

PATRICE: So people stay here when they come in for the executions?

IRENE: You're stayin' here, aren'tcha?

PATRICE: Does it ever bother you that you make money off of other people dying?

IRENE: (*Annoyed.*) No, it doesn't bother me because I don't think about it like that. I provide a service. I'm in the hospitality business, not in the *killin'* people business. Regardless of my proximity.

PATRICE: Have you lived in Chagrin Falls all your life?

IRENE: I've lived in this motel all my life.

PATRICE: Really?

IRENE: Yeah. Not much of a home, is it?

PATRICE: I don't know.

IRENE: I do.

(*Beat.*)

PATRICE: Do you have any idea how many men they've executed at the prison in your lifetime?

IRENE: Haven't the slightest. That'd be a morbid tally to keep, don't you think?

PATRICE: How do you feel —

IRENE: You know, I don't want to answer any more questions.

PATRICE: All right.

(*Patrice turns of the recorder and puts it in her pocket.*)

IRENE: What made you pick such a cheery topic, anyhow? Or was it assigned to you?

PATRICE: No, I picked it.

IRENE: Why?

PATRICE: Well, . . . it's a very controversial issue, right now.

IRENE: There's a lot of controversial issues. What made you pick this one?
(Pause.)

PATRICE: There are some personal reasons I decided to explore it.

IRENE: Fair enough.

PATRICE: Are the Mendozas staying here?

IRENE: Who?

PATRICE: The parents of Maria Mendoza. The girl he killed.

IRENE: I don't give out information on my guests. Everyone has a right to their privacy.

PATRICE: No, I know, I just —

IRENE: You know, I let you stay here because you said you were a student and I need to fill my rooms, but I don't like reporters in here harrassing the family of the victim. I don't mind so much with the accused's family, they can fend for themselves, but the family of the victim — they don't need some insensitive reporter ripping open their wounds. This is a hard enough thing for them anyway, comin' here.

PATRICE: I already interviewed the Mendozas. I was just wondering if I might see them here. That's all.

IRENE: . . . Well, it's still their business to tell you where they're stayin', not mine.
(Irene clears away Patrice's plates.)

PATRICE: No, I understand . . . I should get over to the prison.

IRENE: All right, then.
(Irene exits into the kitchen. Lights fade.)

Scene Three

The lights come up on Thaddeus and Patrice. They sit on the bank of a river, fishing poles dangling over the edge. Patrice peers down at the water.

PATRICE: Are you sure there's fish in there?

THADDEUS: Always has been.

PATRICE: So, basically, fishing is completely tedious.

THADDEUS: Well, it's not the most heart-pounding activity out there, but it's got it's charms. It's peaceful. It's productive. It's something useful you can do without bothering anyone else.

PATRICE: You didn't want me to tag along, did you?

THADDEUS: No, I don't mind. 'Cording to most folks, I spend too much time by myself, anyhow.

PATRICE: So, do you mind if I ask you a few questions about your job?

(Patrice takes a small tape recorder out of her pocket.)

THADDEUS: How 'bout I ask you some questions first.

PATRICE: OK. Why?

THADDEUS: 'Cause I like to know who I'm talking to.

PATRICE: All right. What do you want to know?

THADDEUS: Where you from?

PATRICE: I'm living in the Boston area right now. Getting my degree. I grew up in Oklahoma City, mostly. We moved around a bit.

THADDEUS: I wouldn't've pegged you for a native.

PATRICE: Thanks.

THADDEUS: You're welcome . . . What's your father do?

PATRICE: Both my parents are college professors.

THADDEUS: They got money?

PATRICE: I wouldn't say they've got a lot of money. They're middle class.

THADDEUS: What do they teach?

PATRICE: My father teaches Christian theology, my mother teaches sociology.

THADDEUS: Do you believe in God?

PATRICE: Do you?

THADDEUS: *(With a smile.)* No. But don't tell Reverend Johnny.

PATRICE: I don't believe in a Christian god. But don't tell my parents.

THADDEUS: Fair 'nough . . . What'd you think of your tour of the prison?

PATRICE: It was creepy.

THADDEUS: Yeah, it's a creepy place. They take you through a cell block?

PATRICE: Yeah.

THADDEUS: I bet you've never had so many men tell you were beautiful all at once like that.

(Patrice shudders.)

PATRICE: It made me want to run back to the motel and take a shower.

THADDEUS: Yeah, the whole place does that to you.

PATRICE: I don't know how you can stand to work there.

THADDEUS: Yeah, well, I don't have a whole lot of options. I can either keep people in cages or kill cows. And since I never met a cow that did me wrong . . .

PATRICE: The lesser of two evils.

THADDEUS: I guess.

PATRICE: So, can I ask questions, now?

THADDEUS: Yeah. Sure.

PATRICE: *(Indicating the recorder.)* Is this OK?

THADDEUS: Yeah.

(She turns on the tape recorder.)

PATRICE: I overheard you saying that you're on the tie-down team.

THADDEUS: Yep. I am.

PATRICE: What does that involve?

THADDEUS: I strap his left leg and arm to the table.

PATRICE: You do that in the execution chamber?

THADDEUS: Yeah. They show it to you?

PATRICE: Yes. It's very . . . sterile. All that stainless steel.

THADDEUS: Yeah.

PATRICE: So you watch the execution?

THADDEUS: No. We wait in the hall. The spectators can't see if we're standing in the way.

PATRICE: How many have you done?

THADDEUS: Ten. This'll be eleven.

PATRICE: Do they ever say anything to you? When you're strapping them down?

(Thaddeus thinks about this for a moment.)

THADDEUS: Not really. They maybe say "good-bye." Sometimes "thanks," which is weird. I mean, I know their thankin' me for talkin to 'em their last week, for bringin' 'em their meals, but considerin' the context, "thank you" sounds pretty strange comin' outta their mouths. Anyhow, there's not a lot of time for chit-chat. We get sent out as soon as they get the needle in his arm.

PATRICE: Who starts the machine with the drugs going?

THADDEUS: Oh, they don't tell us that. The executioner's identity is a very well kept secret. They're in a separate room behind a one-way window. It's all done by remote control.

PATRICE: Seems like an awful lot of people to kill one man.

THADDEUS: Oh, yeah. Four guys strap him down, the nurse puts the needle in his arm, the warden signals for the executioner to start, the executioner pushes a button. They certainly do their best to divvy up the guilt. It's such a farce, everyone trying to dodge culpability. You know, when they used to kill people using a firing squad, they'd have five gunmen. And every time, one of the rifle's would be loaded with blanks, but the gunmen never knew which one it was. So when it was done, each man could say to himself, "It was my gun with the blanks. I didn't kill anybody." Now, it's like they're trying to spread the blame around to as many participants as they can. Like if they split up the killing into enough little pieces, no one will feel responsible.

PATRICE: Do you feel responsible? Just strapping him down?

THADDEUS: I feel like I'm doin' my job.

PATRICE: It doesn't upset you?

THADDEUS: It doesn't keep me up nights or drive me to drink like it does some guys. Maybe it hasn't hit me, yet. I haven't done that many. One of our guys just lost it one day. He'd done I don't know how many. A lot. He had to quit, move out of town, everything.

PATRICE: You think that'll happen to you?

THADDEUS: I don't plan on stickin' around that long. Anyhow, it'd be different if I had to be in the room with him, like the Reverend and the Warden do. I leave the room, he's alive. I come back, he's dead. We put the body on the gurney for the funeral people, and we punch out.

PATRICE: So, you don't go home feeling responsible for a man's death?

THADDEUS: I didn't sentence him to die. I'm just doing my job. Maybe if I was sittin' on a person's jury, maybe then I'd feel responsible.

PATRICE: The judge makes the final sentencing decision, not the jury.

THADDEUS: Don't you believe that. In Oklahoma, the jury decides the sentence. The judge does make the final decision, but it's a formality. There's been maybe one time in the state's history when a judge overturned a jury's death sentence.

PATRICE: So, if you were on a jury, would you ever recommend lethal injection?

THADDEUS: . . . Well, that's hard to say. If you're askin' if I'm opposed to the death penalty, well then no, I'm not. Not exactly. I don't think killing is inherently wrong. It's too much in our nature to be wrong. But I do think it's wrong to stick a needle in someone's arm and call it justice. We should call it what it really is — just cold-blooded revenge. Revenge should burn, don't you think? Be passionate and cathartic. Not clinical and sad.

PATRICE: Do you think Jonas Caldwell deserves to die?

THADDEUS: Oh, I think we all deserve to die. I just don't think murder should be as impersonal as all that.

PATRICE: What's he like?

THADDEUS: He's a class-A bastard, from what I can tell. He's not so bad with me on night watch. I think he sorta tires himself out, spewing venom all day. He gives the day guys an unbelievable time. Yellin', spittin' at the Reverend, threatenin' to kill Henry Harcourt nearly every day. He does hate Henry. I think his unquenchable good nature gets on Jonas' nerves. I know it gets on mine.

PATRICE: He does sort of have the personality of a golden retriever.

THADDEUS: Yeah.

PATRICE: So I guess I had the wrong person ask Jonas if he'd consent to an interview.

THADDEUS: You asked Henry to do that?

PATRICE: Yeah.

THADDEUS: I'd like to be a fly on the wall for that conversation. You'd think working on death row would get under anyone's skin, but Henry's impervious to it. He's so fucking happy and naive it makes me want to punch him. Anyway, Jonas is pretty much spent by the time I come on, though he does save a little invective for me.

PATRICE: Is Henry on the tie-down team?

THADDEUS: No. Well, he's backup. Technically, he's my backup, but we have . . . an arrangement.

PATRICE: An arrangement?

THADDEUS: Yeah, well, you know, we get a fair chunk of change for working executions. That's how they get us to sign up for it. And Henry, he really needs the money right now, with the baby comin' and all. But he doesn't have the skin to do tie-down and he knows it. So, he's my backup and, well, . . . I don't ever call in sick anyhow.

PATRICE: That's nice of you.

THADDEUS: Yeah, don't tell anyone.

PATRICE: Would you ask Jonas if he'd let me interview him?

THADDEUS: I can try, but he's liable to be pretty cold on anything Henry suggests.

PATRICE: Does Jonas frighten you?

THADDEUS: No. He annoys the crap out of me more than anything else. He's always insisting I read to him. Says if I want to read on the job then I have to do it out loud so he can hear. I finally found a book he doesn't want to listen to.

PATRICE: What's that?

THADDEUS: *Crime and Punishment.*
(*Patrice laughs. Thaddeus smiles.*)

PATRICE: You read a lot?

THADDEUS: I guess. I figure if I can't go to college, at least I can read the books. And the more I read, the less I have to think about where I am and what I'm doing.

PATRICE: Have you lived in Chagrin Falls your whole life?

THADDEUS: Yep . . . Not much longer though.

PATRICE: Moving on?

THADDEUS: Packing up my things and gettin' the hell out of here. Going someplace where I can disappear into the crowds, and never be heard from again.

PATRICE: When's this gonna happen?

THADDEUS: I don't know. The day I go, that's in God's hands.

PATRICE: I thought you didn't believe in God.

THADDEUS: I don't. But I acknowledge that there are some things I got no control over. Like the day I leave — it's outta my hands. Outta anybody's hands. But it's comin'.

PATRICE: What, are you waiting for some kind of sign?

(Thaddeus looks at her, looks down at her tape recorder, picks it up, turns it off, sets it back down, and focuses his gaze on his fishing rod.)

THADDEUS: I'm waitin' for my mama to die.

(Pause.)

PATRICE: That's her people were talking about, over at Irene's.

THADDEUS: Yeah . . .

PATRICE: She's got cancer?

THADDEUS: She's been sick five years now. Been hangin' on longer than anybody ever thought she could.

PATRICE: Is your father around?

THADDEUS: He died when I was eleven. It's just been Mama and me since then.

PATRICE: I'm sorry.

THADDEUS: Yeah, well, it happens. Just wish it didn't have to happen so slowly. I mean that for her. Not for me. We spent a lot of time bein' hopeful and fightin' it, but now . . . she just wants to go . . . Death shouldn't be so slow that it moves into your home and sets up camp. It should take you by surprise.

(Pause. They both look at their fishing poles and bob them up and down.)

THADDEUS: I was supposed to go to college, get the fuck out of this godforsaken place. But she was diagnosed right about when I graduated from high school. She only had me to take care of her . . . They say she's only got a couple weeks left now, but we've heard that before. Once she does go I'm hightailing it out of here, and I'm never lookin' back.

PATRICE: You don't have any other family in town that you'd come back for?

(Thaddeus lets out a short laugh of contempt.)

THADDEUS: That depends on your definition of family. I don't have any brothers or sisters and all my grandparents are dead. After my mama goes, I'll be the last of what I think of as family. As for relations, I've got relations comin' outta my ears. But when you're related to half the town, it's kinda hard to think of them as family.

PATRICE: Half the town?

THADDEUS: Maybe just a third. It's hard to say after a while.

PATRICE: You're kidding.

THADDEUS: No. Chagrin Falls is a small place. People don't stray too far from the nest. And lord knows we don't attract any outsiders. "Come live in sunny Chagrin Falls — the smallest town in America where you still have to lock your doors and your windows and your barn." Unless you like escapees hangin' out in your place. "Chagrin Falls — a quaint Oklahoma town where the dominant architectural feature is barbed wire."

PATRICE: It's such a funny name for a place.

THADDEUS: It suits us, I guess. We're pretty much an embarrassment as towns go. Not least of all because the people who live here don't even know what "chagrin" means.

PATRICE: So, is there an actual waterfall on this river?

THADDEUS: Oh yeah. It's upstream about a mile. It's a real impressive four-foot drop . . . When I was a kid we used to blow up inner tubes from truck tires and go over the falls. They still do it. Sometimes I'll be sittin' here and a tube'll float down with a couple of little ones clinging to it, screaming for help 'cause they got caught in the current and didn't mean to come down this far. And I'll go wade in and pluck 'em out. And they'll be all breathless and excited and charge up the bank so they can do it again. Sometimes I just want to tell them — this is it. This is the highlight of living in Chagrin Falls. Enjoy it now, 'cause it's all downhill from here.

PATRICE: . . . Are you really related to half the town?

THADDEUS: Why're you so stuck on that?

PATRICE: I don't know. I can't imagine being . . . connected to that many people.

THADDEUS: I'm not connected to them, believe me. I try to be as disconnected from some of them as possible. Henry Harcourt, for instance, is my third cousin, but I don't go around advertising it 'cause he's an idiot. And he's not the worst of them. Why are you shaking your head?

PATRICE: I just . . . I don't have any relatives. I would give my left arm to meet a third cousin, much less a whole town full.

THADDEUS: You don't have any family?

PATRICE: Well, I have a mother and a father and an aunt and uncle and one cousin, but I'm adopted, so technically I'm not related to any of them.
(Pause.)

THADDEUS: So you never met your real mother or father?

PATRICE: I think I lived with my mother until I was almost two, but I don't remember her. I doubt my father is aware of my existence.

THADDEUS: You think about 'em a lot?

PATRICE: Every day. More my mother. My father is probably some bastard Vietnam vet who raped my mother and killed my family and now lives in some pleasant suburb with his oblivious wife and children. So I try not to waste my time thinking about him.

THADDEUS: So, the people who adopted you, are they Vietnamese?

PATRICE: No, they're white. Very, very white.

THADDEUS: How so?

PATRICE: Well, you know, they're conservative Christians. They have very Western values. They're good people, but their view on the world is . . . narrow. They think I've been brainwashed.

THADDEUS: Why's that?

PATRICE: When I left for college, I was just like them. I was a good little Christian. I went to church. I ate meat. I was judgmental. And then I took some classes in the Asian Studies department my junior year. Starting learning about *my* people. About the history of Vietnam. About Buddhism. About pacifism. Now my parents think I'm this vegetarian heathen freak.

THADDEUS: Everybody in town thinks I'm a freak.

PATRICE: That changes when you move away.

THADDEUS: I hope so.

PATRICE: I felt a tug.

THADDEUS: What?

PATRICE: There it is again. Something's tugging on my line.

THADDEUS: Well, pull up. Up! Like that.

PATRICE: I don't know if I can do this.

THADDEUS: Don't be ridiculous. Unless you want to eat fish sticks all week you better start reeling it in.

(Lights out.)

Scene Four

It is morning. Irene stands behind the bar on the phone, looking up at a cow's head mounted on the wall.

IRENE: Desiree? Hi, it's Irene over at the bar. Is your charmin' husband in by any chance? Sleepin', is he? Doesn't surprise me. I don't mind wakin' him. Why don't you just put the phone up to his ear and I'll say what I have to say. Yeah, you can listen on the other line, just don't hold the phone too close, 'cause I ain't gonna be quiet about it. Thank you . . . Reggie, you no good son of a bitch, I know you're responsible for this atrocity hangin' over my bar! I don't know how you got in here last night, much less how you managed to not wake me up, but if you ever come into my bar without my knowin' it again, I'm gonna cut your balls off!

(Irene bangs the mouth piece against the bar a few times, and then hangs it up.)

THADDEUS: *(Offstage.)* Irene, what the hell is wrong with you?

IRENE: You come on out here and see what's wrong with me. Irresponsible idiots. Comin' into my bar in the middle of the night, hangin' dead things on my wall.

(Thaddeus enters from Irene's room. He is fully dressed but has the rumpled look of someone who's just gotten out of bed.)

IRENE: Look at that thing.

THADDEUS: That for Riley?

IRENE: What do you think?

THADDEUS: Well, what did you expect?

IRENE: Whatever I expected, I wasn't thinking it would appear in my bar. Did you hear anything last night?

THADDEUS: No. Not that I recall.

IRENE: What good are you if you're not going to get up and check on things that go bump in the night.

(Irene puts her arms around him and straightens his collar. Thaddeus smiles.)

THADDEUS: You're the one who's supposed to be the light sleeper.

IRENE: I used to be. But ever since you came along I've been sleeping like a baby.

THADDEUS: Is that right?

(She kisses him, then gently pushes some hair out of his face.)

IRENE: You feelin' better this mornin'?

(At that moment Riley swings the door open. Thaddeus pulls away from Irene. Everyone looks embarrassed.)

THADDEUS: I gotta go see my mother.

IRENE: All right. You give her my love.

THADDEUS: Mornin', Riley.

RILEY: Thaddeus.

(Riley steps out of the doorway so that Thaddeus can get by.)

IRENE: Don't look at me like that, Riley MacDougal. It's none of your business. Up there on the wall is what you should be lookin' so appalled about, anyhow. *(Irene points at the cow's head.)* That's what they got you. For thirty years of service. I suppose they think it's funny, but I think it's a disgrace.

Snuck in here in the middle of the night and put it up without my even hearin' it. Go on. Read the plaque. It's got an inscription.

(*Riley walks to his seat at the bar, peers up at the mount, reads it, and shakes his head.*)

RILEY: I told you they were gonna give me something stupid to hang on the wall.

IRENE: Well, I'd be pissed as a wet hen if I was you.

RILEY: You are pissed as a wet hen, and you ain't me.

IRENE: I don't like people comin' into my place without my knowin'.

RILEY: So put bars on the windows. I'm sure they got some spare ones over at the prison.

IRENE: You're not funny. Eggs and toast?

RILEY: Please.

IRENE: It'll be a few. I'm running late.

RILEY: Oversleep?

IRENE: No, and don't use that insinuating tone with me. I was givin' Reggie and Cal an earful about breakin' into my place in the dark of night.

RILEY: Well, it doesn't clash with the decor or anything. I don't know why you're so blustery about it. Not much different than havin' a moose head up on the wall.

IRENE: Then I think you should take it down and put it over your fireplace.

RILEY: Thanks just the same.

IRENE: That's what I thought. It'll be a few.

(*Irene exits to the kitchen.*)

RILEY: No hurry.

(*Riley leans back looks up at the cow head. Then he gets up and goes behind the bar and pours himself a shot of Wild Turkey and downs it. He grabs himself a coffee mug as Patrice enters, looking groggy. She does not notice the cow head.*)

RILEY: Mornin'.

PATRICE: Oh. Good morning. I didn't realize you worked here.

RILEY: I don't. Irene's just runnin' a little late this mornin', so I was helping myself. Coffee?

PATRICE: Please.

(*Patrice sits at the bar. Riley picks up the coffee pot and finds it empty. Riley pushes the door to the kitchen open.*)

RILEY: There's no coffee out here.

IRENE: (*Offstage.*) Then why don't you make some.

RILEY: I don't know where you keep things.

IRENE: (*Offstage.*) Then you'll have to wait a few goddamn minutes, won't you?

RILEY: She's a little sensitive this morning. Doesn't like the new wall hanging.
　　　(Riley cocks his head at the cow. Patrice makes a sound of displeasure.)
PATRICE: Euh! That's disgusting.
RILEY: That's my former colleagues.
　　　(She gets up to get a closer look.)
PATRICE: It's for you.
RILEY: My parting gift.
PATRICE: "Here's one for the road"?
RILEY: They got a morbid sense of humor over there.
PATRICE: You don't like it, do you?
RILEY: It's less tasteless than some things they mighta gotten me. And they sent
　　　it to someone good. To get it stuffed and mounted. Probably wasn't ready
　　　on time on account of the eyes. Can't imagine taxidermists have much
　　　need to keep cow eyes in stock. Did a nice job though. Very lifelike.
PATRICE: "Lifelike" is not the phrase that comes to mind.
RILEY: I suppose not.
PATRICE: You don't seem old enough to retire.
RILEY: Don't I?
PATRICE: No, well, I just mean, you look like you're about the same age as my
　　　father, younger actually, and I can't imagine him retiring. At least not for
　　　a while.
RILEY: He must like what he does, then.
PATRICE: I guess he does.
RILEY: A man like me, living in a place like this . . . you take work where you
　　　can get it, you serve your country, you put in your time, and you retire
　　　as soon as you can.
PATRICE: And then what?
RILEY: That I haven't figured out yet . . . How's your article coming?
PATRICE: All right, I guess. I'm still waiting for Jonas to agree to an interview.
RILEY: I take it Henry was unsuccessful.
PATRICE: Yes. I'm waiting to hear if Thaddeus has better luck.
RILEY: So, what are you doing with yourself today?
PATRICE: I'm supposed to be meeting with the Reverend in a little while. Other
　　　than that my date book's looking pretty barren.
RILEY: If you want, I could take you on a tour of the town.
PATRICE: You mean, there's more of it?
RILEY: Well, you can't judge a place just by it's commercial district. I could
　　　take you around to one of the local ranchers and Randall Cartwright's
　　　wheat farm. And I could always give you a tour of the slaughterhouse.
PATRICE: I don't think I could stomach the slaughterhouse.

RILEY: Well, it's something to see, anyway. Something you wouldn't forget.

PATRICE: I'm sure. I'll think about it.

RILEY: It's an open invitation.

IRENE: *(Offstage.)* Ow!

> *(There is a crash of a metal pot offstage.)*

IRENE: *(Offstage and yelling.)* God Dammit!

RILEY: She's getting off to a rough start this morning.

PATRICE: You know what, I'll just come back later.

RILEY: She'll be out in a minute to take your order.

PATRICE: That's all right. I feel like a walk, anyway.

RILEY: Suit yourself.

PATRICE: That big field of stuff down the road, that's wheat, right?

RILEY: Yeah.

PATRICE: OK. Just checking.

> *(Patrice exits. After a moment, Irene comes in with a plate for Riley and a tray with some covered food.)*

RILEY: You all right?

IRENE: I burned myself making your goddamned bacon.

RILEY: I didn't order bacon.

IRENE: Well, fine then.

> *(Irene grabs the bacon off his plate and throws it in the garbage. Riley begins to eat.)*

RILEY: You know, maybe if you got out of this place a few hours a day, you wouldn't get so wound up.

IRENE: Where am I supposed to go?

RILEY: I don't know. You could go for a walk.

IRENE: Oh, sure.

RILEY: No one's sayin' you can't. No one's sayin' you can't close shop for a few extra hours a day. No one's saying you can't just move on out and get yourself a house like you're always talkin' about.

IRENE: Yeah, then who'd look after the place? There's gotta be somebody on the premises twenty-four hours a day.

RILEY: If I recall, your father made you promise to find somebody to help you run the place after he died. How many years ago was that?

IRENE: Well, I don't see Tom or Clarence comin' back to support the family business, do you? They washed their hands of Chagrin Falls a long time ago.

RILEY: There's other people.

IRENE: I like runnin' this place. It suits me.

RILEY: It suits ya, but you don't hafta make yerself crazy spendin' every last moment of your life in here, just so you can play the martyr with your brothers.

IRENE: What do you know about it?

RILEY: I know you ain't hired anybody.

IRENE: Well, I ain't found anyone I trust with the place.

RILEY: That's 'cause you ain't been lookin'.

IRENE: Will you shut up. You don't have to get in everyone's business just 'cause you retired! Aw. Shit, you made me forget about room six.

(Irene grabs the covered tray and some silverware from behind the bar.)

IRENE: I'm running out to six to give 'em their breakfast. You hold down the fort for a minute.

RILEY: Who's in six?

IRENE: Parents of the victim. Don't try and cook anything.

RILEY: I wouldn't dream of it.

(Irene exits. After a moment, Riley gets up and pours himself another shot of Wild Turkey, downs it, and puts the glass in the dirty-dishes tub. He tops off his coffee. The door to the outside opens and the Reverend enters.)

REVEREND: Morning, Riley.

RILEY: Morning.

(Reverend bellies up to the bar. There is an awkward silence between the two men.)

RILEY: She just went out to —

REVEREND: I saw her.

RILEY: Right. *(Silence. Riley pokes at the remainder of his food.)* Look, Reverend, I'm sorry I haven't called you . . .

REVEREND: You know what, Riley, you don't owe me a phone call. You don't have to come in to talk to me to make me feel better. I'm not the one who needs to feel better, am I?

RILEY: I guess not.

REVEREND: Why don't we make a deal? I'll stop asking you how you are, if you stop apologizing to me for not comin' by. Or calling. Or whatever it is that Irene's made you feel like you should be doing. I am not taking it personally that you don't want to talk to me. My door is always open to you, but you are not under some obligation to have a heart to heart with me, OK?

RILEY: OK.

REVEREND: Good.

(Reverend catches the cow head out of the corner of his eye and steps back in shock.)

REVEREND: That's new.

RILEY: Don't say anything to her about it. She's already pissed.

(Irene returns with an empty tray.)

IRENE: You in for breakfast, Johnny?

REVEREND: No, I . . . I had that talk with Teri this morning.

IRENE: Oh . . . So?

(Reverend glances at Riley. Riley wipes him mouth and pushes away from the bar.)

RILEY: I can go.

IRENE: You don't have to go.

RILEY: I don't want to hear about your sex life.

IRENE: That's not what we're talkin' about.

RILEY: Not yet. I'll pay ya when I come back for dinner.

IRENE: Don't think I'm not keepin' track.

RILEY: I know.

REVEREND: Bye, Riley.

RILEY: See ya, Reverend.

IRENE: You're not givin' me the feelin' it went well.

(She sits down next to him at the bar.)

REVEREND: Well, no. She still doesn't want to see you, but she's gettin' better about it.

IRENE: She say who told her?

REVEREND: No, but I don't think that's important, now. The fact is she knows.

IRENE: Still, whoever told her, they had to've known it would only hurt her.

REVEREND: You'd think.

IRENE: So, she won't see me?

REVEREND: No, she doesn't want you to come by. Or call. She says she's not as upset about it now that she's had time to get used to the idea, but she thinks if she sees you . . . I think it's taken all she's got to not be mad at Thaddeus.

IRENE: If I could just explain to her, how it happened, why it happened, that it's not this . . . this . . . dirty thing that everybody makes it out to be . . .

REVEREND: No one's saying that.

IRENE: Yes, they are. I've heard the whisperin' and the cradle-robbin' comments. They even sit here at my bar and go all silent when I come out with their food. I know what they're sayin'. If it weren't me, I'd probably be sayin' the same thing. I know how it looks. I really don't care what any of the rest of them think, but if I could just explain to her . . .

REVEREND: I don't think explanations are going to improve the situation. It's not the sort of thing a mother wants to hear.

IRENE: What if I don't see her again before she dies?

REVEREND: I think you need to brace yourself for that possibility. She's been pretty bad lately.

IRENE: So she's gonna die mad at me?

REVEREND: No, she's not mad at you. She told me to tell you she's not mad. She's forgiven you, but she can't see you. She just doesn't have the strength to see you.

IRENE: I'd like to think that I don't need to be forgiven. That really we haven't done anything wrong. (*Irene wipes her eyes. The Reverend rubs her shoulder.*) Do you think it's wrong, Johnny? What Thaddeus and I have?

REVEREND: Well, I don't think you're taking advantage of him, if that's what you mean. I worry that maybe you're both deceiving yourselves a little, . . . but I don't know how Thaddeus would have made it through the past few months without you, Irene. And for that alone, I can't say it's a bad thing.

IRENE: He won't even talk to me anymore. It's like he's turnin' colder and harder every day. I know it's not right to say it, but I hope she dies soon before he completely turns to stone. The only reason I know he's still in there anymore is I wake up in the middle of the night and he's cryin' so hard that the whole bed is shakin'. And all I can do is put my arm around him and hold him up close until he stops. (*Reverend hands her a napkin to wipe her sniffles.*) I tell ya, nothin' burns the skin like a man's hot tears . . . I'm amazed I haven't just melted away by now . . . After she goes, I'm gonna take him on a trip. A cruise or something.

REVEREND: Thaddeus? On a cruise?

IRENE: Well, maybe camping. Just get away for a week or two.

(*Patrice enters, holding a sprig of wheat and her backpack. Irene pulls herself together immediately.*)

REVEREND: Hi.

PATRICE: Oh, hi. It's not ten already, is it?

REVEREND: No, I was just stopping by for a minute. Though I've got nothing scheduled between now and then, if you want to do it now.

PATRICE: OK.

REVEREND: Would you mind if we talked here, Irene?

IRENE: I don't mind.

REVEREND: I'm just going to run to the washroom before we start.

PATRICE: Sure.

(*The Reverend exits.*)

IRENE: You want somethin' to eat?

PATRICE: Maybe after we're done. Thanks.

IRENE: All right.

(Patrice begins pulling out her notebook and tape recorder. Irene eyes her while she makes a pot of coffee.)

IRENE: You and Thaddeus have a nice time fishing yesterday?

PATRICE: Well, aside from the fishing part, it was nice.

IRENE: What all else were you doin'?

PATRICE: Oh, nothing. Just talking. I've never killed anything before.

(Patrice nervously twirls the sprig of wheat.)

IRENE: Yeah, I guess you city folk aren't real in touch with your food.

PATRICE: No.

IRENE: So what were you talkin' about?

PATRICE: Oh, you know. I was asking him about his job, about living here.

IRENE: You know, we've got some folks going through some hard times right now. You need to be careful what it is you say to people.

PATRICE: I know, he told me about —

IRENE: Just try to keep some professional distance. Our business is not necessary to your story.

(The Reverend returns from the washroom.)

IRENE: You two have a nice talk.

(Irene exits into the kitchen. The Reverend watches Patrice set down the sprig of wheat.)

REVEREND: It's pretty, isn't it? All that wheat.

PATRICE: It's beautiful . . . I can't believe I've never seen it, touched it, before.

REVEREND: Yeah, it's one of those unexpected pleasures in a place like this. You really get to capture the pastoral elegance of your food. Before they chop it down or kill it.

PATRICE: Or hang it on the wall.

REVEREND: Yes.

(They both look up at the cow.)

PATRICE: Well, I'll try to make this quick and painless. Do you mind?

(She lifts up the tape recorder.)

REVEREND: No.

PATRICE: I never have to worry about misquoting people this way.

(The Reverend leans towards the recorder.)

REVEREND: John-with-an-H-Maycomb; thirty-eight; born and raised in New Canaan, Connecticut; Divinity School at Harvard; did two interim years in Northern Michigan and then came here three years ago.

PATRICE: Do this much?

REVEREND: Every execution. Well, most of them.

PATRICE: Do you miss New England?

REVEREND: The landscape, but not the people.

PATRICE: You said you've been here three years?

REVEREND: A little over.

PATRICE: And how do you like it?

REVEREND: The job or the place?

PATRICE: Both.

REVEREND: The job is . . . challenging. And gratifying, most days. The place is . . . diffr'nt. The people are great. Open. Honest. Where I grew up, it was all closed doors and secrets and things left unsaid. There are no secrets in Chagrin Falls, . . . which is a blessing and a curse, I suppose, but it's a quality I value. But it's a sad place.

PATRICE: How so?

REVEREND: Well, you know, it's a poor, rural community. People here don't really get to reach their full potential. Half the town works at the prison, which doesn't exactly foster a sense of contentment and well-being. The other half kills cows for a living or sits home raising children and watching soap operas . . . Sometimes I think every last person in Chagrin Falls is suffering from clinical depression. Except Henry Harcourt, of course. Henry kind of floats above it all. The rest of the town is steeped in death and Henry floats above it. I think it sort of makes everyone hate Henry, but only because they wish they had it in them. I think he's immune to it, somehow.

PATRICE: To what?

REVEREND: The despair.

PATRICE: Is it contagious?

REVEREND: I think all sorrow is contagious to some degree.

PATRICE: Have you caught it?

REVEREND: I don't know. I think I find it more compelling than catching. I don't know what that says about me, exactly, being drawn to other people's sorrow.

PATRICE: Well, it certainly explains why you've chosen this line of work.

REVEREND: I suppose.

PATRICE: How many executions have you done?

REVEREND: This will be fifteen.

PATRICE: Does it get easier or harder?

(Beat.)

REVEREND: It gets easier to do, and harder to live with it afterwards.

PATRICE: How do you feel about capital punishment?

REVEREND: The Warden has asked me not to discuss my feelings on that issue with any more reporters.

PATRICE: OK. A different question, then. Ummm, during the execution, what exactly do you do?

REVEREND: Well, I walk with him to the death chamber. Stand aside while they strap him down and get the needle in his arm. Talk to him, if he seems to find any comfort in that. And then they pull the curtains so the spectators can see. And I say a prayer. If he wants. After he says his last words. And then the Warden signals the executioner. And we all stand there. Watching . . .

PATRICE: Does he pick the prayer, or do you?

REVEREND: If they have a specific passage they want me to read, I'll read it. Usually, they let me pick it.

PATRICE: What about Jonas?

REVEREND: I believe he's looking for a passage. Not that he can read very well, mind you, but he's enlisted the assistance of one of the corrections officers.

PATRICE: Not Thaddeus.

REVEREND: *(Smiling.)* No. I can't say I've ever seen Thaddeus reading the Bible.

PATRICE: I would think Jonas would enlist you to find an appropriate prayer.

REVEREND: Yes, well, he . . . hasn't asked.

PATRICE: What do you think of Jonas Caldwell?

(Long pause.)

REVEREND: I think he is a very sad human being.

PATRICE: Do you think he's changed at all, since his conviction?

REVEREND: Changed? Well, I didn't know him then, but he hasn't made any kind of grand turn-around or found God, if that's what you mean. I don't think being incarcerated has improved Jonas's personality.

PATRICE: Thaddeus says he spits at you.

REVEREND: Yes, he does. That's really the only recourse he has anymore. That and flinging his feces at people.

(Pause.)

REVEREND: I don't like Jonas Caldwell. I won't lie to you. I'll even go so far as to say I really dislike him. He's a loathsome individual, bubbling over with hate. But I do have pity for him. I mean, he had a terrible childhood, a monster for a father, no one to help him along the way. I don't think an ounce of love was ever put into that man. There's no reason to think we should get any out of him. Still, I expect this will be the most difficult execution for me so far.

PATRICE: Why's that?

REVEREND: Because some very small and dark part of me will be glad when he is dead.

(Lights go to black.)

END OF ACT I

Act II
Scene Five

It's late. The bar is almost entirely dark. Riley stands on the bar holding the cow's head in his hands, staring into its eyes. After a moment, Patrice enters. She does not notice Riley and her presence does not seem to register with him. Patrice steps behind the bar, looking for a glass and some ice. She gasps slightly as she realizes she is not alone.

PATRICE: I'm sorry, I didn't . . . Riley? Are you all right?

(Riley does not appear to hear her. Patrice rushes over to Irene's door and bangs on it.) Irene! Irene! Are you in there? There something wrong with Riley!

IRENE: *(Offstage.)* What?

PATRICE: With Riley. There's something wrong with him.

(Irene emerges tying her robe closed and closing the door behind her.)

IRENE: What's the matter? Oh, good Lord. Riley. Riley, honey? Whatcha doin' up there?

(Riley does not respond.)

PATRICE: I was thirsty and I can't drink water without ice in it, so I came in to get some . . . I didn't think you'd mind . . .

IRENE: He was standing up there when you came in?

PATRICE: I didn't notice him for a minute. He's so still.

IRENE: He say anything?

PATRICE: No.

(Irene opens her bedroom door a crack and looks inside.)

IRENE: Thaddeus, honey, you gotta come out here and help me with Riley.

THADDEUS: *(Offstage.)* What?

IRENE: Riley's up on the bar and I can't get him down myself. Come on out here . . . You can't come out like that. Put something on. *(To Patrice.)* He's groggy.

(Thaddeus comes out zipping a crumpled pair of pants, but wearing nothing else. He is startled and obviously embarrassed to see Patrice, though perhaps not as startled as she is to see him. He quickly evades her glance and his eyes land on Riley.)

THADDEUS: Jesus . . . Riley?

IRENE: He doesn't even look like he knows we're in the room.

(Thaddeus sizes up the situation, then he climbs up on the bar, approaching Riley from behind.)

THADDEUS: All right, Riley? You hear me? I know you hear me. Now, I'm behind you. Comin' up behind you. What's he doing?

IRENE: Just staring at the cow.

THADDEUS: All right. Riley? Riley? I'm gonna touch you now. Just on the shoulders. I don't want to startle you.

*(Slowly Thaddeus grasps Riley's shoulders. Riley shudders violently and lets
out a sob.)*

THADDEUS: All right, why don't you let go of the cow. Riley? Let go. That's
it. Just put your hands down by your side. That's good. All right now.
Let's the both of us sit down on the bar. I'll help ya. Riley? What's he
doing?

IRENE: Still staring. I think you gotta cover his eyes or something.

THADDEUS: All right, Riley? I'm going to cover your eyes now. You ready? OK.
Here we go. OK, now you gotta turn your head. I don't want to try to
get you off this bar with your eyes closed, so you're gonna have to turn
away from the cow. Nice an' easy. There you go. That's it. I won't let you
fall. OK. You're fine. Now, I'm going to take my hand away, OK? So don't
look at the cow, all right? You hear me? Don't look at the cow.

*(Thaddeus takes his hand away but keeps a grip on Riley's shoulder. Riley
looks down at his feet, ashamed.)*

THADDEUS: All right. Now, come on. Sit down with me on the bar. OK? Let
me help you.

IRENE: Careful.

THADDEUS: We're OK. We're fine. We're sittin'. OK . . . Want to get off the
bar, now? Sit on your stool?

(Riley gets off the bar.)

IRENE: Thaddeus, honey, take that thing down. Put it behind the bar or something. Patrice, would you mind pourin' us a shot of Wild Turkey?

*(Thaddeus takes the cow head down and sets it behind the bar, facing the
audience. Patrice fumbles around behind the bar but then deftly pours a generous shot for Riley. Irene helps Riley get seated.)*

IRENE: God, honey, you're soaked with sweat. What were you doin' up there?

RILEY: I wanted to see its eyes.

THADDEUS: Its eyes are made of glass, Riley. You know that.

(Riley mumbles something inaudible.)

IRENE: What, honey?

RILEY: Alice died with her eyes open.

*(Thaddeus and Irene exchange a look. Thaddeus continues to avoid ac-
knowledging Patrice.)*

IRENE: Did she? I didn't know that.

RILEY: Cows always die with their eyes open. When you slaughter 'em, I mean. They don't cut you any slack. They just keep staring right at you with those deep, watery brown eyes. That's why you gotta stun 'em first.

IRENE: You wanna drink something? Patrice poured you some Wild Turkey.

RILEY: Something cold, please. Water.

(Patrice hands him her ice water.)

RILEY: Thank you.

(Riley takes a long drink, about half the glass. He sets the glass down and stares at nothing for a moment.)

RILEY: Alice died with her eyes open.

IRENE: Yeah, honey, you just told us that.

RILEY: Did I? . . . It was strange. I was lookin' in 'em when it happened. It was the strangest thing, watching the life go out of her. You can see it in the eyes. Something changes. They get dull and you can tell they're not see-ing anymore . . . But the thing was, I could still feel her looking at me. From some new place that I couldn't point my finger at. The Reverend was there, and I told him I could still feel her looking at me, and he said it was fine. Natural. My piece of proof that people don't just stop being. How did he say it? . . . "A little gift from God, not meant to replace my grief, but to lighten the load of it." That's what he said.

(Riley drains the water glass.)

IRENE: Well, that's a good thing, isn't it?

RILEY: I thought it was. I did. It made the first few nights easier. I'd be lyin' in bed and a warm feelin' would come over me . . . But after I went back to work, I don't know. I just started thinkin' things.

IRENE: What kind of things?

(Riley rubs his head uncomfortably.)

RILEY: Things about all the cows I killed. I started wonderin' if they was all lookin' at me too.

IRENE: From Heaven?

RILEY: I don't know about Heaven, but from whatever place it is that dead things go to. Did all those cows have souls like my Alice did?

IRENE: I don't know, Riley. I don't know about cows, 'cept for cookin' and eatin' 'em.

RILEY: I mean, it's one thing to have your wife watchin' over you from some other place, but several thousand head of cattle is a completely different matter.

IRENE: Now, Riley you can't let yourself fret over —

RILEY: But I can't get it out of my head. All those big, sad, cow eyes. And I can't tell if they forgive me or not. At least with the other ones, with the people, I know they don't forgive me.

IRENE: Why don't you two go back to bed now. I think we're all right.

THADDEUS: You sure?

IRENE: There won't be anymore walkin' on the bar tonight.

THADDEUS: I'm gonna head home, then. Since I'm up.

IRENE: . . . All right.

(Thaddeus exits into Irene's bedroom without a word to Patrice.)

PATRICE: Goodnight.

(Patrice exits.)

IRENE: You scared the daylights outta that girl.

(Irene downs the shot of bourbon.)

RILEY: You suppose Alice knows things now?

IRENE: Knows what things?

RILEY: Things I didn't tell her.

IRENE: Alice knew you loved her, Riley.

RILEY: That's not what I mean! I mean the secrets I didn't tell her. You suppose she's met some of the soldiers I killed? I don't like the idea of people bad mouthin' me in Heaven.

IRENE: *(Smiling.)* I don't think Heaven works like that.

RILEY: How do you know how Heaven works?

IRENE: I guess I don't.

RILEY: What I mean is, can she see inside of me, now? Can she see the things I've done?

IRENE: Riley, Alice knew you were fightin' in a war. I don't think she had any illusions about what went on over there.

RILEY: That's not it. I just don't want her findin' out things about me now when I can't explain myself to her.

IRENE: What's she gonna find out about?

RILEY: I can't tell you.

IRENE: Well, maybe you should tell somebody. Maybe the Reverend. He knew Alice real well.

RILEY: What's the Reverend gonna say? I may not be the most spiritual man on Earth, but I know you can't have it both ways. Either Alice is in Heaven and she can see everything, or else she's not anywhere. And you can't have your wife still lookin' over you and have the ones you've done wrong just die and stop being. Either you got your ghosts or you don't. You can't have it both ways.

IRENE: Well, maybe Johnny could help you sort it out, Riley. Sounds like you're having a real crisis of faith to me, but you're way outta my area of expertise.

RILEY: Can I sleep here tonight?

IRENE: Course, honey. I'll get you a room key.

(Lights fade to black.)

Scene Six

Thaddeus sits at his fishing hole, taking a fish off his line. He is in a foul mood. Patrice enters behind him.

PATRICE: Hi.

THADDEUS: Jesus.

PATRICE: I'm sorry. I didn't mean to startle you.

THADDEUS: I didn't hear you comin'.

PATRICE: You seemed a little lost in thought.

THADDEUS: Did I.

PATRICE: Are you all right?

THADDEUS: What are you doing here?
(Thaddeus begins to violently gut the fish, throwing the innards into a bucket.)

PATRICE: I wanted to know if — Do you have to do that right now?
(Patrice is clearly repulsed. Thaddeus stops.)

THADDEUS: How are you gonna watch a man die if you can't even stand to see a fish gutted?

PATRICE: Just stop, OK?
(Thaddeus chucks the fish in the bucket and then stares at Patrice waiting for her to continue.)

PATRICE: . . . I wanted to know if you'd had a chance to ask Jonas about the interview. Last night, with Riley on the bar, that didn't seem like the appropriate moment to bring it up and I —

THADDEUS: He said no.

PATRICE: Oh . . . Shit.

THADDEUS: Sorry.

PATRICE: Do you think if I asked him myself —

THADDEUS: I don't know. I can't get into someone else's head.

PATRICE: Well, would they even let me see him —

THADDEUS: I don't know. Why don't you ask whoever it was that got you in for the tour.

(Thaddeus reaches into the bucket for the fish and Patrice turns to go but immediately turns back. Thaddeus looks inside the dead fish, poking it.)

PATRICE: Did I do something to offend you? Because if I did, I apologize —

THADDEUS: You didn't do anything, OK? You just . . . You found out something about me that I didn't want you to know.

PATRICE: You mean about Irene.

THADDEUS: Yeah.

(Thaddeus drops the fish back in the bucket.)

PATRICE: Well, I won't put it in the article or say anything to anyone, if that's what you're worried about.

(Thaddeus laughs.)

THADDEUS: You don't need to say anything. Everyone knows. You can't have a bad haircut in this town without the whole fuckin' world knowing about it. I'm sure Irene and I are a regular topic of conversation at the ladies' bridge club and the Moose Lodge . . . That's why I hate this fucking place. There's no privacy. There's not a person in this town that doesn't know that I got this scar when Roger Delford beat me to a pulp in the fifth grade, or that Riley spent close to a year in a mental hospital after he came back from the war, or that Henry Harcourt was born with a misshapen head and his brother Tom mushed it back into the proper shape when no one was lookin'. It's like you're constantly dragging your past around with you in this town, having your mistakes on display. And then you come along, asking me all these questions and all the sudden I'm talking about myself for nearly the first time in my entire life. And I'm telling you about me. Not about the way everyone else sees me, but about how I see me. And I'm leaving things out, because you don't have to know that I didn't kiss a girl until I was eighteen, and that the girl was old enough to be my mother. That she was best friends with my mother. You don't have to know that the whole town snickers behind my back because I'm screwing the barkeep who's past her prime. But now you do know. Now you're just another person I can't look in the eye.

(After a long moment, Patrice sits down next to Thaddeus. He is trying hard not to cry.)

PATRICE: You shouldn't . . . you don't . . . You shouldn't be ashamed of loving someone . . . You do love her, don't you?

THADDEUS: No, I do. It's just . . . She's the only one who really understands how it's been for me with my mom sick. It's bad enough that they all think of me as the freak-boy with the books. And now that I've been with Irene, none of the other girls will look twice at me, not that they did before.

Not that any of 'em have half a brain in their heads. I don't know why I'm telling you this. It's like you opened up some kind of floodgate in me the other day and now I can't shut up.

PATRICE: Well, I'm sorry if I know too much about you, but I don't think you're a scandal.

THADDEUS: You ought to think I'm an asshole.

PATRICE: Why?

THADDEUS: 'Cause you know I'm planning to leave.

PATRICE: Irene doesn't know you're leaving?

THADDEUS: I think she knows, but not 'cause I told her . . . I've just got to get out of this place.

(Very cautiously, Patrice touches him. He is crying silently now.)

PATRICE: I don't think you're an asshole . . . Will you look at me?

(Thaddeus shakes his head no. Patrice takes his face in her hands and turns his head to face her.)

PATRICE: Does that hurt?

THADDEUS: Yes.

(She kisses him ever so gently on the lips.)

PATRICE: Does that hurt?

THADDEUS: Yes . . . Please don't.

PATRICE: All right. I'll let you be.

(Thaddeus wipes his eyes as Patrice walks away. Lights fade to black.)

Scene Seven

The stage is dark except for a space downstage with a cold light shining on it. Two folding chairs face the audience at an angle. Henry enters, guiding Patrice.

HENRY: You can sit right over there, Patrice. Rickert'll bring him out in a sec —

(The sound of a metal door rolling open.)

HENRY: There they are. I'll be right outside this door if you need me.

PATRICE: OK. Thank you.

(Henry exits. Patrice sits in one of the chairs. She is looking at someone and she is uncomfortable. She has a notebook and her tape recorder in her hands.)

PATRICE: Hi . . . God, you look so different.

JONAS: Who are you?

(Jonas's voice should be piped in through a loudspeaker.)

PATRICE: My name is Patrice Dougherty. I'm writing a piece on capital punishment. I've been trying to contact you about an interview. But I guess you haven't received my letters.

JONAS: I know you.

(Pause.)

PATRICE: I was wondering if I could ask you a few questions. About your . . . situation.

JONAS: You were on my jury.

(Pause. Patrice looks away from the speaker but does not respond.)

JONAS: I thought you were twelve years old, sittin' there in that jury box. You don't look much older now. Bigger tits, I guess. Sort of.

PATRICE: Are you sorry you killed her?

JONAS: Are you sorry you're killing me?

PATRICE: Yes.

JONAS: Yeah, well, your sorry ain't worth much to me, is it? And my sorry ain't worth shit to a dead little girl, so I don't bother with sorry.

PATRICE: . . . Do you hate me?

JONAS: Maybe if I got to know you I would.

(Pause.)

PATRICE: I don't suppose I could ask you a few questions —

JONAS: *(Cutting her off.)* No, I don't suppose you could.

PATRICE: All right.

JONAS: You coming to watch tomorrow night?

PATRICE: Yes.

JONAS: Well, then I guess I'll see you then. OK, I'm done. You can take me back.

(The sound of a metal gate opening, a chair being pushed back, then the gate slamming shut. Patrice sits frozen. After a moment, Henry enters.)

HENRY: You all done, Patrice?

PATRICE: Yes.

(She wipes tears from her eyes but does not move. Henry sits down next to her.)

HENRY: *(Gently.)* Hey now, Patrice, you can't get upset if he was mean to you. He don't like anybody. You should hear the things he says to me.

PATRICE: No, it wasn't anything he said.

HENRY: He didn't spit at you did he?

PATRICE: No . . . No. Actually, I did something to Jonas, a few years ago, and I came to tell him I was sorry.

HENRY: You knew Jonas from before?

PATRICE: Sort of. Anyhow, he didn't accept my apology. Not that I really expected him to.

(Henry takes her hand in his.)

HENRY: Well, I can't imagine you did anything to Jonas nearly so bad as what he done to other people.

PATRICE: I don't know about that.

HENRY: It wasn't nothin' against the law, was it?

PATRICE: No. Still, you can hurt people without breaking the law.

HENRY: I suppose that's true . . . Well, it was big of you to come say you were sorry. Most people wouldn't do that.

PATRICE: Yeah, well, sometimes you don't realize that you've done something wrong until . . . afterwards. When it's too late to do anything about it. I can't undo what I did, but I wanted to come look my mistake in the eye, at least.

HENRY: You know, Patrice, I ain't got no idea what you're talkin' 'bout.

PATRICE: I know, Henry. It's OK. I appreciate you holding my hand. Wish you could do it tomorrow night.

HENRY: Well, you can pretend I'm holding it.

PATRICE: I guess I can.

HENRY: I'm glad I won't be there, though. I'd be afraid to watch someone die. I'd be afraid it would do something to me . . . Are you afraid?

PATRICE: Yeah.

(Lights fade to black.)

Scene Eight

The lights come up on Thaddeus reading at the bar. The remains of a meal sit on a plate next to him. On the end of the bar is an open cardboard box. Irene enters from her room carrying a large basket of laundry. She sets the laundry basket down on a chair and begins to fold towels, stacking them on a dining table when she's done.

IRENE: You done?

THADDEUS: Yeah . . . It was good . . . Thank you.

IRENE: You have the night off, right?

THADDEUS: Yeah.

IRENE: You readin' something good?

THADDEUS: Tryin' to.

IRENE: Well, excuse me. If my presence is disrupting you so, why don't you go read at home? Sit with your mother.

THADDEUS: Because I'm waitin' for someone.

IRENE: Who?

THADDEUS: Is everything your business?

IRENE: What the hell is with you today?

(Riley enters.)

RILEY: Hey.

IRENE: Hi. You in for a late lunch?

RILEY: No. Just a beer. I'll get it.

(Riley goes behind the bar and pours himself a beer.)

IRENE: I notice you've been makin' yourself comfortable behind the bar, there.

RILEY: I ate at McNeally's today.

IRENE: Really?

RILEY: Yeah. Remind me to never do that again.

IRENE: OK.

RILEY: Such a sorry bunch of old farts. Sittin' around, playin' cards. I always thought they were playin' poker or somethin'. I go in there — they're playin' Go Fish. Apparently none of them can remember the rules to anything more complicated.

IRENE: How's the food with that new "chef" over there?

RILEY: Oh, you know. Dead cow. Tastes the same across the street.

(Riley sits down in his seat and looks over at Thaddeus. He continues to stare at him until Thaddeus says:)

THADDEUS: What?

RILEY: Nothing.

(Pause. Irene exits to her room.)

RILEY: You've been spending some time with this reporter girl, haven't you?

(Thaddeus looks behind him to see if Irene is there listening.)

THADDEUS: We went fishin'. I wouldn't call it spending time.

RILEY: But you've talked to her?

THADDEUS: You askin' if she interviewed me?

RILEY: I'm askin' if you talked to her.

THADDEUS: Yeah, we had a conversation while we were fishing. Why?

RILEY: She happen to say if she was born in this country?

THADDEUS: No . . . She said she was adopted.

(Irene returns with another basket full of towels.)

RILEY: She said that?

THADDEUS: Yeah.

(Thaddeus looks at Riley.)

THADDEUS: I suppose you could ask her. She doesn't seem like the type to get offended.

RILEY: I don't think I could ask.

THADDEUS: Suit yourself.

IRENE: Who're you talkin' about?

(Pause.)

THADDEUS: Patrice.

IRENE: I haven't seen her around today, have you?

RILEY: I haven't seen her.

(Thaddeus does not respond. The Reverend enters and sits at the table where Irene is folding. He looks exhausted.)

IRENE: Hey.

REVEREND: Hey.

IRENE: Shouldn't you be at work?

REVEREND: Yeah, I've got to run home and change clothes before I talk to the press.

IRENE: So, they're descending upon us already.

REVEREND: Oh, yeah . . . I just got through talking to Arlene Caldwell.

IRENE: The mother?

REVEREND: The mother.

IRENE: How's she holding up?

REVEREND: Oh she's holding up fine. She'd stick the needle in his arm herself, if they'd let her.

IRENE: Lovely.

REVEREND: Yeah.

IRENE: What is this? Number fourteen?

REVEREND: Fifteen.

IRENE: Startin' to show on you, Johnny.

REVEREND: Is it?

IRENE: Looks like you could use a drink.

REVEREND: *(With a chuckle.)* Yeah.

IRENE: Help yourself.

REVEREND: No, I couldn't.

IRENE: Why not? It's almost happy hour.

REVEREND: It's three.

IRENE: So, It's happy hour in Connecticut. I'm sure your parents are having a drink right about now.

REVEREND: I'm sure they are.

(The Reverend stares at the bar for a moment. Riley sees him thinking about it. Riley gets up, goes behind the bar, pours a shot of whiskey, and brings it over to the Reverend.)

RILEY: There you go. We won't tell anyone.

(Riley goes back to his seat. The Reverend is amused. He downs the shot.)

IRENE: You're not allowed to get fed up and bolt out of town without sayin' goodbye like the last one.

(Thaddeus turns around, unsure of who she's talking to.)

REVEREND: I would never do that to you, Irene . . . All right, well I better go freshen up for the press. Put my collar on. Look professional.

IRENE: Is this Jonas gonna be a big draw?

REVEREND: I'd say you'll pull in a pretty penny tomorrow night. Probably tonight, too.

IRENE: What about protestors?

REVEREND: Oh, yeah. There's a bunch of them out there already, marching in circles, pumping their signs in the air, raising dust. Patrice is out there talking to them.

(Patrice enters.)

REVEREND: Or was. Hi.

PATRICE: Hi.

(Patrice slumps down in the seat the Reverend has just vacated.)

REVEREND: Well, I'll see you all later. Thanks for the drink, Riley.

RILEY: Sure.

IRENE: Don't forget to brush your teeth before you talk to the press.

REVEREND: I won't.

(Reverend exits. Pause. Everyone glances at Patrice who is very down in the mouth.)

IRENE: You were over there interviewing the protestors?

PATRICE: Hmm? Oh, yeah.

IRENE: I bet they talked your ear off.

PATRICE: Yeah, they were a little bit overzealous.

IRENE: They're a weird bunch, those protestors.

PATRICE: I guess.

IRENE: You lookin' for somethin' to eat?

PATRICE: No. Thanks.

IRENE: You ever get that interview with the accused?

PATRICE: Well, I saw him, but he wouldn't talk to me.

(Thaddeus glances over at her, but she doesn't meet his gaze. Irene notices the look.)

IRENE: Oh. That's too bad.

PATRICE: I don't even know if I have a story without that interview. *(Pause.)* I'm gonna go take a shower. I've got to wash his eyes off me.

(Patrice shudders. Irene hands her some towels.)

IRENE: Here's some fresh towels for you. Thaddeus, would you grab her a few bars of soap?

(Thaddeus pulls about six hotel-size bars of soap out of the box and holds them out for Patrice.)

THADDEUS: Here.

PATRICE: I don't need that much.

IRENE: Why don't you just take it.

(She is about to protest, but she finds them all looking at her strangely.)

PATRICE: OK. *(Patrice takes the soap. She takes a few steps toward the door then turns back to Irene.)* This is going to sound stupid, but what do I wear? What's appropriate attire for tomorrow night?

IRENE: I think it's what you'd call business casual. Nothin' too dressy. Nothin' too bright.

PATRICE: OK. Thanks.

(Patrice exits.)

RILEY: This place is so fucking depressing before an execution.

IRENE: I know it.

RILEY: I'll be back later.

IRENE: All right.

(Riley exits. Long pause.)

IRENE: Was it her you were waitin' for?

THADDEUS: What?

IRENE: You said you were waiting for someone. There's not that many people you talk to.

THADDEUS: I wasn't waitin' for her.

(Pause.)

IRENE: You think she's pretty?

THADDEUS: She is pretty. She's empirically pretty.

IRENE: What does that mean?

THADDEUS: It means she's pretty regardless of what I think about it. What are you doing, Irene? Don't I have enough on my mind without you harpin' on me about some girl who's leavin' tomorrow?

IRENE: I'm sorry.

(Henry enters.)

HENRY: Hey, Irene. Thaddeus.

(At the sound of Henry's voice, Thaddeus lunges at him, knocking him to the ground and nearly choking him by the collar.)

THADDEUS: Did you say something to that bastard about my mother?

HENRY: What? Thaddeus! Ow!

THADDEUS: Did you?!

HENRY: What? You're hurting me.

IRENE: Thaddeus! Let go of him.

(Irene tries to pull Thaddeus off Henry.)

THADDEUS: Have you been spouting off about how sorry you feel for me in front of that bastard?

HENRY: No!

(Thaddeus loosens his grip and Irene pulls him away from Henry. Thaddeus bellows at Henry at the top of his lungs.)

THADDEUS: Then how does he know? How does that sick motherfucker know that my mama's dyin'? Do you have any idea what I had to listen to all night?!

IRENE: Oh, God.

THADDEUS: Do you have any fucking idea?!

HENRY: He was sleeping. Rickert asked me how she was doing.

THADDEUS: Have you read the rule book?

HENRY: He was snoring.

THADDEUS: Discussion of your own personal business and that of other corrections officers is strictly forbidden in front of the inmates. Do you remember that one?

HENRY: Rickert was just worried about her. I thought Jonas was sleeping.

THADDEUS: I could kill you, Henry.

(Thaddeus rips away from Irene and storms out. Irene gives Henry a hand up.)

HENRY: I thought he was sleeping.

IRENE: I know, Henry.

(Lights fade to black.)

Scene Nine

It's the middle of the night. Riley sits at the bar drinking. Patrice comes in wearing pajamas and a robe. She sees Riley.

PATRICE: Oh.

RILEY: Hi.

PATRICE: I didn't mean to . . .

RILEY: You're not.

PATRICE: I just wanted a glass of ice water.

RILEY: Can't sleep?

PATRICE: No.

(She gets herself a glass of ice water.)

PATRICE: I think I'm nervous about tomorrow night.

RILEY: It's not easy watching someone die.

PATRICE: Do you mind if I sit in here for a while?

RILEY: I don't mind.

PATRICE: Would Irene?

RILEY: Irene don't mind as long as we don't wake her up. You can help your-self to something stronger than water if you like. On me.

PATRICE: What are you having?

RILEY: Bourbon.

PATRICE: Would it help me sleep?

RILEY: It might.

(Patrice pours herself a stiff drink.)

RILEY: You seemed pretty upset before.

PATRICE: Yeah.

RILEY: You have a lot invested in this story.

PATRICE: Yeah. I do.

RILEY: You gonna be able to write it without Jonas's interview?

PATRICE: I guess I'll have to. Anyhow, I already know how the execution is going to effect Jonas. I guess the more interesting question is: how does it effect everyone else?

RILEY: And how it'll effect you.

PATRICE: Yeah, well. That's only interesting to me, I have a feeling.

RILEY: Did you interview the Reverend?

PATRICE: Yeah.

RILEY: He was helpful?

PATRICE: He was. Has he been helpful to you?

RILEY: I suppose he's tried. You interview Thaddeus?

PATRICE: Yeah.

RILEY: Irene?

PATRICE: Briefly.

RILEY: How come you never asked me? What I thought?

PATRICE: . . . Well, you don't work at the the prison.

RILEY: Neither does Irene.

PATRICE: You and I didn't exactly get off on the right foot.

RILEY: I guess not.

PATRICE: I mean, it was my fault.

RILEY: It's not anybody's fault.

PATRICE: I never know how to behave around veterans. I'm always so uncomfortable . . . I was afraid I'd trigger a flashback or something. I didn't mean to offend you. Not asking.

RILEY: No. No offense taken . . . It's just been pressin' down on me these past coupla months since Alice died. This whole death thing. I've been tryin' to make sense of it. Trying to make sense of what I've done with my life. Fightin' in a war, makin' a livin'. I've always been killing things. I ain't never been in the prison, but I've been thinking a lot about this Jonas fella, this past week and whoever's got to kill him. We got some shitty jobs, the lot of us. Americans eat more beef than any other nation in the world and how many people kill cows? A few thousand? We got how many people on death row? Hundreds? And how many folks who got to put the needle in their arm? Maybe thirty? I'm not sayin' the act itself is wrong. We got to eat. We got to protect ourselves. If we were a tribe, we'd all be hunting, killing our own food. And if there were someone like Jonas who went around raping and murdering little girls, we'd have to execute him. We couldn't just exile him and have him lurkin' around. We couldn't waste able-bodied men to keep him captive when we need them hunting and working in the fields, right? We'd have to kill him to protect the tribe. It'd be the only reasonable thing. But now we got a whole nation of people and everybody's got their job. Some people make shoes, some people push paper, some people keep men in cages, and some people kill cows. And pigs and chickens . . . and other people. I mean, I know we got to do it, but it doesn't seem right that the dirty work should rest on so few shoulders, you know? . . . I don't think the human soul was made to stand it all. All that grief. I know mine wasn't.

(Pause.)

PATRICE: I really need to start carrying my tape recorder everywhere in this town.

RILEY: Oh, don't worry about it. It's just the ramblings of a drunk old man, anyhow.

PATRICE: You spend a lot of nights in here?

RILEY: Lately.

PATRICE: Since your wife died.

RILEY: Yeah.

PATRICE: Maybe you should move to a house with fewer ghosts.

RILEY: My ghosts sit right on my shoulders and follow me around . . . I thought you were a ghost when you first walked in here.

PATRICE: Why?

RILEY: You mind my askin' how old you are?

PATRICE: How old do you think I am?

RILEY: I don't know. That's why I'm askin'.

PATRICE: I'm twenty-six.

RILEY: Twenty-six.

PATRICE: Older than you thought?

RILEY: Older than you look.

PATRICE: I know.

RILEY: Thaddeus said you were adopted.

PATRICE: . . . Yeah. I am.

RILEY: So, were you born here or there?

PATRICE: I was born in Vietnam.

RILEY: What city?

PATRICE: I don't know. I flew out of Saigon.

RILEY: How old were you? When you were adopted?

PATRICE: . . . I was two.

RILEY: *(More nervous and urgent.)* You remember anything? About your mother? You know her name?

PATRICE: *(Getting irritated.)* I don't know her name. I don't know anything about her. There's not much documentation on us half-breeds.

RILEY: You don't remember her?

PATRICE: I remember a woman's face. I don't know who it is.

RILEY: So if there's no record of your birth, you don't really know how old you are.

PATRICE: Not exactly, no.

RILEY: Any chance you could be off by a couple of years?

(Pause.)

PATRICE: What's the matter, Riley? You rape some poor woman and now you're afraid I'm coming back to haunt you?

RILEY: I didn't rape anybody!

PATRICE: So she was a whore.

RILEY: No! She was just . . . a girl. You know. A waitress in a bar.

PATRICE: She speak English?

RILEY: A few words.

PATRICE: You speak Vietnamese?

RILEY: A few words.

PATRICE: So it was a meaningful relationship.

RILEY: No. Patrice, I know . . . I know you probably don't have it in you to understand. That you can't know what it's like to be this stupid farm boy, sent to this foreign place, and ordered to kill people you ain't got nothing against. What it's like to be so homesick that your bones ache, and your nerves are shot from explosions going off all the time, and you can't close your eyes because the things you've seen come to you when you close your eyes. So you go to a bar with the guys to drink away your pain and your fear. And you sit in the corner 'cause you don't feel like talkin' and laughin' and pretendin' there's no war goin' on outside. And this waitress comes up to you and when you look up at her, it's like she can see right inside you. And suddenly you know scared must look the same no matter what language you speak, because she can see how scared you are. And just when you feel your eyes start to water and you're about to come apart, she puts her tiny little hand on your arm and squeezes. And somehow that little gesture, those little hands, they hold you together and keep you from crumbling. You can't believe how strong she is, that she can hold you together like that. And you wait for her every night. You wait for her to get off work so you can walk her home. So she can hold your hand and keep you whole. 'Cause all you need to survive this place, this war, this world, is to know there's a little bit of kindness out there . . . And then they tell you you're being moved out to some other place with a name you can't pronounce and you go to say good-bye to her. And she already knows somehow, and she looks afraid for the first time. And she's saying something to you that you can't understand. But you know it's important. You can see on her face that it's urgent that you know. And while you're standing there looking at her like an idiot with tears running down your face, she takes your hands and presses them on her belly . . . And it's like she's punched you in the gut. It's all joy and horror and confusion. And you hold her and you cry and you kiss her good-bye and you never see her again . . . You look so much like her . . . But she'd be twenty-eight now . . . If it was a girl.

PATRICE: *(Touched, careful.)* I don't think they'd be off by two years. Not with a two-year-old.

RILEY: No. I don't suppose.

PATRICE: Did Alice know?

RILEY: No. Alice couldn't have children. It would have broke her heart . . . I never told anybody.

(Thaddeus comes out of Irene's room. Both Patrice and Riley turn around to see who it is. Thaddeus stops, meeting their gaze, but he says nothing. He exits. Pause.)

RILEY: Do you ever think about going back to Vietnam and looking for her? Your mother.

PATRICE: Well, yeah. All the time, but I think it would be sort of futile. Since I don't even know her name. *(Pause.)* Do you think about going back and looking for her? Now that Alice is gone?

RILEY: *(A heavy sigh.)* Yeah. A bit. It's not a good idea for lots of reasons. For one, she mighta married. Had a good life. How would she explain me showing up on the scene? Who's to say she'd even want to see me? Lord knows she wouldn't recognize me. Maybe she's not even living. . . . I don't know too many men who fought in that war who could set foot on that soil again. I'm not so well-mended that I won't break again . . . I'm a fragile man, now. I wouldn't travel well. Not there.

(The lights fade to black.)

Scene Ten

Riley sits alone at the bar, a beer in hand. After a moment Irene enters with a couple of racks of glassware. She sets them down behind the bar and then leans against it with finality.

IRENE: Well, that should do it. All the dishes are clean, the kegs have been changed, the chili's ready, there's extra soap in the rooms.

RILEY: The quiet before the storm.

IRENE: Yep.

RILEY: You got help coming in?

IRENE: A couple of high school kids.

RILEY: I'll help you tend bar if it gets busy.

IRENE: If?

RILEY: I'll tend bar, then. You can't have high school kids behind the bar with those news people here.

IRENE: There a lot of 'em?

RILEY: Looked like four or five crews when I went by.

IRENE: Vultures.

RILEY: Yep.

IRENE: I hope they leave the parents alone. They're already so fragile as it is.

RILEY: If they were looking for peace, they shouldn't have come here.

IRENE: How could they know? And there's no way to tell them otherwise.

RILEY: I know. Who would have thought we'd be such experts on vengeance and grief?

IRENE: Yeah, well, it's the legacy of being born in Chagrin Falls, isn't it?

(Pause.)

RILEY: Lots of protestors out there, too. I guess I understand their position and all, not that I totally agree with it, but all that hollering and ruckus when someone inside's getting ready go . . . that don't seem so considerate to me.

IRENE: Well, you know how it goes. If you don't make lots of noise, nobody listens to you.

RILEY: Personally, I think the most effective part is the candlelight vigil. The way they stand up there, all silent, with their faces glowing amber. And the way they all blow the candles out when they know it's done. It's fitting. Respectful. None of that self-righteousness and yelling.

IRENE: I think I liked it better when they used the chair. I remember sitting up, watching TV or playing Monopoly. For some reason we always stayed up for it. Did you and Alice do that?

RILEY: We'd sit up reading.

IRENE: It seemed like everybody stayed up for it. There was something about the way the lights dimmed down. That sudden hum of all the appliances and the lights, struggling to stay on, trying to run when most of the town's electricity was being pumped into some sinner. It seemed to take so long. I remember sitting there watching the light bulbs pulse faintly, thinkin' how could it take somebody so long to die with that much voltage goin' through 'em. And then the power would come back in that swelling kind of surge. And there was that moment where we'd all sit there. All silent and knowing. Knowing that someone had just passed on . . . to somewhere. It was sad, but it seemed right, you know? There wasn't any way to pretend it didn't happen.

(Pause. After a moment Henry bursts in, out of breath.)

HENRY: Thaddeus?!

IRENE: Jesus, Henry.

HENRY: Is Thaddeus here?

IRENE: No.

HENRY: *(Breathing hard.)* He didn't come to work. He's supposed to work the execution.

IRENE: Maybe he's sittin' with Teri. She probably took a bad turn.

(Irene goes to the phone and picks up the receiver.)

HENRY: No. No one's there. I went and checked already.

IRENE: No one's there?

HENRY: No. I went inside. Looked around.

IRENE: Teri wasn't there?

HENRY: Her bed was empty.

IRENE: He must of taken her to the hospital.

(*Irene dials some numbers.*)

RILEY: I thought she wanted to die at home.

IRENE: (*Into phone.*) County hospital, please.

HENRY: You gotta tell him to come in to work.

IRENE: He's not gonna come into work if his mama's about to pass on, Henry.

HENRY: But he has to! Or else I have to be on tie-down . . . I don't want to be part of killin' nobody.

IRENE: Yes, hello, I'm trying to find out if a Mrs. Teri Newell has been admitted into the hospital or the ER? . . . Teresa Newell. N-E-W-E-L-L. Yes, I'll hold.

HENRY: (*A little whiny.*) I can't.

RILEY: Did you think your turn would never come up, Henry?

HENRY: The Bible says it's a sin.

RILEY: It may be a sin, but it's in your job description.

IRENE: Yes, I'm here . . . Yes . . . Well, they must be on their way. Could you get a message to . . . If you could just tell him to . . . All right, I'll call back then. (*Irene slams down the phone.*) Bitch.

RILEY: Looks like you're out of luck, Henry.

HENRY: I'm afraid of needles.

RILEY: Well, they're not stickin' you with it. Maybe this Jonas guy's afraid of needles.

HENRY: That don't make me feel better, Riley.

IRENE: You'll be all right. Thaddeus says it's just like bucklin' your belt, except bigger buckles. It's not like you have to watch.

HENRY: But then I gotta unbuckle him after. I never seen a dead person before.

RILEY: You'll just haveta take deep breaths and try to think of somethin' else, Henry.

(*Henry stares at both of them helplessly for a moment and then exits.*)

IRENE: God, I hope Thaddeus is OK. I hope she doesn't die in the car on the way over there.

RILEY: I wasn't under the impression there were going to be any more trips to the hospital.

IRENE: I should go be with him. He shouldn't be there by himself.

RILEY: You should wait and make sure that's where he went before you drive forty minutes.

IRENE: Where else would he go?

RILEY: I'll hold down the fort if you want, Irene, but what if you drive all that way and he's not there?

IRENE: . . . I'll call again in a few minutes.

(Lights fade.)

Scene Eleven

As the lights dim on the previous scene, Riley and Irene sit at one of the tables, waiting quietly for the moment to pass. Specials come up on everyone else. The Reverend is center stage with a Bible in his hand. Patrice stands off to the side, looking on. Henry, a bandage on his face, stands facing away from the Reverend, caught up in his own thoughts. Thaddeus stands, wet and muddy, leaning on a shovel, looking downward at the ground. The sound of rain falling on the earth.

REVEREND AND HENRY: In thee, O Lord, I do put my trust; let me never be ashamed.

REVEREND: Deliver me in thy righteousness. Bow down thine ear to me.

REVEREND AND THADDEUS: Deliver me speedily.

REVEREND AND RILEY: Be thou my strong rock.

REVEREND AND IRENE: A house of defense to save me.

REVEREND: Pull me out of the net that they have laid privily for me, for thou art my strength.

REVEREND AND IRENE: I will be glad and and rejoice in thy mercy, for thou hast considered my trouble; thou hast known my soul in adversity . . .

REVEREND AND RILEY: Have mercy upon me, O Lord, for I am in trouble. Mine eye is consumed with grief, yea, my soul and my belly, for my life is spent with grief, and my years with sighing. My strength faileth because of mine iniquity, and my bones are consumed.

REVEREND AND THADDEUS: I was a reproach among all mine enemies, but especially among my neighbors, and a fear to mine acquaintance: they that did see me without fled from me.

REVEREND, THADDEUS, RILEY, AND IRENE: I am forgotten as a dead man out of mind. I am like a broken vessel,

REVEREND, IRENE, and THADDEUS: for I have heard the slander of many.

REVEREND: Fear was on every side. While they took counsel together against me, they devised to take away my life.

REVEREND AND HENRY: But I trusted in thee, O Lord: I said thou art *my* God.

ALL: Let me not be ashamed, O Lord; let me not be chagrined,

REVEREND: for I have called upon thee. Let the wicked be ashamed, and let them be silent in the grave. Pray for us sinners, O Lord. Now and at the hour of our death.

ALL: Amen.

(Henry reaches up to his face and then looks at the blood on his hand. Lights fade to black.)

Scene Twelve

The lights come up on Irene and Riley playing gin rummy at a table. All the chairs are resting upside-down on the tables. Both Irene and Riley go through several turns of picking up cards and discarding until Riley goes out. Irene is impatient and agitated. There's the soft sound of rain on the roof, with occasional distant rumble.

IRENE: Jesus. How can you win that many times in a row?

RILEY: You're distracted.

IRENE: It's my deal, right?

RILEY: Yeah.

(Irene shuffles the cards. She is tense.)

IRENE: You're a good man, Riley MacDougal. Tendin' bar. Stayin' up with me. Helpin' me clean up after that mob.

RILEY: They were a mob.

IRENE: Always are. Those news people on one side of the place, drinking everything in sight. Laughin'. Makin' fun of the town. Tryin' to pretend they weren't part of someone dyin'. The protesters on the other side, feeling helpless and bein' surly. Nobody tipping for shit. It's always a lousy night.

RILEY: That Patrice girl didn't come in.

IRENE: Nope, she didn't. Johnny didn't come either.

(Irene deals the cards.)

RILEY: He usually come in?

IRENE: He usually helps me close up the place. Maybe he's at the hospital with Teri. Maybe Thaddeus called him and not me.

RILEY: I suppose the breakfast crowd'll be in any minute, now.

IRENE: People won't want much more than coffee today. Did you go?

RILEY: I gotta discard.

IRENE: You know, Thaddeus told me that Teri's leaving me that house in her will.

RILEY: Really?

IRENE: Yeah. I was kinda surprised, you know, with how she felt about me 'n' Thaddeus.

RILEY: I know. Would you move in there?

IRENE: I don't know. I think it'd be too strange. Too sad.

RILEY: Yeah.

> (Pause.)

RILEY: You wanna live in my house?

IRENE: What?

RILEY: Not with me. I'd live here, you could live there.

IRENE: You wanna sell me your house?

RILEY: No. I just don't wanna live there no more.

IRENE: Could I redecorate it?

RILEY: You could do whatever you want to it.

IRENE: And you'd live here?

RILEY: I'll work here, if you want. Watch the place. And you can have that porch and that rockin' chair and that little bit of peace and quiet you're always whinin' about.

IRENE: So, you just retired and now you wanna come work for me?

RILEY: Sure. What the hell else am I gonna do? I can pour drinks as well as anyone. I'm not gonna cook anything, but I could wait on tables and such.

IRENE: You're not gonna drink all the profits, are you?

RILEY: No.

> (The door opens and the Reverend enters. He is wet from the rain and muddy up to his knees with rich brown dirt, which is also smeared on his face a little. The sight of him propels Irene out of her chair.)

IRENE: Oh God, she's dead, isn't she?

REVEREND: Yeah . . . Thaddeus buried her.

IRENE: What? . . . Where?

REVEREND: On the back end of their property. Teri picked out the spot last year.

IRENE: But how could he — he buried her already?

REVEREND: I guess she told Thaddeus to dig the grave a couple weeks ago. He made her a coffin, too.

IRENE: Why didn't you come get me, Johnny?

REVEREND: Thaddeus asked me not to. I went over there to see what happened to him. Why he didn't come to work. When I didn't find anyone in the house, I went and looked for the grave. He was already filling it in when I got there.

IRENE: Well, where is he? I need to see him.

REVEREND: He's gone, Irene. He gave me a couple of letters for you. One from him and one from Teri.

(The Reverend takes two envelopes out of his breast pocket and holds them out. Irene slowly walks up and takes them, walks into her room, and closes the door.)

RILEY: It's a long time comin'.

REVEREND: Yeah. She suffered more than anyone should have to. Thaddeus, too.

RILEY: They were both more than ready to go.

(The sound of something being broken offstage.)

IRENE: *(Offstage.)* Goddamn him!

RILEY: You should probably go in there. You're better with these things than I am.

(The Reverend nods and then follows Irene. Riley starts making a pot of coffee. Patrice enters with her bag. Her hair is wet.)

RILEY: Hi.

PATRICE: Hi.

RILEY: And how are you this fine mornin'?

PATRICE: Well, aside from puking my guts out all night and taking God knows how many showers and not sleeping, I guess I'm all right.

RILEY: Irene was saying folks go through a lot of soap on execution nights.

PATRICE: So when do I start feeling clean?

RILEY: It takes a while.

PATRICE: Does leaving town help?

RILEY: I suppose. It doesn't change what you witnessed, but it . . . fades some. Takes the sting out of it. But it'll come back on you sometimes, when you're doin' the most ordinary things. Washing your face or gettin' caught in the rain. It hits you full force, and you'll feel just like you do right now. That doesn't go away.

(Sobbing emanates from behind Irene's door.)

RILEY: Teri Newell passed on.

PATRICE: Oh. *(Pause.)* So, Thaddeus is gone.

RILEY: Yep.

(The sound of heavy objects thrown to the floor comes from behind Irene's door.)

PATRICE: Should we go in there?

RILEY: Reverend's with her.

PATRICE: Did Thaddeus say good-bye to her?

RILEY: Nope.

(Pause. Patrice looks at the door.)

PATRICE: I need to pay my bill.

RILEY: Oh . . . Any idea how much it was?

PATRICE: No. She put all my meals on my tab.

RILEY: Well, let me see if I can find where she keeps that stuff.

(Riley starts rifling through drawers and cabinets. He jumps back, suddenly.)

RILEY: Jesus!

PATRICE: Are you all right?

RILEY: Yeah, I'm fine. Just a big . . . bug.

(Riley moves out of the way but leaves the cabinet door open, revealing the cow's head propped up inside. He continues looking through drawers.)

RILEY: I gotta be honest with you, I don't really know what I'm looking for.

PATRICE: Well, maybe I could leave my credit card number with you. And the expiration date.

RILEY: Yeah. That would be all right. Here. You can write it on here.

(Riley hands her a pad of paper and a pen. Patrice pulls out a credit card and writes the number down.)

RILEY: Are you sorry you came here?

PATRICE: Sorry? I don't know if that's the right word. I feel like I killed someone last night.

RILEY: You'll be a different person now, havin' seen what you saw.

PATRICE: But not a better person.

RILEY: The person you are is about what you do with what's been handed to ya.

PATRICE: Yeah.

RILEY: You want to put down your phone number too, so she can tell you how much the bill is?

PATRICE: Yeah. OK.

(Patrice writes down her number and pushes the pad of paper toward Riley.)

RILEY: That should do it.

PATRICE: Yeah.

RILEY: It was a pleasure meeting you, Patrice.

PATRICE: Yes. You too.

RILEY: You have a good trip back.

PATRICE: Thanks . . .

(She turns to go, but stops.)

PATRICE: Um . . . I wanted to thank you.

RILEY: For what?

(Pause.)

PATRICE: I came here looking for some kind of absolution. And I definitely didn't get that. But you gave me something I wasn't expecting.

RILEY: I don't follow you.

PATRICE: When I was ten years old my parents told me that there was no record of my birth and that I would never be able to locate my biological parents. I used to lie awake at night trying to imagine what she was like. I thought she must have been young and pretty and poor and afraid for her half-breed baby. The more I read about Vietnam, the more grateful I was to her for giving me up. But my father . . . well, I didn't like to imagine him so much. What kind of person he was. Nothing nice ever really came to mind. Not knowing the circumstances of my conception has always weighed heavily on me. You probably already figured that out. But I wanted to thank you, because I'll never know who my father is, but now I do know who he could be. And that's a gift I never thought I'd stumble across. Certainly not here. So, thank you.

(Patrice pauses a moment and then exits, leaving Riley stunned and still. After a moment he wipes his eyes and pulls the cow head from the cabinet and places it face up on the bar. He touches one of its eyes gingerly. Henry enters. His hair is wet, as if he's just showered. He also has a white bandage on the side of his face. All of Henry's natural enthusiasm is gone.)

HENRY: Hey, Riley.

RILEY: Hey, Henry.

HENRY: Was that Patrice I saw drivin' away?

RILEY: Yeah. She left. What happened to your face?

HENRY: Jonas knocked me down and kicked me when we was walkin' him to the death chamber. I guess he wasn't jokin' about wantin' me dead.

(Henry sits at the bar and begins to pet the cow's head.)

RILEY: They still make you do tie-down?

HENRY: Yeah. They stuck some gauze on me and sent me in.

RILEY: You did OK, though, right?

HENRY: Well, I was all right when we tied him down. I was so mad at 'im for kicking me, I just strapped him down hard as I could. But when we had to go back in . . . after. I don't know, I just . . . I almost started cryin'. You don't tell nobody, though.

RILEY: Course not.

(Henry continues to pet the cow.)

HENRY: Sure is a pretty one.

RILEY: Yeah, they picked a real beauty.

HENRY: Why'd Irene take it down?

RILEY: . . . Some folks found it a little unsettling, I guess.

(Pause.)

HENRY: Riley? You think it's worse to work at the slaughterhouse or the prison?

RILEY: Well, I don't know. They're both pretty depressing vocations. You thinkin' 'bout quittin' your job?

HENRY: Yeah. I don't think I could kill a cow, though.

RILEY: Well, there's other jobs, other places.

HENRY: I know. I just can't imagine moving somewhere else. Everyone I know lives in Chagrin Falls. And Tracey wouldn't want to move away from her folks. And neither of us got a farm in our family.

RILEY: You could always work on someone else's farm.

HENRY: I guess. It sure ain't a steady way to make a livin', though. Support a family.

(Reverend enters from Irene's room.)

RILEY: How's she doing?

REVEREND: She's . . . upset. But she seems to be done throwing things. For now.

RILEY: *(To Henry.)* Your Aunt Teri passed on last night.

(Irene emerges from her bedroom. She sits at one of the tables looking lost. Reverend goes and sits with her. Riley pours a cup of coffee and brings it over to her.)

IRENE: Thanks.

RILEY: What kinda sandwich you want, Henry?

HENRY: I don't care.

(Riley goes back behind the bar. Everyone is silent and still in their own thoughts for a moment. Thunder rumbles gently.)

IRENE: I hate these dark rainy mornings. It makes it feel like the night never ends.

(The lights fade to black.)

END OF PLAY

MUSIC FROM
A SPARKLING PLANET

By Douglas Carter Beane

We are all interested in the future for that is where you and
I are going to spend the rest of our lives.

— Edward D. Wood, Jr.

PLAYWRIGHT'S BIOGRAPHY

Douglas Beane is the author of the plays *The Country Club, As Bees in Honey Drown* (Outer Critic's Circle John Gassner Award), and *Advice from a Caterpillar*. Universal has purchased the film rights to *Bees* and the film version of *Caterpillar*, starring Cynthia Nixon, Tim Oliphant, Andy Dick, and Ally Sheedy, received the best feature film award at both the Aspen Comedy Festival and the Toyota Comedy Festival.

Steven Spielbergy is producing Mr. Beane's first original screenplay, *To Wong Foo, Thanks for Everything, Julie Newmar*. The film, starring Wesley Snipes, Patrick Swayze, John Lequizamo, Robin Williams, and Stockard Channing, was the number-one film in the United States for a month. His second original screenplay, *Rasputin's Penis,* is in preproduction. Plans for the upcoming theater season include a collection of sketches, *Mondo Drama,* and a new musical, *The Big Time*.

Mr. Beane's career as a producer and artistic director began with his creation of the popular New York theater company, Drama Department Productions, which has presented hit revivals of forgotten plays. Among them are Williams's *Kingdom of Earth* (*New York Times* Highlight of '96), Lardner and Kaufman's *June Moon* (Obie Award, Lucille Lortel Award, Encore Taking Off Award), Stowe's *Uncle Tom's Cabin or Life Among the Lowly* (Genie Award, Dramaleague Award), Hart and Berlin's *As Thousand's Cheer* (cast album available on CD), and Kelley's *The Torch-bearers* (Lucille Lortel Award). He has produced world premieres by Frank Publiesi, Paul Rudnick, and David and Amy Sedaris.

ORIGINAL PRODUCTION

Music from a Sparkling Planet was first produced by the drama department at the Greenwich House Theater in New York City on June 20, 2001. It was directed by Mark Brokaw; the set design was by Allen Moyer; the lighting design was by Kenneth Posner; the sound design was by Janet Kalas; the original music was by Lewis Flinn; the costume design was by Michael Krass; and the stage manager was Christine M. Daly. The cast was as follows:

TAMARA . . . . J. Smith-Cameron

HOAGIE . . . . Ross Gibby

MILLER . . . . T. Scott Cunningham

WAGS . . . . Josh Hamilton

ANDY . . . . Michael Gaston

TIME

The play take place in the past, present, and future.

PLACE

In and around Philadelphia.

MUSIC FROM
A SPARKLING PLANET

Act I
"The Past and the Present"

First the past. The early seventies. A woman dressed in a spacesuit (a little too much cleavage) stands before a cardboard set representing a spaceship. She wears a tiny helmet with an antenna. Her name is Tamara Tomorrow and she is a children's television show host.

TAMARA: Boys and girls, this is Tamara Tomorrow from a far-off galaxy in the distant future and I've come to tell you what the future holds for you. By the year 1979 all diseases will be cured by pills and exercise. In the middle of the ninteen eighties people will communicate only by thoughts! Oh what the future holds for the boys and girls of the Philadelphia area! Come blast off with me and I'll show you such a sparkling planet. By the year 2002 most every home will have a computer —
(Now, the present. We see a bar in Philadelphia. Miller, a press representative in a very stylish suit, walks in and Hoagie, a personal trainer in sweats, stands up.)
And all days will be filled with only —
MILLER: *(A desperate cry for life.)* Trivia!
HOAGIE: *(A cry at a sporting event.)* TRIVIA!!!
TAMARA: Scientific discussion.
MILLER: My life is so full of shit I can't even bear it. I need trivia now. Category.
HOAGIE: Best television portrayal of the future. After "Star Trek."
TAMARA: The most scientific discussions.
(She is gone.)
MILLER: "Lost in Space."
HOAGIE: "Lost in Space" sucks. You take the cool robot out of "Lost in Space" and all you have is my family on any trip and who wants to see that?
(Wags, a handsome young lawyer in a relatively conservative suit, enters. Like the other two men, though an adult, there is a something of a child to him.)
WAGS: OK, in like the history of bad days, this is one for the books. I need trivia YESTERDAY!! Category.

MILLER: TV show that is just wrong and so pisses you off.

WAGS: Very good category! TV show that is just wrong? "I Dream of Jeanie."

MILLER AND HOAGIE: Why?

WAGS: This woman is walking around calling her boyfriend "master" and nobody's just assuming it's an S and M thing? Just wrong. Hoagie?

HOAGIE: I'm sorry but for something like this I am going to fall back on an old standby.

WAGS: Howells?

HOAGIE: On "Gilligan's Island" why did the Howells pack all that clothing for a —

HOAGIE, WAGS, AND MILLER: Three-hour tour?

MILLER: One of life's great mysteries. And for me? Show that is just wrong? "H.R. Puffenstuff." What sex was that thing? No, what sexual preference was that thing? It's like some bi-curious Mayor McCheese. Take it from my eyes.

HOAGIE: Miller's got it.

WAGS: Miller wins. Oh, hey, Mills, what's this I hear about Greg?

MILLER: Nothing, he just had an attack or something. Category —

HOAGIE: Most stoned cartoon character.

WAGS: *(Simultaneous with Miller's next line.)* Ahhh, Shaggy, too easy.

MILLER: *(Simultaneous with Wag's previous line.)* Shaggy on "Scooby Doo." Obvious.

WAGS: No, I heard he like fell down and started twitching and —

MILLER: It's nothing, just some seizures. He's at the hospital resting and —

WAGS: Jesus, what is —

MILLER: It's nothing, he's having tests done, I'll pick him up later. Nothing, let me get those beers.

(He leaves.)

HOAGIE: God, Wags.

WAGS: What?

HOAGIE: This is like happy conversation. This is sit-in-a-bar-and-talk-about-nothing-in-a-bar-with-friends conversation. This is unwind time, not wind-up time.

WAGS: I just asked how —

HOAGIE: OK. For the record, when you come in and are like, "Oh my girlfriend Wendy wants me to move in" and all that. "Oh, they're passing me over for partner again this year." We're guys. We don't care. We just want to know who is your favorite James Bond.

WAGS: God. I'm such an asshole.

HOAGIE: Nah.

WAGS: Why do I do this? When exactly am I going to become this sensitive adult who is aware when people want to talk about things and don't want to talk about things?

HOAGIE: Don't stress it.

WAGS: So — who is —

HOAGIE: Sean Connery. Be real.

WAGS: Same here.

(Miller arrives with a tray of beers.)

MILLER: Back with beer!

WAGS: Listen, uhm, Miller. About what just —

MILLER: Quick, who's your favorite local Philly celebrity?

HOAGIE: Very promising category. We can have fun with this.

WAGS: Local Philly only.

HOAGIE: Dr. Dead.

WAGS: Oooh. Good call.

HOAGIE: Friday nights at eleven. Watch "Creature Double Feature" with Dr. Dead.

WAGS: Very good call.

MILLER: I found him ghoulish.

HOAGIE: A little Christopher Lee, a little Peter Cushing. Dr. Dead would come out of his casket introduce the next movie —

MILLER: Very big on the puns that one.

WAGS: "Grave evening, I've been lurking to meet you."

HOAGIE: And then Dr. Dead would say good night.

WAGS: "Pleasant nightmares."

HOAGIE: And he'd slowly close his casket. The lightning would flash and that creepy creepy music would — I hear it now in my head and I get goose flesh.

MILLER: Tchaikowsky's *Swan Lake*. Oh the terror.

HOAGIE: Dr. Dead. Wonder where Dr. Dead is now?

WAGS: He died. Brain cancer. It was really —

(Hoagie shoots him a look.)

My favorite James Bond is Sean Connery.

MILLER: So. Wags. Favorite local Philly celeb.

WAGS: Uhm. Tamara Tomorrow.

HOAGIE: Oh my God, Tamara Tomorrow, I change my vote.

WAGS: She was rocking my six-year-old world.

HOAGIE: Race home from school. Get that TV set on. There's Tamara Tomorrow.

WAGS: And the cleavage. And talking about the future and all. And introduc-
ing an "Astroboy" cartoon.

MILLER: Best Japanese animation we have to do someday soon.

HOAGIE: She was so sexy and happy and positive and sexy.

(The others agree.)

WAGS: And all those just happy predictions for the future. She was hope, right?
Dr. Dead was how awful things could be and Tamara Tomorrow was how
good they could be.

MILLER: The conflict of light and darkness. Oh look. This conversation has
depth after all. So there.

HOAGIE: Nah. Tamara was hope.

WAGS: And the first stiffy, man. I tell you, her and that cleavage. First time
boner material.

MILLER: Well, I'm afraid, for favorite local Philly celeb, my votes gonna be —

(Hoagie is about suggest someone else, but he's cut off by Miller.)

Don't say the newscaster with the gerbil rumor or I will abruptly leave
this bar. No. For me. Tamara Tomorrow.

HOAGIE: But you're —

MILLER: Boys, when we were growing up in Cherry Hill, New Jersey, I knew
then and there that I was . . . artistic. And one look at Tamara in that
ensemble and anyone could see there was a very unique aesthetic at work.
Tamara Tomorrow. Love. Her.

WAGS: That is so — wonder where she is now?

MILLER: Around I guess.

HOAGIE: We should call her.

MILLER: What do you mean "call her"?

HOAGIE: Look her up in the phone book.

MILLER: Hoag. And I need you to really concentrate. I think Tamara Tomorrow was a stage name. That probably is not her real name. I am willing
to hazard a guess that there are no Tomorrows in the Philadelphia phone
directory.

*(In the past, the early seventies, Andy, a producer, walks up to an impromptu
curtain backstage of a community theater.)*

HOAGIE: What is her real name?

ANDY: Sharon Phipps?

MILLER: I would be having no idea.

(The present is gone. In the past, the curtain parts, and there is Tamara To-morrow or who she really was. Sharon Phipps. She has on a very old bathrobe.)

ANDY: Sharon Phipps?

TAMARA: And then Leo, we gotta Dutchman those flats.

(She sees Andy.)

Hello, sweetheart. You gotta wait outside for the cast.

ANDY: Actually, I'm here to see you.

TAMARA: Outside, in the house, I'll be there in —

ANDY: I'm a producer.

TAMARA: Hi. Sharon Phipps. I'll change it.

ANDY: Andrew Connelly.

TAMARA: Nice to meet you, Mr. Connelly.

ANDY: Very good performance. The *Inquirer* was right when they said it was a highlight of the 72-73 season.

TAMARA: I don't read reviews. And it was the *Courier-Post*.

ANDY: The kids really liked you.

TAMARA: Thank you, sweetheart. And you're calling me Sharon.

ANDY: You have a real presence.

TAMARA: I like to think so. It's a hell of a lot of fun. It's community theater, doing a children's matinee. Most people just do the musical version, but we're doing the original. More dark, more disturbing, more literary. So, a producer. How long have you been a producer?

ANDY: First time at it. I have to direct too, so — you have a great quality. And when the pirate ship fell down. You just kind of made a joke and pushed it back up and . . . kept going. I admire that.

TAMARA: I always wonder what goes on in the minds of producers. Is that it?

(Her robe comes undone. He looks. She catches him as she quickly closes it.)

ANDY: Listen Miss Phipps, could we go out for a drink? I have something I'd like to discuss.

TAMARA: Coffee. Drink and me don't mix. I've found out. And my name is Sharon.

ANDY: Sorry, Sharon. I'll tell you here. I'm in kind of a bind. I have this role that should have been cast about a month ago. And I happened to be here with my daughter — who loved you by the way — and I saw you and if there's anyway that you could come and help us out it would be —

TAMARA: Of course. Of course, I'll — this is an actor's dream. What are the particulars? I'd —

ANDY: I'm over at Channel Thirty-six and we just bought this package of Japanese animation, and we're going to need a host to introduce —

TAMARA: Oh. I'm sorry. You're a . . . television producer. I thought you were a theatrical producer.

ANDY: In Philly? Not likely.

TAMARA: Oh.

ANDY: You seem disappointed.

TAMARA: I — I'm sure you're wonderful people over at Channel Thirty-six and you all do lovely work. But I'm an actress of the theater. I'm not —

ANDY: You don't like television? I think you'd be very good at it.

TAMARA: I might just. But it — I don't like it. I got this philosophy. That people go to the theater to be told the truth and that they watch television to be lied to.

ANDY: Why you picking on TV? I don't say bad things about theater. I think it's a great place to find talent.

TAMARA: Hey. What can I say? I'm just carny, cousin. It's been nice talking to you. I should get ready for the next show.

ANDY: It's only a little local television show. No adults will see it. It's on opposite Mike Douglas for Christ sake.

TAMARA: I really don't want to do television.

ANDY: You're a good actress, this could be a lot of exposure.

TAMARA: Mr. —

ANDY: Connelly.

TAMARA: I just — later on in life if you will. I am getting to do what I always wanted to do. I just got divorced and now I get to do for me. I am going to be a stage actress. I know you can't comprehend that but — I don't wanna be somebody on TV that never gets to meet people. I like being in a theater, live, where you know what the audience is feeling. My ideal is like what Melvin Siders has got. You know Melvin Siders? Runs a small Yiddish language theater here in Philly. And each night, 'cepting Fridays, he's there affixing his makeup in a theater no bigger than a storefront. With a cast of —

ANDY: Wait. Melvin Siders?

TAMARA: Yes.

ANDY: The Jew theater guy?

TAMARA: You know him?

ANDY: He's gonna be Dr. Dead over on Channel Forty-eight.

TAMARA: Sorry?

ANDY: Dr. Dead. Kaiser Broadcasting bought a package of old Hammer films. He's gonna introduce them. There's this Uncle Ted guy doing really well in Scranton and —

TAMARA: I had no idea.

ANDY: Hey and Helen Hayes is a Snoop Sister, so what the hell?

(In the present, Miller appears. He is at Greg's bedside.)

MILLER: Hey, Greg.

TAMARA: I have to follow my —

(In the present, Hoagie appears. Sporting a T-shirt that proclaims "Trainer," he is at his gym talking to his manager.)

HOAGIE: Yeah, Joe?

ANDY: Do both. I think it would be a real good career choice.

(In the present, Wags stands before his girlfriend, Wendy.)

WAGS: Wendy just don't. For once.

TAMARA: I'm sorry, I have flats to Dutchman.

(She leaves.)

ANDY: *(Shouting off.)* 'Cause for all the stuff you love about your theater, there's one thing that television is that theater isn't. It's a living.

(Andy smiles smugly and walks off, taking the past with him. We are in the present.)

HOAGIE: Things are —

MILLER: Things are a little —

WAGS: I'm not happy, OK?

HOAGIE: Fucked up.

MILLER: Up in the air, let's say. They're running all these tests on you and there's still no reason for the seizures, not drugs, not AIDS, and the doctor is being real comforting and supportive. He keeps saying over and over again, "This is very rare, this is very rare" like, "You're gay and you have money, this is rare, you'll want this."

HOAGIE: The lady is crazy is the deal, Joe. She's like, you know, all business-woman flirty and flirting with me during her ab work and I say one little thing flirty back and she's like, "I'm sorry I don't date people whose jobs are written on their sweatshirts." And then complaining to you. Like I was going to date her. Like I don't know it's gym policy that trainers can't date clients. And I've gotten offers to break that rule with girls a lot younger and better looking than her so — well, not lately, but —

WAGS: "What is the future of our relationship?" Wendy, why do you even ask something like — Future? Where do you — Relationship? What is a person supposed to do with that kind of a — Future? Of our relationship — Don't — That's every — don't do that. Future thing. Of the — Don't do that.

MILLER: Greg, the deal is — they don't seem to be having a — you know, notion of what your deal is — so, I know they said you were going to go home tonight — well they want to admit you. For more tests. But the good news is what it isn't.

(He starts to cry, he turns his back.)

HOAGIE: I've been at this gym longer than any other trainer and this is the first complaint you ever got. Just . . . put me on warning, OK? Suspension is a little intense for some crossed-wire thing.

WAGS: We're only talking about moving in, like if we were talking about marriage or having a kid then we would talk about future stuff or — what do you mean?

HOAGIE: Assign her to somebody else.

WAGS: How many months along?

MILLER: I know we talked about me moving in this week but, you know, my landlady said I could stay on for another month, at my place, so I won't move in right now.

(In the past, Tamara in her Tamara costume walks onto the set for the first time. Andy is there, clipboard in hand.)

TAMARA: Mr. Connelly?

ANDY: Please, call me Andy.

WAGS: How long have you known?

TAMARA: Andy.

HOAGIE: No hard feelings with her. What's past is past.

MILLER: Let's figure out the present before we move on to —

WAGS: Well then. We should talk about our future.

(Hoagie, Miller, and Wags and the present are gone. Only the past now.)

TAMARA: Geez those lights are bright, what are ya, opening a supermarket or something?

ANDY: TV needs bright lights.

TAMARA: Looks like a Penn Fruit and Dales or some — so I memorized all my lines and —

ANDY: Don't do that again. We got the idiot cards, just read off this.

(He shows her a large cue card.)

TAMARA: How am I gonna find my character if I don't have the lines etched across my soul?

ANDY: Sweetheart, this is television, we don't have time for a character 'cause there's a Frank's Cola commercial coming up our ass ninety miles an hour.

TAMARA: I want this to be good.

ANDY: And you will be. Don't worry about it. You have plenty personality. Like you were in the play, just be yourself.

TAMARA: I was playing an elfin boy.

ANDY: So you say your I'm-from-the-future crap here — then you walk down to this tape mark —

TAMARA: Spike mark, I'm a pro.

ANDY: And you say your "Astroboy" intro crap.

TAMARA: What's my motivation?

ANDY: Sorry?

TAMARA: For that move, what's my motivation?

ANDY: This is the camera that's going to be on then. If you don't move, no one will see you.

TAMARA: I can make that work.

ANDY: So that should do the intro for "Astroboy," now for "Ultraman" —

TAMARA: *(To herself.)* I'll be going for my ray gun and be interrupted by thought.

ANDY: We'll start over at the launchpad.

TAMARA: Wait, aren't we going to rehearse it? The "Astroboy" section?

ANDY: Rehearsal? Wait, are you gonna make me nutty with this method acting stuff?

TAMARA: Hey, I'm sorry but I'm from the legitimate theater where we take a little time with what we do —

ANDY: Amateur theater —

TAMARA: Hey, amateur is Greek Latin talk for something you do from the heart and I do everything from the heart so I don't take umbrage at that!

ANDY: Just smile and talk.

TAMARA: I am an actress! I'm not some—— Jessica Savitch smile pretty girl spokesmodel. I have emotions. Enough to share. The world needs me to show my emotions because they're all so cut off they can't express their own!

ANDY: OK, OK — calm down. You're gonna be great. Just wonderful. You've memorized your lines and you're enough of an old pro that you can waltz through this no sweat.

TAMARA: Thank you.

ANDY: You just do the intro, do "Astroboy," then we have plenty time during the cartoon.

TAMARA: You're real kind.

ANDY: You want a quick snort before?

TAMARA: I don't partake. Anymore.

ANDY: Right. Sorry.

TAMARA: And that wouldn't be very professional.

ANDY: Very good. So. Greeting and intro of Tamara Tomorrow — just be yourself. Then you walk over to the —

TAMARA: Spike mark.

ANDY: Spike mark —

TAMARA: Spike mark, I'm a pro.

ANDY: And you do your intro into "Astroboy" and then there's a cartoon.

TAMARA: Easy as pie.

ANDY: Easy as pie. And at the end, I'll be right by the camera.

TAMARA: Spike marks.

ANDY: And if I go like this —

(Makes an "OK" sign.)

TAMARA: OK.

ANDY: Right. Or I'll go like this.

(Indicates — stretch.)

Which means?

TAMARA: Taffy? I'm guessing.

ANDY: No, stretch.

TAMARA: Stretch?

ANDY: Just keep talking.

TAMARA: Keep talking. Keep talking what?

A VOICE (WAGS): On in fifteen Andy.

TAMARA: Where is this talk going to come from — idiot cards?

ANDY: OK people — let's look alive! *(Offhandedly to Tamara.)* Just make something up.

TAMARA: Make somethi — ad lib? Improv?

(Lights change.)

ANDY: You'll be great — have fun out there.

(A voice [Hoagie] begins a countdown from ten.)

TAMARA: Improv? Improv? DO I LOOK LIKE I'M FROM CHICAGO???!
— give me that snort.

(She takes a swig. The countdown is done. We see the nervous energy of the room slide into a calm hum. Red lights on the TV come on. Tamara's face appears on the monitor. She is a natural.)

Hey, space kiddets. Lucky for you, you've tuned in. This is your friend Tamara Tomorrow and her theater of the future and we'll be here on Channel Thirty-six until I am called back to the year 3000 to bring you "Astroboy," "Ultraman," and "Tobor, the Eighth Man." And I'll let you in on a secret. Tobor is robot spelled backwards. Oh yeah. Now I'm gonna tell you about "Astroboy" and I'm gonna walk over here to do it because, well quite frankly, I want to be close to my ray gun. You never know who doesn't want you kiddets to see these things. Astroboy is a cartoon friend and he's a robot boy being raised by Professor Elefun. And he can fly by turning his feet into flames. So — let's all meet Astroboy!

(A beat of silence, She looks over at Andy. He is making the stretch sign. A quick look of panic on Tamara's face. Then a mischievous grin slowly arrives on her lips.)

TAMARA: Well, how much time we got, Andy?

(Andy drops his clipboard.)

TAMARA: Here also, but you can't see him, is another friend of the future . . . Andy. Asteroid Andy. Asteroid Andy how much time have we got before the "Astroboy" cartoon?

ANDY: Uh — mayb — one minute five.

TAMARA: That's metric futuretalk for one minute and five seconds. Well in that time let me tell you about what the future is gonna be like. I know a lot of people out there because of the Russians and their bombs are real real worried that there's not gonna be a future.

(Andy is now shrugging in disbelief up to men in the booth.)

TAMARA: Well, space kiddets, there is a future and I'm it and here's what to expect. OK. By the year 2005 all meals will just be a pill. It will taste just like food and you'll be full afterwards but it's just a pill.

(Andy looks at her — "What?")

TAMARA: And by the year 1996 — everyone will have a personal jet pack to go to school in.

(Andy shakes his head as he picks up his clipboard.)

TAMARA: And by the year 2047 there will be only one sex.

(Andy drops his clipboard again. The monitor flashes to the face of Astroboy as we hear his opening march. The lights go down and Andy runs up to Tamara.)

ANDY: Where the hell did you come from?

(In the present, Wags, Miller, and Hoagie at a bar.)

TAMARA: The future.

ANDY: No, really.

MILLER: Tie breaker.

(All three take a swig of beer.)

TAMARA: No. Really. That's my character — I just thought if I really was from the future, I'd probably be very confident. I mean, what's 1973 if you're living in the year 3000.

(Andy, Tamara, and the past are gone. Wags and Hoagie are ready to play, very competitively.)

MILLER: Tie breaker. In case of tie, three questions, same category, loser chooses category. Category is — Superhero relatives.

HOAGIE: *(With Wags.)* Yesssssss!

WAGS: *(With Hoagie.)* Fuck me! OK.

MILLER: Who are Racer X's parents?

(Both slam the countertop with an open palm, Wags a little quicker.)
Wags.

HOAGIE: Damn!

MILLER: Racer X's parents are Moms and Pops Racer, because — *(Doing an imitation of a voice-over.)* Unknown to Speed, —

HOAGIE, WAGS, MILLER: *(All doing the same voice.)* Racer X is actually his long lost brother, Rex Racer.

HOAGIE: *(Regular voice.)* I so knew that.
(He's now pacing around the bar.)

MILLER: Correct, one point for Wags. Question two. Who is Astroboy's father?
(Both slam the table, Wags again a little quicker.)
Wags!

HOAGIE: *(Pointing at the countertop.)* My buzzer's not working, man.

WAGS: Professor Elefun.
(Miller makes the sound of a losing buzzer on a game show.)

HOAGIE: No!

WAGS: What?

MILLER: Hoagie?

HOAGIE: No. No no no no no no. No. *(Quickly and in Wag's face.)* Astroboy was created by the head of the Scientific Institute, Dr. Bointon, who was grieving over the death of his son, Astor Bointon, but when Astroboy refused to grow older, Dr. Bointon went mad and sold him to a robot circus where he was freed when the robots achieved equal rights and he went to live with Professor Pachydermus J. Elefun and you can eat my hairy ass and suck on my fat one!

MILLER: That's one point for Hoagie and two offers I notice are never thrown in my direction. Final question. The tiebreaker of the tiebreaker. Category? Relatives. What is your maternal grandmother's maiden name?
(Wags and Hoagie just look back at Miller confused.)
Just kidding. Who are Batman's parents?
(Wags and Miller slam the countertop at the same time. A crashing boom and we are in the past with Andy and Tamara seated at a table in old, original Bookbinders.)

TAMARA: Woo hoo. Bookbinders. Somebody's trying to impress somebody.

ANDY: Only the best for Tamara Tomorrow. I ordered shrimps as an appetizer. It's on its way.

TAMARA: Shrimps? This is either a thanks-for-doing-a-good-job-kiss-off meal or this is a re-sign.

ANDY: Have whatever you want, don't even look at the right side of the menu.

TAMARA: Sounds like a kiss off to me.

ANDY: Don't say that.

TAMARA: Hey you said six weeks, I did six weeks. We went opposite Mike Douglas —

ANDY: Don't —

TAMARA: We didn't even make a dent in his ratings. So I got a little coin put away and now I can go back to doing plays. Lump crab meat for me.

ANDY: Well. Actually? I know and you know the ratings are not good. And we said we'd only do this for six weeks and all. But there's something we didn't count on happening. And it happened.

TAMARA: What's that? I hope our waitress brings some bread for the table.

ANDY: Second TV sets. Most houses, a lot of families today they have a second television set. So Mom is in the kitchen watching "Mike makes your day" and the kids are in the rumpus room. Watching "Tamara Tomorrow." And Mom feels safe 'cause the kids are just watching a nice clean lady introduce some cartoons. And the kids like her 'cause a grown-up is talking to them very matter-of-factly and not down to them and the sponsors are happy 'cause the kids are believing anything the nice lady is telling them and the parents aren't around.

TAMARA: Isn't that nice we get to leave on a high point? I hear they're doing Strindberg this season. *(That doesn't sound fun. She tries to convince herself that it will be.)* That should be fun.

ANDY: Actually, we got an offer. From Frank's Cola. To go to an hour and a half. Ninety minutes. So we can get the kids just when they get home from school. We're gonna add three more Jap cartoons —

(The present appears; the trivia game is going strong.)

HOAGIE: Best Japanese Animation!

ANDY AND WAGS: "Marine Boy" —

ANDY: and —

ANDY AND MILLER: "Speed Racer."

HOAGIE AND MILLER: *(To Wags.)* Why?

ANDY AND WAGS: Marine Boy chews oxygum and can breathe underwater —

HOAGIE AND WAGS: *(To Miller.)* Why?

ANDY: and —

ANDY AND MILLER: Speed Racer has a car with gadgets —

MILLER: and really tight pants.

MILLER AND WAGS: Hoag?

ANDY: And —

ANDY AND HOAGIE: "Johnny Cypher in Dimension Zero."

MILLER AND WAGS: Why?

HOAGIE: The name, man. It's way cool.

(Miller and Wags groan; they all walk off; the present is gone.)

ANDY: Frank's will sponsor the whole thing. All they need is for you to sign on for two years.

TAMARA: I don't know if I have ninety live minutes a day in me.

ANDY: You got a great presence, and you're quick on the feet. I don't know if you noticed but we haven't written a line for you in near two weeks. You just get up and wing it and it's great.

TAMARA: But I — I really should do a play.

ANDY: You can do both — I, if I may speak my mind, really think you should do this. It would be real good for your career.

TAMARA: How do you know what'll be good for my career? You don't know me. We've worked together every day for a month and a half, right hand up, this is the first time we ever talked.

ANDY: We're busy, we have a job to do, we don't have time to know each other, that's business.

TAMARA: OK. You put too much sugar in your coffee. And you don't stir it, you stab it with the stirrer. When you laugh, before you laugh, just before you laugh, you look around like you want to make sure you heard what you just heard, then it sounds like somebody popped a balloon. You don't follow sports except hockey and your socks have really only matched twice.

ANDY: What are you a spy?

TAMARA: So. You tell me about me.

ANDY: You? I don't know. You're funny. Very good on the show.

TAMARA: Yeah, yeah, so are you. So me.

ANDY: You love theater. Uh, you got a divorce from a guy. Who you didn't like, I guess. And that gives you time to do theater. Which you love.

TAMARA: And?

ANDY: And?

TAMARA: Jeez, I wish that waitress would get here with some bread for the table. I tell you Andy that was really pretty pathetic.

ANDY: So you won't stay on, 'cause I didn't get to know you?

TAMARA: Pretty much.

ANDY: Uh. Well, I noticed that you're funny and easy to work with and, uh, very good on the show and —

TAMARA: Lonesome.

ANDY: Sorry?

TAMARA: Lonesome. Like they say in country western songs. I'm lonesome, Andy. Mighty lonesome. Television, is so lonely. I'm spending my days, talking in an empty room into a machine. And I never hear anything back. I miss people. I'm sorry. But the answer is no. A friendly no, but a no.

ANDY: Well if it's people you want —

TAMARA: What's with the extra napkins, you expecting a spill?

ANDY: The hostess recognized you, she asked me to get you to autograph it for her daughter

TAMARA: Oh. OK.

(She starts to sign.)

ANDY: She'd like you to sign it, "your friend."

TAMARA: That's sweet.

(She signs it; he hands another napkin to her.)

ANDY: This one is for the dishwasher.

(She signs it; he hands her the stack of napkins.)

ANDY: And these are for the kitchen staff and the waitresses.

(She smiles. Turns and waves at the staff.)

ANDY: And uhm, while you're doing them, could you do one for me?

(She looks at Andy, then starts to write a long message.)

ANDY: What you writing?

TAMARA: "I should tell you. Our show isn't going to be on. After next week. Tamara Tomorrow." *(She writes now as she talks.)* "Will be on a half an hour earlier."

(Andy looks up.)

TAMARA: "We're adding three more cartoons. 'Speed Racer,' 'Johnny Cypher,' and 'Aquaboy.'"

ANDY: "Marine Boy."

TAMARA: He chews gum.

(In the present, we are back in the bar.)

HOAGIE: Category.

ANDY: Champagne!

TAMARA: All right. Just this once.

HOAGIE: Biggest cartoon character slut.

MILLER: Excluding Disney?

HOAGIE: Yes. You first, Wags.

TAMARA: "See you in the future, Tamara Tomorrow."

(The past is gone.)

WAGS: I — uh — sorry — my mind is — off somewhere.

HOAGIE: Mills, biggest cartoon character slut!

MILLER: OK, we are really scraping the bottom of the —

HOAGIE: Good, I'll go. Biggest cartoon character slut? Betty Rubble.

MILLER: *(Appalled.)* Not Betty!

HOAGIE: Hey, check it out. Bamm Bamm looks nothing like Barney.

MILLER: I find your view of womanhood questionable.

HOAGIE: Hey Wags, biggest cartoon character slut?

WAGS: I — I'm sorry I wasn't paying attention. I shouldn't have come out tonight guys, I've got a lot on my mind. Wendy and I are — and the firm is a real pain lately and — Wendy is on and on about getting married. I mean, more than usual. And nothing I do is right anymore and — My apartment is too small and hers is too faraway and —

MILLER: What is going on with you?

WAGS: Well —

MILLER: What?

WAGS: Well, whether or not I will be a husband, it looks like I'm going to be a daddy.

HOAGIE: Oh shit.

MILLER: You've had that straight boy panic look all night. I knew somebody somewhere must be pregnant.

WAGS: Fuck. I mean I want to. Down the road. But.

MILLER: Look at us. Life presents itself. Life and death present themselves and we're —

HOAGIE: And we're not going to talk about it anymore we are distracting each other from our —

MILLER: Just . . . trapped.

WAGS: Yeah. Trapped. And I want to escape.

MILLER: Escape. Any old excuse. To — so what are you going to do?

HOAGIE: We're not — who had a better car — Batman or James Bond?

WAGS: Like you know, OK, when something bad happens, the very first instinct you get or I get is to run away. But you don't dream of heeding it 'cause like well, you have commitments and — even if it were just for a day, but you don't.

HOAGIE: Who had nicer Nazis, "Wonderwoman" or "Hogan's Heroes"?

WAGS: Like, at work, a partner will come by and say something so, you know, snotty to me, like if it were a stranger saying it at the gym you would just have to clock him. And I don't. Clock. Or say something. Or just take my fucking attaché case and leave. I don't. I just smile at him. Like, "Oh, you devil." 'Cause I can't leave, I'm thinking of my future.

(Somewhere, Tamara appears, signs an autograph, and leaves, over and over again.)

TAMARA: See you in the future, Tamara Tomorrow.

WAGS: So you don't run away, you stay, but all the time with the run away like feeling going.

MILLER: I know. Exactly. I want to — get away.

WAGS: Run away.

MILLER: Yeah.

HOAGIE: We're not talking about these things. We're talking about —

TAMARA: See you in the future —

HOAGIE AND TAMARA: Tamara Tomorrow.

MILLER: What about her?

HOAGIE: I was talking to somebody at work, she said she saw her.

TAMARA: See you in the future!

HOAGIE: Like about six months ago.

MILLER: No way.

WAGS: Who saw her?

HOAGIE: Brenda the stretch instructor told me. She was at the Granite Run Mall and on this wall they had all these celebrity handprints from when the mall opened of like —

(In the past, Tamara speaks at the mall opening.)

TAMARA: It's an honor to be opening this new mall with my television friends: Dr. Dead, Larry Ferrari, Wee Willie Webber,

HOAGIE AND TAMARA: Sally Starr —

HOAGIE: Al Alberts, what have you, only like since the mall opened nobody knows who most of those people are anymore so they put a earring hut in front of it so anyways Brenda walks by and she sees this woman looking at the wall behind the pagoda. Looking real sad.

TAMARA: I place my handprints on this wall for all time, space kiddets —

HOAGIE: And in a second, Brenda knew that it was Tamara Tomorrow.

TAMARA: And I sign my name.

HOAGIE: So she says,

TAMARA AND HOAGIE: "Tamara Tomorrow?"

TAMARA: And —

(She begins to write something on the wall.)

HOAGIE: This woman looks at her real sad, puts on her sunglasses and walks
away.

TAMARA: I'll see you —

MILLER: That is so wild.

TAMARA: in the future.

WAGS: Evidently nobody knows where she is. She's in hiding.

MILLER: A sort of Delaware Valley Greta Garbo.

WAGS: Wouldn't it be great to meet her?

MILLER: Oh God yeah. The best — but —

HOAGIE: I would like to go to thank her for my first erection.

WAGS: Wonder what she looks like?

TAMARA: See you in the future, Tamara Tomorrow.

WAGS: We could —

TAMARA: See you —

MILLER: What?

WAGS: Go find her —

TAMARA: in the future —

WAGS AND TAMARA: Tamara Tomorrow.

WAGS: it would be fun.

MILLER: And fucked up.

HOAGIE: And fucking crazy. Fucked up and fucking crazy.

MILLER: Really. But I do wonder what she looks like.

WAGS: It would be an escape.

MILLER: A getaway.

HOAGIE: Guys, no way.

TAMARA: See you —

WAGS: Could you, guys — I'm owed so many sick days I could — It's only
going to take a day at the most and —

MILLER: And I have tons of work, but no clients breathing down my neck right
now, so I could —

WAGS: Run

MILLER: Yeah.

WAGS: Find Tamara Tomorrow.

TAMARA: See you —

WAGS: Hoag, could you?

HOAGIE: I can't, work is —

MILLER: Hoag, you're a trainer at a gym. Call in and say you've sprained
something.

HOAGIE: Yeah. I could.

TAMARA: See you in the future.

(The present is gone. Tamara is in the past stamping a stack of eight-by-ten glossies one after the other. Next to her, a glass of Kirin.)

See you in the future, see you in the future, see you in the future, see you in the future, see you in the future.

(She begins to sort of sing it as Andy walks in.)

ANDY: Well, look who went and got happy all a sudden.

TAMARA: What?

ANDY: Singy-songy. You always do that when you're in a good mood. You must be liking TV all a sudden.

TAMARA: It's OK, I don't understand it. I mean they shoot my picture out into the atmosphere and it gets picked up by all these antennas and whatnot. What leaves me scratching my head is — what about all those things of me that don't get picked up, where do they go?

ANDY: *(Chuckling.)* That's the damnedest question I ever heard. We'll ask Phil sometime.

TAMARA: Now movies, I understand how they work.

ANDY: Can you stay a little later today? Frank's Cola people want you to tape a commercial once and for all, to play so you don't have to do the setup every day. The promotional tie-in. The doll and the badge spiel.

TAMARA: Good idea. Put it on tape. More time to think of what the hell I'm gonna say next.

ANDY: Yeah.

TAMARA: Yeah.

ANDY: *(He stares at her working for a while — she looks up.)* So if it's movies you understand, we could go check that out. Sometime.

TAMARA: What are you saying?

ANDY: I'm saying, we should go see a movie sometime.

TAMARA: Oh. That. That would be — a movie. That would be — is this what I'm thinking?

ANDY: Probably.

TAMARA: I don't know what to say to that.

ANDY: How about yes? We have a good time, you know? I can laugh with you. We got laughs. And you're not like — you're more modern in your thinking. You're divorced for chrissake. And you're . . . easy on the eyes, that's for sure.

TAMARA: Be still my girlish heart.

ANDY: And in case you didn't notice, I am noticing a lot more things about you. Like you make songs out of anything when you're in a good mood.

See I noticed that. And you, just before the cameras go on, you whisper, "sell it!" Two days a week you're on a diet, two days you're not. The fifth day is anybody's guess. All these things, I noticed on account of you told me that I didn't notice things. And I did and that made me want to — ask you to see a movie. Look I'm not good at this.

(A nervous pause, She goes back to stamping. He turns to leave. Without stopping, she says absently.)

TAMARA: I noticed you're married.

ANDY: That is the, with the exception of my two girls, that is I would say the mistake of my life. My wife and me, we don't — I haven't loved her for a very long time. It just evolved into nothing.

TAMARA: Get a divorce.

ANDY: I'm . . . Catholic.

TAMARA: I'm sorry. Get it annulled then.

ANDY: I don't make that much. It's just a movie. And, for what it's worth. That lonesome thing you talked about. I've got it too. Mighty lonesome.

TAMARA: I . . . would like to but I —

(They never look at one another, but as they speak, their hands slowly reach across and find one another.)

See I got this sixth sense that knows what nothing can come of.

ANDY: I know. Instincts, like.

TAMARA: And nothing can come of this.

ANDY: Nothing. We shouldn't even —

TAMARA: It's, whattayacall. Futile.

ANDY: We don't then, that's OK.

(They are holding hands.)

TAMARA: There's no future in this. *(She looks at him. She abruptly gets up.)* I got a commercial to do.

(The past fades. We see the present. Hoag, Wags, and Miller in a car. Miller is driving.)

MILLER: I so cannot believe we are doing this. I feel like I'm playing hooky.

HOAGIE: Somebody from work is going to see me, I know it.

WAGS: Stop whining, we are having an adventure. We've just been to a great place — how did you know about that place, Miller? Nothing but old TV toys and shit. And that place is wild. I had no idea how much . . . just junk goes with all this stuff we know in our heads.

HOAGIE: Or things I didn't even know were in my head, I'd see a board game and be like, "Oh my God, I remember that show."

MILLER: And she — the lady who runs the place REALLY knows her stuff. I mean REALLY. And she knows all the local celebs, 'cause, you know she gets them autographed. The Lorenzo the clowns, the Captain Noahs. The Pixannes.

HOAGIE: Drag she didn't know how to find Tamara Tomorrow.

MILLER: I think this is going to be tougher than we expected.

WAGS: This lady in the store, I think her name was Eadie —

MILLER: If not it should be.

WAGS: Anyway, she was real helpful, and I kind of thought it would be nice to buy something, so I bought something.

MILLER: You are such a softie. I was wondering what was in that bag. What did you buy?

WAGS: It's great, man. Unbelievable. Actually in the box. You know? This is so valuable. I can't believe I got one.

MILLER: Would you show us what the hell you bought — I was coveting the Mork and Mindy game — so you know.

WAGS: I got — I found — and it's so rare —

MILLER: WHAT?

(In the past, Tamara is doing her commercial.)

TAMARA: This doll looks like your best friend, me —

WAGS AND TAMARA: Tamara Tomorrow —

WAGS: Doll.

(He presents it, his friends can't believe him.)

MILLER: You are so high.

WAGS AND TAMARA: And —

WAGS: Look —

WAGS AND TAMARA: In —

WAGS: *(Simultaneous with Tamara's next line.)* The —

TAMARA: *(Simultaneous with Wag's last line.)* My —

WAGS AND TAMARA: Utility pocketbook both lipstick and a weapon.

(Tamara is gone.)

WAGS: I mean these are so rare. The people who have them don't ever want to sell them so that just drives the price right up.

HOAGIE: How much did it cost?

WAGS: And the demand is huge.

HOAGIE: How much?

WAGS: I was lucky to get it.

MILLER: How much did it cost?

WAGS: Two hundred and fifty dollars.

HOAGIE: WHAT?!

MILLER: You crazy?

HOAGIE: Man, do you know how hard I have to work for two hundred and fifty dollars?

MILLER: Seriously Wags, you've snapped something now.

WAGS: No, but — in addition to the fact that I will enjoy it and I will, I'll also put it in my office and people can come in and talk to their lawyer and this will be an ice breaker because — AND best of all. This is an investment — something like this will increase in value should I choose to sell and I never will because Goddamn it, I've got a Tamara Tomorrow doll.

HOAGIE: You're wasting money.

MILLER: I can't believe you spent that much money. I mean, I got something, because I felt gratitude —

WAGS: What did you get?

(Tamara appears.)

TAMARA: Now —

MILLER: But I didn't make a Christie's level bid —

WAGS: What'd you —

TAMARA: For the boys —

MILLER: I didn't —

WAGS: What did you get?

MILLER AND TAMARA: The —

TAMARA: equally amazing and wonderful —

MILLER AND TAMARA: Tamara Tomorrow badge.

WAGS: How much?

MILLER: It wasn't two hundred doll —

WAGS: How . . . much?

MILLER: Ninety-five.

WAGS: NINETY-FIVE???!!!!

HOAGIE: You guys are like working for the government or something.

MILLER: A little steep.

WAGS: It's just a piece of faded plastic.

MILLER: Not to me. Not what I bought.

TAMARA: This will shield you from the forces of evil as you embark on your journey.

MILLER: I like it for all the reasons you like your stupid doll. I can wear it, people will love it and —

TAMARA AND MILLER: And it glows in the dark.

MILLER: Or it did.

HOAGIE: The next time you guys have three hundred and forty-five dollars to just throw into the wind, throw it in my direction, OK?

MILLER: This is cool stuff.

HOAGIE: Yeah, if you find it at a flea market for ten bucks maybe.

WAGS: Hey, how I spend my money is my —

HOAGIE: All I know is, if I had money like you guys make it, I wouldn't waste it on toys. *(Silence. This is awkward.)* Actually I would, probably. I need a drink.

MILLER: OK, let me find a space.

HOAGIE: And then I can show you what I bought.

MILLER: You, after all this —

WAGS: What did you —

HOAGIE: Oh yeah. Poor, stupid Hoagie actually got a good thing that actually might helps us find Tamara Tomorrow. And it only cost six bucks.

WAGS: What ya get Hoag?

HOAGIE: A scrapbook. Some little girl fan of Tamara Tomorrow put together. Of articles she cut out and then rubber cemented in.

WAGS: Good one, Hoag.

MILLER: Let me see —

HOAGIE: No, you have to find a parking space.

MILLER: Pass it up to Wags, he'll show it to me, I'll find a space. *(It happens, as Miller tries to find parking.)* Ohhhhhh. Cissy signed it. And she doted her "i'" with an enlarged happy face. I just look at that and I wonder where she is today. How she's doing? Was her divorce bitter? Read to me, Wags.

WAGS: Uh. Oh it's all chronological. Sweet. Uh. "Meet Tamara Tomorrow. The word over at Channel Thirty-six is she may just be what the kids want, they've extended the six weeker for a whole season. Tamara adds a little more to the mix, sez she . . ."

(In the past, Tamara appears.)

TAMARA: I believe in hope. I believe in the promise of tomorrow. I'm just an old-fashioned girl from the year 3005.

WAGS: Whoa. "Will Tamara Tomorrow dethrone King Mike?"

TAMARA: I do not believe in competition. By the year 2252 all wars will be settled by lawyers in negotiation.

WAGS: Tamara Tomorrow sells out appearance at the Franklin Institute. In a telephone interview from the set.

(We begin to see pictures of Tamara at publicity events.)

TAMARA: The Franklin Institute experience was great. It just shows there is a tremendous interest in the future in the —

(The pictures are too numerous and begin to overlap, as do Wags and Tamara's next two lines.)

WAGS: But who is Tamara Tomorrow? Is there an actress portraying this character? All those at Channel Thirty-six are mum, including Miss Tomorrow herself and program director Andrew Connelly.

TAMARA: I'll be opening a great new mall, called "Granite Run," and then I will be receiving the key to the city from Mayor Frank Rizzo. I hope all my fans can be at both of these events.

HOAGIE: Tamara Tomorrow opens new pediatric wing of Thomas Jefferson hospital. Extra police brought in for quote mob control. Man!
(All three are reading now, simultaneously. The stage is covered with articles.)

WAGS: Here Tamara takes a first ride on SEPTA's new trolley of the future. Miss Tomorrow gives us her own recipe for space food snacks. Tamara Tomorrow shows three easy exercises for the whole family. Tamara Tomorrow: Why I hate pollution.

MILLER: Tamara Tomorrow seen here having lunch with the amazing Kreskin in town to do the "Mike Douglas Show." They discuss mental telepathy in the future and its impact on the stock market. Tamara Tomorrow on hand to open the new modern wing of the Philadelphia museum. Gazing at a Warhol, she claims, "I like the old stuff."

HOAGIE: Latest craze in South Philly? Girls and boys in zippered jumpsuits. According to local stores, they can't keep the stuff in stock. Tamara Tomorrow to license her name to Shapiro shoes for new line of sneakers. Tamara Tomorrow, that girl that loves to tell us all what we'll be doing, has us wondering, what will she be doing next?
(Just as they end, all the other articles vanish and the stage is covered with one large Philadelphia Magazine *cover. On it Mike Douglas and Tamara Tomorrow in a mock "put up your dukes" pose. And the headline, "The Battle for Three Thirty." Tamara steps forward.)*

TAMARA: I like Mike Douglas. His week with John Lennon and Yoko Ono was wild and wonderful. And I hope our week with the real Ultra Man, flying in all the way from Japan, will be equally wild and wonderful.
(She is gone.)

HOAGIE: For the first time in his ten years, Mike Douglas has fallen into the number two spot. And it's behind Tamara Tomorrow. Though this is a one show phe-mon-mon —

MILLER: Phenomenon.

HOAGIE: She has done what Merv never could do. Which has national buyers looking. Will "Tamara Tomorrow" be the biggest thing to come out of Philly since Bandstand?

(The next three lines overlap.)

MILLER: "Tamara Tomorrow" producer, Andrew Connelly.

HOAGIE: Phone went unanswered by Andrew Connelly.

MILLER: Rumor has it show is being shopped by Andrew Connelly.

(Andy appears.)

ANDY: If a national market would be interested in "Tamara Tomorrow," and I don't see why they wouldn't be, I can easily see —

MILLER: We should call over to Channel Thirty-six —

ANDY: Channel Thirty-six allowing us to produce the same kind of —

WAGS: Right.

(Pulls out cell phone.)

ANDY: of fun show that we have now —

WAGS: Maybe he still works there —

ANDY: And this season we're going to go to tape —

WAGS: knows how to get a hold of her.

ANDY: So, if need be the folks on Central and Pacific time can see it.

WAGS: *(Into cell phone.)* Channel Thirty-six, please. Yeah, general information, sure.

MILLER: Get the number and we'll call from the bar. It's much more professional.

ANDY: But I have no doubt that Tamara could maintain that air of spontaneity that makes the show work.

(In the past now. An elegant mid-seventies apartment on Rittenhouse Square. The house is decorated for Christmas, and Tamara is wearing an elegant Christmas robe.)

HOAGIE: *(Still reading from the scrapbook.)* Don't think that Tamara Tomorrow and her constant escort Andrew Connelly are anything more than business partners. He is a happily married man and father of two girls, and she's a woman who prefers to live in the future.

(The present is gone. Tamara has a drink in her hand and is a little tipsy. A jangle of keys. Tamara turns toward the door and puts a bow on her head.)

TAMARA: Ho ho ho!

(Andy enters and puts the keys back in his pocket.)

ANDY: Hey, baby.

TAMARA: Come over to Sandy Claus and get your candy.

ANDY: What you got on your head?

TAMARA: Aren't I a regular Christmas present with a bow on my head?

ANDY: What a present you are, baby.

TAMARA: You're a little late —

ANDY: Things are nuts down at the studio, just got out.

TAMARA: If the ham is dry, you have no one to blame but yourself.

    (They kiss.)

ANDY: Having a little Christmas cheer?

TAMARA: Sure, you want some?

ANDY: Nah. Have to drive.

TAMARA: Drive? Oh no! And! You promised. Christmas would be us this year. You said you'd tell her that you had to work late at the studio it would be your year to do it and —

ANDY: She put the girls on the phone. She doesn't play fair.

TAMARA: You don't play fair, and you know it.

ANDY: Baby, I'm worried about you, you're putting to much into us, I told you when we started —

TAMARA: I'm not putting too much, just something. The least you can do is —

ANDY: You gotta get outside interests.

TAMARA: Like what?

ANDY: Like — I don't know — your theater stuff — or — You gotta do something.

TAMARA: I — I enjoyed doing theater. But I've moved on. To — I've moved on. This is my life now.

ANDY: I'm sorry.

TAMARA: And it's good.

ANDY: I'm sorry. I'm sorry. I should call her, tell her I'm coming.

    (Andy picks up the phone.)

TAMARA: It's just Christmasses are tough, usually on a holiday, there's a parade for me to be in so it's not a big whoop. Thanksgiving, I did the Gimbles parade, so — just Christmas is hard, because I — there's no parade.

ANDY: And New Year's —

    (Andy dials the phone.)

TAMARA: Mummers. I'm an honorary Mummer this year. So —

    (Andy on the phone. He indicates Tamara should be quiet, She does so. In a bar in the present we see Wags on a cell phone.)

WAGS: Hello, Mr. Andrew Connelly.

ANDY: Honey, it's Daddy, can you put Mommy on?

WAGS: Mr. Connelly, my friends — colleagues are doing an article for the *Philadelphia Inquirer* on TV in its heyday.

ANDY: Yeah, so I talked to some guys at the station, and Phil —

WAGS: And we're so so worked — very excited to find out that you were still employed by Channel Thirty-six.

ANDY: Let me finish, Phil says he'll cover for me.

WAGS: Could we — interview you about your work? Just the three of us. No cameras.

ANDY: Yeah, but because this is Christmas, and I said I would work it, you know, seven months ago —

(Tamara downs her drink.)

WAGS: Well the thing of it is, we're under a deadline.

ANDY: I — I'm going to have to work some other holidays a lot, OK?

(He looks at Tamara, who looks away and pours herself another Kirin.)

WAGS: How about in about an hour?

ANDY: OK, I'll be there in a half an hour.

(The present leaves us, Andy puts down the phone and looks at Tamara, who gazes sadly into the future.)

TAMARA: There should be a parade. A Christmas parade.

ANDY: You got friends, right? You can be with your friends.

TAMARA: Or a special maybe. We should talk to Thirty-six. The Tamara Tomorrow Christmas Special.

ANDY: Call up your old theater pals.

TAMARA: Uh. Oh. No. I've got work. So much WORK to do.

ANDY: On Christmas?

TAMARA: Letters. All these letters to answer. From all these kids. I've got to sign them. There's this thing that happens, when I'm on the street, Andy. Children, small children, they come up to me and put their arms around my neck and even though you think they can't speak, they do. And they say —

(In the present, Hoagie, Wags, and Miller walk into the studio.)

"I love you." And it gets to me. Then their parents come up and take them away. And that gets to me, too.

(Tamara takes a long sip of her drink, and the past fades. Andy turns to the boys in the studio. He is older.)

ANDY: You the boys from the *Inquirer*?

WAGS: Yes, hello. I'm David Wagner. I'm a reporter. With the *Inquirer* and these are my colleagues. Also reporters. With the *Inquirer*. This is Miller.

MILLER: Hi. Miller Burke. Style section.

HOAGIE: Hey. I'm Hoagie.

ANDY: Hoagie?

WAGS: Mr. Connelly, we were developing a series of articles on a sort of Golden age of television in the Philadelphia area. "Bandstand," John Facenda —

HOAGIE: Gene London

ANDY: Gene London, geez you guys are doing your research. Well that was a different time then. The local stations — they had more time to fill back then. Networks didn't put on so much. There was more of a local feel to TV. TV then, they wanted it to reflect the community. Now, soaps and talk shows.

WAGS: Exactly the point of our article. We were wondering what you could tell us about Tamara Tomorrow.

ANDY: Why, what have you heard?

WAGS: Well, you were friends with her.

ANDY: What does this have to do with anything?

WAGS: I mean you produced her show and directed it at first and —

ANDY: Yes, we had a package of Japanese animation. And guys in rubber suits. "Astroboy," "Ultraman" —

HOAGIE: And later "Johnny Sokko and His Flying Robot"

MILLER: Hoagie works in research.

ANDY: And we . . . came up with the idea of Tamara and . . . it was very successful.

MILLER: And wasn't there talk of going national?

ANDY: That was — that wasn't meant to be I guess. That fell apart.

WAGS: Really, why?

ANDY: Well, no need to go into that.

WAGS: We would love to include it in our article.

ANDY: Look, we worked very hard not to have anybody write about it then, we're not going to have it dug up now.

WAGS: Not — write about —

ANDY: You don't do your research. Jesus, everybody knew about Tamara Tomorrow. Philly's a real big city that happens to be a very small town. Everybody knows everybody's business. You don't know about this Hoagie?

HOAGIE: I — uh — don't.

ANDY: Well. I'll forgive you. Maybe. Tamara had a fall. We kept it away from the kids. But word got around.

(In the past. Tamara stumbles on and looks at Andy. She is drunk.)

ANDY: Where have you been?

TAMARA: Lunch.

ANDY: Where?

TAMARA: Without you.

ANDY: That doesn't make any sense. *(The sound of a countdown from "10.")* Jesus! You can't go on like —

TAMARA: It's my usual lunch spot. I'm ready, I'm ready. Put a camera on me and catch some magic.

ANDY: I can't — I'll go on.

TAMARA: You have no charisma.

ANDY: We're on. Someone get coffee.

(In a second we are on the air.)

TAMARA: Well. Look who's here. Space kids. Hello space kids. This is your old, old, elderly friend. Tomorrow Tomorrow. And — so. What do we do first? Let's do mail capsule. MAIL CAPSULE!!

(Andy waiting off to the side, waits till he knows Tamara is ready to catch it.)

TAMARA: *(She hisses.)* I see the damn thing, Andy. Just chuck it.

(He throws it. It lands perfectly on to the ground right in front of her. She looks at it, then puts her hands in a catching position.)

TAMARA: I'LL GET IT!! *(She looks down at the ground again.)* Oh forget it. Probably just junk mail any — so, what next Asteroid Andy? *(This is suddenly the funniest thing she's ever heard.)* Hemorrhoid Harry? Mongoloid Morty? HEY! Let's watch an "Astroboy" cartoon. Let me tell you something, spacecritters. Astroboy is your Aunt Tamara's boyfriend. OH YEAH!! Astroboy is the ooooooooooonly man who loves your Aunt Tomorrow. Did you know —

(The monitors are suddenly alive with the "Speed Racer" theme song. Tamara is gone and as the music fades, Andy is in the present. The three reporters are shocked.)

ANDY: She went for a rest up at Chit Chat Farms. She . . . got better. But that's what happened. You'll hear all kinds of whispering, but that's the truth and you heard it from me. But don't you print that, OK? She's away. Hiding. She doesn't need to be . . . what do you call? Reminded of things.

WAGS: Where — uh, where is she hiding?

ANDY: I don't know definitely, but I have some ideas of how to reach her. If I wanted to.

WAGS: What are those ideas?

ANDY: Didn't you hear me? I'm not telling.

WAGS: What —

ANDY: Hey I don't like your way of talking, what are you grilling me for? I'll pick up that phone right now and call Patty Shirk over at the city desk, so help —

MILLER: NO no, that's not —

WAGS: DON'T DO THAT!!

ANDY: Who are you guys? You ain't from the *Inquirer.* Patty Shirk died three
years ago. What do you guys want?

HOAGIE: We want to find Tamara Tomorrow.

ANDY: Why?

HOAGIE: It seemed like a good idea at the time.

MILLER: We were fans, when we were kids. We thought it would be —

ANDY: Why would you go through all this and put me through all this just —

WAGS: *(Suddenly exploding.)* Because our lives suck, OK?!! Because our lives
are ghastly fucking messes, OK?!! And we remember this moment, this
aspect of our life with some fondness, JESUS!! But we don't want it to
be this. This horrible story about public humiliation and —

(A shaft of light hits Andy. We are in the past, all others are gone.)

ANDY: Hello Space Kiddets. This is your friend Asteroid Andy. Yesterday,
Tamara Tomorrow was sick. Very sick. She had an inner ear infection,
which caused a sort of a balance problem — you can ask your family physi-
cian or school nurse about it they can explain it in detail. So. Tamara is
going to a place where she can get well and we're lucky enough that Chief
Halftown, from Sunday mornings, will be able to substitute host for the —
till she gets back.

*(In the present. A car in the rain. Miller and Wags sit. And stare. A moment.
They then sing the Roadrunner song. Absently. Then silence again. Then —)*

WAGS: I'm sorry I included you in my life-is-a-mess speech.

MILLER: Well. That's OK. It kind of is.

WAGS: Yeah?

MILLER: Yeah. I mean, yeah. I'd be further along in my job if I were better at
it. And — I really should be further along at it. Nothing is turning out
the way I thought it would — I started in advertising because, well the
whole "Bewitched" thing, and I thought I could flourish. But I didn't really. So, kind of got into public relations 'cause I thought it would be interesting. And a breeze. Breeze, it ain't. And Greg.

(He looks out a window.)

Remember how, before Greg I was only dating really younger guys. Like
college age. Because there was never really the THREAT of responsibility, which, you know worked for me. And if things got too deep they'd
have mid-terms or something and I was on to the new —

WAGS: I don't remember you dating younger guys.

MILLER: Wags, you fully do remember. You told your mother that my new nick-name was "short eyes."

WAGS: Yeah. That was funny.

MILLER: So then I met Greg at this bar I can't even stand and we started just talking, I mean I wasn't looking for anything and just everything I said, all my pat answers — he would call me on it. And I knew that part of what it's all about is having someone to call you on it. If you want the mature relationship. So the second Greg is not there to call me on any-thing and he needs me. Look what I choose to do. No I would say fuck-ing ghastly mess to describe my life would be a euphemism. Wonder how Hoagie's doing with that community theater lady? Supposed to be some friend of Tamara's.

WAGS: Mine is. Life a mess. I really should have been a partner two years ago easy. I'll have to leave soon. Try to be partner somewhere else. Or stay. Become one of those little gray guys in the gray suits we all whisper about. "Never made partner." And Wendy is — I mean she tells me she's preg-nant and I leave and I haven't spoken to her since and now she can't find me. The running away thing that's just — not helping matters. Anywhere.

MILLER: Infantile. Both of us.

WAGS: Right now there are two people on this shitty stormy night, two peo-ple who were told by someone that they were loved. And right now those same two people are alone. And scared. And wondering. I mean, it's only been a day, but — we suck.

MILLER: I would say so.

WAGS: We should —

MILLER: I think so —

WAGS: Call the whole running-away thing —

MILLER: Give it a rest —

WAGS: Call it quits.

MILLER: Head back.

WAGS: Yeah. Return. Soon as —

MILLER: Wonder what poor Hoagie is doing with the community theater lady? Maybe they've put him in the chorus.

WAGS: Now, Hoagie, I love him like a brother but he's —

MILLER: More of a mess than we are.

WAGS: Seriously, he struts around in sweats all day, like the world is still high school gym class or something. He's like, in denial, about life, right?

MILLER: Dead end job, different girl all the time. So much growing up to do, he is so nowhere fast, right?

WAGS: Absolutely.

MILLER: Seriously.

> *(They stare forward for a bit.)*

WAGS: Good lead. That Connelly guy put us on to.

MILLER: Wonder what the story was there. He got real supportive of us finding Tamara. After your life-is-a-mess speech.

> *(In the past, at the studio, Tamara returns from Chit Chat Farms. She walks over to Andy.)*

WAGS: Well, we should —

MILLER: Let's go —

WAGS: Go —

TAMARA: Hey ho. Nobody —

WAGS, MILLER, TAMARA: Home.

MILLER: Yeah.

WAGS: Right.

TAMARA: Meat, nor drink, nor money have I none. Especially the drink.

ANDY: Don't you look great.

TAMARA: Feel great. Clean bill of health from our friends over at Chit Chat Farms.

ANDY: That's great. How's it going?

TAMARA: One day at a time, sweetheart. I'm ready for work. I'm a pro. I honor a contract.

ANDY: We have a problem. With the sponsors.

TAMARA: Oh. Really?

ANDY: Word is out on the streets about your . . . illness.

TAMARA: It is an illness. I was sick and now I'm well.

WAGS: Chasing after some poor lady. Who probably didn't want to see us anyway.

ANDY: Frank's Cola, in addition to being the manufacturer of children's colas, actually primarily is —

WAGS: I think it's best we — give up. Bite the bullet.

ANDY: The manufacturer of cocktail mixers for adults.

MILLER: It's time to go back.

WAGS: Go back.

ANDY: Ginger ale, club soda, lemon lime. They don't want — you know how this town talks. They don't want the image of a —

TAMARA: Ahhhhhhh.

ANDY: I don't have to say this. Of course Channel Thirty-six will honor your contract. They'll continue to pay you.

TAMARA: And what about us?

ANDY: What they also volunteered, and this is very generous, you will have the rights to the name Tamara Tomorrow. If you want to shop it around to another sponsor and take it to over to Seventeen or Twenty-nine or Forty-eight or —

TAMARA: And what about us?

ANDY: I have a contract with Channel Thirty-six, I can't —

TAMARA: WHAT ABOUT US WHAT ABOUT US WHAT ABOUT US WHAT ABOUT US WHAT ABOUT!!!!! US?!!!!!!!

ANDY: For God's sake be professional. People are listening.

TAMARA: Sorry. Real big city, very small town.

(In the present, Hoagie jumps into the backseat.)

ANDY: I have other commitments, but —

HOAGIE: Guys!

ANDY: If you want, I have a friend over at Channel Eight in Lancaster. He might be able —

(Tamara begins to leave.)

HOAGIE: The community theater people just gave us the mother lode.

TAMARA: No, I'm not doing Tamara anymore.

HOAGIE: We've found Tamara Tomorrow. The costume lady keeps in touch.

TAMARA: We'll just end it here.

HOAGIE: She's in Wildwood, New Jersey.

(Wags and Miller look at one another for a moment.)

HOAGIE: We going?

(Miller just looks forward.)

TAMARA: She'll be forgotten in no time.

ANDY: Sharon!!

MILLER: You wanna go, Wags?

ANDY: You can do television somewhere else.

WAGS: After all we just said, after all we just talked about?

TAMARA: No thank you.

MILLER: But to see Tamara Tomorrow?

TAMARA: Tamara Tomorrow will just go away.

WAGS: We can't.

HOAGIE: Why can't we?

WAGS: We shouldn't.

MILLER: Why shouldn't we?

TAMARA: She'll just disappear.

WAGS: Let's go.

MILLER: All right!

HOAGIE: YES!

ANDY: Sharon!!

TAMARA: And no one will find her.

WAGS: *(Starting the car up.)* Let's go find her.

TAMARA: No one will ever find me.

END OF ACT I

Act II
Scene One: "The Future"

Darkness. And from that darkness the triumphant march that is the open-
ing theme of "Tobor, the Eighth Man." Along with the music, onstage an in-
cessant banging in time. As the music fades we are in Wildwood, New Jersey,
and in the lobby of the Star-luxe Motel. The banging continues. It is Wags
knocking on a door. Hoagie and Miller sit in awe on some very old modern
furniture.

WAGS: Ms. Phipps? Ms. Phipps? We don't want to hurt you, Ms. Phipps.

MILLER: Feature this architecture, please. You really have to go to Wildwood,
New Jersey to see architecture like this. Wildwood, New Jersey or, of
course, Pluto.

WAGS: Ms. Phipps?

HOAGIE: She's not coming out, Wags.

MILLER: She's not coming out, Wags. *(To Hoagie.)* Isn't this just the setting you
would want Tamara Tomorrow to be living in? Do you think she has a
time share with Electro-woman and Dyna-girl? Just wondering.

WAGS: Ms. Phipps? We mean you no harm.

MILLER: Say, "We come in peace," Wags.

WAGS: We come in peace.

HOAGIE: Man did you see her run? She's standing there behind the desk there,
we walk in, Wags says, "Ms. Phipps." And somehow she knew what was
up and she just, you know, bolted. Bolted for the room over —

WAGS: *(To Hoagie and Miller.)* She's not coming out.

HOAGIE: This one lady at the community players said she's been in hiding ever
since a very ugly theater-in-the-round incident.

MILLER: I really thought I might get through my whole life without hearing
you say a sentence like that. You know I'm kinda going for this decor right
about now. This sort of "we're in the sixties but we're looking forty years
into the future, only we're forty years into the future now and it looks
nothing like this." There's nothing so reassuring as the past's view of the
future.

HOAGIE: How did she know what was up?

MILLER: She saw it in our faces. That unmitigated hope. For her to be Tomorrow. She probably sees that look on three adult men and is out of
here like a tornado already.

HOAGIE: What is with you? You've been this way since we stopped for gas.

MILLER: Just. Once I was doing it. This. It wasn't a . . . fun quest. It was invasion of privacy or something I don't — and Greg and — Wags, she's not coming out. Why don't you just sit down on the least Venutian furnishing?

WAGS: I feel so bad.

MILLER: We all do.

WAGS: This woman must feel so awkward. I mean, I thought we'd come in and be like — "Ms. Phipps, weren't you Tamara Tomorrow?" and she'd by like — "Oh shoot that was so long ago how sweet of you to remember" and she'd make us tea and we'd get some pictures and we'd leave. But we just walk in and — she must just be embarrassed is what it is. She must just feel like — "What did I do with my life? I used to be a star and now I'm a front-desk clerk at a motel in Wildwood. Off-season." *(A moment of silence as all three just sit there and ponder this. Miller then rises, walks over to the door, taps on it gently.)*

MILLER: Ms. Phipps? All your choices were valid. *(He looks at the door. Nothing. He looks at the other two, then throws his arms up and walks over to the others.)* Let's go.

(He begins to leave. Wags soon joins him.)

WAGS: I can't believe after all that, that's how it ended.

MILLER: Yeah. Welcome to most things, right? Lots of stuff, then nothing.

(They're at the door.)

MILLER: You coming with, Hoags? *(No response from Hoagie.)* Hoagie?

(Miller and Wags are stymied as Hoagie walks over to the door and leans into it. His quiet plea is plaintive and very sincere.)

HOAGIE: Miss Tomorrow. My name is Hoagie. Actually my name is James, my nickname is Hoagie. Anyways. I came here with my friends, on account of. Well for me, on account of when I was a kid I was so fearless, right? I was athletic and easygoing and all those kind of things. And girls wanted me for a boyfriend when we got older. And I was . . . sure of myself. And it's not that way now. Nothing I do is that way these days. Fearless. I'm fearful, I would say. And the reason I came is because — when I think about those fearless times and such. You were there. And if I could see you again. Maybe, I would — I'm sorry, we shouldn't have bothered you.

(He walks away from the door and joins Wags and Miller. Just as they are at the door, the other door unlocks. They turn and watch as the door slowly opens. For Tamara, years have gone by, but they don't show much on her.)

MILLER: And the sun becomes the moon and the moon becomes a sun, the earth becomes the sky and the sky the sea and fantasy and reality jitterbug around the room like mice in old black-and-white cartoons. Three mere mortals are meeting Tamara Tomorrow.

TAMARA: Now you know why I hid in the office.

WAGS: Wow. This is — WOW!! Tamara Tomorrow. You're a legend.

TAMARA: Now you've seen me. You want some rooms or did you just come for the show?

(A phone rings.)

WAGS: Actually —

TAMARA: Hold that thought, I gotta get the phone. There's a machine out there if you want coffee or pop.

WAGS: Or maybe some Frank's Cola.

TAMARA: What?

WAGS: Frank's Cola. You used to do the commercials for them.

TAMARA: Right you are.

WAGS: "Is it Franks? Thanks."

TAMARA: Of course, I forgot. They went out of business, you know.

(She picks up the phone, which has become quite annoying by now. Miller punches Wags in the shoulder.)

WAGS: OW!! What is that all —

MILLER: Frank's Cola, Wags?

TAMARA: (Into phone.) Sorry it took so long. Reservations?

HOAGIE: I mean good one, that's only who fired her.

WAGS: Awww. Dammit. I'm not thinking.

MILLER: She looks good. You think she's been tucked?

HOAGIE: A time machine.

WAGS: I don't want it to end.

MILLER: This has gone very nicely and we should end it now because I don't want it to end with you getting slapped and us being asked to leave.

WAGS: It can't end.

(Tamara hangs up the phone.)

TAMARA: So, gents, what'll it be? Rooms or gawkin'. 'Cause if it's gawkin' it's five more minutes and then I'm asking you to leave.

MILLER: This isn't what we want.

WAGS: You were Tamara Tomorrow.

TAMARA: So?

WAGS: How great is that?

TAMARA: I take it you don't want rooms then.

WAGS: How have you been?

TAMARA: I been great kid. Now do you have something for me to autograph?

HOAGIE: Would you do that? I have a scrapbook.

WAGS: I've got a doll. Sitting in my car.

TAMARA: You boys need to get some sun. Get a hobby. Have sex with a partner. All right, I'll sign and then you'll leave.

WAGS: Sure, I mean, I w — we will. But that's not what we — I mean, we really liked you. The work you did before really affected us. On TV. And even though we're adults —

MILLER: On paper only.

WAGS: We cherish — I'm gonna use that word here, and I can't think of another time that I have — we cherish the memory of you.

TAMARA: I got three whole fans. I'm touched. Get me your dolly and you can leave.

HOAGIE: You were great.

TAMARA: I wasn't anything.

HOAGIE: No you really —

MILLER: You really were. Are. Great.

TAMARA: I'm a reference. I'm the answer to a trivia question. I'm whattayacall. Camp.

MILLER: Trust me. I know camp. You're not camp. You're a . . . a . . .

TAMARA: Nice try.

MILLER: Is there nothing we can say to let you know how much you mean to us?

HOAGIE: We're fans. No lie.

WAGS: We're not just fans. We're more than fans.

MILLER: Stalker talk. Keep going.

WAGS: We. The three of us, just dropped out of our lives to find you. And you — we found you and you're not that easy to find. OK?

TAMARA: You want me to say "thank you" here?

WAGS: No. But we're not just coming to you as . . . admirers. We're here for something else.

HOAGIE: Huh?

MILLER: Shhhhh.

WAGS: We're here . . . for . . . on business.

(Hoagie is about to say something; Miller grabs his arm.)

MILLER: Let him go.

WAGS: A — we — we feel that if we would want to see you. Others might — will want to see you. Like everyone our age from Philadelphia would want to see you. So —

MILLER: This isn't what we wanted, but by God, he's going to make it something we want.

WAGS: We could help you . . . orchestrate . . . your comeback.

(A pause. Everyone looks at one another incredulously. The phone rings.)

TAMARA: *(Running to the phone.)* Conventions! Come next week we'll be ass to elbows in old men on tiny motorcycles. *(She picks up the phone.)* Starluxe Motel.

HOAGIE: What are you talking about Wags?

WAGS: Just, it's not enough. Now that I'm here I want more. And — dammit, for all she's done for me, I want her to know she is something.

HOAGIE: But — what is this comeback thing?

MILLER: I for one applaud Wags. Every once in a while, I look at this fourteen-year-old trapped in the body of a nearly forty-year-old —

WAGS: Fuck you.

MILLER: And I say, "Oh right. He is a lawyer. Who's successful. And thinks of things and knows how to settle things. Right."

HOAGIE: Can we do that?

WAGS: I know a lot of people would be interested, I know I am.

HOAGIE: It seems dangerous. And foolish. At the same time.

WAGS: I gotta think. Of stuff.

HOAGIE: But —

MILLER: Hoag, the time for buts is done. We're in it now. And Wags is, Goddamn it, a lawyer. And the thing about a lawyer is, it's like opera. All that recitative and then, they land on an idea and it's aria. And you gotta just sit back and listen.

(Hoagie looks back with no response. Miller explains in words Hoagie will grasp.)

MILLER: All that dribbling and then he shoots.

HOAGIE: Oh.

MILLER: Wags has a seriously good idea here. And it would be a hell of a lot of fun. *(He looks at Wags.)* And maybe for once in our gleamingly selfish lives. We could do something, anything for someone else. Imagine that.

WAGS: You in Hoagie?

HOAGIE: I'm in though I don't know what I can do or anything.

WAGS: Yes! Kick. Ass. We should concoct this really wisely. We could —

(Tamara is back.)

TAMARA: So. Sorry, where were we? Oh right, you had that foolhardy idea and I was trying to come up with a kind way of rejecting it.

WAGS: Well I don't know that you're taking everything into consideration. You could be famous again.

TAMARA: I'm retired from —

WAGS: I think there is money to be made here.

TAMARA: I get by.

WAGS: Real money.

TAMARA: How many people are your age and from Philly? Not many.

WAGS: How many people are my age and from Philly and parents now themselves and afraid of all the shit — may I speak frankly?

TAMARA: Go ahead.

WAGS: Afraid of all the shit they see on TV now. And would like a figure they can trust. And who gives them optimistic views of things to come. I remember, as sure as I am talking to you, that you once said that after the year 2001 most homes would have a computer. Most homes do now.

TAMARA: I was lucky on that one. I think I also said dogs would have full voting rights. I made it up, it was whimsy.

WAGS: Your whimsy turned into our hope.

TAMARA: Oh jeez. So what would I do? Just stand there peelin' potatoes? I didn't do a lot on that show in case you don't remember.

WAGS: You could —

MILLER: Personal appearances. Hi, Miller Burke. This is where I kick in. I work in public relations. In life. First of all, let me say, loved your work. You made the early seventies a great place to grow up. Totally overshadowed Watergate and the escalation of Viet Nam. Ms. Phipps. You can make so much money from personal appearances

TAMARA: I don't think —

MILLER: Five thousand dollars a night. Easily. You've kept yourself off the market, you're very desirable.

TAMARA: I can't believe anyone would pay that much to hear me —

MILLER: Ms. Phipps, may I call you Tamara? Do you know what a Tamara Tomorrow doll goes for? Two hundred and fifty dollars. People our age have a lot of disposable income at their fingertips. And they will do anything to keep themselves young, why do you know what someone paid for just the plastic glow in the dark badge? Now if we repackaged the old shows, it would be a license to print money. Set up a few speaking engagements.

TAMARA: You boys are very sweet to think of me, but you all have a bolt loose. Thank you so much for stopping by. Let me sign your old pieces of junk that you probably paid too much for and I'll let you get back on the road. I think there's supposed to be bad traveling tonight.

HOAGIE: Miss Tomorrow. I'm James. People call me Hoagie. I talked to you earlier through the door. I really think you should do this. It could mean a lot to a lot of people.

TAMARA: Why?

WAGS: Because we were close to you. And we lost you. And now we've found you. The way things are now, everything is so fast. A best friend is a casual acquaintance is a name on a Christmas card list is an obituary that makes you sigh only. Just like that. We all have one person we've lost track of and would like to get in contact with. You're ours. And I think you'd be a lot of other people's too.

TAMARA: How did you even find me?

HOAGIE: Community Players.

TAMARA: Jeez, how did you find them?

MILLER: This guy at the TV station.

WAGS: Andrew Connelly.

HOAGIE: Right.

TAMARA: You boys done your homework.

WAGS: We're serious about this.

TAMARA: If I ever did this . . . comeback thing. I should tell you. Warn you. People are gonna want to know why I left and went away. And they're not gonna want to hear the how come. I had a substance abuse problem.

MILLER: People are going to want hear about that. People are going to require it. That's a whole other lecture circuit.

TAMARA: What you're saying is starting to make sense, you better leave.

WAGS: Kids today would love you as much as their parents do.

TAMARA: You got kids?

WAGS: I — actually — not yet.

TAMARA: Well when you do, get back to me. And what's your participation in this, huh? What kind of ungodly percentage would you take?

MILLER: Nothing. We're doing this because we love you.

TAMARA: Oh, now —

MILLER: We . . . love . . . you. We have left behind all kinds of commitments to find you.

TAMARA: Yeah, like what?

MILLER: I — well — commitments.

TAMARA: Well, thanks, I think. Now, you should get going and —

HOAGIE: Ms. Phipps, it's me, Hoagie again. When you opened the pediatric wing at Jefferson, they had to bring in police there were so many people.

TAMARA: So.

HOAGIE: Those people all loved you. And that doesn't go away. People just have to be reminded of it.

TAMARA: This is silly talk.

HOAGIE: If they just reran your old show and you made some appearances, it's not that much work and you could remind people.

WAGS: Exactly! That's what we should do! Rerun the old shows. People would love it.

TAMARA: That's just scary.

HOAGIE: In my personal experience, I have found that it's not the stuff that scares you that winds up being a problem.

WAGS: We show the old shows, you show up at a couple of events, you could have that whole world back.

TAMARA: Nobody cares.

HOAGIE: You're the first girl I loved ever.

WAGS: Same here.

MILLER: Absolutely.

TAMARA: That's sweet.

HOAGIE: And that's like the love that stays with you your whole life.

WAGS: And there must be a lot of other people who could say the same thing.

MILLER: And I would give anything to hear you do those predictions one more time.

HOAGIE: YES!!

MILLER: To tell me how possible it all is.

WAGS: Seriously!

MILLER: Reassure us.

HOAGIE: Tell us it's all gonna be all right again.

WAGS: Remind us of all the good things we can expect.

(The phone rings. She reaches for it, stops, then looks at them.)

TAMARA: You're talking talk that is just — *(She looks at the phone, then back at them.)* And it's not like I haven't thought about it before, but — *(She looks at the phone and abruptly presses a button.)* The answering service'll get it. *(She considers their faces for a moment.)* Give me. Let me have a sec. I'll be right back. *(She is gone.)*

WAGS: She'll do it.

HOAGIE: How do you know?

MILLER: Maybe.

HOAGIE: What just happened? In my head, I'm halfway back home. Now I'm staging a comeback. What the —
(He mouths the word "fuck.")

WAGS: She'll do it. I have to think.

(He looks out the window.)

HOAGIE: This is like a major fucking event and we have to stage it.

MILLER: We need to think. We should come up with a cohesive plan.

WAGS: We're gonna have to spend the night.

HOAGIE: How come?

WAGS: It's snowing.

HOAGIE: She said it was going to snow.

MILLER: Tamara Tomorrow. Clairvoyant still.

(Tamara walks in with a cardboard box.)

TAMARA: So I got this cardboard box, right?

MILLER: Sorry?

TAMARA: Where I just chuck any of my Tamara Tomorrow stuff actually all my showbizzy things. Anyways. Contracts and such are in here. I have no idea what I have.

(She sets down the box. The others gather around.)

WAGS: So, I take it you've signed on?

TAMARA: I have decided nothing. Just thought we'd look through this — see what we have on our hands.

WAGS: Hand me the contracts.

HOAGIE: You know what is so cool? We all like can have like a little task in this. Like Wags is lawyer so he can handle all the business stuff. Miller is the only PR person so he can plot out the career and all and I'm a personal trainer so I can help get her back into shape.

TAMARA: OK. The one with the sandwich name? I want him dead.

MILLER: You can't kill him, after a while you learn to love him. Wow. Lot's of programs.

WAGS: Contracts? No, income tax.

MILLER: I don't see any more pictures of you as Tamara or —

TAMARA: Pictures and costumes I have off in a storage. All I have is contracts, odds and ends, and —

(Hoagie reaches for something. He and Miller suddenly gasp.)

TAMARA: My antennae.

(Hoagie reverently pulls out a rusty antennae.)

MILLER: I am blacking out.

(He touches it.)

WAGS: Cool. Hey, a contract, thank you. This must have been your first, it looks like it's only for a month or so.

MILLER: Read it, Wags.

WAGS: Witnesseth. The party of the first part, Sharon Phipps, hereafter referred to as, "the artist" shall —

MILLER: Wags no longer read aloud please. Just speak when you fall on to something of pertinence. Whoa, here's a program, I didn't know you did this play. At Valley Forge Music Fair. Nice.

TAMARA: I used to be an actress, dabbled in theater. Community level, nothing big. Before Tamara.

MILLER: But this is after — It says Tamara Tomorrow on the program. Right at the top.

TAMARA: Oh yeah. That billing. My swan song, if you will.

HOAGIE: What do you mean?

TAMARA: It wasn't a . . . great experience.

MILLER: What happened?

TAMARA: This isn't about Tamara Tomorrow, you wouldn't be interested.

MILLER: I would.

HOAGIE: If it's about you, we would.

TAMARA: It was a play I had done before the television stuff. That I did again, right after. You don't want to hear this.

MILLER: Tell us.

TAMARA: It's no big story.

HOAGIE: You can tell us, if you want. We're friends.

TAMARA: Some friends of mine ran a small theater company I had worked with before. They were broke, they approached me to, for one night, recreate a successful role I had done for them and rent the Valley Forge Music Fair. And it was a bad experience — you didn't hear about this?

HOAGIE: All the community theater lady said was there was an ugly thing that happened. Was that the ugly thing?

TAMARA: Yeah. And it started with that program.

MILLER: What do you mean?

TAMARA: Well, that night I was in the dressing room, and I felt more alive than I had in so long and — there's this tradition, right? You never have a playbill in your dressing room. And they did this time, right? And — the program, the billing was — TV's Tamara Tomorrow parenthesis lettering so small it looks like an eye chart Sharon Phipps end parenthesis in J. M. Barrie's — maybe that's how come they have that superstition. So the actors don't have to feel queasy just before —

(The lights change. They are odd. Hoagie and Miller continue to watch; Wags continues to read the contracts. But they will supply all the background noises

MUSIC FROM A SPARKLING PLANET   167

in the next section. First, the growing sound of an audience grumbling in anticipation.)

WAGS: *(As stage manager.)* Places.

TAMARA: And I got to the wings and I wanted to cry and —

WAGS: *(As stage manager.)* Places for act one scene one.

TAMARA: And then for that moment, for that instant everything was better than all right. The house lights down, the stage lights up. The silent sound, the audience's rapt attention. The sound of scenes going along well enough. Then the cue light and my doubt. A tug of the harness. Because we were in the round my entrance was to fly over the heads of the audience on to the stage. And my doubt had a voice —

HOAGIE: *(Quietly.)* Tamara Tomorrow is really flying now!

WAGS: *(Quietly.)* Look at Tamara soar, what's she been drinkin'?

TAMARA: And the voice of my doubt grew louder and with it, the cold realization.

MILLER: *(A little louder than the others.)* Had a drink, Tamara?

TAMARA: That wasn't my doubt talkin' to me that night onstage.

HOAGIE: *(A little louder.)* She's way in the air, she's three sheets to the wind again.

TAMARA: It was the audience. Children, no longer young but gangly and spotted in their preadolescence with all that pent-up sexiness taking out their rage on me that evening on stage.

WAGS: *(Openly loud now.)* Hey, Tamara, can I have a drink?

(The others laugh derisively.)

TAMARA: And it was in the round so everywhere I turned —

(Miller hiccups, the others laugh as teenagers.)

TAMARA: Humiliation after humiliation. They piled up on the small round stage. A reminder by another character to "take my medicine" and a whole three-act play was performed by the audience for the actors onstage to watch. And I, well — *(Lights and everything back to normal.)* When it was over. I never wanted to act on stage again. How my life had turned out. Wanting to be a stage actress, becoming a TV personality, ending up a joke.

MILLER: Life is very cruel to a great many people.

TAMARA: Life's a pain in the ass to most everyone. It's how you take it that counts. Hey, and if anyone's to blame for me not being a actress any more. It's me. I coulda stuck with it. Maybe done a play under my own name only. Or done a play far away from Philadelphia. But. For all my talk. I didn't love theater. Enough. When you love something, it's no great shakes to say you love it when it's all sweeties and dearies. But when it turns mean.

The true colors time. That's when love is. And I didn't have it. Wish to hell I did. Regret of my life, maybe. You know?

(*She hands the program to Miller. He has found something else in what she has said. He gets up and walks to the window and looks out.*)

TAMARA: He got quiet all a sudden. He wasn't in the audience at Valley Forge, was he?

HOAGIE: Nah, he's just moody lately.

WAGS: This is discouraging.

TAMARA: What's discouraging, sweetheart?

WAGS: These contracts. Did you have a lawyer?

TAMARA: Well, I —

WAGS: I mean who was your lawyer, their lawyer?

TAMARA: I take it there's a problem of some sort or another?

WAGS: Let's just say these contracts are . . . more than a little one-sided. I mean the first one is straightforward enough —

(*Andy appears as Tamara remembers him.*)

ANDY: I'll tell you here. I'm in kind of a bind.

WAGS: You're hired at a salary to act on a television show.

ANDY: I have this role that should have been cast about a month ago.

WAGS: I mean a nice enough salary for back then.

ANDY: If there's anyway that you could come and help us out, it would be —

WAGS: But nowhere does it mention you as originator of this role.

TAMARA: What does —

ANDY: I'm over at Channel Thirty-six and we just bought a package of Japanese animation and —

TAMARA: What does that have to do with anything?

WAGS: Well, you should have been compensated for that. And nowhere does it suggest in anyway your ownership of the name Tamara Tomorrow.

TAMARA: It was a six-week job. And what do I care who owns the name?

WAGS: Well if you walk around saying you're Tamara Tomorrow, Channel Thirty-six could come along and say, "not without us, sister." And their lawyers should be fired if they don't.

TAMARA: This is all Hollywood talk, this.

WAGS: Now for your second contract —

ANDY: We got an offer from Frank's Cola.

WAGS: Again, a nice salary for back then.

ANDY: To go to an hour and a half.

TAMARA: Hey that's a nice salary for now.

WAGS: Nowhere does it mention residuals from rebroadcasting. Reruns.

ANDY: And Frank's will sponsor the whole thing —

WAGS: Or a percentage of the dolls and toys or public appearances.

ANDY: All they need is for you to sign on for two years.

HOAGIE: You know all that stuff? That kind of stuff sounds small but it adds up, I'll bet.

TAMARA: We didn't think about those things then. Andy just wrote something up and I signed it.

WAGS: You let the producer draw the contract and then you — Why would you —

ANDY: In case you noticed I am noticing a lot more things about you —

WAGS: let the management arrange your terms?

ANDY: Like you make songs out of anything when you're in a good mood.

TAMARA: It was a different time.

ANDY: See I noticed that.

TAMARA: I knew I could trust him.

ANDY: And you,

WAGS: Why?

ANDY: Just before the camera goes on —

WAGS: I mean you couldn't trust him.

ANDY: You whisper

WAGS: I mean he did fire you —

HOAGIE: Geez, Wags.

ANDY: Sell it.

HOAGIE: You're gettin' harsh.

TAMARA: *(Evenly.)* It was a different time. We trusted then.

ANDY: Two days a week you're on a diet —

WAGS: You trusted and you got screwed.

MILLER: Wags, chill.

ANDY: Two days you're not —

WAGS: I mean, I'm sorry —

ANDY: The fifth is anyone's guess.

WAGS: But we're starting a new venture here with nothing.

ANDY: All these things I noticed on account of you told me I didn't notice things.

TAMARA: I never said we were starting it!

WAGS: We have to go to Channel Thirty-six, hat in hand, begging. Why did you even bother to keep these contracts? They're useless.

TAMARA: I don't — They call me an artist. That's nice.

ANDY: But —

WAGS: But they're worthless.

ANDY: For what it's worth.

HOAGIE: Wagner, lay off!

ANDY: That lonesome thing you talked about.

WAGS: Why would you trust the producer to take care of you?

ANDY: I've got it too.

WAGS: I mean he's given you nothing.

ANDY: Mighty lonesome.

WAGS: Why did you trust him?

TAMARA: Because I loved him.

(Silence for a moment. The three just stare at her.)

ANDY: And nothing can come of this.

TAMARA: I loved him and I'd like to think he loved me.

(She takes the contracts from Wags. Andy disappears.)

WAGS: I'm sorry I didn't know.

TAMARA: And he hurt me. But what I wonder — as I stand here listening to you berate me and all — is how do you live? When you say something to a girl you love, when you promise things, do you have loopholes already concocted in your mind? When a pretty girl says she loves you, do you get it in writing? And in triplicate? How do you live at all in your world of negotiated agreements? And who trusts you to do anything? Who trusts you?

(This hits Wags hard. She returns the contracts to the cardboard box.)

TAMARA: And what frosts me is I'm the one who's getting looked at with the loser eye from you three. Like I did the coward thing, the stupid thing. When truth told, I'm the one that trusted. I flew into it, no parachute. *(She is rifling through the box.)* I hope you learn to. I hope to God, you do, cause — wait I wanna show you something — 'cause if you don't trust somebody and somebody don't trust you, your life is null and void. Here. *(She finds an envelope.)* And though I got burned, I don't doubt what I did for a minute. I don't regret — *(She hands the envelope to Wags.)* Here, read this.

WAGS: This is a letter —

TAMARA: Read.

WAGS: I read contracts, not love letters.

(Indicates that he should read; he does so.)

HOAGIE: I don't think Wagner meant to hurt you, ma'am. He just, doesn't have good people skills. I think he was trying to figure out —

WAGS: Oh.

ANDY: *(Offstage.)* What they've volunteered.

MILLER: What?

ANDY: *(We see him.)* And this is very generous.

TAMARA: I trusted.

WAGS: Oh God. They gave it to her.

ANDY: You will have the rights to the name Tamara Tomorrow.

HOAGIE: Gave what?

WAGS: The copyright for Tamara Tomorrow.

ANDY: If you want to shop it around to another sponsor.

MILLER: What good's the name if we don't have the rights to the old shows?

WAGS: No. That's not the question.

ANDY: Take it over to Seventeen or Twenty-nine or —

WAGS: The question is — what good are the old shows without the rights to Tamara Tomorrow? She owns everything.

(Like that, Andy is in the present talking to an unseen superior.)

ANDY: It was an amicable parting at the time.

TAMARA: I trusted.

ANDY: The station was trying to get out of an awkward situation.

HOAGIE: What do you know? She can go anywhere and be Tamara Tomorrow. Even to another station.

ANDY: I negotiated that contract. Contract. It was a letter I wrote and the owner of the station signed.

HOAGIE: Whoa.

ANDY: Don't. You. Talk to her. I'll talk to her.

TAMARA: Wags, Miller, Hoagie. I think it's time for us to get to Philly.

ANDY: Let me do this meeting. We have history.

TAMARA: *(She looks over at Wags.)* I trusted someone and even though I got hurt, I did OK. So. Who trusts you?

(Wags looks away. She walks over and touches his cheek gently.)

TAMARA: I do. Right now, I do. You won't let me be hurt again.

(A flash, we are in Andy's office at Channel Thirty-six. Tamara, Wags, Miller, and Hoagie stand before Andy.)

ANDY: Sharon. God.

TAMARA: Look at you, Andy.

ANDY: You look great.

TAMARA: You look old. Geez you keep it cold in here, the whole left side of me is near froze off.

ANDY: Come and give us a hug.

(They do so. Timidly at first, then desperately clinging to one another.)

ANDY: I missed you.

TAMARA: Missed you too.

ANDY: Now don't start crying.

TAMARA: I can't cry no more. I'm all cried out. I make a cry face, nothing comes out.

(They pull apart.)

ANDY: Like old times.

TAMARA: Could be.

(Andy looks at the boys.)

ANDY: Hey, you found her.

(They smile awkwardly.)

ANDY: They brought you back to me. It's a miracle. I talked to the station manager, actually, it's not a station manager it's a divisional chief, we're all bought up by Info, Inc. You know them? Anyway, I mentioned that you were coming back and they expressed some interest. We don't have that much time for local during the day just after one a.m., but still. Maybe you could introduce some old movies or — episodes of "Star Trek" or — cards on the table, not a lot of air time, bad slots, not a ton of interest, but interest.

TAMARA: Interest. Well. I haven't worked in twenty years and a division chief has interest. How do you like that?

ANDY: Just having you back in the old building. I didn't know how great it would be.

TAMARA: How you been Andy?

ANDY: Busy. Tired. Lot of changes.

TAMARA: I read in the *Inquirer* your wife passed on. I was sorry to hear that.

ANDY: She died very sudden.

TAMARA: People our age do.

ANDY: I miss her. I've been in grief more than I thought.

TAMARA: How long has it been now? Five years?

ANDY: Six, almost.

TAMARA: Men your age don't grieve that long. They remarry. Quick and to something younger and thinner. I read that in the paper too.

ANDY: Stephanie is . . . you would like her. You should meet. I tell you, once we hear back from the folks at Info, who knows? Maybe we'll be working together again. You could meet her then.

TAMARA: No.

ANDY: No?

TAMARA: No. I don't need to hear back from anyone at Info to make my next step. Andy, I'd like you to meet David Wagner. Mr. Wagner is my attorney.

ANDY: Really? Yesterday he was a reporter.

TAMARA: Mr. Wagner.

WAGS: Channel Thirty-six is squandering one of its greatest commodities of the past. There is an opportunity for unprecedented revenue. Tamara Tomorrow remains a brand of integrity. Untarnished by time, this property has only garnered potential value. Now. According to a letter, dated July 12, 1977, Channel Thirty-six relinquishes all rights to the name and character of Tamara Tomorrow to Ms. Sharon Phipps.

ANDY: All right all right. You're a lawyer. And I know that letter, I wrote it. But what does all that have to do with gettin' air time here?

TAMARA: You'll have to speak to my publicist, Mr. Burke.

MILLER: Any television station in the Delaware valley would give their eye-teeth to put Tamara back on the air. Channel Thirty-six should get in the game very quickly. She is a beloved local icon. Her appeal? Somewhat across the boards. Nostalgia and the future. Baby boomers, Gen Xers, Gen Yers. Gay men and lesbians? Don't get me started. Adult children of alcoholics and alcoholics? A role model. And a lot of people grew up in the Philadelphia area watching Tamara. Some even have moved across the country and with the influx of cable? National is a real consideration.

(Andy is in shock. He looks at Hoagie.)

ANDY: National? And what do you do?

HOAGIE: I'm her lover.

(Tamara laughs.)

MILLER: *(Simultaneous with Wags.)* Hoag!

WAGS: *(Simultaneous with Miller.)* Way to be!

TAMARA: No, Hoagie is a friend. A friend until yesterday I didn't even know I had. And my feeling is there are a lot more.

ANDY: What do you want?

TAMARA: I want the old videos of my show. First broadcast to last, in order. I own them, they're going back on the air. We start entertaining offers tomorrow afternoon. Have your division chief come up with an offer.

ANDY: Sharon —

TAMARA: I'm sorry to be hard-nosed but that's me now.

ANDY: Sharon. I would like to give you the old shows, but I can't.

TAMARA: If you want a court case, I'm sure David can make it very ugly.

ANDY: Not that. Sharon. I would give you the shows if I could. This isn't about ownership. The truth is — we don't have them anymore. We . . . taped over them.

(Tamara is devastated.)

WAGS: What?

ANDY: No one thought we'd ever rebroadcast them. We didn't have use for them. We taped over them for some Flyers games.

WAGS: Not your property, we'll sue!

MILLER: Wags, quiet! *(To Andy.)* What are you saying?

HOAGIE: You're bluffing!

ANDY: I wish I was. That was my work too. I checked into it.

MILLER: How could they do that?

ANDY: We don't have acres of storage here.

WAGS: So, there's nothing?

ANDY: The only tape I could find was the commercial for the merchandising. The news department has it on file. For your obituary. I'm real sorry.

TAMARA: Well now.

MILLER: I can't believe they would do that.

HOAGIE: And we were so close, too.

WAGS: *(To Tamara.)* I didn't know this would be such a waste of time. I let you down.

MILLER: *(To Tamara.)* If I'd — we'd known — we never meant to put you through this.

HOAGIE: Yeah, I really sorry they erased everything you did. That it's not around anymore.

TAMARA: No, it's around.

HOAGIE: Huh?

TAMARA: It's around.

MILLER: What do you mean?

TAMARA: Andy, you remember Phil, the technician.

ANDY: Sure, still works here sometimes on weekends.

TAMARA: You remember when I asked you and Phil, "Where does all the stuff broadcast of me that doesn't get picked up go?" And you and Phil laughed your asses off. And Phil said, "Just goes into the atmosphere, I guess."

ANDY: Damnedest question I ever heard.

TAMARA: I'm thinking Phil guessed right. It got put into the atmosphere. All that laughing and hoping. It was music like. And people heard it. Some right away, some a while later. They heard it. And I wasn't alone.

ANDY: I'm sorry there's only one thirty-second tape.

TAMARA: Get it for me, will you sweetheart? We're gonna need it to show around. Because. Because, we're doing a new show. Better than ever.

HOAGIE: Really?

MILLER: Are you serious?

TAMARA: I own my name right?

WAGS: Absolutely.

TAMARA: I'm doing a new show. I got a tingling in my fingertips telling me that this is the right thing.

ANDY: I'll get a copy of the merchandising video from the news department for you. No hard feelings.

TAMARA: No. Not a one. Go. Get the tape.

ANDY: And maybe Channel Thirty-six will make an offer. Who knows?

(He exits. Cheering and hugging from Tamara and her boys.)

TAMARA: All right, space kiddets, here's what the future holds for us! I predict. By the end of 2002 — Tamara Tomorrow will reappear on the local Philadelphia screen. In the year 2003, Tamara Tomorrow will be the number one show in Philadelphia! And by 2004 —

(Hoagie steps forward and addresses the audience.)

HOAGIE: Her left side being cold was the first signal.

TAMARA: By 2005 — Tamara Tomorrow will be the highest rated local show in America.

HOAGIE: The tingling in her fingertips was the second.

TAMARA: 2006? Dolls and badges reissued, and me getting a percentage.

HOAGIE: After her predictions she felt tired and we started to drive her back to Wildwood. She complained of nausea.

TAMARA: By 2007 Tamara Tomorrow will be in national syndication.

HOAGIE: And we pulled off to the side of the road and she had her first stroke.

WAGS: *(Stepping forward and addressing the audience.)* We quickly drove her to Jefferson. Where she had her second stroke.

MILLER: *(Stepping forward and addressing the audience.)* God. Jefferson. The same hospital Greg was in. Of course, it's like fate was guiding me back or something. So convenient. So — So we admitted her. And waited while they ran tests and —

WAGS: That's when we first saw the candles, that evening.

MILLER: Astonishing. First a few flickering across the street from the hospital.

HOAGIE: Some local radio guy announced it. That Tamara Tomorrow was sick in the hospital. And people — adult children like, just started showing up and the candles got more and more to where they had to block off Market Street.

MILLER: And the next day —

HOAGIE: The next day. All of Philadelphia called in sick to work. And people just showed up and waited. Like vigil-like.

WAGS: I'd like to think she saw it. She was gone a lot of the time. And kind of in a coma or deep sleep. Occasionally saying words that didn't make much sense. And when dusk came —

HOAGIE: Four forty-five.

WAGS: When the candles started again. She had her third stroke.

(Andy on television that night.)

ANDY: Channel Thirty-six regrets the loss of it's former colleague —

HOAGIE: People who probably hadn't thought of her in years showed up and just cried their eyes out. Real people with suits and cell phones and appointments.

ANDY: "Tamara Tomorrow" first appeared on the television screen in the fall of 1973 —

MILLER: I mean, OK, you can say, Philadelphia is not really that big a city. But the fact is, she shut it down.

ANDY: Watergate, Vietnam, and inflation, her brand of optimism —

HOAGIE: They dropped everything to be there. All the boys and girls —

ANDY: Boys and girls —

(Tamara appears as she does on the last remaining video tape.)

TAMARA: Boys and girls, this is Tamara Tomorrow from a far-off galaxy in the distant future and I've come to tell you what the future holds for you.

ANDY: Tamara or as she was really known Sharon Phipps quickly became —

(Wags is at Wendy's door with the Tamara doll.)

WAGS: I'm sorry I left, Wendy.

(Miller appears at the foot of Greg's bed.)

MILLER: Greg, I'm sorry.

WAGS: It was bad of me to go.

MILLER: Terrible of me to go.

WAGS: But.

MILLER: I had to —

WAGS: I had things I had to say good-bye to.

MILLER: and I won't do it again.

WAGS: I won't leave again.

MILLER: I'm sorry. But —

MILLER AND WAGS: I'm here now.

HOAGIE: All of Center City glowed with candlelight —

ANDY: All of Center City glowed with candlelight as Tamara's space kiddets, all grown up with space kiddets of their own.

(Wags places a hand on Wendy's belly.)

WAGS: Look what I bought for the baby.

TAMARA: The amazing and wonderful Tamara Tomorrow doll.

MILLER: You can trust me, I'll be here.

TAMARA: This doll looks just like your best friend.

MILLER: I'm your best friend.

WAGS: I'm your best friend.

TAMARA: Me, Tamara Tomorrow.

WAGS: I belong here.

MILLER: Just breathe. I'm here.

TAMARA: And in the utility pocketbook both lipstick and a weapon.

WAGS: I'm here for you. And the baby. OK?

ANDY: Ms. Phipps had no children of her own. Other than the entire tri-state area.

HOAGIE: Just silence and candles. And everybody knowing that they weren't a kid anymore.

TAMARA: Now.

MILLER: I have something for you.

TAMARA: For the boys.

(Miller pulls out the small plastic shield.)

MILLER: I got this. For you.

(He places it on the bed.)

HOAGIE: Everybody knowing.

TAMARA: This will shield you from the forces of evil.

MILLER: Just breathe.

TAMARA: As you embark on your journey. And it glows in the dark.

WAGS: I'm here.

MILLER: *(Coming in after Wag's "I'm.")* I'm here.

ANDY: On a personal note. I, along with everyone at Channel Thirty-six, will miss her immensely.

TAMARA: Come blast off with me and I'll show you such a sparkling planet. There will be joy and laughter and music and hope, always hope, and everywhere the unmistakable sound of little boys and girls growing up and watching all of their dreams coming true.

(Wags, Miller, and Hoagie look off into the future. Frightened, but ready.)

TAMARA: Oh, what the future holds! What the future holds!

END OF PLAY

DIVA

By Howard Michael Gould

For Russ — and for the rest of his family
on his porch that night

And Albert began to feel fear. Real fear of never working
again. Real fear of not having the one thing he needed —
the love and respect of the people he hated.

— from *SoCal* by Jerry Belson

PLAYWRIGHT'S BIOGRAPHY

Howard Michael Gould graduated from Amherst College, where he wrote and directed plays and musicals, and worked for five years as a Madison Avenue copywriter, winning three Clios and numerous other awards, while continuing to write and direct Off-Off Broadway.

He moved to Los Angeles in 1989 and spent the next ten years writing for television shows, such as "Home Improvement" and "The Jeff Foxworthy Show." Mr. Gould was head writer and executive producer of *Cybill* when it won the 1996 Golden Globe for Best Comedy Series.

Since 1999, he has worked primarily in features and is cowriter of the DreamWorks movie *Surviving Christmas*, starring Ben Affleck and James Gandolfini.

In 2001 his play *Diva* was produced at the Williamstown Theatre Festival, starring Bebe Neuwirth and Eric Bogosian, and then at La Jolla Playhouse, with Susan Blakely and Jere Burns. *Diva* was published in 2002 by Samuel French.

ORIGINAL PRODUCTION

Diva was produceed as a workshop in the Williamstown Theatre Festival (Michael Ritchie, producer) in Williamstown, Massachusetts, in July 2001. It was directed by Neel Keller; the set design was by David Korins; the costume design was by Denitsa Bliznakova; the lighting design was by Jeff Nellis; th sound design was by Matthew Burton; and the original music was by Robert Reale. The cast was as follows:

DEANNA DENNINGER	Bebe Neuwirth
ISAAC BROOKS	Eric Bogosian
EZRA TWAIN	Darryl Theirse
PETEY RYAN	C.J. Wilson
BARRY JOSHUA	John Michael Higgins
KURT FAST	Kurtwood Smith

Diva received its world premiere at La Jolla PLayhouse (Des McAnuff, artistic director) in LaJolla, California, on September 23, 2001. It was directed by Neel Keller; the set design was by Andrew Jackness; the costume design was by Nadice Donnelly; the lighting design was by David Lee Cuthbert; the sound design was by Robbin E. Broad; and the dramaturge was Shirley Fishman. The cast was as follows:

DEANNA DENNINGER	Susan Blakely
ISAAC BROOKS	Jere Burns
EZRA TWAIN	Tim Maculan
PETEY RYAN	Timothy Warmen
BARRY JOSHUA	Paul Provenza
KURT FAST	Jonathan Hogan

CHARACTERS

DEANNA DENNINGER: an actress, forties
ISAAC BROOKS: a television writer-producer, forties
BARRY JOSHUA: an agent, thirties
KURT FAST: a studio head, fifties
EZRA TWAIN: an actor
PETEY RYAN: a gaffer, thirties

SETTINGS

ACT I

Scene One: A television soundstage.
Scene Two: Isaac's office, one week earlier.
Scene Three: A restaurant, four weeks earlier.
Scene Four: Isaac's office, two months earlier.

ACT II

Scene Five: A ballroom, one night earlier.
Scene Six: Isaac's office, eight months earlier.
Scene Seven: Isaac's office, six months earlier.
Scene Eight: The restaurant, two nights earlier.
Scene Nine: A cocktail party, five years later.

It is strongly suggested that the time change (e.g., "one week earlier") be made clear to the audience at the beginning of each scene, via projection or narration or both.

DIVA

Act I
Scene One

*A television soundstage. The set represents an official government office, per-
haps with a false vista of Washington, D.C. visible through a false window.
A rehearsal in progress. Ezra Twain pours his heart into a scene he plays with
Deanna Denninger. She sits behind the desk and mostly pays attention to the
messy shrimp salad sandwich with which she's struggling. Isaac Brooks watches
the rehearsal from a director's chair.*

EZRA: "How did I tell my mom? Well, I said I found someone and I was getting married. And she said, That's wonderful, and naturally she asked,
What's her name? What does she do? And I said, Her name is Warren,
and she plays right field for the Yankees."
(Ezra, as "Jeremiah," laughs at his own joke, into tears.)
DEANNA: *(Mouth full.)* "I'll bet your mother's disappointed. I know she was
hoping for a . . ." — shit! *(Scrubs at the stain.)* Fucking carrots. *(Calls
off.)* Petey! *(Back to Ezra.)* What's your line?
EZRA: *(Struggling to hide his irritation.)* "Her name is Warren, and she plays
right field for the Yankees."
DEANNA: *(Turns.)* Isaac — why am I saying this line?
(Ezra crosses away and sits down, begins to read a magazine.)
ISAAC: For seventy-five thousand dollars an episode, that's why you're saying
the line. Stop trying to do everyone else's job. Just do your own, and let
us get on with rehearsing this scene. The network'll be here for the run-
through at four-thirty.
DEANNA: But when I say —
ISAAC: *No.* Stop talking. No more talking.
DEANNA: But I think —
ISAAC: No more *thinking.* These little "inspirations" of yours just waste our
time and suck all the energy out of the room. Just say the lines, *as writ-
ten.* Period. I am the organ grinder; you are the little dancing monkey.
DEANNA: This little dancing monkey happens to be the executive producer of
this show, which gives me the right to contribute a good idea whenever
I want. *(Then.)* Ezra says . . .

EZRA: *(Without looking up from his magazine.)* "Her name is Warren, and she plays right field for the Yankees."

DEANNA: *(To Isaac.)* And you have me saying, "I'll bet she was disappointed. I know she was hoping for a dentist." It would be funnier if I said, she was hoping for a woman. You know, because he's gay.

(Isaac looks over at Ezra, who shrugs and goes back to his magazine.)

ISAAC: No, that would not be funnier.

DEANNA: Well, I think it would be funnier.

ISAAC: The Goddess of Humor speaks.

DEANNA: Don't take that attitude with me. I didn't fuck Harvey Korman for two years without learning a little something about comedy. *(Snaps.)* Line, Ezra.

EZRA: *(Again without looking up.)* "Her name is Warren, and she plays right field for the Yankees."

DEANNA: "I'll bet your mother's disappointed. I know she was hoping for a woman." *(To Isaac.)* See?

ISAAC: See what? That you're comedically tone deaf?

DEANNA: That's clever. Maybe next time you could find a way to put a funny line in the script. *(Calls off again.)* Petey?! Somebody page Petey! *(Back to script.)* I don't like this: "She must be disappointed." His mother should be tolerant and accepting. *(Crossing out part of her script.)* Instead of this, I want to give a speech about how it's really all right to be gay. By the way, why haven't we had a lesbian wedding on the show?

ISAAC: In case you haven't actually watched our series, we don't happen to have any lesbian characters.

DEANNA: America likes lesbians better than homosexual men. My assistant should be a lesbian instead.

ISAAC: That might be a hair outside of Ezra's range.

DEANNA: Excuse me. I will not stand still for the writers on the show putting down the actors. *(To Ezra.)* If I haven't said this before, I think you're fabulously skilled, although you do tend to mug a little, but even so I'm proud to have you on my show. And by the way, it wasn't me who told *People* magazine that thing about the syringes in your dressing room, I don't care *what* they say. Fuck them. You should be a lesbian.

EZRA: Could I say something about the lesbian idea?

DEANNA: Yes. I for one would like to hear what the only homosexual working on the production has to say about the subject.

EZRA: Just a reminder: I'm not gay, my character is. And I don't want to make trouble, but . . . I really think that even if my character got a sex change, he would still prefer men.

DEANNA: Don't be so sure. I didn't fuck David Bowie three ways from Sunday without learning a little something about lesbians.

ISAAC: Tell you what, Deanna: I don't want to hear any more about how you want things done, or who you fucked to get your brains. I want you to put down the sandwich, say the words, and not bump into the actors with talent.

(He resets Ezra in front of Deanna.)

EZRA: "How did I tell my mom? Well, I said — "

(Petey Ryan bounds in, carrying a six-pack of soda, and slaps Ezra on the back, interrupting him.)

PETEY: Here's your soda, Dee. *(To Isaac.)* I had to drive around half the Valley to find a diet cream.

DEANNA: Don't talk to him.

PETEY: *(To Isaac.)* Sorry.

DEANNA: Apologize to me, not him, numb nuts. We paged you.

PETEY: I didn't hear it.

DEANNA: And where are your headphones? Put them on.

(Petey scrambles to put on a headphone remote pack.)

DEANNA: I swear to God, Petey, if you weren't such a good lay, I'd fire your ass.

PETEY: *(Grins.)* You can't fire me — you're not paying me. *(Then, gesturing toward Isaac and Ezra.)* Did you tell them?

DEANNA: Oh, yeah. We got hitched.

EZRA: Hitched, married — hitched?

(Petey proudly shows the ring.)

EZRA: Mazel tov.

PETEY: Thank you.

ISAAC: Nice going, Petey. What does that make you, number five?

PETEY: Four. Only number four.

ISAAC: Well, keep working at it.

PETEY: I will.

DEANNA: Stop talking to him.

PETEY: *(To Isaac.)* Sorry.

DEANNA: And stop apologizing to him!

PETEY: Did I walk in on something? 'Cause there's like a vibe in here.

DEANNA: I don't want to talk about it. I came up with a line that was not only funnier, but made a lot more sense, and Isaac got all threatened and went bat shit. *(Turning on Isaac.)* And by the way, next week's script sucks. I refuse to even read it at the table on Monday.

ISAAC: What's your problem with it?

DEANNA: All of it. I hate it. Start over.

ISAAC: Start over? It's Wednesday — by Monday, you want me to write a whole new script?

DEANNA: Two scripts.

ISAAC: *Two* scripts.

DEANNA: This is intelligent management. How good can a script be if you're writing it at the last minute? But if you write two, it doubles my chances that one of them is at least salvageable.

ISAAC: "Salvageable," meaning, you can save it with your brilliant notes.

DEANNA: Exactly. And I want them both by eight p.m. on Sunday so I can read them before I go to bed. Understood?

ISAAC: No. I'm not doing that.

DEANNA: *No?*

ISAAC: Damn straight.

DEANNA: Don't say "damn straight." It's homophobic.

ISAAC: What?

DEANNA: "Damn straight" implies that "straight" is a good thing, so "gay" is a bad thing. *(Indicating Ezra.)* And to say something like that in front of a gay man is remarkably insensitive.

EZRA: I'm not gay!

DEANNA: Yeah, yeah, save it for "Entertainment Tonight." Those of us who actually know you detect a little hint of mint, OK?

EZRA: If you need me, I'll be in my dressing room, listening to Ricky Martin and picking out new drapes.

(He goes, passing Barry Joshua, thirties, and Kurt Fast, fiftyish, as they enter.)

BARRY: What's up?

ISAAC: What the hell are you doing here?

BARRY: I was having a little powwow with Kurt, and we heard there was a problem on the set.

DEANNA: I'm very glad you're both here. The behavior on this soundstage has been entirely inappropriate for a professional production.

ISAAC: Behavior? Jesus, start with her. She eats all through the fucking rehearsal —

DEANNA: I'm hypoglycemic. *(To Barry.)* I'm simply trying to stay lucid. He'd rather have me black out.

ISAAC: Eating nonstop does not make you lucid. It makes you rude and fat.

DEANNA: *Fat?!*

ISAAC: She eats because she's got the munchies. She's stoned half the time —

DEANNA: *Who's* stoned?!

ISAAC: Don't stand here and tell me you've never smoked marijuana before walking onto this set.

DEANNA: One time. Two weeks ago, when Ezra was being a bitch on wheels. And how did you even hear about it? *(Realizes.)* Wardrobe. I left that joint in my pocket and they found it, didn't they.

ISAAC: No, I smelled it when I came to talk you out of your trailer.

DEANNA: *(To Barry.)* I want the entire wardrobe department fired.

BARRY: I'll take care of it. *(Turns.)* Kurt?

KURT: Done.

ISAAC: Don't blame wardrobe for this. I'm telling you, I smelled it when —

BARRY: Did you hear him, Isaac? They're already gone.

ISAAC: Oh, now we hear from the lapdog. Fuck you too, Barry.

KURT: Isaac, maybe we should go to neutral corners and cool off —

ISAAC: I'm tired of your cool-off talks, Kurt. You're paying her salary. Tell her to start acting professionally. Shit, at least tell her to start *acting*.

DEANNA: What is that supposed to mean?

BARRY: Stay calm, Deanna; this is what you have me for. *(To Isaac.)* What is that supposed to mean?

ISAAC: It means every week she's getting paid twice what the average American family makes in a year, and she doesn't even bother learning her lines. The last three weeks this psycho bitch from hell has asked for cue cards. She looks like fucking Estelle Getty out there.

(The others all gasp at this last, even Petey. Kurt steers Isaac to a downstage corner. Barry steers Deanna to the opposite upstage corner.)

KURT: Let me tell you a story, Isaac. When I first came out to Hollywood, I met a great and famous novelist who had moved here to write screenplays. He told me, working in this town is like sitting down to dinner at a beautifully set table, where they bring you the most perfect meal you can imagine. One great big plate with every one of your favorite dishes, each prepared to succulent perfection. And you cannot believe that fortune has chosen you to smile upon in this way. And then you notice something, and you look a little closer, and you realize that in one corner of the plate, there's this little piece of steaming shit. And you stop, and you curse, and you stew. In the end, there's only one thing you can possibly say: "That's all right, I'll eat around it." *(A beat, then.)* Look, Isaac, as I've told you before, every hit show goes through a period of high tension. You created a series called "Deanna," and like it or not, Deanna is what you've got. Tough it out with her for a few years, get very rich, then say your fuck you's — to her, to me, to all of Hollywood if you want. But don't squander this. You know how much luck goes into putting together a hit show. And you know the odds against lightning striking you a second time.

ISAAC: A good writer can always find a job.

KURT: How old are you?

ISAAC: Forty-six.

KURT: Forty-six. How many TV writers do you know over fifty?

ISAAC: *(Beat.)* Working ones?

KURT: Working ones.

(Isaac says nothing.)

KURT: So as a friend, I would advise you to find a way back down off this ledge before the network hears about it and this becomes a full-blown crisis. Make your peace with Deanna. Let her know you're on her side. Eat around it.

(Isaac looks at him for a long beat, sighs.)

KURT: OK?

ISAAC: OK.

KURT: Come on. I'll help you.

(They turn back to Deanna and Barry.)

ISAAC: Listen, Deanna, I don't know what to say. I'm sorry I went off like that —

DEANNA: *(To Kurt.)* I want him gone. Now.

BARRY: Simple equation: He's gone or she walks.

KURT: Isn't there something we can —

DEANNA: No.

KURT: *(Turns to Isaac.)* Well, that's that.

ISAAC: That's what?

KURT: Go home, Isaac. You're fired.

ISAAC: *What?!* Just like that?

KURT: Don't worry about the money. You're well protected in your deal.

ISAAC: You can't fire me — the voice of this show is mine. Without my voice, what do you have?

DEANNA: *My* face. *My* voice.

KURT: We'll be fine, Isaac.

ISAAC: I don't think so. If you did this, I don't see how you would ever be fine.

KURT: I'm not denying that you're a talented writer. But the business of television is the business of getting the audience into a habit. Happily, people are now in the habit of watching Deanna.

ISAAC: Shit, no wonder people are sick of network TV. Quality television is about vision. This series isn't just a "vehicle" to let Deanna Denninger strut her stuff — this is a deeply personal concept which I've been nursing for ten years. I'm spilling blood on every page. Sure, you'll find some hired gun to replace me, somebody who'll put up with this loony toon because you'll pay him two million bucks a year, but you know and I know that the show will suffer. And the audience will notice, and the ratings will drop. In the long run, you cannot make money feeding people garbage.

KURT: Of course you can. That's the beauty of television. Look at almost any hit, how the "quality" deteriorated after the original writers left or the premise just grew tired. Once the audience is in the habit of watching, they'll keep coming back, no matter how lousy the show gets. The good news for someone like me is that, basically, people are stupid. *(Then.)* Go home, Isaac.

(Isaac starts off, defeated, all eyes on him. Then:)

DEANNA: *(Holding her temples.)* This is so painful . . .

(Isaac stops, turns, and looks at her in disbelief.)

BARRY: It's OK, Deanna. It's over. He's gone.

DEANNA: That's not enough. Petey!

(Petey jumps up and rushes over to her She hands him the unopened can of diet cream soda.).

PETEY: Yeah, Dee?

DEANNA: Throw this at him.

PETEY: Dee?

DEANNA: Throw this can of soda at Isaac. Hard.

PETEY: Really?

DEANNA: Throw it.

(Petey looks dubious, then starts to cock his arm.)

KURT: Don't throw it, Petey.

PETEY: No?

DEANNA: Petey, I said, throw the soda at him.

ISAAC: You're not serious.

(Petey fires the can. It just misses Isaac and smashes through the scenery flat just behind his head.)

ISAAC: Jesus!

PETEY: *(Regarding his miss.)* Oops. Sorry, Dee.

(She tosses him another can.)

DEANNA: Go for two out of three.

(Petey cocks his arm.)

KURT: Petey — *(Then.)* Deanna, I would prefer it if Petey didn't happen to throw another soda at Isaac.

DEANNA: Oh yeah, Kurt? *You* would prefer it, huh? Throw it, Petey.

(Barry steps forward.)

BARRY: *Whoa, whoa, whoa!!* Maybe we can work something out. *(Then.)* Deanna wants a bigger trailer.

DEANNA: *(Quickly.)* Twenty-two hundred square feet.

KURT: Twenty-two hundred? We didn't even give that to Ted Danson —

DEANNA: Throw the soda, Petey.

(Kurt pauses. Petey hesitates. Isaac looks at them all like they're crazy.)

BARRY: *Whoa, whoa, whoa!!* *(To Kurt.)* There's a deal to be made! Kurt, Petey played quarterback at Ohio State. If he wails that thing at Isaac and whaps him in the head, we're talking concussion at least, possibly brain damage.

KURT: But *twenty-two hundred square feet . . .*

BARRY: Guy could end up a vegetable. Think of the lawsuit, amigo. You've made a lot of money over the years. Do you really want to have it all taken away? And by a *writer?*

(Beat.)

KURT: *(Sighs, then to Deanna.)* I'll give you the trailer.

(Beat.)

DEANNA: Petey? I'm thirsty.

(Petey brings her the soda, opens it for her.)

ISAAC: *(To Deanna.)* You are one very sad, deluded, deeply fucked-up human being.

(He starts to exit. Barry steps into his path.)

BARRY: You know, I just saved you from bodily injury. A simple "thank you" would not be inappropriate. *(Off Isaac's look.)* OK, fine.

(Isaac shakes his head, turns away, . . . then spins and punches Barry clean on the jaw, knocking him down.)

ISAAC: *(Mutters.)* Fucking agents.

(He exits.)

BARRY: *(On the ground, checking for blood.)* OK, so he's pissed. Fine. He was fired; we've all been there; it sucks. But you don't fucking coldcock somebody, you know what I'm saying? I mean, it's not even professional.

DEANNA: Petey? *(Fragile.)* Would you go get me another sandwich?

PETEY: Sure, Dee.

(He goes.)

DEANNA: Barry, you too.

BARRY: *(From the floor.)* Me too? Can't he get it himself?

DEANNA: *Just go.*

BARRY: A sandwich you want, a sandwich you shall have. *(He jumps up and exits. And then, Deanna starts to cry. She collapses on her desk and sobs. Kurt comes over to her.)*

DEANNA: I'm sorry. I knew I'd start bawling my eyes out, and I didn't want to do it in front of everyone

KURT: *(Putting a hand on her shoulder.)* It's OK. It's OK. It's me.

DEANNA: You have no idea how hard it is to be the only woman, surrounded by men.

KURT: I know. It must be hell.

DEANNA: It is hell. For twenty-five years, I've been world famous, and everyone has wanted to have sex with me.

KURT: I can't even imagine.

DEANNA: I know that sounds like it would be a good thing, but it's awful, it really is. It's like I'm an object. Everyone only wants me for what they can get from me. When I meet people, I can never trust them. I get so lonely. So lonely.

KURT: It's not easy, being successful. I have the same kind of feelings sometimes. It must be that much harder to be famous, too. I really admire you, Deanna.

(Deanna looks searchingly into Kurt's eyes. There's a magic — maybe a black one, but a magic nonetheless — in the intensity of her gaze. And Kurt is a goner.)

DEANNA: They all want to ruin me, Kurt. It's like I'm too perfect, and they need to destroy me.

KURT: Not me, Deanna.

DEANNA: I need you to help me, Kurt.

KURT: I will, Deanna. I'll do everything in my power. The best writers, directors. Every penny I have to spend to get the show right.

DEANNA: The way I want it.

KURT: Of course.

DEANNA: I need you, Kurt. I know you're the man I should have counted on a long time ago.

KURT: I'm here for you now.

DEANNA: I know you are.

(She leans against him, and he holds her.)

DEANNA: *(Crying softly.)* This is the same thing they did to Marilyn Monroe, you know.

KURT: I know.

DEANNA: The same thing they did to Marilyn . . .

KURT: *(Holding her.)* Shh.

DEANNA: The same thing they did to Marilyn . . . *(Beat.)* And Jesus. *(Blackout.)*

Scene Two

Isaac's office, one week earlier. Kurt sits on a sofa. Isaac paces.

ISAAC: She eats all through rehearsals. She fired two script supervisors last week alone. The second one bit the dust for correcting her when she called the actor "Ezra."

KURT: That's his name.

ISAAC: That's the *actor's* name; the character is "Jeremiah." This was *on camera*. Then she said we should change the character's name, make it easier for her to remember. It's the second year of the show.

KURT: *(Laughs.)* Our Deanna.

ISAAC: Yeah. It's real cute. But not if you're the poor schmuck who got fired because this woman can't tell the difference between real life and television. You know what she's asking for now? This is why I had to talk to you.

KURT: I can't wait.

ISAAC: This week we're doing the episode about Deanna finding her birth mother. Heavy stuff, right? And believe me, the writing staff has slaved over this one for months, trying to nail that balance of emotion and laughs. Well. Deanna calls me up yesterday — from her bathtub, no less — and tells me that America won't care about "this birth mother thing." What America cares about, according to Deanna Denninger, is her hair.

KURT: Can't you just stick in a couple of hair jokes? I'm sure that would satisfy her.

ISAAC: Nope. Her shrink says it has to be the A-story.

KURT: Her shrink?

ISAAC: Oh, didn't I tell you? I do a notes session every week with one Dr. Kenneth Olshansky. Plus, believe it or not, I've had two script meetings with her nutritionist, and once I got three single-spaced pages from her animal psychic.

KURT: Animal psychic?

ISAAC: Yes, sir.

KURT: The psychic is an animal, or?

ISAAC: The psychic is a person, but he channels the souls of pets who've gone to the great kennel in the sky.

KURT: You've got your hands full. *(Sighs.)* People have no idea how difficult television is, how the pressure brings out the worst in everyone. Even a small personality conflict has a way of mushrooming because you know you're looking at years and years together, shackled at the ankle.

ISAAC: I know all that. But you have to admit, some of this stuff she's doing is pretty outrageous.

KURT: I've never heard of a show that was easy. Not one. The writers hate the actors, the actors hate each other, everybody hates the network. There's always something. And it's eighteen hours a day, week after week, ten months a year.

ISAAC: *(Sighs.)* I think the only saving grace is that it keeps me away from an empty house.

KURT: I heard Meredith is moving up to Napa with the children.

ISAAC: Can't stop her. It's in-state. *(Beat.)* You know, you work eighty, ninety hours a week, there's nothing left for your family. Maybe you get a couple hours on the weekends to ride bikes with your kids, take your wife to dinner. You barely have enough time to remind yourself what it was all for in the first place. *(A deep breath.)* And then you run into a season like *this* . . . and on the weekends you can't even *see* your kids . . . *(A deep breath.)* If I had it all to do over . . . well, let's face it, I fucked up. *(A silence.)*

KURT: Look, I know it's a difficult time for you, and this is a particularly difficult show for many reasons. Just try as best you can to keep your cool until things settle down.

ISAAC: I'm not a prick, Kurt. I'm not one of these asshole show-runners who tells the star just to say the lines and not bump into the furniture.

KURT: I understand. We'll talk to her when she gets here. I'm sure she'll be reasonable.

ISAAC: I just want what's best for the show.

KURT: As do I.

(The door bursts open dramatically and Deanna leans in.)

DEANNA: Knock knock!

KURT: Deanna! Come in, come in.

DEANNA: Good morning, Kurt.

ISAAC: Hello.

DEANNA: Darling! How *are* you?

(She kisses him on both cheeks.)

ISAAC: Very well. How about yourself?

DEANNA: *(Stricken, on a dime.)* Oh! Don't ask! Did you ever meet Middi?

ISAAC: No, but you've certainly talked about her.

DEANNA: *(To Kurt.)* Middi is this incredibly spiritual African-American woman who's worked for my family since before I was born. A very soulful, extraordinarily beautiful woman, who practically raised me. She crashed her car on the 405 this afternoon, broke her collarbone.

ISAAC: Oh, I'm so sorry to hear that.

DEANNA: *(Nods.)* Sixty-eight years old.

KURT: Oh, my.

DEANNA: That's not the worst part. The worst part is, her family is blaming *me.* They say the only reason she got *into* the crash is that she was so upset because I had just fired her.

ISAAC: You fired her?

DEANNA: I had to. She was stealing.

KURT: No!

DEANNA: Mm-hmm. Jewelry.

KURT: I hate that. It's so difficult, when you trust people, take them into your home.

DEANNA: Isn't it?

ISAAC: How did you find out?

DEANNA: Well, I didn't have any actual *proof,* but, I mean, how many times can you lose *one earring* without getting a little suspicious?
(Isaac looks to Kurt, who doesn't look back. Then:)

KURT: Should we start?

DEANNA: Let's wait a moment — Barry's right outside. *(Hollers.)* Barry?!

ISAAC: Barry's coming?

DEANNA: Do you have a problem with that?

ISAAC: It's awkward.

DEANNA: It doesn't have to be.

ISAAC: I didn't want it to be that kind of meeting. I mean, there are issues to work out, but —

DEANNA: What kind of meeting *is* it, Isaac? I'm not Roseanne, for crying out loud. Stop treating me like I'm Roseanne. You don't know how hard it is to be the only woman in these meetings. Always. I wasn't about to walk in here unprotected.
(Barry enters.)

BARRY: *(To Kurt.)* Asshole!

KURT: Shithead!

(They hug.)

BARRY: *(Extending a hand to Isaac.)* Isaac. Feels like a while since we talked.

ISAAC: *(Pointed.)* Gosh, it does.

(They all sit.)

DEANNA: Can we please get to it?

KURT: Let's.

DEANNA: I want to speak first. Barry?

BARRY: *(Deep breath.)* Deanna believes — and I stand squarely behind her on this — that everyone is against her and is trying to ruin her show.

ISAAC: *What?*

KURT: Could you be more specific?

BARRY: Specifically, Isaac.

ISAAC: *(To Barry.)* What the hell are you doing? *(To Kurt.)* I don't have to listen to this.

KURT: *(To Deanna.)* In what way do you feel Isaac is hurting the show?

DEANNA: I'll tell you. *(Then.)* Barry?

BARRY: Deanna is unhappy with the writing.

ISAAC: The writing won an Emmy last season.

DEANNA: *Last* season.

(Isaac reacts.)

KURT: *(Quieting him with a subtle wave; then, to Barry.)* Was there a specific script which disappointed Deanna?

DEANNA: Talk to *me.* I'm sitting right here.

KURT: I'm sorry, that was rude. Did you have a problem with a specific script?

DEANNA: Thank you.

(She turns to Barry, who again answers.)

BARRY: Deanna has been pitching story ideas all season, and every single one of them has been ignored. She's not just an actress, you know. She's a primary creative talent, and the executive producer of this show.

ISAAC: *An* executive producer, not the executive producer.

KURT: Well, as *an* executive producer myself, I'd like to hear the concepts Deanna has pitched.

DEANNA: My hair story, for starters.

BARRY: Which was brilliant.

ISAAC: All you said was that America cared about your hair.

DEANNA: And it does.

BARRY: It really does. America is fucking in love with Deanna's hair. We were in a town car going to Letterman, and that's like all the English the driver knew — *(With accent, holding a finger to his head.)* "Oh, Deanna, I love your beautiful hair." *(Laughing hard at his own anecdote.)* Tell 'em, Deanna. It was a riot. There's an episode, I'm telling you.

ISAAC: That's not a story.

BARRY: Look, if a great writer like you can't find the comedy in that . . .

ISAAC: A story, Barry, is conflict. A story is something which transacts between your characters, which challenges them, which forces their relationship to shift or grow or deepen. A cab driver with a funny accent and a thing on his head is not a story. Kurt, help me.

KURT: *(To Barry.)* What other ideas did — *(Turning to Deanna.)* — did you have?

BARRY: Deanna pitched a primo story about the book *Little Women.*

ISAAC: She didn't pitch a story.

DEANNA: Did I or did I not tell you I wanted to do an episode about *Little Women?*

ISAAC: That doesn't suggest a story to me.

DEANNA: Then put some writers on it. The good ones. And when the script is finished, I want credit.

ISAAC: What do you mean, credit?

DEANNA: On screen. "Written by."

ISAAC: I can't do that to the writer who actually sits down and writes the script.

DEANNA: Based on an idea which he stole from me, thank you very much.

ISAAC: The writer would quit. I guarantee it.

DEANNA: We have too many writers anyway. I can't remember their names, it's embarrassing. Kurt, can we at least make them wear numbers? Let me tell you something: *Little Women* was a very, very important part of my childhood. Now at this moment in time, I can't remember why — but that doesn't matter, and I'm sure a lot of women feel the same way. I am trying to enrich the series with moments from my own life. So if I'm going to be taken seriously as executive producer, when I say I want to do an episode about *Little Women* —

BARRY: Which, by the way, made a fucking awesome flick.

KURT: Wonderful film. Did you see it, Isaac?

ISAAC: They did a terrific job. But that still doesn't —

BARRY: Then you see how it can work. And you never know, maybe you could even stunt-cast Winona Ryder.

DEANNA: Ooh, I love her. Let's try to get her. *(To Isaac.)* And I'm saying this as the executive producer of the show.

ISAAC: Again, you are not *the* executive producer, you are *an* executive producer, which is a vanity credit Kurt gave you because he'd rather cheapen *my credit* than give you more of *his money.* Meanwhile, as the only executive producer who actually does any producing, I'm telling you that even *if* Winona Ryder would guest on the show, which she won't, *Little Women* is not a story.

BARRY: Hey, Bruce Willis did a *Mad About You* couple years ago. You get Bruce Willis, you don't need a story. Did you see that thing?

ISAAC: Kurt, please speak.

KURT: Personally, I would love to have Winona Ryder on the show. Or even Susan Sarandon.

DEANNA: No! No Susan Sarandon. I hear she's difficult, and I certainly don't need *that* around here. *(To Isaac.)* Remind me later, I have to give you those names for the casting people. There are some women I keep seeing on their lists, and I never want to see them again. Susan Sarandon, Cybill Shepherd, Bernadette Peters, who's a fucking bitch. Goldie Hawn, who used to be funny until she had all that work done. Oh, and Faye Dunaway. Are you writing these down? Faye Dunaway deliberately spilled cranberry sauce down my Mizirahi one time at the Golden Globes when we were both trying to fuck James Earl Jones. And no Candice Bergen, who is so stuck up I want to puke. We were at this state dinner at the White House, and I was telling Barbara Bush this story about how Orson Welles pulled out my tampon with his teeth, and Candice Bergen gets up and walks away. Frigid bitch, like she never gets her period. I really wish you would write that one down.

ISAAC: Oh, I'll remember that one.

DEANNA: You say you'll remember, but you never do. Last week, you had Ezra do a joke about Lyle Waggoner.

ISAAC: Got a big laugh.

DEANNA: I told you when I first read that script that Lyle Waggoner happens to be a very, very close, personal friend of mine. *(To Barry.)* Is he still alive?

BARRY: I think so. *(To Kurt.)* Is he?

KURT: *(Thinks.)* Yeah. Yeah, he's still alive.

DEANNA: Good. Because I will really miss him when he goes.

KURT: I'm sure you miss Orson Welles.

DEANNA: Every day.

ISAAC: At least every month.

KURT: Anything else you'd like to discuss while you have us all here?

DEANNA: The character of Ezra is overwritten.

ISAAC: The character is Jeremiah. Ezra is the actor.

DEANNA: Whatever. Either way, he's boring.

ISAAC: Ezra, who gets standing ovations from the audience every week, is boring.

DEANNA: I'm not saying we should fire him.

ISAAC: That's big of you.

BARRY: You know, that's exactly the kind of attitude that makes Deanna feel undermined.

DEANNA: Jeremiah is a side dish. He's funny because I made his career by putting him on a show called "Deanna." When he gets the last joke of a scene, it's boring to the audience, no matter how much it sounds like they're laughing. *(Beat.)* I just want the character of Deanna to be as much like me as possible.

KURT: I think we all do.

BARRY: You're the one the audience is coming back to see every week.

DEANNA: I want her to make the choices I would make.

KURT: Absolutely.

DEANNA: To say the things I would say.

KURT: Exactly.

DEANNA: Because then I can play it honestly. The audience is intelligent, and we mustn't underestimate them. They know the difference.

KURT: They certainly do.

DEANNA: That's all I ask.

(Beat.)

ISAAC: Deanna, what's confusing me is that you and I talk through these stories in detail before we write each script, so it surprises me to hear that you're dissatisfied with what you're reading. Could you point to one specific place where I have your character do something that feels wrong to you?

DEANNA: Yes. Easy. The act break of this week's episode. Right before we go to commercial, Ezra has that joke about my feet.

ISAAC: Right.

DEANNA: In real life, if it were really me, I would say something smart after that. You know: a great comeback, one that's not only meaningful but also gets a bigger laugh than Ezra got.

ISAAC: Like what?

DEANNA: Oh . . . well . . .

ISAAC: What would you say? You know, if this were real life?

DEANNA: Well, I don't have the line right at my fingertips, but —

ISAAC: That's real life, though. You don't get a dozen writers staying up until four in the morning to make you look good. Real life, where you say you'd be so pithy and hilarious, is coming up with the line right on the spot.

So why don't you give us the line right now — *(Snaps his fingers.)* — and we'll just go with it.

DEANNA: I don't know, I'd say . . .

ISAAC: *(Snaps his fingers again, moving closer in on her.)* Give me a line. *(Snaps.)* Go ahead. *(Snaps.)* Real life! *(Snaps.)* No time to think! *(Snaps.)* Come on!!

KURT: *Isaac.*

DEANNA: *(Tearing.)* You see what I'm dealing with?

KURT: Isaac, that was way out of line.

(Barry comes over to Isaac and puts a hand on his shoulder.)

BARRY: What have I been telling you? Keep your cool, no matter what.

ISAAC: *(Beat.)* I'm sorry. *(To Deanna.)* I'm sorry. This is just . . . very fucking hard.

(Beat.)

DEANNA: Barry: I cannot operate one minute longer with this conflict of interest. You have to make a choice right now.

BARRY: *(Sighs.)* I'm sorry, Isaac. I can't be your agent any more.

(Beat.)

ISAAC: Oh. There's a big surprise. *(Then.)* How did we get to this place? I want you to look me in the eye and explain it to me.

BARRY: Hey, you're making this impossible. You cannot expect me to represent a guy who refuses to do his job.

ISAAC: I'm *doing* my job!

BARRY: What, screaming at your star?

ISAAC: The job is *writing.*

BARRY: Oh, please, not the "Real Writer" speech. Jesus. Isaac. You want to live in the woods? You can do all the real writing you want — novellas, haiku, knock yourself out. You want a million four a year? Then give 'em something they can run between the commercials. That's the gig, amigo, and it's not like we haven't talked about this before.

(A silence.)

(Kurt approaches Deanna.)

KURT: Look, I was saying to Isaac before you got here that television is the most emotionally grueling medium to work in. These hours, this pressure, people can start to wear on each other. Good people. Let's not forget that this team got us where we are. It earned us ratings and won us awards. And together, we're going to make a big pile of money. So I think we should all just call a truce, cool down, appreciate one another, and move forward.

BARRY: Amen.

KURT: OK, Isaac?

ISAAC: Yeah.

KURT: Deanna?

DEANNA: *(Sniffs.)* OK.

BARRY: So what about Deanna's stories? *Little Women* and the hair concept.

KURT: I think they're great.

ISAAC: You've got to be kidding. I cannot rewrite this episode at the last minute to be about Deanna's hair.

KURT: Next week's show, then.

DEANNA: Fair enough.

(Petey sticks his head in the door.)

PETEY: This where the party's at?

(Isaac reacts with a little shock.)

KURT: *(Rising.)* Petey Ryan! How the hell have you been?

PETEY: Damn fine

KURT: We've missed you.

PETEY: Well, I'm back now.

DEANNA: He certainly is. *(To Petey.)* You're just in time to drive me home. *(Taking Kurt's hand.)* We'll have to have dinner one of these nights. The two of us.

KURT: *(Holding on a beat.)* I'd like that very much.

DEANNA: *(That smile.)* Great. I'll call you.

KURT: *(Walking her to the door.)* By the way, I've always loved *Little Women.* The original novel, I mean.

DEANNA: Isn't it brilliant? It was such an important book in my life before I even read it. And it meant so much more when I realized they weren't actually *small* . . .

(And she exits with the others, leaving Isaac alone. Blackout.)

Scene Three

A restaurant, four weeks earlier. Isaac and Deanna sit at a table, kissing and nuzzling.

ISAAC: You really don't mind that people are staring?

DEANNA: I've told you: people always stare at me. I am world famous.

ISAAC: That's the point. That busboy could be a stringer for the *National Enquirer.*

DEANNA: Isaac, once you get used to being larger than life, it's actually very liberating. People are going to believe what they want to believe anyway, so I might as well do whatever I want, whenever I want, with whomever I want.

ISAAC: Sounds nice. But I'm not a star.

DEANNA: You are when you're with me.

(Beat, as Isaac takes this in.)

DEANNA: Enjoy it, Isaac. You're with Deanna Denninger. Right this minute, every man in this restaurant wishes he could trade places with you. Get used to it.

ISAAC: I think I could.

DEANNA: I'll teach you how to enjoy the spotlight. Just give me time.

ISAAC: My time is nothing but yours.

DEANNA: I know. I have the best writer in town working for me. Day *and* night.

ISAAC: Have you had a lot of writers?

DEANNA: Mm, I'm more of a director gal.

ISAAC: Is that so.

DEANNA: Uh-huh. I gave Frank Capra his last blow job.

ISAAC: Bravo.

DEANNA: The rewrites are divine, by the way.

ISAAC: Thank you. We were there until two-thirty last night.

DEANNA: I remember. *(Taking his hand.)* Sometimes I can't imagine where you find the energy.

ISAAC: Caffeine, megadoses of ginseng. Did I tell you? Yesterday I had a nurse come to my office and give me a B-12 shot.

DEANNA: Such a devoted worker.

ISAAC: Recognize the restaurant?

DEANNA: *(Getting it.)* It's where we met! That's so romantic. Who would have thought this would turn out to be such a satisfying relationship?

ISAAC: Amazing how it worked out. *(Pause.)* So how was today?

DEANNA: I have to tell you: I had a remarkable moment this morning. I was sitting off to the side, reading the rewrite, and I was laughing and laughing, and then I looked up, and saw all these hardworking people from the crew, and the director, and the supporting cast, and especially Ezra Twain, and I thought, I am surrounded by so much damn talent, I have to be the most fortunate woman in show business. It was bliss. Truly, that was the word that came to mind. Bliss.

ISAAC: And after that . . . everything went all right?

DEANNA: Yes. *(Then.)* Why, did you hear something?

ISAAC: Um . . . no. You know, not anything, really.

DEANNA: It's the guacamole joke, isn't it. What, is Ezra going around saying that I "stole" it or something?

ISAAC: Well . . . it is a funny joke, and I guess he feels he was getting a good laugh on it.

DEANNA: It is much funnier coming from my character than from his. You have to admit that. Frankly, it was a blunder on your part to give it to him in the first place. I wish you would just let me see the rewrites before anybody else.

ISAAC: But when we finish working at two-thirty in the morning —

DEANNA: When we're in production, I wake up at five-thirty. I could give you notes at six-thirty or seven, and you'd still have time to make changes before rehearsal begins.

ISAAC: I don't know how funny I'll be at six-thirty in the morning if I don't come home until three.

DEANNA: Then wake up the other writers and have them do it. They're getting paid a lot of money, and this is important.

ISAAC: It's not that important. It's about Ezra not losing his jokes, that's all. Believe me, the writers will make sure you have plenty of funny stuff of your own, working the normal eighteen hours a day.

DEANNA: But darling . . . I want the jokes that I want.

(Isaac just looks at her.)

DEANNA: What else did he say?

ISAAC: Ezra?

DEANNA: Yes.

ISAAC: Well, there was some issue about the coverage?

DEANNA: Alvin was shooting all the wrong angles.

ISAAC: He's one of the best half-hour directors around —

DEANNA: Excuse me. I didn't fuck Marty Scorcese for an entire summer without learning a little something about where to put the cameras. Alvin didn't have me in close-up during Ezra's first line. Here Ezra was going to get this enormous laugh — which I generously let him keep, by the way — and what should the audience be seeing there? What is the most important thing?

ISAAC: Ezra, delivering the line.

DEANNA: *(Patronizing.)* I don't think so. I think my reaction is the most important thing. I think the show is called "Deanna," thank you very much, not "Here Comes Deanna's Funny Assistant."

ISAAC: True. But it's an ensemble comedy, you know, like "Mary Tyler Moore," or "Barney Miller" —

DEANNA: Christ, that little prick really carried on, didn't he.

ISAAC: He comes from the theater, and a whole different way of working —

DEANNA: What did he think when he decided to go into television? This isn't New Haven any more. This isn't thirty people yawning in the audience at the Yale School of Drama. He's damned fortunate that I discovered him and made him all that money.

ISAAC: He's the first person to tell everyone how fortunate he is —

DEANNA: He should come in every morning and kiss my ass. There are thousands of unemployed actors out there who would kill to be on my show. Do you know what he does? He comes into my trailer when I'm not there and uses the toilet and doesn't flush. I mean it.

ISAAC: How would you know that?

DEANNA: Please, who else would it be. He really is quite the little faggot. And, by the way, I say this as the Grand Marshall of the Pasadena Gay Pride Parade, so it comes from a good place.

(Long pause.)

ISAAC: Look, none of this is that important. What do you say we put it away now, and not let it ruin our evening?

DEANNA: Good idea. I won't let him get to me. He doesn't realize how lucky he is.

ISAAC: He is lucky. We're all lucky. *(Taking her hand again.)* I'm particularly lucky.

DEANNA: *(Mollified, playful again.)* You are lucky.

(They kiss some more, then gaze into one another's eyes.)

ISAAC: I knew we could get back on track tonight.

(Deanna nods, but then a cloud passes over her.)

ISAAC: What?

DEANNA: When did you talk to him?

ISAAC: Who?

DEANNA: Ezra. What, did he just drop into the writers' room and interrupt everything?

ISAAC: No, no. He called Meg and made an appointment.

DEANNA: Made an appointment. Uh-huh. To talk to you in private, without me? Did he forget that I'm one of the executive producers now?

ISAAC: It wasn't that big a deal. He'd like to do a play over the hiatus, so mostly he wanted to know how firm the production schedule was.

DEANNA: He brought up the preshoot, didn't he. The scene in the car.

ISAAC: Come on, why don't we talk about it tomorrow?

DEANNA: *(Locked in now.)* The second take was brilliant.

ISAAC: Yes, I know why you liked it —

DEANNA: You're going to use the second take, of course.

ISAAC: I'll have to look at them both.

DEANNA: Oh, it had better be the second take.

ISAAC: Well, in the first take, when you tell him that his cat was found dead, and he cried a little bit?

DEANNA: That was way over the top.

ISAAC: But you did such nice work reacting.

DEANNA: We had to pull him back, though. I asked Alvin to pull him back, because it was just way too much.

ISAAC: But then in the second take —

DEANNA: Yes?

ISAAC: In the second take, you cried. A lot.

DEANNA: I was in the moment.

ISAAC: Well, look at it from his perspective. He learns his cat is dead, and he cries a little bit, the director asks him to pull back, and he does, and in the very same scene, you start sobbing.

DEANNA: I've heard this, Isaac. You're repeating yourself. Get to the point. What is your point?

ISAAC: From his perspective —

DEANNA: You said that. Stop repeating yourself. You're boring me.
(A pause.)

ISAAC: What is the motivation for your character crying there?

DEANNA: I had to tell my assistant, my confidante, my best friend in the world, some terrible news, which I knew would break his heart.

ISAAC: I know, but it's *his* heart —

DEANNA: Pets mean a lot to me.

ISAAC: Oh, I understand, but —

DEANNA: I lost a puppy once. *(Tearing up.)* We called him Ringo. When I was seven, I lost him in the most traumatic way.

ISAAC: I'm sorry.

DEANNA: Ringo ran away from home.

ISAAC: That's tough.

DEANNA: I was inconsolable. My father drove around the neighborhood for two days and nights looking for that poor, lost puppy. Finally, on the third night, Daddy found poor Ringo lying by the side of the highway.

ISAAC: Dead?

DEANNA: No, he was fine, thank God. Daddy brought Ringo home to me, and I was so happy to see him, I cried and cried. But I was angry, too, that this puppy could be so stupid and reckless. So, I made him eat two of my jacks, and then he died.

(Deanna weeps softly.)

ISAAC: That must have been awful.

(Deanna nods.)

ISAAC: Plus then you only had eight jacks.

DEANNA: *(Wiping her tears.)* Isaac, you have to understand. I am not some kind of mannered, British-style stage actor, who can hit the same exact note take after take. I'm more organic. More spontaneous. There's something larger at work. It's beyond my mortal will. Do you understand?

ISAAC: Kind of, but not completely.

DEANNA: My work is very spiritual. There's a transcendent power in the universe which gave me my talent, and which speaks through me. I am merely an instrument. It took me a long time to realize this.

ISAAC: So not crying in that scene — that wasn't even an option.

DEANNA: Not at all. And that's why it's crucial that you use the second take. This isn't just me speaking.

ISAAC: It's divine intervention.

DEANNA: Exactly.

(A long silence.)

DEANNA: Look, Isaac, while we're on the subject . . . I need to sing more.

ISAAC: Sing?

DEANNA: In the show. I should be singing almost every week from now on.

ISAAC: Well, that's hard to work in. I mean, we did it once, but . . . you're playing a United States senator.

DEANNA: Bill Bradley played basketball, and he was a senator.

ISAAC: I get C-Span, and I'm pretty sure I never saw Bill Bradley shoot hoops during a floor debate.

DEANNA: I don't know why you're being difficult about this. It's totally true to the concept you created. Brassy, independent woman comes to Washington and shakes everything up. I want to sing "Bridge Over Troubled Water," by the way, and "Pink Cadillac." This week I want to sing a spiritual.

ISAAC: A *spiritual?*

DEANNA: I'm not saying "Please" now; I'm saying "Do it."

(A pause.)

ISAAC: You never said that before.

DEANNA: Well, maybe you're just starting to get a little too lax about everything.

ISAAC: The show is doing very well —

DEANNA: I don't want to hear, "I can't." Those words aren't in my vocabulary, and they shouldn't be in yours.

(A silence.)

ISAAC: I didn't want tonight to turn into a fight.

DEANNA: It's not a fight. We have a professional relationship, and there will be creative tensions from time to time. From those, the show will only get stronger. It's the nature of the beast.

ISAAC: We'll work it out, though.

DEANNA: Of course we will. We're adults.

(Another silence.)

ISAAC: Listen, the rest of my furniture came today. So don't be surprised if my place is kind of a wreck tonight.

DEANNA: I don't think we should go to your place tonight.

ISAAC: But didn't you say you have your kids?

DEANNA: I don't think we should spend tonight together.

ISAAC: Look, if this is about Ezra —

DEANNA: This is about you and me. I think that the professional relationship and the personal relationship are in conflict, and I don't think it's good for either of us to continue this way. I hope you can be adult about this.

ISAAC: Sure. Adult as hell.

DEANNA: It is the wisest course. You know what they say about shitting where you eat.

ISAAC: Which part was the shitting?

(Blackout.)

Scene Four

Isaac's office, two months earlier. Isaac nurses a hangover, sips from a bottle of water. Barry, fully awake and spry, looks directly at Isaac while he carries on a conversation over a hands-free telephone plugged into his ear, a thin cord running down to his belt.

BARRY: Big night.

ISAAC: Big, big night.

BARRY: Client's show wins two Emmys, hasn't even been on for a full season yet? Can't get much prouder than I am today.

ISAAC: Thank you.

BARRY: But enough chitchat. About my car.

ISAAC: What?

BARRY: My Boxster, Gunther. You promised me I'd have it back this morning, and I'm still stuck with the piece of shit loaner you gave me.

ISAAC: You're on the phone. Don't do that to me when I'm hung over.

BARRY: Yes, my client's TV show won two Emmys . . . Isaac Brooks . . . No, he's not *on* the show — Gunther, I don't want to talk about the Emmys, I want to talk about how I'm supposed to drive onto the Fox lot this afternoon in a Goddamn Taurus.

ISAAC: Don't make eye contact with me when you're talking to somebody else. It's creepy.

(He leans back and closes his eyes.)

BARRY: Yeah, fine. *(Then.)* Too bad Deanna didn't win. Fucking Helen Hunt. Isn't everyone sick of her already?

(Isaac doesn't answer.)

BARRY: I'm talking to *you.*

(Isaac doesn't respond.)

BARRY: *I'm talking to you.*

(Isaac opens his eyes.)

ISAAC: Me?

BARRY: Yes, *you,* amigo. I'm on hold. You look like shit.

ISAAC: Yeah, well, I feel worse then that.

BARRY: Champagne hangover's brutal. Didn't think you were going to make it to your limo last night. *(Beat.)* In fact, you didn't make it to your limo last night

ISAAC: You noticed.

BARRY: Rumor is you found your way into Deanna's, and Petey was left at the Governor's Ball with his dick in his hand. Be careful, Isaac.

ISAAC: Media?

BARRY: *(Shakes his head.)* The very fact. Unacceptable.

ISAAC: What?

BARRY: Unacceptable, amigo. Absolutely unacceptable.

ISAAC: Look, I'm not entirely proud of it, either, I was drunk, OK, but you of all people —

BARRY: I've got a Boxster under warranty, not two thousand miles on it, it's unacceptable.

(Realizing, Isaac groans and closes his eyes again.)

BARRY: Gunther, how come whenever you have bad news about my car, your accent gets thicker? Let me put it in language you can understand: Boxster, *ja,* Carrera, *ja,* Taurus, no fucking way, *jawohl?* My show won two Emmys! *(Then.)* Don't give me that shit, Gunther, have you ever taken a meeting at Fox? . . . Of course not. You know what makes Fox different from all the other networks? At Fox, when you drive onto the lot, *they can see you.* Those fucks can look right out their windows at the valets, make up their minds about your pitch before you even walk in the building. And be-lieve me, Gunther, nobody ever drove off the Fox lot in a fucking Tau-rus with even a mid-season six. Now I'm coming to the dealership at eleven-thirty sharp, and if my car isn't ready, you're going to loan me a Porsche. Not a Taurus, not a Miata, not a Jaguar XK8 convertible — a Porsche. A red one. And you know why you're gonna do that for me? *'Cause last night, I won two Emmys. Auf Wiedersehen.*

(He hits a cutoff button and pulls the earpiece out of his ear.)

BARRY: Now. You. *(Beat.)* Isaac Brooks. *(Then.)* Emmy winner Isaac Brooks, who spent last night schtupping America's sweetheart, Deanna Denninger.

ISAAC: *(Eyes still shut.)* Tell me when you're off the phone.

BARRY: I'm off. Asshole.

(Isaac finally looks at him.)

BARRY: You really slept with her.

(Isaac grunts.)

BARRY: Just be warned, my friend. That's a well-trodden path you journeyed.

ISAAC: Lovely metaphor.

BARRY: Just speaking the truth. The woman has her own little Vietnam down there. A lot of good men have gone, and not come back the same.

ISAAC: Look, I know how you have some issues with her.

BARRY: Issues? Not at all. In fact, I've been thinking I'd like to represent her. *(Off Isaac's look.)* What?

ISAAC: What do you mean, "what?" You? Represent her?

BARRY: You have to allow individuals credit for human growth. The better I get to know Deanna, the more I appreciate how things look from her perspective. *(Then.)* Hey, she's been looking for a new agent.

ISAAC: Really? For how long?

BARRY: A while. I wanted to see how you would feel about it before I did anything, naturally.

ISAAC: Naturally.

BARRY: Stop looking at me like that. It's business.

ISAAC: But you're concerned about how I would feel. From the standpoint of the conflict.

BARRY: *(Waves it off.)* Conflict. There won't be a conflict

ISAAC: Barry . . .

BARRY: You've got a hit show, and the two of you are a fabulous team. Even if, you know, the shared-limo thing doesn't entirely work out. Hey — you gave her back her career. She tells everybody that. I've never seen an actress so grateful.

ISAAC: I don't know, I don't feel good about this.

BARRY: Look, if I was even the least bit worried, I wouldn't bring this up. In fact, it'll be good for you.

ISAAC: Good for me?

BARRY: Two Emmys, the ratings'll get a nice bounce — sometime this year the network'll start talking extension. And *then* — you and Deanna negotiating together? Can you imagine how far we'll be able to ram it up Kurt's ass?

(A silence.)

BARRY: Look, as agents and clients go, I think we have something special.

ISAAC: I like to think so.

BARRY: You're not just any client to me, you're one of my closest friends.

ISAAC: And you're one of mine.

BARRY: If we do this, a time ever comes where there's a *hint* of conflict — *anything* — just say the word and I'll let her know she has to find someone else. You will always come first. Always.

ISAAC: Enough said. It's an opportunity. Go for it.

BARRY: You're sure.

ISAAC: And she couldn't ask for better. I'll tell her that myself.

BARRY: Would you? That'd be great.

(A silence.)

ISAAC: I can't believe I did that last night. It doesn't even seem real

BARRY: Well . . . speaking as your agent, this could be a good thing. *(Off Isaac's look.)* Scandal gives you character. People want to know you, get into business with you. Elizabeth Hurley, most beautiful woman in the world, nobody gives a shit. Then her boyfriend gets a blowjob from a hooker with no teeth, boom, everybody wants to take a meeting.

ISAAC: It's a sick industry.

BARRY: Come on, you know that's how it works. So you're a family man, I respect that. I'm just saying, if you're screwing around anyway —

ISAAC: I'm not screwing around.

BARRY: Well, whatever you want to call last night, I'm just saying as a friend that I won't be judgmental, and, as your representative that, at the end of the day, there may actually be a professional upside.

ISAAC: Deanna's not a career tool, she's a *person*. A terrific person.

(Beat.)

BARRY: Is this love? Shit man, don't tell me this is love.

ISAAC: It's not love. It was a stupid, one-night, too-much-champagne thing, and I'm kind of embarrassed about it, and I'd like it all to just go away before there's any real damage.

BARRY: Oh, man. She really rotated your tires, didn't she.

ISAAC: Stop it.

BARRY: Look at you. She really reupholstered your sofa.

ISAAC: Come on . . .

BARRY: She really deboned your fish — Deanna!

(Deanna appears in the doorway, looking great.)

DEANNA: Good morning, Barry. Isaac.

ISAAC: Hi.

(A moment between Isaac and Deanna. Barry jumps in.)

BARRY: Deanna, you looked unbelievable last night. Who did your dress?

DEANNA: Vera Wang. Wasn't it divine?

BARRY: Green was made for you.

DEANNA: Thank you, darling.

BARRY: Green is your color. You own green.

DEANNA: Thank you, darling.

BARRY: Green should be embarrassed to be seen on another woman.

ISAAC: *(A bit sickened.)* Or even on a plant.

BARRY: You should have won, if there was any justice in the world. Helen Hunt is a no-talent piece of shit. You know, in my opinion.

DEANNA: That's nice of you to say.

BARRY: Anyway, I was so upset that you didn't win, I took the liberty of getting you a little consolation gift.

DEANNA: You didn't have to do that, Barry. How thoughtful.

BARRY: Well, I would love the chance to break bread with you some time. Talk about your career.

DEANNA: I would like that, too.

BARRY: Good. I'll have my office call you to set something up.

DEANNA: It's a date, then.

(That look. That smile.)

BARRY: Wonderful. See you soon.

(He starts to move off, transfixed.)

ISAAC: Bye, Barry.

BARRY: Bye, uh . . .

ISAAC: Isaac.

BARRY: Isaac.

(And he goes.)

DEANNA: *(Looking after him.)* Nice man.

ISAAC: Yes.

DEANNA: You're happy with him? As an agent?

ISAAC: He's the best.

(She turns her attention to Isaac. They look at one another for a moment, break into embarrassed grins, then laughter.)

ISAAC: How the hell do you look so good? I mean, I *know* how little sleep you got.

DEANNA: Professional secret.

ISAAC: You doing OK?

DEANNA: I'm doing fine.

ISAAC: Good.

DEANNA: I don't remember whether I told you, but I was very proud of you last night. For winning.

ISAAC: Thank you.

DEANNA: And the things you said about me in your speech, they were lovely.

ISAAC: You had a tough category. Everyone's commented on that. Helen Hunt and all . . .

DEANNA: That was last night, and now we move forward. The beautiful thing about the Emmys being on Sunday night is that we all go right back to work on Monday morning.

ISAAC: That's very healthy.

(They smile at each other for a beat.)

DEANNA: So. This week's script. There's something that jumped out at me —
you know, just thumbing through this morning.

ISAAC: What's that?

DEANNA: The blows, at the end of the scenes? In five scenes Ezra and I are on
stage together at the end, and in three of them, Ezra has the last joke.

ISAAC: *(Thumbing through a script.)* Really? I don't tend to pay attention to that.
(Sees something and smiles.) Some good jokes.

DEANNA: But darling, don't you think the audience would rather see me have
the funnier lines?

ISAAC: You want me to start counting jokes now?

DEANNA: No, no. I'm not saying that. Just . . . think about taking care of me.
You do have an aptitude for it.

(They hold each other's gaze, the moment growing a little more charged.)

DEANNA: I hope I didn't get you in too much trouble last night. Your poor
wife in bed with the flu, and all . . .

ISAAC: Well, as a matter of fact . . .

DEANNA: I knew it. Sorry.

ISAAC: . . . Meredith and I had a long talk after I got home. I'm going to move
out for a while. It's going to be hard, with the kids and all, but . . . I think,
well . . . considering everything . . .

(Beat.)

DEANNA: *(Realizes.)* You're in love with me.

(Beat.)

ISAAC: Yes. I have been. From the beginning. From before the beginning.

DEANNA: My, my.

ISAAC: So. I said it. *(After a moment.)* Are you just going to stand there?

DEANNA: What do you want me to do?

ISAAC: I want you to tell me what you think about that. About what I just
said.

(Pause.)

DEANNA: I like it. I like it a lot.

ISAAC: *(Smiles.)* What about Petey?

DEANNA: Petey? I hope he had the sense to find a cab. *(Then.)* I'll send him
packing.

(She goes to him.)

ISAAC: I left my wife.

DEANNA: I know.

ISAAC: But I feel good. I mean . . . I don't feel any doubt . . . I don't feel frightened . . . I'm just . . . *happy.*

DEANNA: I'm happy too.

ISAAC: Are you?

DEANNA: Mm-hmm.

(They begin to kiss, but Deanna starts laughing.)

ISAAC: What?

DEANNA: Just imagining Kurt's face when he hears about all this.

ISAAC: *(Laughs too.)* Kurt . . . shit . . .

(Then Isaac looks at her, and kisses her deeply.)

DEANNA: Is the door locked?

ISAAC: It doesn't matter. I'm way too tired to do anything.

DEANNA: *(Gently pushing him down on the sofa.)* Who said you had to do anything?

(Isaac is speechless. Deanna begins unbuttoning his shirt.)

DEANNA: Anything you'd like to tell me?

ISAAC: I love you.

DEANNA: Anything else?

ISAAC: *(After a beat.)* The door locks by itself . . . ?

DEANNA: *(Laughs, then, unfastening his pants.)* Anything else?

(Beat.)

ISAAC: I'll look at the ends of those scenes?

DEANNA: *(A big smile.)* Thank you.

(And she continues. Blackout.)

END OF ACT I

Act II
Scene Five

*A ballroom, one night earlier. The "Deanna" table at the enormous indus-
try bash which follows the Emmys. Seated, from left to right: Barry, Petey,
Deanna, and Kurt. Everyone's already had a drop too much to drink, and
Deanna a little more than that. While Kurt and Deanna talk, Barry scans
the room and Petey focuses on the rolls and butter.*

DEANNA: I just came here wanting the show to win *something*. For me personally, just being nominated for an Emmy was more than enough.

KURT: But think about it. What did Ray Romano say? "The Emmy goes to
Isaac Brooks, *for 'Deanna.'*" Your name was all over that show tonight.
Every award, every *nomination*, is a victory for you personally.

DEANNA: I look at it that way, too.

KURT: Everyone knows it's all about you. From day one, I never even considered calling the show anything but "Deanna."

DEANNA: Was that *your* idea? Because I really like it.

KURT: Television is a medium of personalities. Take a strong personality whom
the audience loves and connects with, and everything else that surrounds
that personality basks in it and is nourished by it.

BARRY: By the way, you should've won, Deanna. Helen Hunt is a no-talent
piece of shit.

PETEY: I know *I'm* sick of her.

(But Deanna doesn't acknowledge Barry, and Barry doesn't acknowledge Petey.)

KURT: This is why I'm happy to have a star be executive producer of her own
show. Especially when we're blessed with such an intelligent star.

DEANNA: I can see that.

KURT: So feel free to be more active in that role this season. Feed Isaac ideas:
enrich the series with incidents from your childhood, moments from your
own everyday life.

DEANNA: I have those.

KURT: I'm sure you do. And believe me, Isaac will be happy to have you contribute. *(Then.)* Speak of the devil!

*(Isaac enters, carrying his Emmy. The others clap for him, and he holds the
statuette aloft.)*

ISAAC: Can you believe we won these! *(He lets out a howl.)*

(Ezra enters, also carrying an Emmy.)

DEANNA: Ezra!!

(She rises and looks at him from across the stage. The others look on and await this moment with trepidation.)

DEANNA: I am so unbelievably . . . incredibly . . . wildly . . . *proud* of you!

EZRA: Thank you. This really belongs to both of us.

DEANNA: I know!

EZRA: I want to dance with you, Deanna —

DEANNA: Yes, let's dance.

EZRA: — in just a few minutes. First I have to find Candice Bergen. She has a story to tell me about the White House. She said to remind her, "Orson Welles."

(He shrugs at the incongruity and starts off. Barry follows him.)

BARRY: Ezra — wait up. *(As they go.)* I got you a little present . . .

(They exit. Deanna downs her drink and holds out the glass to Petey.)

DEANNA: Petey, I'm tired of champagne. Get me a margarita.

PETEY: Jeez, the lines at the bar were so long.

DEANNA: Why do you think I'm sending *you?*

PETEY: Good point. *(He takes a roll and goes.)*

(Isaac begins lovingly polishing his Emmy with the tablecloth. Deanna watches unhappily. Isaac realizes she's watching, and her displeasure, and quietly places his Emmy on the floor, under the table.)

DEANNA: The important thing here is perspective. I am a star. Ezra is a *co*-star. And what's he going home to? That wife of his? That mousy little fag hag? I, on the other hand, live a rich, full, sexually adventurous life. *(Turns to Isaac.)* So. How did you manage to ditch *your* wife tonight, anyway?

ISAAC: *(Laughs.)* I didn't ditch her; she has the flu.

DEANNA: Mm. What a shame. That's certainly one hell of a shame. *(Then.)* What's *her* sex life like?

ISAAC: . . . My wife's?

DEANNA: When she doesn't have the flu. I've been wondering. I bet it's pretty damn good. *(Looking straight at him.)* Don't look so confused, Isaac, this is called flirting.

KURT: *(Rising.)* I should go find my date.

DEANNA: *(Without looking.)* Sit down.

(He does.)

DEANNA: *(Turns to him.)* Your "date." That manager, what's her name — ?

KURT: Alicia.

DEANNA: Alicia. Golub. Kurt. I know you are not fucking Alicia Golub.

KURT: I don't think I'm going to comment on that either way.

DEANNA: Jesus Christ, you don't have to. It's obvious. Alicia Golub is so clearly that sort of convenient business friend who's perfect for the Emmys: you can ignore her all night while you work the room, and she can ignore *you* all night while *she* works the room. Plus, you've got nothing to lose being seen with her, because everyone already knows you date twenty-two-year-old actresses. Of course, if you're both drunk and bored enough, you and Alicia Golub *could* end up fucking tonight, but I don't think that's the way this evening is going to play out.

KURT: No?

DEANNA: No. *(Looks right at him.)* Personally, I think tonight you'll be tempted by something a little more . . . adventurous.

(Now Isaac rises.)

ISAAC: I'm going to go say hi to Reuben.

DEANNA: *(Again without looking.)* Sit down.

(He does. Deanna takes a seat between the two men.)

DEANNA: Nobody's going anyplace. Not until we find out just *how* adventurous everyone here *is*.

(Deanna reaches and slides Kurt's champagne glass next to hers. Then she slides Isaac's glass over to join them. With the three glasses lined up in front of her, she faces forward and waits for the other two to figure out what she's talking about. It dawns first on Kurt, then on Isaac. Each man takes a moment to steal a self-conscious glance at Deanna, and the other man beyond her. Deanna simply and quietly relishes the moment. At length, Petey returns with her margarita.)

PETEY: Man, I got lucky with that line. One bartender went off duty just when I got there, and now there's a fifteen-minute wait, easy. Here you go, Dee. Margarita.

DEANNA: Thank you, Petey. *(To the others.)* Do you fellows need refreshers?

KURT: Yep.

ISAAC: Uh-huh.

DEANNA: Petey, would you be a real dear and fetch a couple margaritas for the boys?

PETEY: *(Starts to object, but.)* Sure, Dee.

(And he starts off, but comes back and picks up his roll and a couple more from the tray in the center of the table. Then he exits.)

DEANNA: *(After him.)* Make sure the bartender uses enough triple sec! *(Turning to Isaac, laughing.)* Get it? Triple sec? *(Then, serious.)* Isaac, a writer needs to feast at the table of experience. Have you ever tried any sort of . . . triple sec? *(She giggles again.)*

ISAAC: No.

DEANNA: Kurt?

KURT: Yes.

ISAAC: Really?

KURT: Two women, though. Actually, I paid one of them.

DEANNA: Cool.

(Isaac reacts, looks at each of them. Then starts to settle into the idea. Beat.)

KURT: I'll let Alicia know she can take the limo.

(He jumps up and goes. Deanna sips her drink, a triumphant grin on her face. Beat.)

ISAAC: I have fantasized about you since I was — *(Off her warning look.)* — well, since *you* were — *(Again.)* — OK, but I've fantasized about Deanna Denninger for a long, long time. And since I've met you, I've been fantasizing more than ever. And you know what else? If *I* had to go and shake off *my* date, I know damn well that Kurt Fast wouldn't be sitting around here waiting for me to come back. The man pays my salary, and he isn't going to like what I'm doing now, but damn it, this is the biggest night of my life, and I want you, and I want you for myself. *(Forcefully.)* I don't want to share you.

DEANNA: But Isaac. Darling. I've already got my heart set on something more . . . elaborate. Why should I settle for just you?

ISAAC: *(Looks straight at her, dead serious.)* Because when I'm finished with you, you're going to feel like you've been with *three* men.

(Beat. Then Deanna picks up her purse, stands, and begins to walk off. She pauses and looks back over her shoulder.)

DEANNA: Let's take my car. *(And she goes.)*

(Isaac, not quite believing that this worked, swigs the rest of her margarita and follows. Long beat. Kurt returns, finds the table empty. He cranes his neck, looks around the room. Then he thinks he's figured it out . . . smirks . . . and looks under the table. But of course, all he finds down there is Isaac's Emmy, which he picks up and regards. Then Petey returns, carrying two margaritas. He gives one to Kurt, puts the other down, and returns to his rolls and butter. Then Kurt hands him Isaac's margarita. Dumbfounded, Petey takes it. They silently toast one another, Kurt knowing they are both now odd men out, Petey still happily oblivious. Blackout.)

Scene Six

Eight months earlier, Isaac's office. Isaac and Deanna sit opposite Ezra, who stands, auditioning. Deanna reads with him.

DEANNA: "It's not easy being a woman senator. Everybody wants a man."

EZRA: "Lord knows I do. You don't know what it's like out there. All the good ones are either married or straight."

(Isaac and Deanna laugh.)

ISAAC: Very nice work, Ezra. Cool, man.

EZRA: Well, this character is a hoot. My agent said you already shot the pilot?

ISAAC: Yeah, but we'll reshoot the Jeremiah scenes. The actor we had was fucking great, but . . . you know how it gets with the network.

EZRA: Oh. Been there. Reuben Hanover?

ISAAC: Mm-hmm. Reuben Hanover wouldn't know he was sitting on a good actor if he had half of John Malkovich sticking out his ass.

DEANNA: To be honest, talented as the other actor was, I could never quite believe he was gay. You on the other hand . . .

EZRA: *(Laughs.)* That just made my week.

DEANNA: I hope I didn't offend you.

EZRA: No, not at all. I take that as the highest compliment to my acting, all things considered.

ISAAC: Meaning?

EZRA: First of all, I'm married and I have three kids.

ISAAC: And second of all?

EZRA: Well . . . *(Smiles at Deanna.)* . . . let's just stick with the first of all. *(Then.)* Hey — good luck with this.

ISAAC: Really nice work, Ezra. We'll be seeing you again, I'm sure.

EZRA: Thank you.

(And he exits, laughing, closing the door behind him.)

ISAAC: What was that about?

DEANNA: Beats me.

ISAAC: He's good, though, don't you think?

DEANNA: Best yet. By far.

ISAAC: Mm-hmm. I bet even the network's going to love him.

DEANNA: He's cute, too. Queer as a three-dollar bill, but adorable.

ISAAC: *(Checks his sheet.)* That's the last one for today. *(Looks at her.)* You still having fun?

DEANNA: *(Smiles.)* Time of my life.

(She takes his hand and gives it a squeeze. A knock on the door, then Ezra sticks his head back in.)

EZRA: Sorry — forgot my bag.

(He crosses to pick up a portfolio beside a chair.)

DEANNA: *(Flirty.)* Couldn't stay away from me, could you.

EZRA: Glad you remember, after all these years. I almost thought you forgot.

ISAAC: You guys know each other?

EZRA: Well, I wasn't going to say anything, but since Deanna brought it up . . . we had an affair — just a long weekend, really — about eight years ago, in Miami. *(Back to her.)* Anyway, Deanna, great seeing you again. *(Then, to Isaac.)* Bye. *(And again he leaves.)*

ISAAC: Well.

DEANNA: *(Flustered.)* You know, he *looked* familiar.

ISAAC: And gay.

DEANNA: I remember now. Miami. Yes. He looked absolutely gay, but turnable. And that's exactly what happened. My, my. If he has three kids, they certainly have *me* to thank, that's for sure.

(Kurt enters.)

KURT: Am I interrupting something?

ISAAC: No, we just finished a casting session. I think we found our new Jeremiah.

KURT: Well, he'd better be good, because a lot of people are going to be watching him every week.

ISAAC: You have news?

KURT: Just talked to the network: we go on in March . . . Thursday, nine-thirty.

ISAAC: No!

KURT: Yes.

ISAAC: No!!

KURT: I kid you not.

DEANNA: Yay!!!

(She hugs Kurt and then Isaac.)

ISAAC: That's great. Would you call Reuben and set a casting session so we can bring this guy in?

KURT: Sure. In fact, why don't you step down the hall and talk to Sherwin about getting a test deal started.

(Isaac nods and exits.)

DEANNA: You're going to love this actor, Ezra Twain. He's fabulously talented. And . . . *(Significantly.)* . . . a graduate of the Yale School of Drama.

KURT: While I have you . . . *(Closes the door.)* Something has come up. The network is not entirely happy with how Isaac handled the issue of replacing Paul Nardino.

DEANNA: He thought Paul was great in the pilot.

KURT: But the network didn't.

DEANNA: Isaac spoke his mind. He went to the mat for the actor he believed in. They should respect him for that.

KURT: He pushed too hard. And he didn't have many friends to begin with.

DEANNA: What are you saying?

KURT: They'd like to add someone to the mix. Another show runner.

DEANNA: In addition to Isaac.

KURT: Yes. To team up *with* him. Someone they feel they can talk to.

DEANNA: Someone above him.

KURT: They'd have the same title.

DEANNA: But someone above him.

(Pause.)

KURT: Isaac hasn't worked on a hit in a long while. And he's never created one. It's not like one man writes a series by himself, anyway. Isaac will be hiring a whole team under him —

DEANNA: *Under* him.

KURT: Plus maybe we'll bring on one above, too.

DEANNA: He'll walk. You know that. He'll quit the project if you do this to him.

KURT: Perhaps he will . . .

DEANNA: Not perhaps. He's gone. And you know it.

KURT: *(At length.)* Isaac is talented, but he's . . . volatile. Look, we are where we are because of him, as I'll be the first to admit. For that, he's been well compensated. If the series has legs, he'll continue to be compensated, and quite generously, I might add. The way these things are structured, he could leave the show before episode two and still end up making fifty million dollars.

DEANNA: You're rationalizing.

KURT: Isaac Brooks may not be the man to take us to the next level.

DEANNA: I think he is.

KURT: Your opinion matters, but it's not the only one that matters.

DEANNA: What's your opinion, Kurt?

KURT: The network would prefer someone else.

DEANNA: But what's *your* opinion?

KURT: My opinion is . . . the network would prefer someone else.

(After a moment.)

They told me this when they mentioned the strong possibility of the Thursday time slot.

DEANNA: "Strong possibility"? I thought you said . . . *(Realizes.)* We get Thursday nine-thirty, but only if you get rid of Isaac.

(A silence.)

DEANNA: What did you say?

KURT: I said I would talk to you. Nothing is going to happen without your blessing. But if you want the time slot, and if you want the network behind the show. *(He lets the thought hang.)*

DEANNA: Rather desperate of them, to want to make a change so quickly.

KURT: Everyone's in panic mode. Overall viewership keeps shrinking, what with cable, new networks, the internet. We're watching a grand business slowly die.

DEANNA: You've done quite well.

KURT: True. But the networks are making it harder and harder for independent studios like ours. Throw in the prime-time game shows, those reality shows . . . it's a grim picture. I'd like to be a nice guy here, but you know what they say: nice guys finish on Showtime.

DEANNA: When I first considered doing TV, everyone told me it was a kinder business than features.

KURT: It was. I used to think of television as the happiest confluence of art and commerce. People made good shows and made good money, and there was room for kindness.

DEANNA: But not any more.

KURT: Unfortunately, no.

(A long silence.)

DEANNA: Part of me wants this show so badly that I'm willing to go along with what you're asking. The other part of me knows that I only *have* this opportunity because I believed in Isaac Brooks, and Isaac Brooks believed in me. I've been around long enough to know how you suits operate. You can't write the shows, you can't act the shows; on your own, you couldn't generate one single laugh in front of the camera or behind it. But you can divide and conquer. If Isaac Brooks is gone, Kurt Fast becomes a hero to the network, and the one life jacket left for me to cling to. Well, forget it, mister. I have to look myself in the mirror. And I know that if my career has one more life left in it, it's because Isaac Brooks decided to give it to me. So if Isaac Brooks is going down, I'm going down on him. With him. *(Blackout.)*

Scene Seven

Six months earlier. Isaac and Barry in Isaac's office.

BARRY: *(Significantly.)* Howie . . . Long.

ISAAC: The football player?

BARRY: Thirteen.

ISAAC: No. Where?

BARRY: Where. Fox, where. They think he's a breakout star on their pregame show. The feature thing didn't pan out, now he's looking at sitcoms, and Fox'll go thirteen on the air. I know his manager. Howie's in town next week — I can get you in a room.

ISAAC: It's not like I have any Howie Long ideas floating around.

BARRY: You don't even need one. Kim Markowitz says they want him to be a football coach at an inner-city high school. Lot of black kids with dope attitude.

ISAAC: Barry, what the hell do I know about an inner-city high school?

BARRY: You know that it's thirteen on the air. Should I set a meeting?

ISAAC: Let me think about it.

BARRY: How's Meredith?

ISAAC: She's good. We're good. We're going to Laguna next week.

BARRY: Nice.

ISAAC: Sixteenth anniversary. We really liked meeting Stacy, by the way. She's gorgeous.

BARRY: She's history.

ISAAC: You said you were in love.

BARRY: Body that wouldn't quit, no denying it, but you weren't exactly going to see her on the awards platform at the science fair, know what I mean?

ISAAC: You're dating somebody else already.

BARRY: *(Shrugs.)* A couple. *(Off Isaac's laugh.)* Hey, if I could find myself a Meredith, I would settle down in a heartbeat. *(Then.)* Your papers are up.

ISAAC: Already? Send over the new ones.

BARRY: Oh, don't worry, the agency is sending them. They never forget that. Point is, I'm not sure I want you signing them.

ISAAC: Why not?

BARRY: Listen, you're the only client I'm saying any of this to.

ISAAC: What's going on? You making a move?

BARRY: There are moves to be made. If I want to make them, there are moves to be made.

ISAAC: I thought you loved it there.

BARRY: It's not the same. The new guys, they're assholes. I mean, I was in the mailroom with fucking Brendan, we sat right next to each other when I was on Irv Mechanic's desk and Freddie Kovell was busting his balls. Now, just because he's in features and I'm in TV, he treats me like a fucking peon.

(A silence.)

ISAAC: You're in trouble.

BARRY: *(Quickly.)* No. No. *(Beat.)* I mean, not *trouble* trouble. You know, like I said . . .

ISAAC: There are moves to be made.

BARRY: Right.

ISAAC: If you want to make them.

BARRY: Exactly.

ISAAC: Look, whatever. You've been my guy for eight years. You move, I go with you. Even if you decide to hang your own shingle and go it alone.

BARRY: That means a lot to me, man. *(Changing the subject.)* Howie Long.

ISAAC: Forget Howie Long a minute. I might have something.

BARRY: What, a concept?

ISAAC: Talent.

BARRY: Really? Who?

ISAAC: Deanna Denninger.

BARRY: Pass. Pasadena. That is one piece of business you want to run away from. That's run, not walk.

ISAAC: Well, she called me.

BARRY: Deanna Denninger called you? Herself?

ISAAC: She saw a "Frasier" rerun, the one I freelanced, and she was talking about it at dinner with some mutual friends. So they gave her *Off the Rack,* remember that one?

BARRY: The screenplay.

ISAAC: Right.

BARRY: Sure. I love that one.

ISAAC: She did too, and the friends gave her my number. John and Jan Polachek.

BARRY: John Polachek, I know that guy. How does he know Deanna Denninger?

ISAAC: Through the kids.

BARRY: Fuck, I need some kids. So what did she say when she called?

ISAAC: She wanted to buy me dinner. I freelance an episode, two years later Deanna Denninger wants to buy me dinner. How's that for a residual?

BARRY: Dinner? You two and the Polacheks?

ISAAC: Just me and her.

BARRY: Bullshit. You're not going to go, are you?

ISAAC: Already went.

BARRY: What did Meredith say?

ISAAC: *(Laughs.)* Come on, if Meredith can't trust me after sixteen years . . .

BARRY: This is Deanna Denninger.

ISAAC: And this is me, Barry, not you.

BARRY: Yeah, yeah. Deanna Denninger is a praying mantis. She will fuck you
and then eat your head.

ISAAC: Hey, I've heard the stories. I figured it was a pass, no-brainer, but come
on, how do you say no to *that* dinner?

BARRY: Fine. It's still a Pasadena. But go on, what happened?

ISAAC: Well . . . she surprised me. She's charming. She says she's learned. She
says she's changed. Smart, funny, no attitude, no ego. She still looks great.
I mean, *great.* I'm telling you, Barry: you put this woman on the air, and
America is going to fall head over heels in love with her.

BARRY: *(Sighs.)* You poor bastard.

ISAAC: So I pitched her that Washington idea I had a couple years ago.

BARRY: *(Remembers.)* The woman senator, right? You pitched it to Jobeth
Williams.

ISAAC: Yeah —

BARRY: And Geena Davis.

ISAAC: Yeah —

BARRY: And Olympia Dukakis.

ISAAC: That's the one.

BARRY: And after they all passed, you told me you were relieved — you said
it was the hackiest idea you ever had in your life.

ISAAC: It is the hackiest idea. But when I was sitting there the other night, it
hit me: you tailor it to her personality, maybe you have something. And
anyway, she likes it.

BARRY: So what. She's ice cold.

ISAAC: So am I.

BARRY: You're not ice cold. You're underrated right now, that's all. I ever tell
you my theory? At any given moment, nobody in Hollywood is where
he should be. Everyone is either overrated or underrated . . . and it keeps
changing, so there's always hope. Look at Mel Brooks. Seventies he's doing
fart jokes — that sells, the studios treat him like he's a fucking genius,
they'll make any piece of shit he wants. Overrated. Then a couple of 'em

bomb, for ten years the poor guy can't get a green light on Ventura Boulevard.

ISAAC: Underrated.

BARRY: Exactly. Then he takes an old movie, writes a couple songs, puts it on Broadway — now he's a genius again. You watch, not only will Hollywood welcome him back, but they'll start teaching "Spaceballs" in film school.

ISAAC: Well, I've been overrated and I've been underrated, and believe me, overrated was better.

BARRY: And we'll get you there again, amigo. But in the right way. Trust me. You're a good writer. A quality individual. You've got a family, you've got your priorities, all of that comes through in every script you write. You just need the right project.

ISAAC: I need a star.

BARRY: Howie Long.

ISAAC: I don't have Howie Long.

BARRY: I can get you in a room. Deanna Denninger . . . well, let's just say she's no Helen Hunt.

ISAAC: Maybe all she needs is a real writer who can put good material in front of her every week. Don't forget, *she* sought *me* out; going in, there's already a relationship based on respect.

BARRY: I hate to burst your balloon, but this isn't the first time I've heard about this. Her agent called me, sniffing around about you and a couple of other people.

ISAAC: Really?

BARRY: So I ran it by Kurt.

ISAAC: What did he say?

BARRY: Pasadena. Kurt hates her. His words: "Deanna Denninger's only appeal was that every straight man in America wanted to fuck her, and she actually let enough of them that the rest figured they had a shot." He says she's a tough sell at any network.

ISAAC: Kurt doesn't know everything.

BARRY: Look, if Kurt Fast says he can't sell the buyers on Deanna Denninger, you don't want to try to push that boulder uphill alone.

ISAAC: She has a network if she wants it.

BARRY: *(Skeptical.)* She tell you that?

ISAAC: John Polachek plays tennis with Reuben.

BARRY: With Reuben? Really?

ISAAC: Yeah.

BARRY: John Polachek plays tennis with Reuben Hanover.

ISAAC: Mm-hmm. At Riviera.

BARRY: Where the fuck does John Polachek get off playing tennis with Reuben Hanover?

ISAAC: Who cares? It's tennis.

BARRY: How does John Polacheck even *know* Reuben Hanover?

ISAAC: Through the kids.

BARRY: *Fuck.*

ISAAC: Anyway, apparently Reuben says Deanna's not a big commitment, but there's definitely a script deal.

BARRY: *(A deep breath.)* I'm telling you, not just as your agent, but as your friend: stay away from this person. She is not a quality individual.

ISAAC: You really got a bug up your ass. You know her or something?

BARRY: Not really.

ISAAC: Then what is this? I mean you do business with some of the biggest scumbags in town.

BARRY: You kidding? I *represent* some of the biggest scumbags in town.

ISAAC: Then what is your problem with her?

(Long pause.)

BARRY: Oh, there was a thing with my sister. *(Then.)* But that's not your concern.

ISAAC: What with your sister?

BARRY: No, I shouldn't have even said that much. You're the client, I work for you. Your best interests are the only thing that matters.

ISAAC: Is this the one I met? Twin sister, right?

BARRY: Barbara.

ISAAC: I met her at your house. She lives in Vermont or something.

BARRY: Maine. We're close. Very, very close. Twins — you know. She used to live out here. She was married to Stan Brody.

ISAAC: Director, right? MOW guy.

BARRY: Yeah.

ISAAC: He's your brother-in-law? I never knew that.

BARRY: *Was* my brother-in-law. Deanna busted it up. Barbara never got over it. Took my nephew and moved clear across the country, put on fifty pounds.

ISAAC: Aw, shit.

BARRY: It's a very small business, Isaac. You screw somebody, somebody screws you, the next day you still meet the guy for breakfast at the Peninsula.

It's business, so you get over a lot of shit in a hurry. Still, there are some things that . . .

(A silence.)

ISAAC: Then I can't do this. How can I do this? This is beyond business. This is real life.

BARRY: Well . . . if working with Deanna Denninger was the right career move for you, I would suck it up. I'd have to.

ISAAC: No. Forget it. (Beat.) Look, she's just a script deal anyway, right? Howie Long's thirteen on the air. Get me in a room.

BARRY: Proving once again: you are a quality individual. (Beat.) But look: if — if — it didn't work out with Howie, and we went through all your other options, and there was nothing else out there for you that was halfway decent, we would go with Deanna Denninger and I would suck it up. I'm your guy, first and foremost.

ISAAC: I appreciate that, but I'm telling you, no way, I'm not going to put you in that position. I would never do that to you. (Beat.) Howie Long.

BARRY: Howie Long.

ISAAC: Fuck Deanna Denninger.

(Blackout.)

Scene Eight

The restaurant, two nights earlier. Isaac and Deanna, well into dinner and well into a bottle of wine.

DEANNA: Let's talk about you now.

ISAAC: All right.

DEANNA: Which of my movies was *your* favorite? (Then.) I'm joking. You.

ISAAC: Me. Well, I've been married sixteen years. We have two girls, twelve and nine.

DEANNA: Family man.

ISAAC: That's me.

DEANNA: And what would you *really* like to be doing?

ISAAC: What do you mean?

DEANNA: Surely you're dying to write the Great American Novel. Or at least the Great American Screenplay.

ISAAC: No, not at all. The Great American Sitcom would do it for me.

DEANNA: Is that so.

ISAAC: It is. Novels are dying. Theater is already dead.

Movies are all about the director, and besides, TV comedy has been better than movie comedy for a good thirty years now.

DEANNA: I never thought of that.

ISAAC: And with the amount of material required, television truly is a writer's medium. Over five or six years, you can get to know those characters better than any character in a movie, or even a book. I actually believe TV is the last great refuge for a real writer. Plus, when you make twenty million people laugh all at once — that doesn't suck. *(Then.)* "Hearts of Stone."

DEANNA: What about it?

ISAAC: My favorite movie of yours. "Hearts of Stone," easily.

DEANNA: The one where I take off my shirt.

ISAAC: Well, yes. Now that you mention it. And, may I add, truly first-rate . . . cinema.

DEANNA: Thank you.

ISAAC: *(Looking back over his shoulder.)* They keep us sitting at the bar for forty-five minutes, and now we can't even get a waiter to bring us a menu. It's like going out to eat at the DMV. Which one do you think is ours?

DEANNA: That one keeps looking over here.

ISAAC: Probably has a crush on you. You must get stared at all the time.

DEANNA: Oh, I used to, but not so much any more. *(A quiet moment, then:)* You know, last year I went to Kansas City and did dinner theater. I did. I hadn't had a job in L.A. in two years, so I went to Kansas City and played Abigail Adams in *1776*. First time I had ever been on stage. I'd been a movie star. I had an Oscar Nomination.

But I was petrified — *petrified* — to get up in front of all those people. Opening night, my first entrance, my first cue . . . and the words just didn't come. *(Laughs.)* The local critics had plenty of fun with that, boy, and I thought, I've really hit bottom. But I went back out on that stage the next night, and the next, and the night after that, and conquered my fears. And then I started learning how to make a connection with those people beyond the lights. And I liked it. And it made me determined to come back to L.A. and get my own sitcom, so I could make that kind of connection week after week. It's not the money; I have plenty of money, I was always very careful that way. It's the work, in its purest form. I miss it so, Isaac. I never realized I would.

ISAAC: You could find a hotter writer, you know.

DEANNA: I did my homework. They all say you were the flavor of the month about ten years ago.

ISAAC: Closer to fifteen.

DEANNA: I read two more scripts since we talked on the phone. *Days of Lemon* is hilarious.

ISAAC: Thank you.

DEANNA: And the woman in *Powder Blues* reminds me so much of my own mother.

ISAAC: Really?

DEANNA: I actually cried a little at the end. Isaac, writers may lose their heat in Hollywood, but they don't lose their talent. Those are the best scripts I've read in a long time. That's why I went after you.

ISAAC: Thank you. *(Then.)* You know, it's funny. Almost any other business, we'd still be in our primes.

DEANNA: I wasted some of my prime. I didn't always behave as well as I should, and that probably cost me some opportunities. It all came so easily, I didn't really appreciate what I had. If I get another chance, I'll do some things differently, that's for sure. I bet that waiter is ours.

ISAAC: If he is, he isn't very good. Let's hope he can act, so he has something to fall back on.

(Petey enters, comes to the table.)

PETEY: Hey, Dee.

DEANNA: Petey!

(They kiss. And kiss. And kiss.)

DEANNA: Isaac, this is Petey Ryan, my fiancé.

ISAAC: Good to meet you.

PETEY: Good to meet you.

(Isaac withers at Petey's handshake.)

ISAAC: Strong grip, there.

DEANNA: *(To Petey.)* What are you doing here?

PETEY: I was on my way to my session with Rory, and I stopped by to kiss you.

DEANNA: Aren't you sweet. *(To Isaac.)* Petey has a personal trainer work him out four times a week, and I pay for it. I figure, I'm the beneficiary. *(Provocative.)* Right, Petey?

PETEY: Yeah. *(Laughs, then matching her tone.)* You're the beneficiary, all right.

DEANNA: Uh-huh. I'm the beneficiary.

PETEY: Yeah. You're the beneficiary.

ISAAC: I feel like I'm in a Noel Coward play.

PETEY: I'm gonna be late. Nice meeting you, Isaac. Later, Dee.

DEANNA: Bye, darling.

(He goes.)

ISAAC: Nice guy. Your fiancé?

DEANNA: Yes, but . . . it's not really serious. *(Off his look.)* He fucks like a bull and he walks the dog.

ISAAC: You're a little . . . how should I say this? You're saltier than I expected.

(Deanna laughs.)

ISAAC: I mean, in your movies, you have this . . . elusive . . . ice princess thing going. But in real life . . .

DEANNA: I fuck and I'm proud.

ISAAC: Yeah.

DEANNA: Do you find it off-putting?

ISAAC: No not in the least. There's something very refreshing about it. Very winning.

DEANNA: It's who I really am. That ice princess image is just something these male directors kept imposing on me. I never wanted it.

ISAAC: The real you — this should be the TV series.

DEANNA: *(Laughs.)* You think America's ready for that?

ISAAC: Oh, yeah. I do. *(Beat.)* You know, I wasn't going to pitch you anything tonight, but I've had one idea for a while which I really love, and I've been waiting for the right person to make it work. Senator's wife, living in Washington, *in* that world but not *of* that world, you know what I mean? Then, halfway through the pilot, the senator dies . . . and they ask her to finish out his term.

DEANNA: Me? A senator?

ISAAC: Yes. But one with exactly your personality: real, honest, earthy, an every-woman who's movie-star beautiful . . . America would eat it up.

DEANNA: I would love to play a character who's actually close to me.

ISAAC: And you should. That's the thing that works on TV — that marriage of character and actor that's so natural, you almost can't tell the difference between real life and television.

DEANNA: I like the sound of that.

ISAAC: Yeah?

DEANNA: Yeah. *(Then.)* Let's do it.

ISAAC: *(Surprised.)* Let's do it.

(They smile and they clink glasses.)

DEANNA: Isaac, if you get involved with me, I make you one promise.

ISAAC: What's that?

DEANNA: I'll make your life a lot more interesting.

ISAAC: Somehow, I don't doubt you.

(*Ezra enters, wearing a waiter's uniform and carrying menus.*)

EZRA: Sorry for the delay. My name is Ezra and I'll be your waiter tonight . . .

(*Blackout.*)

Scene Nine

A Malibu cocktail party, five years later. Deanna looks out over a railing at the Pacific. Isaac enters and approaches.

ISAAC: Pardon me: didn't you used to be Deanna Denninger?

DEANNA: (*Without looking.*) No, sorry; you must be mistaken.

ISAAC: Mm . . . I couldn't be: I've seen all your movies. And weren't you on television? Briefly?

DEANNA: Television . . . oh yes, that. Bad move. Some writer talked me into it.

ISAAC: So. How've you been? The papers don't mention much about you any more.

DEANNA: Did you come out here just to take snide potshots?

ISAAC: No, I came out to get some air. The snide potshots are a bonus.

DEANNA: And here I was, sure you were just drawn by my natural magnetism.

ISAAC: (*Laughs derisively.*) If anything, I wanted to tell you that I survived your natural magnetism. And it was a lot easier than you'd think.

DEANNA: Well, bully for you. Did you ever get another show on the air?

ISAAC: I can't believe you don't know the answer to that.

DEANNA: Tell me. Please.

ISAAC: No.

DEANNA: No, you won't tell me?

ISAAC: No, I did not get another show on the air. Are you happy?

DEANNA: Happy? Me? Of course. Wasn't I always the happiest person you know?

ISAAC: Yes. Always.

DEANNA: Did you ever remarry?

ISAAC: No. Heard your marriage ended, too.

DEANNA: Mm. Couple of them.

ISAAC: Actually, I've been with someone for almost a year.

DEANNA: Really? Is she here tonight? I'd love to meet her.

ISAAC: No such luck.

DEANNA: Hm. Home with the flu?

ISAAC: Delivering a baby. She's an OB, works at a free clinic downtown.

DEANNA: How very noble.

ISAAC: Helps me keep perspective. You wouldn't believe how many things in her life are more important than her hair.

DEANNA: Too bad Petey didn't hit you with that can.

ISAAC: Petey. How did things go south with you and old Petey?

DEANNA: The usual.

ISAAC: Hard to believe a crackling wit like his couldn't keep you amused.

DEANNA: Don't be so smug. I've slept with smarter men than you.

ISAAC: Never a better comedy writer, though.

DEANNA: That's a presumptuous statement.

ISAAC: Not really. I kept watching the show.

DEANNA: Good. That's the one question I've always wanted to ask you. It wasn't very strong after you left. I often wondered what you thought.

ISAAC: I thought Ezra was funny.

DEANNA: You're still a prick.

ISAAC: I heard you banned Kurt from the set.

DEANNA: He's an evil man. And his dick is not nearly as big as they all say.

ISAAC: Good. That's the one question I always wanted to ask *you.*

DEANNA: By the way, regardless of what he tells everyone, I never slept with Barry. Never.

ISAAC: Is that a fact.

DEANNA: It is.

ISAAC: Well, the poor boy doesn't know what he missed.

DEANNA: *(Looks at him.)* Why, thank you. *(Then.)* I didn't fuck Warren Beatty when I was nineteen without learning a little something about fucking. *(They both break into grins, then real laughter. They regard each other for a long time, smiling now.)*

DEANNA: *(Off his look.)* What are you thinking?

ISAAC: I'm trying to figure out how long ago you were nineteen.

DEANNA: I am not that old, mister. Believe it or not, plenty of men would still sleep with me.

ISAAC: Hey, *I'd* still sleep with you.

(Deanna takes a step closer to him as he drains his drink.)

ISAAC: If I didn't know you so well.

(He slaps the drink down on the railing and crosses off.)

DEANNA: *(After him.)* Fuck you! You don't know me.

ISAAC: *(Offstage, screams.)* Don't know you?!

(Isaac runs back on.)

ISAAC: Don't *know* you? After I got fired, I didn't work for two seasons because I came away with a reputation for being difficult! I went into therapy for the first time in my life — four sessions a week! My two daughters, I only see them summer and Thanksgiving! What the fuck more could I possibly need to know about you?

DEANNA: *(Turns on him.)* If I still had a dozen writers, I could come back at you with something really . . . you know, good. *(Then, softening.)* But all I can think of on my own is, it's nice seeing you again. *(Beat.)* Can I buy you dinner?

(Isaac looks at her, stunned. Finally.)

ISAAC: All right.

DEANNA: What do you feel like eating?

ISAAC: I'm easy. *(Then.)* Anything but jacks.

(Blackout.)

END OF PLAY

BE AGGRESSIVE

By Annie Weisman

For my sister

. . . what would the music
be without you
since even through
the chorus of pure joy
the tears hear you
and nothing can restrain them.

— from "To the Sorrow String" by W. S. Merwin

PLAYWRIGHT'S BIOGRAPHY

Annie Weisman's latest play, *A Totally Meaningful Ritual,* was commissioned by A.S.K. Theater Projects and has received developmental support from the Sundance Writers Retreat, Manhattan Theatre Club, and the Mark Taper Forum. Her play *Hold Please* was produced Off Broadway in February 2003 by Working Theatre Company after being commissioned and produced by South Coast Repertory. *Be Aggressive* premiered at La Jolla Playhouse in July 2001 and went on to production at Theatreworks, Palo Alto, and Dallas Theater Center in 2002 and to publication by Dramatists Play Service. Ms. Weisman is now collaborating on a new musical for Trinity Repertory and has recived an NEA/TCG grant to develop a new play with South Coast Repertory. She has received commissions from the Mark Taper Forum and La Jolla Playhouse. She has had short pieces in the Aspen Comedy Festival and the Actor's Theater of Louisville Humana Festival and has written teleplays for HBO. Ms. Weisman is a Southern California native, a member of the Dramatists Guild, and a graduate of Williams College.

ORIGINAL PRODUCTION

Be Aggressive premiered at the La Jolla Playhouse in July 2001. It was directed by Lisa Peterson. The cast was as follows:

LAURA	Angela Goethals
HANNAH	Daisy Eagan
PHIL	Mark Harelik
LESLIE	Jennifer Elise Cox
JUDY	Linda Gehringer
CHEERLEADER CHORUS	Tamala Horbianski, Carly Kleiner, and Joy Osmanki

CHARACTERS

LAURA: seventeen

HANNAH: eleven

PHIL: forties

LESLIE: seventeen

JUDY: forties

CHORUS: three young women who play Cheerleaders, Cops, and
Protesters

*Note: It is my intention that Laura, Leslie, and Hannah be played young
adults, not children.*

TIME

The present.

PLACE

Vista Del Sol, a Southern California community by the sea,
and on the road.

BE AGGRESSIVE

Prologue

In darkness, we hear the sound of the ocean, then the sound of the freeway, then the sound of a horrible car crash. Silence. Lights up. Bright sunshine. Vista Del Sol High School by the sea. Cheerleaders in formation. The sound of pom-poms shaking.

CHEERLEADER 1: Did you guys hear?

CHEERLEADERS 3 AND 4: Dead.

CHEERLEADER 2: Who?

CHEERLEADER 1: Dead.

CHEERLEADER 2: Who?

CHEERLEADERS 1, 3, AND 4: Dead!
> *(Beat.)*

CHEERLEADER 3: Our maid's their maid's daughter.

CHEERLEADER 4: Our lawyer's their lawyer's son!
> *(Beat.)*

CHEERLEADER 3: My dermatologist lives on her cul-de-sac!

CHEERLEADER 4: My gynecologist lives next door!

CHEERLEADER 1: Dead. On Impact.

CHEERLEADER 3: Nuh uh! Vegetable. All night.

CHEERLEADER 2: Fifteen feet it threw her.

CHEERLEADER 3: Fifty feet, I heard.

CHEERLEADER 1: The hole in her head was the size of a golf ball.

CHEERLEADER 2: Bocce ball!

CHEERLEADER 3: Honeydew!

CHEERLEADER 4: Cantaloupe!

CHEERLEADER 1: It was on Avenida Avocado.

CHEERLEADER 2: That's where my stepmom power walks!

CHEERLEADER 1: They said that her dad had to come identify her mom's mangled body.
> *(They gasp. Pause.)*

CHEERLEADER 1: I heard it's at the Surfswell Plaza Freeway Project.

CHEERLEADER 3: I heard she got so crushed that they're gonna pave part of her right into the new road.

CHEERLEADER 4: I heard that too.

CHEERLEADER 3: I heard her head hit like a hackey sack on a handball court.

CHEERLEADER 2: Like boobs on a boogie board.

CHEERLEADER 4: Splat!

CHEERLEADER 1: They drove away.

CHEERLEADER 2: Who?

CHEERLEADER 3: The ones who killed her.

CHEERLEADER 4: They hit her into a hole and they drove away. *(Beat.)* Vista Del Sol is like, a dangerous place.

(Pause.)

CHEERLEADER 1: 'K guys! Practice!

CHEERLEADER 2: Without her?

CHEERLEADER 1: Without her.

CHEERLEADER 4: Is she coming back?

CHEERLEADERS 2 AND 3: Yeah, can she cheer any more?

CHEERLEADER 1: She'll be back. *(Beat.)* HANDS ON HIPS!

ALL: SMILES ON LIPS!

CHEERLEADER 1: *(A cheer.)* READY?

ALL: OK!

CHEERLEADER 1: H! *(Clap! Clap!) (Clap! Clap!)*

CHEERLEADER 2: E! *(Clap! Clap!) (Clap! Clap!)*

CHEERLEADER 3: L! *(Clap!)*

CHEERLEADER 4: L! *(Clap!)*

(They wait for the "O." It doesn't come. They continue.)

CHEERLEADER 1: H! *(Clap! Clap!) (Clap! Clap!)*

CHEERLEADER 2: E! *(Clap! Clap!) (Clap! Clap!)*

CHEERLEADER 3: L! *(Clap!)*

CHEERLEADER 4: L! *(Clap!)*

(Clapping, stomping. Lights shift.)

ACT I
Scene One

Lights up on Laura in her room with her little sister Hannah. They are getting dressed.

LAURA: O.

HANNAH: What?

LAURA: Nothing.

(Pause.)

HANNAH: It's not fair.

LAURA: I know.

HANNAH: I don't have a whole black outfit. And you do. I only have separates. My blacks don't even match. It's not fair!

LAURA: Then change.

HANNAH: Into what?

LAURA: I don't know.

(Beat.)

HANNAH: Is everyone in all-black outfits, or just us?

LAURA: Um, I don't know. People wear brown too. I'm pretty sure. Earth tones.

(Pause.)

HANNAH: Is our age group expected to wear dark sunglasses? 'Cuz I only have pink ones and purple ones and teal ones.

LAURA: Well, tough.

HANNAH: My new tortoise tee has some black in the trim. Can I wear that?

LAURA: Why are you asking me?

HANNAH: Well who am I supposed to ask?

(Beat. Pause.)

LAURA: OK, no. I don't think you should wear your tortoise tee.

HANNAH: How come?

LAURA: DUH! It's COMPLETELY inappropriate!

HANNAH: How would YOU know! How would you know anything!

(Laura throws an item of clothing at Hannah.)

HANNAH: Ow! Bitch!

LAURA: Oh, please!

HANNAH: You hurt me!

LAURA: Stop being a baby!

(Pause.)

HANNAH: What's she gonna look like?

LAURA: We don't have to look at her.

HANNAH: How do you know? You're older. They'll put you in front. You'll have to look.

LAURA: No they won't.

HANNAH: They'll put you in front, and they'll put me in back, with Grandma. It's not fair! She gives me dirty cough drops from the bottom of her purse. She makes that clucking sound 'cuz we don't know the prayers. I don't see why you get to sit in front and look.

(Pause.)

LAURA: It's just 'cuz I'm older.

    (Beat.)

HANNAH: Who's gonna make my waffle?

LAURA: Dad, I guess.

HANNAH: And my hot chocolate?

LAURA: Yeah.

HANNAH: He can't do the hot chocolate.

LAURA: He can too.

HANNAH: From scratch? No way! Mom doesn't use a mix. She starts with Ghi-radelli Bitter Chocolate. I put my finger in it once and it was like dirt. Dog crap. It was awful tasting. You have to know how to make it.

LAURA: You just mix it with sugar and milk.

HANNAH: But you have to know exactly how much. And I don't know and he doesn't know and neither do you! *(She turns and looks at Laura.)* When did you get boobs?

LAURA: Hannah . . .

HANNAH: When did they get so big?

LAURA: Hannah.

HANNAH: I swear you got them today! You're not supposed to have big fat boobs! *(Beat.)* Are you sexually active?

LAURA: Where did you hear that?

HANNAH: When are we going back to school?

LAURA: I don't know.

HANNAH: Are you going to cheer practice?

    (Beat.)

LAURA: I don't know.

HANNAH: Are you gonna be in the game one greeting cheer?

LAURA: Of course!

HANNAH: Not if you don't go back to practice! *(Beat.)* If you're not in the game one greeting cheer, you can forget about being a stunter this year. You're gonna be a spotter again, senior year, the last cheer year of your life!

LAURA: That's none of your Goddamn business!

HANNAH: Are you still going to work?

LAURA: I don't know!

    (In silence they pick up brushes and brush their own hair. Lights shift revealing their dad, Phil,. somewhere else, just looking out.)

LAURA: Everybody's gonna be looking at us! It'll be sort of like a pep rally, but quiet, and we're the pom squad. So we have to think about how we're gonna look! Come here.

(Hannah is making a mess of her hair. Laura reluctantly goes to her and begins to comb it.)

HANNAH: When's Dad coming back?

LAURA: I'm not sure.

HANNAH: I heard something from the other room. When Dad was calling everybody. He said something about the size of the hole it made in her head. When her head hit the ground! *(Panic. Builds.)* Are we gonna have to look at it? The hole? *(Laura accidentally pulls Hannah's hair.)* Ow! Bitch!

LAURA: Fine! Then do it yourself!

(Laura moves away from her.)

HANNAH: Do you think the stuff from my old room is still in the storage facility? I'd like to get that mobile back I had over my bed. That circled around and played those stupid tinkly little songs? I bet Dad has it logged on a list on his computer. I want to get it back! My mobile? *(Beat.)* You have humongous disgusting tits.

(They hold a tableau. Hugging themselves. Lights shift. Phil, still in a pool of light. A cop speaks to him in voice-over.)

COP: We're very sorry for your loss.

PHIL: Thank you.

COP: This is really just a technicality. We just have to clear up a few facts with you regarding your whereabouts on the afternoon of the eighth of September.

PHIL: I was at work.

COP: You were at your office.

PHIL: No. I was out in the field, actually. At the survey site.

COP: So you were out at the wetlands.

(Beat.)

PHIL: No.

(Beat.)

COP: I'm sorry, sir, to have to answer these questions, in light of your loss, it must be very difficult, but we do need to verify —

PHIL: No. It's not that. It's that . . . *(Beat.)* They are not "wetlands." That's a myth generated by the environmental lobby. It is a man-made bog. We're draining and reclaiming it for the community.

COP: OK.

PHIL: I was doing a check-in at the survey site on Camino Del Mar. It was only the first day of our hydrology study and we're already two weeks to public review. I walked the site, did a quick touch base with the team heads. Routine stuff. *(Beat.)* And when I got back to the office, the message light was blinking, so I pressed the button and the machine said, "You have one message." And then my daughter Laura said, "Dad come home. Mom is dead." And then the machine made a very long beeping sound and said, "To erase press two. To save press three." *(Beat.)* You don't think you're ever gonna hear that.

(Pause.)

COP: Sir, was your wife an avid jogger?

PHIL: She was very physically fit.

COP: She jogged routinely?

PHIL: After breakfast. That was her morning.

COP: And she was aware of the dangers of jogging on the old bluff road? The traffic diversions being caused by the Surfswell Plaza Freeway Project?

PHIL: We were always telling her. I would tell her.

COP: Because where her body was found . . . she was jogging in a very dangerous place. Any car doing fifty, particularly if you're not local and they don't know how to take the Caminito Curve . . .

PHIL: I told her! I bought her a treadmill and put it in the atrium where there's plenty of natural light. But she wanted to jog on the old bluff road. Look out at the ocean. "Why else live here?" That's what she'd say. I told her she was nuts. The traffic. The erosion. *(Beat.)* She's the one who found this neighborhood. We drove up the coast looking for a place to live, when she was pregnant with our first child. A place with ocean views, reasonable seafood restaurants, and good schools. Eighteen years, we've been here. That's a lifetime in this community. Got in on the first tract development they cut into the hill. The iceplant hadn't grown over the retaining walls yet. The cement dividers were still soft. We got a Spanish stucco ocean view unit for forty-five thousand dollars. It's worth ten times that now, as a tear-down! *(Beat.)* She planted this eucalyptus seedling when we got here. It's a huge thing now. Towering over the breakfast nook. Dropping leaves in our jacuzzi. *(Beat.)* I tried to tell her that things had changed.

COP: I think we have the information we need to pursue the matter. Thank you for coming in. I want to tell you, how our hearts and prayers go out to you and your family.

PHIL: We're Jewish people actually. My family. We don't practice, not since we moved here. But just so you know, if you are gonna pray. Pray Jewish. *(Lights shift. The sound of the freeway.)*

Scene Two

Laura's house. Laura is sorting through her dead mother's clothes with her dad.

LAURA: We're out of stuff.
    (Phil holds up a hat.)
PHIL: Keep?
LAURA: I don't know.
PHIL: Give away?
LAURA: I guess.
    (Beat.)
PHIL: What stuff?
LAURA: *(Irritated.)* Stuff me and Hannah eat! Like, food!
PHIL: Didn't people leave all that . . .
LAURA: It's weird casseroles. And like, pies. It's not stuff we eat.
    (She holds up a jacket. He points to a pile. She throws it in.)
PHIL: Well, then, you'll need to go to the market, I guess. Can you do that?
LAURA: Yeah.
PHIL: You know what to get?
LAURA: I used to push the cart sometimes. I know her pattern.
PHIL: What was it?
LAURA: What?
PHIL: The pattern.
LAURA: Just her way of going! The order of things?
PHIL: What order? What order was it?
LAURA: It was just the way she went, that's all!
PHIL: Tell me the pattern.
LAURA: Produce, dairy, frozen stuff. Bread, drinks, checkout. And she tells Hannah "NO!" when she picks up a Snickers and then she pays, and that's all.
    (Beat.)
PHIL: We may have to set you up with a checking account.
LAURA: I don't want a checking account! I'll use her ATM card.
PHIL: Do we know the code?
LAURA: She told it to me.
PHIL: She did?
LAURA: Yeah.
    (Beat.)
PHIL: So you'll go to the market, and you'll get what she got. And you'll make something. You'll do that chicken that she does.

LAURA: With sun-dried tomatoes?

PHIL: That's the one.

LAURA: I don't know how to do that.

PHIL: Why don't you look at her cookbooks and figure that one out.

LAURA: She didn't use cookbooks.

PHIL: Well then just figure it out, somehow, and we'll sit down to a nice family dinner. I think it's important that we do that. For Hannah.

LAURA: Can't we just order something?

PHIL: No.

LAURA: But, that's gonna take all afternoon, and I just —

PHIL: You just what?

(Laura holds up a shirt to her chest.)

LAURA: Keep?

(Phil looks at it for a long beat. A memory. He touches the shirt.)

LAURA: Keep or give away?

(He smooths the shirt over Laura's shoulders.)

PHIL: Looks like you could wear this one.

(Beat. Laura pulls away.)

LAURA: Can't we get a nanny?

PHIL: I don't want some person in our house.

LAURA: What if she was here after school, only?

PHIL: I don't want a stranger here that I don't know.

LAURA: What about Grandma?

PHIL: Your grandmother lives far away from us, and it's going to stay that way.

(Beat.)

LAURA: But I want to go back to my work.

PHIL: You don't have to work! We've told you that.

LAURA: I like my work.

PHIL: You need to be here.

LAURA: But.

PHIL: But, what?

LAURA: I want to go back to cheer practice.

PHIL: What?

LAURA: If I don't go back to cheer practice now I won't learn the game one greeting cheer and if I don't know the game one greeting cheer they'll cut me and I'll never make varsity!

PHIL: Varsity? For jumping up and down?

LAURA: That's not what we do!

PHIL: You jump up and down . . . and you yell.

LAURA: That's not what cheerleading's about!

(*Laura holds up a sexy black nightgown. They freeze. A sad and awkward silence. Phil takes the nightgown and lays it gently on the bed.*)

PHIL: Your mother was planning a family trip to Israel. You didn't know that. After the project, she wanted me to take the family on a trip to Israel. I said, are you nuts? The violence, the heat! But she said, no. Not by the coast. The coast is temperate and mild. Like here. Which makes a lot of sense for the promised land. Paradise. (*Beat.*) I have to work very hard and very late until the freeway opening. The project is at its most critical phase and your little sister and I will need you here!

LAURA: The freeway blows! Everybody says! It's gonna destroy natural resources!

PHIL: Do you have any idea what kind of population growth our country has seen in the last ten years? If we don't make a freeway to accommodate the Surfswell Plaza congestion, then before long, every four-by-four in the Inland Empire is gonna be gunning through our formerly walkable and charming downtown shopping district. You won't be able to park on Caminito Del Mango and walk to Krissie's Muffins without taking your life into your hands! And before we know it, they'll start bringing their inner tubes and their boom boxes full of John Cougar Mellencamp to our beaches. You won't be able to lay out on the sand anymore without some morbidly obese family eating their surplus cheese sandwiches and having a domestic dispute! Everything we have will be ruined!

LAURA: Krissie's Muffins is closing. Everybody has to go to the Breads Etc. Megastore!

(*Pause.*)

PHIL: I don't want you doing things. I want you here.

(*Lights shift.*)

Scene Three

Sound of a blender. Then two. Then six. Then all the blenders of the southland, whirring at top speed. Lights up on the smoothie shop. Laura with her hand on the top of a blender. Her body shakes. Then stops.

LAURA: 'K. First you add the Basic Boost.

(*Adds something to the blender. Puts on the top. Loud blending sound again. Her body shakes. It stops.*) Now the All-Pro Protein. (*Adds something.*) Then, ask if they've tried any of our Smoothie Madditives, which are: Mood Lift,

Memory Boost, Energina, Youth Jolt, and Mega-Cleanse. Then, tell them about this week's promotional madditive, which is — *(Checks a list.)* Moby Thick! — a fiber blend made from the baleen of humpback whales whose healthful benefits have been enjoyed by the Inuit people for centuries. And we guarantee these whales died naturally by old age and not poaching or disease. *(Beat.)* Then, they pick their fruit. Oh, you're supposed to try to push the new fruits. Otherwise, people will just get like, strawberry or banana. There's a new hybrid of kiwi and cassava melon — it's called Kissava — and it has twice the mineral content of an average serving of fruit. You're supposed to say that. *(Beat.)* Oh, and the cool thing is, no matter what you put in, you always add our special smoothie starter at the end. That way, the color always comes out the same. The healthful rosy flush that customers want. If you forget this final additive, the color will be a grayish brown. And when they see it, they won't like it. *(Beat.)* Oh, and if you mess it up, just throw it away and do it over. We never run out of anything. Somebody comes in at night and stocks it all, I guess. *(Pause.)* I don't know how. Some of the stuff is like, really heavy. *(Beat.)* K, that's it. That's all you need to know. *(Pause.)* Now blend! *(Noise of a thousand blenders. Lights shift.)*

Scene Four

Transition. Cheer practice. The sound of stomping. They come together into a tight Fosse clump and hit a solid frozen pose. Tight. Serious faces. On another beat, they smile. On another beat, they sneer. On another beat, they do a sexy, wild dance, then freeze. They do a bunch of military-style moves. They freeze.

CHEERLEADER 1: READY?
CHEERLEADERS: OK! *(Beat.)*
    GO!
    FIGHT!
    WIN!
    GO!
    GO! FIGHT! WIN!
    (Music stops.)
LESLIE: I have an idea!
CHEERLEADER 1: Excuse me!

LESLIE: I made something up.

CHEERLEADER 2: YOU made something up?

LESLIE: Well, since we don't have Laura anymore, I thought I would make up a new game one greeting cheer that works without her. And I thought I would up the ante a little too, while I was at it.

CHEERLEADER 3: Up the what?

LESLIE: Make it BETTER! 'K?

CHEERLEADER 1: OK, Leslie. Show us your cheer.

LESLIE: *(Builds.)* Thanks. OK. It goes, "Seagulls, DOMINATE! This is our year — make it great! Victory! Is our fate! Our battlefield is your booty. Our field is your behind. We'll stomp you down we'll beat your butts I SAID WE'LL BLOW YOUR MIND!" *(Beat.)* And on "mind," we're gonna basket toss Katie into a double "V" toe-touch jump, and while she's in the air, we're gonna turn out and do a fully extended "happy face with jazz hands," then we'll catch Katie, slap back to buckets, smile, sneer, and then here's the thing . . . *(Beat.)* Simultaneous standing back tucks. *(Cheerleaders gasp.)*

LESLIE: 'K?

CHEERLEADER 2: Um, what?

LESLIE: Simultaneous standings! It's de riguer among competitive squads. *(Beat.)* And we could get butt patches that say stuff when we flip! *(Beat.)* 'K? *(Silence. No one responds.)*

CHEERLEADER 1: Um, I'm glad you took the initiative to make up a cheer, but . . . standing back tucks? Isn't that where you fling your body upside down? Backwards?

CHEERLEADER 3: You basically throw your head on the ground. *(Beat.)*

LESLIE: Yes, it'll take some commitment. But together we can conquer it. *(Beat.)* And it'll be thirty-two karat when we nail it, I swear to you. *(Beat.)* 'K? *(Silence. Laura walks out from behind the pack of cheerleaders. She is not in her practice uniform. Everybody except Leslie sees her. They freeze. It's her first time back since it happened.)*

LESLIE: *(Continued.)* I said . . . 'K? *(Silence.)* You guys? *(Beat.)* 'K? *(The cheerleaders exit. Laura slowly approaches Leslie. Long pause.)*

LAURA: 'K.

(Lights shift.)

Scene Five

Laura's house. Hannah is hysterical.

HANNAH: A chains aw! With a chain saw!

LAURA: What kind of chain saw?

HANNAH: That kind that makes the loudest noise ever and cuts down trees! He was cutting it down!

LAURA: When did he do this?

HANNAH: He said, "It would fall down on the house at any time." He said we were in danger. He said, "They're notoriously shallow-rooted trees." He researched it.

LAURA: What are?

HANNAH: Eucalyptus!

LAURA: Where did he get a chain saw?

HANNAH: We had one in the garage.

LAURA: We did?

HANNAH: Under stuff. Under all the late-night television fitness machines. *(Beat.)* It was SO LOUD! Like somebody making a smoothie out of a tennis racket! It sounded AWFUL! *(She cries.)*

LAURA: He cut down our eucalyptus tree?

HANNAH: It tipped over our property line and onto the Stevenson's Sports Court. And that's grounds for a lawsuit! And then he just sat down on the stump and goes, "It's over. It's over. It's over."

LAURA: Like that?

HANNAH: Three times. *(Beat. Then hysterical.)* We have a murdered mom!

LAURA: It's not murder!

HANNAH: Murder happens here!

LAURA: It's not murder! It was a hit-and-run. A terrible accident.

HANNAH: But they said it was a death trap and she jogged right into it!

LAURA: Shhh!

HANNAH: What killed her?

LAURA: Just, a car. Hit and run.

HANNAH: But what EXACTLY? What?

LAURA: The impact, I guess.

HANNAH: How? Did it crush her heart? Did her brain just pancake? Did it make a hole that made all her living parts come out and mix with the dirt in the road?

LAURA: No! She died instantly. She just closed her eyes and died.

HANNAH: Whose fault is it?

LAURA: It's not anybody's fault. It was an accident.

HANNAH: There's faults! There's always faults! Underneath us! Cracks in the earth that open up and shake and swallow things.

(Beat.)

LAURA: Shhh, no. She closed her eyes and died.

HANNAH: How do they make asphalt?

LAURA: I don't know.

HANNAH: Cement is one thing, and asphalt is a lot of things mixed, right? Gravel and cement and tar. How do they mix things that are so hard?

LAURA: They have to heat them up, I guess.

HANNAH: When they're hot they're soft and when they get cold they're hard!

LAURA: That's right.

HANNAH: Our mom got crushed in the road!

LAURA: No! shhh. Come here. It's OK. Come here.

(Hannah falls heavily into her arms. Laura rocks her, strokes her hair. She tries to sing the tune their mother used to sing to them. Hannah begins to calm.)

LAURA: Shhh. I'm here. I'm here.

(Lights shift.)

Scene Six

Cheer practice has just ended. It's just Laura and Leslie.

LESLIE: I'm so glad you're allowed to come back to practice now.

LAURA: Thanks.

LESLIE: We missed you. (Beat. Serious.) I missed you.

LAURA: I wasn't sure you knew me.

LESLIE: We're squadmates!

LAURA: Well, yeah, but. I just didn't think you could really tell me and Laura Lesterson apart sometimes.

LESLIE: Well, now I can. 'K?

LAURA: 'K.

LESLIE: I'm pregnant.

LAURA: Oh.

LESLIE: Sean Ashton, that needle dick prick wank. He said he'd pull out right away. Well so did Nixon in 'Nam!

LAURA: Who?

LESLIE: You know, Sean. He drives the magenta Jetta! We hooked up at Kira Kartanian's Labor Day Weekend pool party on Friday night and then we cruised to TJ on the school day off. His mom LIVES in the Seabluff Bungalow Suites! I dumped him the day after. And Stacie said he bragged to the whole long-boarding team that I swallow. *(Beat.)* And then I skipped my P and now I have to get the dustbuster!

LAURA: What a jerk. Are you telling your mom?

LESLIE: She'll just be SO "unconditionally supportive." She'll just hold my hand and be all, "I remember my first abortion." And then she'll "treat me" to that stinky Iraqi facialist on coast highway that I HATE. And then she'll buy me a "cozy" brown sweater.

LAURA: OK.

LESLIE: That's all?

LAURA: Yeah. *(Beat.)* OK.

(Pause.)

LESLIE: I'm just kidding. Wanted to see how you'd react. Bravo. You were totally mellow. I knew you could be my best friend.

LAURA: I can?

LESLIE: Yes. I mean I did get pregnant last year and I got an abortion. But not by Sean Ashton. He asked for my number and I was like "1-800-AS IF!!" *(Pause.)* I knew you were my best friend.

(Long pause. They slump down. The sound of the ocean.)

LESLIE: There is absolutely fucking nothing to do in this stupid boring town. *(Beat.)*

LAURA: Do you want to go shopping?

LESLIE: I was just joking about joking. I am pregnant. But you are my best friend.

LAURA: 'K. Do you want to go to the beach?

LESLIE: I'm too white.

LAURA: Me too.

LESLIE: I'm chalk.

LAURA: I'm butt.

LESLIE: Let's get smoothies.

LAURA: Had one at work today.

LESLIE: Let's get wraps.

LAURA: 'K. Have you tried the sprouted cajun?

LESLIE: I get the cumin-scented barbeque tofu. No cheese no sour cream.

LAURA: They have the new ocean size sodas. We can get sixty-four ounce diet cokes.

LESLIE: 'K. You work?

LAURA: Yeah. At Smooth Talk.

LESLIE: Oh. Are they hiring?

LAURA: You need to work?

LESLIE: If I want department store cosmetics! If my mom had her way I'd be the Maybelline monster that she is. I used to work at Krissie's Muffins, but they're on the path of the Surfswell Plaza Freeway Project. Everything's changing you know. We can't even park our own cars at our own beach anymore! They're putting in a PAY LOT with SEVERE TIRE DAMAGE and everything! We're all getting paved right under. *(Beat.)* At RJRJ — R.J. Reynolds Junior High School where I went in Winston-Salem — cheerleading was WAY more important than it is here. At RJRJ we had a weight limit and if you exceeded it, you were dismissed in a very solemn ceremony. With paddles and everything.

LAURA: Wow.

LESLIE: But these bitches are dedicated to nothing but fear and mediocrity. Won't practice basket-tossing on the quad just because it's kind of cementy? Have they ever heard of TRUSTING their spotters?

LAURA: I couldn't more totally agree.

LESLIE: We're never gonna convince these guys to care about cheer as much as we do. They just don't have our commitment to the sport. *(Beat.)* We should go to a professional cheer-training program. Like the Spirit Institute of the South.

LAURA: What's that?

LESLIE: It's actual professional cheerleading. The Competitive Sport of Cheer. Cheer for cheer's sake. We're talking Bible Belt intensity not this perky coastal shit. *(Beat.)* I have a brochure. It's very compelling. They have a standing back tuck. Pre-req. It's hard core.

LAURA: Do you have a standing?

LESLIE: Not yet. Do you?

LAURA: Not yet. *(Beat.)* Wait, standing back tuck? Isn't that where you like fling your body upside down?

LESLIE: Backwards! *(Beat. Leslie approaches Laura.)* There is a stirring passage in the brochure from the founder of the institute. She went from doing a dozen doughnuts and a fistful of quaaludes a day to being the first person to execute a flying heel stretch on an all-girl competitive squad. Today, she offers the skills and experience garnered on her journey to girls like us. *(Beat.)* It's two weeks. A thousand bucks. We should go.

LAURA: To S.I.S.

LESLIE: To their winter training intensive. We'd have to nail our standings. And get the cash. We could do it. It's a leadership seminar as well as a professional cheer training program. This year's spirit slogan is "Believe to Achieve." And they televise the final session. Let's pick weights. I say ninety-five 'cuz the camera adds ten so that's really one hundred and five.

LAURA: So we should just say one hundred and five then.

LESLIE: But the camera adds ten.

LAURA: OK so let's say eighty-five, 'cuz that's like ninety-five, then.

LESLIE: Eighty-five pounds. Done.

LAURA: Um, why don't they have cheerleader anchors like they have sports anchors? People who are experts on who the cheerleaders are and what they're doing. Everyone likes to look at girls more than guys, so looking at the cheerleaders at professional sports events could become like the most popular spectator sport! *(Beat.)* God, I don't usually talk so much!

LESLIE: It's called spirit! We should go.

LAURA: But we'd have to train. We'd have to get good. Maybe we should get private coaching!

LESLIE: Yeah!

LAURA: Like the little gymnasts do.

LESLIE: Yeah! But they start when they're like, three. And the good ones are all from countries with harsh dictators. But no, we have to live in America, land of the "rugged individual"! What a fucking joke!

LAURA: We'll just have to do it ourselves!

LESLIE: My mom is part of the coalition fighting the Surfswell Plaza Freeway Project. They raised money by selling this promotional cellulite cream called "Firm Up Against the Freeway."
(Beat.)

LAURA: Um, I heard we need the freeway. 'Cuz otherwise fat people are gonna clog up our charming downtown shopping district.

LESLIE: The freeway blows! It's gonna destroy natural resources! *(Beat.)* I know. I'm gonna make my mom get me fake boobs. Only instead, I'll use the money for S.I.S.!

LAURA: But won't she know when you don't get the boobs?

LESLIE: I'll just tell her they're subtle. Like yours.

LAURA: I don't have fake boobs!

LESLIE: We're squadmates. You can say you had your tits done. Gillian did.

LAURA: She did? I didn't know that.

LESLIE: You can just say!

LAURA: But I didn't! *(Beat.)* They feel fake sometimes. I swear. They're kinda hard. Kind of high up. They're like aggressive. *(Beat.)* But I swear to God they just came out of my own skin. My body must have made them. Fast! *(Beat.)*

LESLIE: My mom is totally flat. That's one of the reasons I hate her.

LAURA: Yeah.

> *(Long pause. The sound of the ocean. Laura stares out. She closes her eyes and throws her head back. Feels it.)*

LAURA: Standing back tuck.

LESLIE: Pre-req.

LAURA: Hard core!

> *(Leslie and Laura do one loud simultaneous clap, their hands in prayer pose. They turn and stare at each other, thrilled.)*

LAURA AND LESLIE: OH MY GOD!

> *(Transition. From the chorus, we hear "Got to go! Uh huh! Got to go! That's right! Got to go!")*

Scene Seven

> *Laura's house. Dinner. From the outside, the chorus continues:*

CHORUS: BIG N! LITTLE O! The Surfswell Freeway's got to go! Uh huh! Got to go! Say what? Got to go! *(Etc.)*
> *(Phil slams the window shut. Sits.)*

HANNAH: Who are they?

PHIL: They're wealthy women with nothing better to do.

HANNAH: How come?

PHIL: Because they have teenagers who . . . drive themselves.

HANNAH: How come?

PHIL: Because time passes! I don't know. They are bored women . . . They have nothing to do. So they've decided to take a swing at the freeway development.

LAURA: They're sponsored by the Earth Watch coalition. It's national.

PHIL: Is that right?

LAURA: They're a fully accredited environmental group.

PHIL: They're a bag of hammers. They've already cost taxpayers three hundred thousand dollars with this sham of a lawsuit. They're suing on behalf of some special breed of gopher which they claim Surfswell will make no more. Well I'll tell you something, this woman, the "leader" of the "coalition" — I'll tell you where her sympathy for the gopher comes from. Have you seen the woman's overbite? This girl could eat an apple through a picket fence! *(He chuckles. They don't. Beat.)* They are suing on behalf of some pellet-crapping pests.

(Pause.)

HANNAH: I thought . . . Remember, Yosemite? When she took us there. And we stayed in a cabin. And we had that nature guide who was her old friend from her Berkeley days? Who had the longest hair ever and the guitar with stickers on it? And remember how she talked different with her old friend from her Berkeley days? She called things "far out." Remember? Well didn't she say something like, how gophers do something super important, really? Remember?

LAURA: Pockets of air in the soil. They give the ground its very life.

HANNAH: Remember?

(Laura and Hannah share a moment.)

HANNAH: I like gophers.

PHIL: What's in this rice?

LAURA: I need some money. Our cheer team, we're raising money to go to this special cheer-training camp. We want to get really good.

PHIL: So?

LAURA: So, I want to go.

PHIL: How long?

LAURA: Two weeks. They have a land-a-standing-re-req. *(Beat.)* That means something.

PHIL: What about school?

LAURA: It's two weeks.

HANNAH: Where's North Carolina?

PHIL: What?

HANNAH: That's where it is, right?

PHIL: It's WHERE?

LAURA: I know you think it's nothing but it's not. We really want to go.

PHIL: Who's we?

LAURA: *(Beat.)* Our squad.

HANNAH: No, it's just her. And her one friend. They're the only ones that —

LAURA: It's our squad!

(Pause. Phil takes a bite of his food.)

PHIL: What's in this?

LAURA: Miso broth. I cooked it with miso broth.

HANNAH: What's a miso?

PHIL: It's related to the gopher!

HANNAH: Ewww! Laura!

LAURA: No, honey. It's made from a soybean and it's very good for you. He's teasing.

PHIL: Miso broth?

LAURA: I got it at the supermarket. They have this new world cuisine section? I just, got it.

PHIL: And you put it in our rice?

LAURA: She used to put stuff in it.

PHIL: She never put stuff in it. It was rice. She made us our rice.

LAURA: She put stuff in it. You don't know. I was making it. I didn't even know I could. My hands just put in the olive oil and browned the onions and toasted the rice and then I reached up like her to the cupboard above the stove. And there was the beef broth. She used to put in a can of beef broth instead of water and it would simmer in and soften it and make it rich. That's how she did it. OK. All this time.

PHIL: I don't want it different. I liked it before.

(Long pause.)

HANNAH: I love these wrinkly tomatoes, they're so weird. It looks like you're eating your ear or something.

PHIL: Your sister wouldn't put a — wait, uh-oh, my ear is gone! Laura came in my room, while I was sleeping, and she cut it off and threw it in the pasta sauce! Oh no!

(Phil chases Hannah around the table with a sun-dried tomato, she squeals and laughs. They spill out into the living room. Phil returns. To Laura, final.)

PHIL: Um, no.

(He exits. Sounds of chasing, playing, laughter. Laura lifts the window. We hear:)

CHORUS: Oh Yeah! Got to go! That's right! Got to go! You know it! Got to go! Now show it! Got to go! *(Etc.)*

(Lights shift.)

Scene Eight

Cheer practice.

CHEERLEADER 1: READY!

CHEERLEADERS: OK! —

> *(Loud clapping sound, first from the chorus, and then louder, like a hundred kids stomping in a gymnasium. Laura and Leslie stand together. The other cheerleaders surround them. Sweet, light.)*

CHEERLEADERS: B-E-A-G-G-R-E-S-S-I-V-E!

SO BE!

AGGRESSIVE!

BE! BE!

AGGRESSIVE!

LAURA AND LESLIE: *(Loud, violent.)* AGGRESSIVE!

CHEERLEADER 1: You guys, that was to loud.

CHEERLEADER 2: And too late!

CHEERLEADER 3: It was totally too loud and late!

CHEERLEADER 1: Do it —

CHEERLEADER 2 AND 3: With us!

CHEERLEADER 2: With us! What were you guys doing?

LESLIE: We were being what we're saying! FOR ONCE!

> *(Cheerleaders look at each other. Puzzled. Pause.)*

CHEERLEADER 1: We don't do the being. We do the cheering.

LESLIE: But —

CHEERLEADERS: Yeah?

LESLIE: I want MORE!

> *(Beat.)*

CHEERLEADER 1: It's gonna get cloudy out!

CHEERLEADER 2: Yeah, k'we just cheer?

CHEERLEADER 3: You guys? Spot us?

LAURA: No! We're not spotting!

CHEERLEADER 1: What?

LAURA: We're not! No!

CHEERLEADER 2: Why?

LAURA: 'Cuz, um, I mean, oh, I'm sorry. I don't know. I'm sorry.

> *(Leslie glares at Laura for a long moment. Laura shrugs and joins the squad. The cheerleaders go back to building their stunt.)*

CHEERLEADERS: B-E-A-G-G-R-E-S-S-I-V-E!

SO BE! AGGRESSIVE!
BE, BE! AGGRESSIVE!
(Laura moves into a spot position. Leslie refuses. Loud sounds of clapping, stomping. Lights shift.)

Scene Nine

Lights up on on Leslie's house. Smoke. Dinner.

LESLIE: You smoke!

JUDY: Smoke put food on your table.

LESLIE: Well I want boobs.

JUDY: You have boobs.

LESLIE: No, I don't!

JUDY: You've got plenty.

LESLIE: I'm a B!

JUDY: That's fine. That's good.

LESLIE: That's shit. B is for below the radar. I need a C.

JUDY: How much?

LESLIE: Five grand.

JUDY: Five grand? That's too much. It should be cheaper.

LESLIE: Well I'm sure I could get it done for a sixer of Dos Equis in a Tijuana parking lot. But do you WANT me to look like a thrift-shop water bed?

JUDY: It can be done for less.

LESLIE: Not with the skill I deserve and the discretion you desire.

JUDY: Discretion?

LESLIE: I'll tell unless you get me them.

JUDY: Tell what?

LESLIE: Tell why we have this pile of money now after you resigned from R.J. Reynolds. And even in a white-collar prison for women, I assure you, nobody likes a tattletale.

JUDY: You are way out of line. *(Beat.)* Four grand is the going rate.

LESLIE: I've done research. It's five grand. Five installments. One thousand up front. That's less than the lease on your Lexus. All you gotta do is say yes.

JUDY: Why don't you eat?

LESLIE: You know. I hate.

(Holds up a green leaf.)

JUDY: No daughter of MINE doesn't like cilantro!

LESLIE: I hate being in the same room as cilantro. It smells like burnt eyebrows and it tastes like potting soil.

JUDY: You're just trying to upset me. You know I chose it as the patio ground cover. Next you'll tell me bougainvillea is ugly.

LESLIE: Tacky! It looks like the front of a Mexican groomsman's polyester tuxedo shirt.

JUDY: Who taught you to be a racist?

LESLIE: Grandpa!

(Beat.)

JUDY: I bought this condo at the top of the market, bankrupted myself for you, so we could have a bougainvillea-covered stucco wall and the aroma of fresh local herbs wafting in through an ocean breeze. I got us out of the dead air of the humid shitty south, and I found a house, a semi-detached home, so we could make a fresh start. *(She lights another cigarette.)* Will you please eat something tonight? At least your crust.

LESLIE: I don't eat crust anymore.

JUDY: You used to only eat the crust.

LESLIE: I'm off carbs!

JUDY: But I made the fat-free chedderella mexipizza because I thought you'd eat it. I know it's a little bland, that's why I added the cilantro!

LESLIE: No carbs, no sugar, no crust.

JUDY: But it's a honey corn crust, from the *Sauce of the Southwest* magazine I've been getting. And I used the low-fat preparation option. *(Beat.)* You used to slide off the whole top, no matter what I put on it, and just eat the bottom. Even in front of company. It looked like the under side of skin. *(Beat.)* When I had my face-lift, I looked.

LESLIE: I eat the top now.

JUDY: You've become more and more like your father.

LESLIE: That's because, like him, I hate you!

JUDY: You've gotten that lip thing. That ugly lip thing.

LESLIE: It's called an adolescent sneer!

JUDY: No, it's him. *(Beat.)* I spent a thousand dollars on that low-fat lifestyle cooking class. And now it's "no carbs"?

LESLIE: For now. I'm flirting with the lifestyle of all-engineered nutrition. Powders, bars, and shakes. That's it. Laura and I are losing weight for cheer.

JUDY: Why do you hate me?

LESLIE: Because you're old and ugly.

JUDY: I'm forty-three.

LESLIE: He left you.

JUDY: He left us.

LESLIE: Get me my boobs. Or I'll go too.

JUDY: Where?

LESLIE: To my father.

JUDY: You don't even know where he is.

LESLIE: Yes I do.

JUDY: You're a little liar.

LESLIE: We have an epistolary relationship!

JUDY: You heard that word on Oprah!

LESLIE: He writes me all the time. I can smell his cologne on the paper. Obsession for Men. I write him all about my feelings. And all about you. He loves me.

JUDY: Your father wouldn't piss on your burning ponytail! He always thought you were a worthless ugly little girl from the time you were born till the time he walked out our sliding-glass doors. *(Beat.)* No offense, sweetie. He ended up hating me, too.

LESLIE: You'll never fit in here, Mother. You can't master the local vernacular like I have. You've got dirt under your pastel french tips and everybody knows it.

JUDY: What do you want from me?

LESLIE: Tits.

(Lights shift.)

Scene Ten

The phone zone. Leslie and Laura talk on the phone. Late at night.

LAURA: So?

(Beat.)

LESLIE: She's in.

LAURA: How?

LESLIE: Blackmail.

LAURA: What?

LESLIE: Told her I'd alert the media to her tattletaling against the tobacco company. It was such a bluff. I mean I know she's an asshole, but I wasn't sure she was a professional one. Now she's margarine on my toasted sesame bagel. *(Beat. Then angry.)* You can just say!

LAURA: What?

LESLIE: I've been let down before! You can just say you're not in any more. I knew you couldn't cut it anyway. You're just not Ginsu, like me. YOU'RE A FUCKING BUTTER KNIFE! You believed that crap about "We're not being, we're cheering!" You swallowed their horse pill of lies!

LAURA: No, no, no. I swear. I just didn't know how to do it. To my dad.

LESLIE: I thought you were gonna cash the death card!

LAURA: I couldn't do it. *(Beat.)* He just sits in the backyard, on this stump that used to be our eucalyptus tree? I have to walk over and say, "Dad, come inside. I already put the fajitas into the tortillas and they're getting all gummy." I have to make him come in and eat. Or he just sits there.

LESLIE: OK. *(Beat. Calm.)* Then, what vulnerability does your father have left? We went through everything else. What does he do for a living?

LAURA: He's a development consultant.

LESLIE: What does he do?

LAURA: He . . . consults.

LESLIE: Who?

LAURA: Developers!

LESLIE: Of what?

LAURA: Of, lots of stuff. Places. Things. You know.

LESLIE: No, what?

LAURA: Well, at this particular point in time, of the Surfswell Plaza Freeway Project.

LESLIE: Your dad's building the freeway over the endangered wetland and through our second favorite muffin place?

LAURA: He's not building it, he's consulting! He is mitigating its harmful environmental impact through the implementation of certain standards. Or something.

LESLIE: This could be perfect.

LAURA: How?

LESLIE: We find some flaw in his study, or make one up. Then we blackmail him to reveal it to the press. I'll pretend my aunt is an investigative broadcast journalist.

LAURA: What does your aunt really do?

LESLIE: She's a whore.

LAURA: Oh, OK.

(Beat.)

LESLIE: You have to think of yourself as powerful. Like . . . an interior decorator! You just fan out the fabric swatches and go, "HERE THEY ARE." *(Beat. Serious.)* You think I know how to do stuff? I don't. I just do it.

(Beat.) Sneak over tonight and stretch my middle splits for me. And spot my standing?

LAURA: You have your standing?

LESLIE: Almost. You?

LAURA: Um. I'm closer.

LESLIE: Come over!

LAURA: I can't leave. Yet. *(Beat.)* Sometimes I wonder . . . no it's stupid.

LESLIE: What?

LAURA: It's just, I wonder sometimes. Sometimes I think that I don't know what I look like. That I don't really have any . . . traits. That I might look at a picture I'm in and not know it's me. *(Beat.)* Ever think that?

LESLIE: You have low self-esteem.

LAURA: I do?

LESLIE: There's a whole-day self-esteem seminar at S.I.S.

LAURA: Do you have low self-esteem?

LESLIE: Yes! I hate myself! Duh!

LAURA: Oh.

(Pause.)

LESLIE: There's three kinds of cheerleaders, Laura. There's flyers, bases and spotters. Flyers and bases make stunts. And spotters, they get to stand around with their hands up making sure Laura Lesterson doesn't fall on her tennis elbow again. Spotters. IS THAT WHAT WE'RE GONNA BE FOR THE REST OF OUR LIVES?

(Lights shift.)

Scene Eleven

Lights up on dinner at Laura's house. Laura lights a candle at the empty place at the table. It burns silently. Phil and Hannah eat. Laura tries to get up the nerve to say something to her dad, but can't. Lights shift. Lights up on dinner at Leslie's house. Leslie uses her silverware to do little cheers, while she mouths the words. Her mother eats. She looks up. Leslie continues to silently cheer. Lights shift.

Scene Twelve

Laura's room. Laura and Hannah on the bed. Laura sits behind Hannah, brushing her hair.

HANNAH: *(Gently.)* Ow! Bitch!

LAURA: Sorry!

HANNAH: How come it was so quiet at dinner?

LAURA: I was thinking.

HANNAH: About what?

LAURA: I have a lot of stuff to think about now.

HANNAH: Can I go with you to cheer camp?

LAURA: It's not cheer camp. It's the Spirit Institute of the South.

HANNAH: Are the rest of the cheerleaders going?

LAURA: I didn't say I was going.

HANNAH: Well, are they?

LAURA: No.

HANNAH: Why not?

LAURA: Because they don't care like we do.

HANNAH: Like you and Leslie?

LAURA: Yes.

HANNAH: Are you guys same-sex lovers?

LAURA: Hannah!

HANNAH: Kelly Kembrook said you guys are total lezzies. I think it's OK if you
    are. I would be your ally. How come you don't hang out with any of the
    other cheerleaders? How come you and Leslie are never in the stunts? How
    come you guys are always on your knees, with your hands in the air?

LAURA: The girls on the squad are jealous of us because we have Bible Belt in-
    tensity. They're just perky coastal pep girls who want to hang at the games
    to get guys. They know us 'cuz we dare to care for cheer for cheer's sake,
    and we have our sights set high!
    (Beat.)

HANNAH: Dad wants you to start co-coaching my soccer team. She was going to.

LAURA: When?

HANNAH: Now, tomorrow. Two days a week. And he wants you to supervise
    my piano lessons. He doesn't want me alone with that Hungarian woman.
    So that's another day a week. And I might start taking classes to learn the
    ancient language of our people.

LAURA: Latin?

HANNAH: Hebrew!

LAURA: Where do they have Hebrew lessons?

HANNAH: At Temple Del Sol. It's the temporary temple in the coastal civic center. There's this Israeli woman, Shoshana Levis, and she's starting a Hebrew school class and Dad says I should go and learn it, and you should drive me there and read a beauty magazine in the car until it's over, and then drive me home. Like the others.

LAURA: I don't think . . . it's "Levis." *(Pronouncing it like the jeans.)*

HANNAH: Oh.

LAURA: I think it's "Levy." *(Rhyming with "heavy.")*

HANNAH: Oh.

LAURA: Since when are we Jewish?

HANNAH: Since ever.

LAURA: Well yeah but, Hebrew?

HANNAH: Dad says it will be meaningful to me. *(Beat.)* So that's every day of the week. That means no sneaking away to cheer any more and leaving me here to cover for you. *(Beat.)* Besides, you don't have a thousand dollars, or the balls to ask Dad for it!

LAURA: Who said it's a thousand dollars! Are you spying on me?

HANNAH: Yes. Somebody has to. Ow! You're pulling my bangs too hard!

LAURA: Sorry.

HANNAH: The mobile doesn't work anymore. The tinkle stopped!

LAURA: I'm sorry.

HANNAH: I don't want you cheering! I need you here!

(Lights shift.)

Scene Thirteen

Laura and Leslie at the freeway. At night. Alone. They cheer together over the loud sound of the freeway.

LESLIE: READY?

LAURA: OK! WE'VE GOT SPIRIT!
YES WE DO!
WE'VE GOT SPIRIT!
HOW 'BOUT YOU?

LESLIE: WE'VE GOT SPIRIT!
YES WE DO!

WE'VE GOT SPIRIT!
   HOW BOUT YOU?
LAURA: WE'VE GOT SPIRIT!
   YES WE DO!
   WE'VE GOT SPIRIT!
   HOW 'BOUT YOU?
LAURA AND LESLIE: *(Builds.)* WE'VE GOT SPIRIT!
   YES WE DO!
   WE'VE GOT SPIRIT!
   HOW 'BOUT YOU?
   WE'VE GOT SPIRIT!
   YES WE DO!
   WE'VE GOT SPIRIT!
   HOW 'BOUT YOU?
   (A loud, echoing boom is heard.)
LAURA AND LESLIE: HELLO? HELLO?
   (Loud, strange music. Laura and Leslie dance along, in a building frenzy as the cheer chorus chants.)
CHEER CHORUS: What? What? What? What What What What!
   Can you hear it? Can you hear it?
   Deep inside our pom-poms
   Something shushes when we cheer
   In the crack of our ligaments
   When we high kick
   The sound of our fingernails
   Growing from their quicks
   Our shoes could make a squeak
   That could shatter glass
   We could shake the bleachers
   Under everybody's ass!
   In our face in our fists
   In our knees in our knuckles
   In our bras in our jaws
   In our teeth there are muscles
   We could throw our bodies up totally high
   We could turn our sneakers
   Into pieces of the sky!
   (Music stops. Freeway sounds. Pause. Laura and Leslie catch their breath, entranced. Lights shift.)

Scene Fourteen

Sound of a thousand blenders. The smoothie shop. Laura has her hand on top of a blender. Her body shakes. It stops.

LAURA: 'K. This month's smoothie madditives have a spiritual theme. We have Buddhaberry, Messianic Mango, and Kabbalah-Cran. *(She goes to add one. Stops. A pause.)* You're supposed to know this prayer. The Kaddish? You say it at people's funerals. He was faking it. He put his head down, so the rabbi couldn't see his mouth. He didn't know the words to say. Not any of them. I could tell. He was embarrassed. There are words you're supposed to say and he didn't know them. *(Beat. She opens the cash register.)* We never run out of anything here! Everything gets filled back up. They put it all back! *(Beat.)* It doesn't matter what goes away! 'K? *(Beat.)* THEY JUST REFILL IT!
(Sound of a thousand blenders. Lights shift.)

Scene Fifteen

Lights up on the phone zone. Late at night. Laura and Leslie in their respective rooms. Hannah leaning against the wall overhearing. Judy and Phil in their respective beds, alone. Laura and Leslie whisper ferociously.

LESLIE: READY?
LAURA AND LESLIE: OK! B-E-A-G-G-R-E-S-S-I-V-E-
   SO BE! AGGRESSIVE! BE, BE AGGRESSIVE!
   (Beat.)
LAURA: We're going! As soon as they go to sleep.
   (Pause.)
LESLIE: Can you hear your dad sleeping yet?
LAURA: I'm not sure.
LESLIE: I hear my mom.
LAURA: She snores?
LESLIE: She just breathes. And I hear it. *(Beat.)* What killed her?
LAURA: Hit and run.
LESLIE: But what, what killed her?
LAURA: The impact. I guess. *(Beat.)* There was a logo from a car in the skin of her back. A brand-name fingerprint.

LESLIE: What kind of car?

LAURA: A Lexus.

LESLIE: What do you guys drive?

LAURA: A Cherokee Chief.

LESLIE: And?

LAURA: A Lexus. *(Beat.)* I hear him!

LESLIE: Breathing?

LAURA: Snoring.

LESLIE: It's time. I told you you could do it!

LAURA: What?

LESLIE: Get the money! From your dad.

LAURA: Right. *(Beat.)* Got yours?

LESLIE: Got it.

LAURA: Got the brochure?

LESLIE: Zipped in my duffel!

LAURA: Got the car keys?

LESLIE: Warm in my pocket!

LAURA: Which car?

LESLIE: The Lexus. My mom can drive the Jetta for once. *(They giggle, then silence.)* Ready?
(Beat.)

LAURA AND LESLIE: OK.
(Blackout.)

END OF ACT I

Act II
Scene One

Loud loud music. The music resolves itself into a loud loud sucking sound. Lights up. Laura and Leslie in the car. Leslie drives. They both have harnesses around their waists into which are fitted sixty-four ounce diet cokes. The music stops. The loud loud sucking sound continues, then breaks into individual sputters. Then stops. Long pause. Laura and Leslie breathe, very full of air and liquid.

LAURA: Did you know that sea horses are the only animal species in the oceanic kingdom or otherwise, in which the male carries the babies? *(Beat.)* And the males are nesters, too. They can stay on one blade of sea grass for like, three whole years. Hence, their vulnerability.
    (Pause.)
LESLIE: You're not gonna be one of those people who fills the quiet spaces with like, metaphors, are you?
LAURA: Guy! I was just . . . thinking.
    (They both slurp their drinks, then sputter to a stop. Empty. Pause.)
LESLIE: So, what else?
LAURA: *(Pouting.)* What?
LESLIE: About the sea horses.
LAURA: Well, Chinese herbalists use their desiccated and pulverized corpses to heal many injuries and ailments. Like gout, rheumatism.
LESLIE: What are those?
LAURA: Diseases.
LESLIE: Oh. *(Long pause.)* What else?
LAURA: That's all I remember.
    (Beat.)
LESLIE: Where are we?
LAURA: We're getting closer.
LESLIE: How much longer?
LAURA: *(Refers to map.)* Like, eight inches.
LESLIE: Good. We'll be there soon.
LAURA: But in the last eight hours we went like, half an inch.
LESLIE: Laura, I'm the one who remembered to steal my mom's triple A card, get the maps with it, split the line into three, and pick the stop points. So, if you have a better plan than mine for getting us there then say so. 'K?

LAURA: Well, I got the ATM card.

LESLIE: I know, and I'm grateful for that. That was a good call on your part. *(Beat.)* What's the code? I need greens bad. Let's stop and get cash and get salads.

LAURA: Um.

LESLIE: Oh my God.

LAURA: No, I know it. I know it.

LESLIE: You don't know the fucking code.

LAURA: No, no. I knew it. I swear.

LESLIE: We were relying on that card. I got the car, you got the cash. What the hell are we gonna do?

LAURA: I know it, I swear. I'm just nervous, I'm not thinking right. *(Beat.)* It's my sister's middle name! No, that's our security system disarmer. I know it stands for something. It's some important thing in our lives. Fuck! What is it?

LESLIE: This is just great. Great! The one thing I ask you to take care of, and you don't have the courtesy to follow through. You are totally careless, you know that? *(Beat. Stunned.)* That was my mother!

LAURA: I'm sorry, it's just that somehow it's out of my head, out here. I look out and see all these, like, the lands, and somehow, that code, just, isn't there anymore.

LESLIE: You didn't get any extra cash? No spending money?

LAURA: I just got the tuition. Eight hundreds, two fifties, and five twenties.

LESLIE: You didn't even get any ones?

LAURA: I didn't think about it.

LESLIE: What about tipping? Huh? How are we gonna tip?

LAURA: I don't think you tip at like, motels.

LESLIE: We're gonna have to live off the Mobil card.

LAURA: You got the Mobil card?

LESLIE: Yes, of course I got the Mobil card. I said I was going to and I did. That's how I work. Great. We're going to have to eat off the gas station now. This is just great. For three days. What are we gonna eat?

LAURA: They have yogurts there. Sometimes.

LESLIE: Yeah, like whole-fat banana flavor.

LAURA: Well they have those turkey things don't they, those triangle sandwiches?

LESLIE: Those cat-food-quality cold cuts, on Wonder bread, with iceberg, and mayonnaise? *(Beat.)* Why don't we just get a brick of pork lard, and a couple of soup spoons?

(Long pause. They have reached an open place. There are fields.)

LAURA: What do you think they're growing?

LESLIE: I don't know. Corn. Cotton. Hay. Something.

LAURA: Hay?

LESLIE: I don't know.

LAURA: How many corns on a plant? Like three? Or like twenty? Do they rip 'em out and redo 'em every year, or do the corns just sit under the weather and come back in the sun?

LESLIE: I don't know.

(Pause.)

LAURA: Have you ever tried the wrapless protein wrap?

LESLIE: We already talked about that.

LAURA: Who's your favorite trainer at Vista Del Sol Body and Soul?

LESLIE: We already talked about that, too.

LAURA: 'K. *(Silence. More fields.)* Why don't we open the windows?

LESLIE: I have the AC on.

LAURA: Yeah, but why don't we try it for a bit. Let something in.

(Leslie opens the windows. A short silence. Leslie closes the windows.)

LESLIE: That's enough.

LAURA: What did your dad do?

LESLIE: A spokesmodel. She sold resistance training rubber bands gym to gym. He moved away with her. He hasn't communicated with me in a calendar year.

(Pause.)

LAURA: Elastercizers?

LESLIE: Yeah, those.

LAURA: Nobody uses those anymore. Now that there's the new latex bands.

LESLIE: I know. They're twice as supple without compromising any of the strength. *(Beat.)* I don't know what he does now. *(Pause.)* Are we in Utah yet?

LAURA: I haven't seen a sign.

LESLIE: My neck hurts.

LAURA: Well, pull over. It should be my turn to drive by now.

LESLIE: I'm not pulling over until we get to Utah.

LAURA: Our Lexus has a weight-sensitive neck support.

LESLIE: So does Tracy's mom's Lexus. So does Stacie's mom's Lexus. But my mom has to get the stripped model, of course! Everybody else gets the turkey, and my mom gets the carcass! *(Beat.)*

LAURA: Is Utah . . . on the way to the south?

LESLIE: Look, I've skied there. Do you have a plan?

LAURA: No.

LESLIE: *(Final.)* Then, Utah.

LAURA: 'K.

(Lights shift.)

Scene Two

Laura's house. Phil practices a speech in front of Hannah.

PHIL: It's a draft.

HANNAH: Don't apologize. Just read it!

PHIL: OK. *(Beat.)* My fellow Vista Del Solians.

(Hannah shakes her head.)

PHIL: Solites?

(Hannah shakes her head.)

PHIL: Soltans?

(Hannah shakes her head.)

PHIL: People of Vista Del Sol?

(Hannah nods.)

PHIL: People of Vista Del Sol. We live in paradise. Not a tropical place. There are no coconuts falling onto beds of moist ferns. This is a paradise of geological variety. We have high desert bluffs, deep sandstone canyons, a soft, shifting ocean floor. This is tectonic territory. There are fractures beneath it that make it violently slip and change. Our temperamental paradise has been created by eons of constant destruction. *(Beat.)* What a shock and a revelation it must have been for our ancestors to encounter this stunning topographic diversity after crossing endless miles of flat dusty empty plains in their covered wagons. *(Beat.)* Well, not my ancestors. My ancestors were busy fleeing the Balkan pogroms.

HANNAH: Digression!

PHIL: Sorry. But nevertheless, that's why these people who talk about losing something when the Surfswell Plaza Freeway Project comes cutting through the bluff and into our town, they don't have the slightest idea what they're talking about. Destruction is what the edge of the world is made of. These people, the "coalition," they don't understand that. What we're doing is not just important, it's inevitable. These people don't know shit about losing anything!

(He stops, agitated.)

HANNAH: Well it's edgy.

PHIL: That last part, that's not gonna be part of it.

HANNAH: That's probably good.

PHIL: Isn't her practice over by now?

HANNAH: She probably just stayed late.

PHIL: How late?

HANNAH: She'll be back soon.

PHIL: What about dinner?

HANNAH: I'll make something.

PHIL: You will?

HANNAH: I know how. I've watched. *(Beat.)* She'll be back soon.

    (Lights shift.)

Scene Three

    The Mobil station. Laura reads from the back of a bag of pretzels.

LAURA: Yep. Palm oil.

LESLIE: Jesus Christ! Even in the pretzels! And the only crackers they have are "savory flavored!" Do you know what that means, "savory flavored"?

LAURA: No.

LESLIE: Me neither, but I'm sure it's horrible.

LAURA: I think I'm starving. I think I'm really really hungry.

    (Leslie grabs packages, two, three at a time.)

LESLIE: "Covered in creamery butter"? Mother of God!

LAURA: Does caffeine make you more or less hungry?

LESLIE: More. Less. More. I can't remember!

LAURA: My head is hurting. From hunger. We have to eat something here. We just have to find something that we can eat.

LESLIE: My head hurts too. But it's not hunger. I'm just pissed at you 'cuz you're such a useless dumb ass. Just think of the Goddamn code and we could at least get the dinner salad at Denny's with the dressing on the side. Can't you think of it? *(Beat.)* Caffeine Free Regular Coke. WHERE ARE WE?

LAURA: My head hurts. We have to get something.

LESLIE: What? What are we gonna get? Huh? Yes, excuse me, I'd like a tall, cold BACON CHEDDAR SODA PLEASE!

LAURA: *(Loud, shocking.)* WE HAVE TO GET SOMETHING HERE!

    (Beat.)

LESLIE: What?

LAURA: Something we want.

LESLIE: What?

LAURA: OK. What do you feel like?

LESLIE: Feel?

LAURA: Let's just close our eyes and try to think about what we feel. What. Feels?

(Laura closes her eyes. Leslie reluctantly closes hers. Then, immediately.)

LESLIE: I want a corn dog.

LAURA: What?

(Leslie opens eyes.)

LESLIE: I used to eat them at the Winston County Fair, when I was a kid. With my dad. *(Beat. Closes eyes again. Opens them.)* Orange soda. Do they still have that?

LAURA: Yeah. It's on the thing. It's always on the thing. It's right next to the diet coke.

LESLIE: I'd like the regular size one of those. The regular size.

LAURA: OK. Let's get in line. I think I might want to get us another map. I think there might be a better map than the one we've got. I'm gonna take a look.

(Lights shift.)

Scene Four

Hannah standing in a pool of light. A cop speaks to her in voice-over.

COP: We're very sorry about this.

HANNAH: OK. Can I go now please?

COP: I'm sorry, but I need to clarify, you said, she . . .

HANNAH: I just said they take things more seriously than the other girls.

COP: Like what?

HANNAH: Like cheer! She said they take it more seriously than the other girls, that's all.

COP: Did she say why?

HANNAH: She said that the other girls are interested in the football guys and they're not. They're interested in achieving together.

COP: Did she say what they were interested in achieving?

HANNAH: Cheerleading! They were interested in achieving cheerleading!

COP: I'm sorry. What does that mean?

HANNAH: They were sick of how mediocre their peers were. She wanted to go to a better place.

COP: Did she use those words — "a better place"?

HANNAH: Yeah. Can I go now? 'Cuz, my friend's mom is taking me home.

COP: Did she make any other comments that you thought were a little strange?

HANNAH: Strange?

COP: Did she say anything about her connection to Leslie? Did she use any other words that you might remember?

HANNAH: Other words?

COP: Like, "love" or . . .

HANNAH: OH! You think this is some sort of inscrutable sapphic suicide pact?
(Beat.)

COP: How old are you?

HANNAH: Look, she and Leslie are different. The other cheerleaders don't ever invite them to their preparties. They don't get to stand in the middle. They're terminal flanks. And they always carry other people's megaphones to the cars after the games. They call them the spot sisters, 'cuz they never fly or base. I listen to them talk on the phone. I hear what they say to each other. I take my hair dryer and stick it up to the wall. The heat coils conduct vocal sound waves with surprising clarity. Sometimes it's so quiet for so long. And sometimes it's just like hours of "uh-huh, uh-huh" and "totally." And sometimes they say things that are very frightening indeed.

COP: Hannah Rachel Green, your sister has committed theft. Do you know where she is?

HANNAH: You know how if you look at a picture just one year later, you can look back and see exactly what kind of haircut you really had? Well that's what I think she's doing. But with space instead of time. *(Beat.)* I'm eleven years old.
(Lights shift.)

Scene Five

Motel room. Leslie is alone. The TV flickers in her face. Rhythmically, every six seconds, she laughs along with the laugh track, then stops. Every fourth time, she sighs. Then the laugh track stops. She still laughs, every six seconds, three more times. Then sighs. Laura enters.

LESLIE: What did you say?

LAURA: It's done.

LESLIE: Yeah?

LAURA: It totally worked.

LESLIE: What did you say?

LAURA: You don't have to worry about it. I took care of it.

LESLIE: Well I'd like to know the plan. What did you tell the guy?

LAURA: I told him you were pregnant and that my mom died and I totally cried. I couldn't believe it, I was just crying and crying. I think he just wanted me out of there. I said our dad was paying and couldn't we just stay here till he came tomorrow.

LESLIE: You played the death card.

LAURA: Yep.

LESLIE: He bought it?

LAURA: Cash and carry baby! Look what they had in the lobby!
(She holds up a Twinkie.)

LESLIE: I can't believe they didn't insist on an imprint. Don't they have to have an imprint? Isn't there some kind of law? The center of a Twinkie is made with lamb lard!
(Laura devours the Twinkie.)

LAURA: This is the best food I've ever had. Why haven't I had this before? This is . . . exquisite.

LESLIE: What if they catch us?

LAURA: We sleep and we scram!

LESLIE: But . . . did you look at that man in the lobby? He had more piercings than teeth!

LAURA: We have to keep going.

LESLIE: I'm cold.

LAURA: Shhh, it's gonna be OK. Here.
(Laura throws a sweater at Leslie.)

LESLIE: Ow! Bitch!

LAURA: I'm sorry.

LESLIE: You hurt me!

LAURA: I'm sorry, shhh . . .

LESLIE: I don't like it here.

LAURA: Shhh. It's gonna be OK. Just, shhh . . .

LESLIE: I don't want to wear this stupid fucking sweater!

LAURA: Be quiet!

LESLIE: I hate being away from my stuff!

LAURA: Shhh! Just be quiet, OK! Just, Shhh!

LESLIE: I want to go home and be with my stuff!

LAURA: Shut up.

LESLIE: I have a corn dog inside me. I want to go home!

LAURA: I SAID, SHUT UP!

(*Lights shift.*)

Scene Six

Laura's house. Phil and Judy sitting in the living room, where nobody ever sits. Judy has tea, Phil doesn't.

PHIL: It's not too strong?

JUDY: It's fine, thank you.

PHIL: I don't usually make tea. Or, really, never. I've never made tea. (*Beat.*) Ever.

JUDY: Well, it's lovely. (*Pause.*) Is this one of those antique door tables? I've seen these.

PHIL: Yes, yes. It's a table made of an old door.

JUDY: They're so clever. What they think of. I have a mirror that's made from an old window. It has a sill still.

(*Pause. She doesn't drink her tea.*)

PHIL: You're sure that's not too strong —

JUDY: No, no it's just right. (*Beat.*) What kind is it?

PHIL: Um, Chinese. I believe. Or Irish. No, it's Indian. Well, it's from somewhere else, I can't remember.

JUDY: Well it's lovely.

PHIL: We have so many teas.

JUDY: Then this was a very nice choice. (*Pause.*) What do you do for a living, Phil?

PHIL: I am an environmental impact consultant.

JUDY: Oh! (*Beat.*) What is that exactly?

PHIL: I consult on issues involving the impact to the environment of various development projects. And yourself?

JUDY: I was a consultant, too. A marketing consultant for a large corporation in the south. You know, there's a familiar smell here.

PHIL: I'm sorry.

JUDY: No, no. It's not an odor. It's not unpleasant at all. Just, a smell. That's familiar. That's all. *(Beat.)* I'm sorry. Sometimes I just say things. *(Pause.)*

PHIL: The girls —

JUDY: Yes.

PHIL: What are we going to do?

(Lights shift.)

Scene Seven

Motel room. Laura and Leslie stand next to twin beds, holding their thin motel bedspreads.

LAURA: Just pull it off.

LESLIE: Won't we be cold?

LAURA: You don't sleep with these. They're universally yucky. Just strip 'em off.

LESLIE: But I'll get cold.

LAURA: You should have brought more sweaters.

LESLIE: How many did you bring?

LAURA: Five.

LESLIE: How did you get five sweaters in your bag?

LAURA: I made it a priority. It's cold in other places.

LESLIE: There's no way you fit five sweaters in that one bag.

LAURA: Yes I did. *(Beat.)* I left my whole hair-care product pouch at home. All of it. Conditioner, retexturizer, straightening balm, pomade, paddle brush, round brush. Comb. It was so heavy. So I chucked it onto my comforter. *(Beat.)* Tomorrow I'm gonna have to use whatever complimentary product they have in the shower here. I'm gonna have to just wash it and let it be. *(Beat.)* I have no idea what it is going to actually look like. *(Beat.)* Now stuff the spreads in the corner and help me move the twins to the wall. Let's spot each other's standings.

LESLIE: But this carpet.

LAURA: So?

LESLIE: It's like, military surplus.

LAURA: Yeah?

LESLIE: It could sand our faces off.

(Beat.)

LAURA: In the tuck section of the brochure, it describes how a girl landed face first trying to nail her standing, and she swelled so high she couldn't see for a week. Now help me.

LESLIE: You don't have any hair product?

LAURA: Not an ounce.

LESLIE: But I have coarse, dry, chemically treated hair and you have limp, fine, oily hair so you can't even borrow mine! There's a whole day competitive grooming seminar at S.I.S. It's a big part of the point system if you wanna win the spirit stick at the final award ceremony. You're gonna look . . . I don't know what you're gonna look like!

LAURA: So?

LESLIE: Well it's just . . . I think maybe we should turn around and go home. My mom . . .

LAURA: Yeah?

LESLIE: She's probably freaking by now.

LAURA: *(Firm.)* You said you hate her.

LESLIE: Well yeah, but . . .

LAURA: There's a picture in the brochure of a girl named Jolene. She and her team just won the all-girl squad professional nationals. She's the only one smiling with a closed mouth. Why? Because in the first flying stunt her mounter kicked her coming down from a heel stretch and knocked her two front teeth clean out. They flung across the gym like a couple of peppermint Chiclets. And while her mouth was welling with blood, Jolene nailed that routine to the final tumbling pass. She took that intensity and used it. *(Pause. A plea.)* Remember?

LESLIE: Yeah. It's just that she's my mom.

LAURA: And I'm your squadmate. I'm squatting for my standing. Spot me?

(Laura looks behind her, then looks to Leslie. Leslie doesn't move.)

Scene Eight

Laura's house.

JUDY: Do you sit in this room a lot?

PHIL: It's the living room.

JUDY: But do you really, LIVE here?

PHIL: The TV's in the other room.

JUDY: So for you this is sort of a parlor.

PHIL: I suppose.

JUDY: That's what I would call it. This is lovely. Your house. I enjoy this whole development. I have a friend in this subdivision with this very same model of home. I enjoy her. Her living room looks much smaller than this. But she has a tendency to overfurnish.

PHIL: Actually, this area is unique in that the homes, although built in a tract style, are each, in themselves, unique. It's unique in that way. And they're unusually large.

JUDY: Yes, it's very spacious here. *(Beat.)* My friend actually uses this as an office.

PHIL: Really?

JUDY: Yes. It's an unconventional choice. But she runs a gift-placement service out of her home so she likes an open office area.

PHIL: Where is her living room?

JUDY: Right through that hall and to the right.

PHIL: That's my office!

JUDY: Isn't that funny? Opposites. She says she likes the living room to feel confined. Makes her feel like she's in the mountains.
      (Pause.)

PHIL: Does your daughter cook?

JUDY: Leslie! My daughter wouldn't know a saucepan if you used it to split open her tiny little head!

PHIL: Does your daughter, eat?

JUDY: None of them eat today. Don't you watch prime-time news magazines? They all "suffer" from low self-esteem. I try to work around it. Does your's puke? Now that I won't tolerate. Vomit erodes the porcelain. I have a friend with four teenage daughters and she has had to revarnish their toilets every summer.
      (She notices a silver family picture frame on a piece of furniture. She puts down her tea cup, picks it up. Looks to Phil. Beat.)

PHIL: Yes.

(Judy puts down the picture, picks up her tea cup.)

JUDY: I used to have a deep fat fryer. I put everything into that. I'd make tempura and serve it with chop suey and water chestnuts. I'd have to slap her little hand 'cuz she'd try to eat it off the serving platter. I remember that deep bubbling sound. The oil sound. I haven't heard that in years. That was just their favorite thing. They just loved my oriental night. *(Beat.)* I had a husband at the time.

PHIL: The neighbors sometimes make bacon. We can smell it from our breakfast nook. They're from Chicago. *(Beat.)* It reminds me of grad school. I have a master's. In public policy.

JUDY: Oh.

(A sound. They both jump.)

JUDY: Was that — ?

PHIL: No. Just the security system. Every few hours it checks on us. It beeps. *(Beat.)* How did I let this happen?

JUDY: We're doing everything we can. You made sure the ringer's on "high"?

PHIL: Yes.

JUDY: We're doing everything we can. *(Pause.)* There's that smell again. What is it? It's so familiar. But I can't quite place it.

(Long beat.)

PHIL: Eucalyptus.

JUDY: Eucalyptus! *(Judy looks out the window. Sees the stump.)* Oh!

PHIL: I had to cut it down. It was time.

JUDY: Oh yes. They can fall right onto the house at any time. They're supposed to be very shallow-rooted trees.

PHIL: That's what I've heard too.

(Lights shift.)

Scene Nine

The car. Laura drives. Her hair is wild.

LESLIE: We give the money back. And say sorry.

LAURA: No!

LESLIE: It'll be snap crackle pop! I give the money back to my mom, and you give the money back to your dad, and we just cry, and say that our blood sugar was low, and our hormones were high and . . . we were menstruating, and all that blood loss was really depleting our ethical stores. We play the period card!

LAURA: We're not going back!

(Beat.)

LESLIE: What about the groundbreaking? Aren't you supposed to be there? Don't you have to be there, for your dad? (Beat.) You're going ninety! You're not supposed to go ninety!

LAURA: Look if we're gonna get into an accident, we might as well get into a big gnarly one and die. If we're gonna go, we're gonna go SMOOTH-IED! NO TRACE!

LESLIE: Please slow down! I'll be your best friend!

LAURA: You ARE my best friend.

LESLIE: Fuck. (Beat.) You're going a hundred! I don't think Lexuses go a hundred! It's gonna break!

LAURA: You can go a hundred and fifty in a Lexus and not feel a thing. IT'S A LUXURY SEDAN!

(Beat.)

LESLIE: OK, this isn't cheer any more.

LAURA: This is just starting to be cheer!

LESLIE: I don't know who you are.

(Beat.)

LAURA: Know what? I didn't get the money from my dad. I stole it. From the Smoothie Talk smoothie shop. I committed an actual crime. With actual consequences.

LESLIE: You stole?

LAURA: You blackmailed!

LESLIE: Yeah, my MOM! You stole from one of the pillars of the community!

LAURA: You talk a lot of shit. You know that?

(A scary pause.)

LESLIE: Did you look around where we are right now. How it's all dead flat here? Well some of us have actually lived in shitty places like this! We didn't get to live where it's nice and perfect and new. Where there's bougainvillea walls and streets called Avocado. We lived in places that were dead, dead flat! Like my mom. And me! (Beat.) You STOLE?

LAURA: Yep. I have focus and intensity!

LESLIE: You don't even have your standing!

LAURA: Yes I do!

LESLIE: You threw yourself onto the bed.

LAURA: We just have to "Believe to Achieve!"

LESLIE: We also have to be able to do it, though. And we can't. We can't do standing back tucks. Our CARTWHEELS are for shit! We don't weigh eighty-five pounds! And, your hair! It's like, alive! It's like a living thing! *(Laura screeches to the side of the road. Stops.)*

LAURA: I'm doing it. I can. You watch.

(Lights shift.)

Scene Ten

Laura's house. Phil, Judy, and Hannah in the family room.

HANNAH: Theft.

PHIL: What?

HANNAH: That's what he said. Grand theft. *(Beat.)* He knew my name. He pulled right up after soccer practice and it was so embarrassing. I died. Crishelle Kravitz's mom was taking me home and she had to wait! He talked to me against his car. He said he needed to talk about my sister. Laura. And he knew my name. He had three long hairs gooed on the shine of his head.

PHIL: He said, theft?

HANNAH: Grand or petty or something. He said theft.

PHIL: What did you tell him?

HANNAH: I just said she left. I just said what's true.

JUDY: Are you sure it was a cop?

HANNAH: Yes. He showed me his I.D. card.

PHIL: You mean badge.

HANNAH: No, it was a card. In his wallet.

PHIL: Was he driving a black-and-white squad car? With a light bar?

HANNAH: No, it was more like a . . . Honda.

PHIL: A Honda.

JUDY: A light blue Honda sedan?

HANNAH: Yeah.

JUDY: Was it a laminated yellow card that he showed you?

HANNAH: Yes.

JUDY: Vista del Soldiers. The private security force. What did he say was stolen?

HANNAH: Money. He said Laura stole money from the smoothie shop. Lots of it. They're looking for her.

PHIL: Go to your room.

HANNAH: I'm in trouble?

PHIL: Go to your room. That's where you go.

HANNAH: We're supposed to have dinner.

PHIL: Oh. Well, have dinner. And then, go to your room.

(Pause.)

HANNAH: Daddy, what does this mean?

(Hannah exits. Judy and Phil face each other.)

PHIL: Theft?

JUDY: It's not REALLY theft.

PHIL: She said —

JUDY: They won't contact the police. They're at fifty percent capacity and this is the last thing they'd leak. They'll handle it within the jurisdiction of the mall. They're looking for sushi and dry-cleaning tenants not pawn shops and check cashers! You need to eat. Sit down at your table. I'll cook you something. We'll have dinner.

PHIL: I'm not hungry.

JUDY: What is that sound?

PHIL: What sound?

JUDY: From outside. It sounds like some kind of chanting. Hear that? Let me open your window.

PHIL: No! Please. I think I'm hungry after all.

(Lights shift.)

Scene Eleven

The side of the road. Laura is in the prep position to do a standing back tuck. Leslie spots, tentatively.

LESLIE: Don't do it!

LAURA: I'm gonna. I know I can.

LESLIE: You're gonna get hurt!

LAURA: SO?

LESLIE: So this isn't what cheer is about!

LAURA: This IS what cheer is about. We're only seventeen years old. Seventeen! We're not supposed to have to take care of other people. We're not supposed to have to drive them to their piano lessons and their Hebrew lessons and make them their chicken and rice! We're seventeen! We're supposed to be reckless and careless! We're supposed to do stupid dangerous shit and learn from it! *(Beat.)* There's a hole in the ground where we live, and I really honestly think that voices could come out of it. And I think they're ugly. Really loud, and ugly. It's not nice and new where we live! They just pave over what's there! There's big ugly holes and they pave on top of them, that's all! *(Beat.)* I'm doing it!

LESLIE: I'm not spotting! I'm not gonna spot!

LAURA: I don't need a spot!

LESLIE: Please, don't. Please? Oh my God!

(Laura preps to flip, and just at the point of no return . . . Lights shift.)

Scene Twelve

Phil and Judy in the phone room.

JUDY: What did they say?

PHIL: Nothing. Still.

JUDY: You're sure you have the call waiting activated?

PHIL: Judy, you've —

JUDY: Asked you that ten times already. Sorry.

PHIL: It's OK. I understand.

JUDY: They're looking. They have the number. You have call waiting. We're doing everything we can. *(Beat.)* We only have three days left you know.

PHIL: Three days?

JUDY: Until the Surfswell Plaza Freeway Project groundbreaking. The end of our town as we know it. The coalition is kicking into high gear. They're picketing the house of Mr. X, some bigwig in the project. I've got the graveyard shift tomorrow night. We all need to do our part.

PHIL: Oh God. Oh God.

JUDY: Shhh, shhh. *(Beat.)* I know.

(Pause.)

PHIL: Do you like your daughter?

JUDY: No. Do you?

PHIL: No. Wait. Which one? The older, or the younger?

JUDY: The older.

PHIL: No. She scares me.

JUDY: She scares you?

PHIL: She makes me scared.

JUDY: But we love them so much.

PHIL: Yes.

JUDY: And we know them so well.

PHIL: Yes. *(Beat.)* There's something I have to tell you.

JUDY: Yes?

PHIL: I've never said it before.

JUDY: Yes. I know.

    (Beat.)

PHIL: But I can't. I haven't yet.

JUDY: You can. *(Beat.)* READY?

PHIL: OK! *(Starts out speaking, builds to a cheer.)*

    She's D-E-A-D

    And she ain't comin' back to me.

JUDY: Uh-huh. That's right. And say it one more time.

PHIL: My wife is dead

    She hit her head

    I'll never smell her on my bed

JUDY: Uh-huh. You got it. A little louder now.

PHIL AND JUDY: We got our houses

    In the sun!

    But our spouses

    Had to run!

    We're lonely!

JUDY: Say what?

PHIL: We're L-O-N-E-L-Y

    And we ain't got no alibi!

    We're lonely!

JUDY: Uh-huh!

PHIL: We're lonely!

JUDY: That's right!

PHIL AND JUDY: We're spent!

    (Long pause.)

PHIL: What was that?

JUDY: A cheer.

PHIL: For what?

JUDY: For ourselves.

    (Lights shift.)

Scene Thirteen

Lights bump up on Leslie and Laura. Laura lies face down on the road.

LAURA: I did it.

LESLIE: You fell on your face!

LAURA: I DID IT!

LESLIE: Let me see!

(Laura's head pops up. She's bloody. She spits. A gasp.)

LAURA: OCEAN!

LESLIE: Oh my God!

LAURA: It's ocean!

LESLIE: There's road on your face!

LAURA: How could I be so stupid!

LESLIE: You're bloody!

LAURA: It's O-C-E-A-N!

LESLIE: What is?

LAURA: The ATM CODE! It's the ATM code! How could I just forget things. Of course she picked that, because that was her place. She used to take us there. A long time ago. Before we started just laying out in the sand. We used to swim for hours in the ocean and when it got cold, we would run out and my mother would have a wide, white towel open and she would clutch us up in it and rub us warm and dry. She'd call us her baby burritos. That was before we had wraps. There used to be this old pier. They tore it down. It's something else now.

LESLIE: The Seabluff Bungalow Suites. I know.

LAURA: Yes. A long time ago. I remember I was throwing these rocks hard against the old pier, just enjoying how it made a cracking and smacking sound against the posts. And my mom yelled at me, "Stop it!" And she grabbed me by the wrist and led me under the pier and showed me the mussels. There were mussels that made their homes there. I was cracking and killing them. She showed me what came out. It was little pieces of flesh. Living tissue from a living thing. *(Beat. She cries.)* I felt like a terrible awful person, the worst. But she said, it's OK. Someone just has to teach you that you have impact. Someone has to teach you about impact.

(Pause.)

LESLIE: My dad used to take me onto rollercoasters. That was our thing. I would ride the scariest loopiest roller coaster when I was legally way too little. He used to call me Ironsides. That means I'm really fucking strong.

LAURA: I hate my dad! I'm sorry, but I hate him so much! How could he just keep going! I don't understand how he could just keep going!

LESLIE: Oh my God! Do you smell that?

LAURA: What?

LESLIE: Don't you smell it?

(Laura sniffs.)

LAURA: Yeah. What is it?

LESLIE: Tobacco! It's a crop that we grow. In the south. I can't believe it.

(Beat.)

LAURA: We made it.

LESLIE: Oh my God!

LAURA: Get in the car!

LESLIE: We're here!

(Lights shift.)

Scene Fourteen

Laura's house. Dinner. Phil, Hannah and Judy quietly eating.

PHIL: This is lovely.

HANNAH: What is it?

JUDY: I had to work with what was here. You have quite a few sun-dried tomatoes.

HANNAH: *(Trying to revive the joke.)* Oh no! Wrinkle tomatoes!

(Phil gives her a token chuckle.)

JUDY: They're very high in sodium. And there were quite a few dusty cans of beef broth in the back there. I used one in the rice.

PHIL: I can tell. It's very hearty.

JUDY: We almost never cook with beef any more. It's mostly chicken and the fresh fish I get from Hattie's heart-friendly butcher on Camino Del Mar. My friend Hattie opened that place after her husband had a massive infarction three years ago. That shop saved their life and their livelihood. Of course, they're right on the path of the Surfswell Plaza Freeway Project. She's the one who got me involved with the coalition to fight the freeway. It's been very fulfilling for me. *(Chanting is heard.)* There's that noise again. What is that?

PHIL: Pass the rice please.

HANNAH: You have the rice.

PHIL: Then pass something else!

JUDY: What is that sound?

(Hannah opens the window. We hear the protest.)

CHORUS: H *(Clap! Clap Clap! Clap!)*

E *(Clap!Clap! Clap!Clap!)*

L! L! *(Clap!Clap!)*

N-O!

SURFSWELL PLAZA FREEWAY PROJECT *(Clap!)*

HELL NO! *(Etc.)*

HANNAH: My dad did it.

JUDY: Pardon me?

HANNAH: It's Dad's freeway.

JUDY: Is that so?

PHIL: I'm consulting.

HANNAH: It's my dad's project.

JUDY: You're Mr. X?

PHIL: I'm a development consultant, which means I'm mitigating its harmful environmental impact through the implementation of certain civic standards.

HANNAH: There's a groundbreaking ceremony in two days. Did he invite you?

JUDY: A groundbreaking?

HANNAH: Yeah. They're tenting the whole area. They're already setting up the grandstands and the carnation arch and the beer garden. There's gonna be complimentary muffins courtesy of Breads Etc. There's gonna be news vans and roving photographers and man-on-the-street opinion polls. And my dad is gonna cut the ribbon. Aren't you, Dad?

PHIL: That hasn't been determined.

HANNAH: *(To Judy.)* Did he invite you to come?

(Pause.)

JUDY: I will be there. *(Beat.)* Hannah, more broccoflower?

HANNAH: I've consumed quite enough.

JUDY: Phil?

PHIL: Yes. Thank you. *(He doesn't take any.)*

(Lights shift.)

Scene Fifteen

An abandoned schoolyard. Laura and Leslie run in.

LESLIE: Nobody.

LAURA: Did you run around the back again?

LESLIE: Four times!

LAURA: Me too!

LESLIE: I looked under rocks! I looked under leaves! There's no one here.

LAURA: What happened?

LESLIE: Let's look at the brochure again. Maybe we got it wrong.

(Laura looks at the brochure.)

LAURA: Where did you get the brochure?

LESLIE: I found it.

LAURA: Where?

LESLIE: In the library. I went to the mag rack at recess to put on some perfume from a *Mirabella*. And I saw it poking out of a shelf.

LAURA: When?

LESLIE: A while ago.

LAURA: Do you see what this says at the bottom. Right here? In solid black ink? *(Beat.)* Copyright 1971. 1971! See how the print's all weird? How the letters are like, all, flared at the bottom?

LESLIE: I thought it was retro.

LAURA: Oh my God!

(Long pause.)

LESLIE: My mom says everything comes back. Shoulder pads, everything. She says you just keep it in your closet and you hold on tight. 'Cuz everything comes back! My mom says it does!

LAURA: No, it doesn't. In 1971, my mom was alive, and she's dead now. In 1971, my mother was alive, and today, she's gone.

LESLIE: But she's always in your heart.

LAURA: Is that all there is to say? 'Cuz that doesn't mean anything. *(Beat.)* She used to tell us things, but I barely remember and I can't ask her again! I can't say hey, Mom, tell me things I never listened to! Tell me how to do things! Tell me how to bake sugar cookies so they're soft in the middle! Tell me how to sweep my hair up so it holds with just a pin! Tell me what it feels like when your water breaks and a baby comes out! I don't have anybody to tell me that! *(Beat.)* In 1971, she had a gray streak in the front of her hair. Premature gray. She had it for years until she finally got sick of the giggles and stares and she dyed it like the rest of them. I don't even remember barely. I was so little. *(Beat.)* Is that what happens? You're young, and you believe in things, and then you, what? You get married, you have kids, you move into a Spanish stucco ocean-view unit and you forget? One day you wear your white streak like a peacock's tail, and the next day you're letting them paint it with bleach and toner and wrap it in tin foil and you're sitting under a hair dryer to cook for an hour while you learn lightening tips from a beauty magazine! Like everybody else! *(Beat.)* When you sit under those dryer domes, you can't see or hear a thing. You just have to sit there quietly and let all that stuff soak into you. *(Beat.)* She's really kind of been gone for a long long time. *(Pause.)* I don't want to be a dead girl. I want to be a person who's alive. *(She turns and starts to slowly walk away.)*

LESLIE: Where are you going? Laura? Where are you going?

(Laura turns. A beat.)

LAURA: Home.

(Lights shift.)

Scene Sixteen

Hannah's room. Judy sits on Hannah's bed, brushing Hannah's hair.

JUDY: They're not wetlands. That's a myth generated by the environmental lobby. It's a man-made bog. They're draining and reclaiming it for the community.

HANNAH: What about the gophers!

JUDY: There's been a gopher agreement. In the settlement. There's a gopher provision in the project!

HANNAH: What are they gonna do to them?

JUDY: They're building a temporary burrowing facility.

HANNAH: They're gonna build gopher condos?

JUDY: It's only temporary.

HANNAH: Out of what?

JUDY: Out of the project budget, I suppose.

HANNAH: Out of what material will they build these condos? Are they gonna protest big time? Are they gonna hang my dad in effigy? Is he gonna have to testify?

JUDY: No, there's been a settlement. That means they've dropped the lawsuit. It's over.

HANNAH: They're gonna build them out of tar and gravel. The gophers have to settle for the gravel!

(Beat.)

JUDY: Here's something I have to teach you. You'll learn that you can live with almost anything. You can find a way to make it work and move on. Do you hear me? You can make it work and keep going.

(Lights shift. Phil, isolated in a pool of light.)

PHIL: The bluffs crumble to the beach. The waves wash the sand away and for a while there are jagged rocks and trash all over the shore. But the city comes in with trucks and deposits a fine layer of sand over the broken glass and the discarded feminine hygiene products and replenishes the smooth recreational surface we've come to know and rely upon. With just a little help from man, nature's cycle continues. In a year, this very ground upon which we stand will be racing with high-speed cars. Today we move forward. We don't look back. We proudly pave our way to tomorrow.

Scene Seventeen

Lights up on the groundbreaking ceremony. Phil is flanked by Judy, Leslie, and the cheerleaders. He holds a ceremonial shovel.

PHIL: Thank you. Thank you. I played only a small part in this. I consulted, only. But I thank you. For your support.

(He goes to dig, but stops. He can't. Judy approaches and helps him dig. They wait for applause, none comes. They look to Leslie. She gets the crowd to applaud by cheering. The sound of applause. Lights shift.)

Scene Eighteen

Lights fade out on everyone but Hannah and Laura, who stand at the beach, using their toes to write in the sand.

LAURA: What does yours say?

HANNAH: I'm not done, wait!

LAURA: Let me see!

HANNAH: Wait! There.

LAURA: What does it say?

HANNAH: You first.

LAURA: OK. Mine says, "lying." I lied about stuff. What does yours say?

HANNAH: Forgetting. I'm afraid I'm forgetting her. I can't remember what it
  tasted like when she leaned over to kiss good night and some of her hair
  would get in my mouth.
  (Beat.)

LAURA: We're not gonna forget her.

HANNAH: Well Shoshana said whatever you want to wash away. You can write
  it. *(Beat.)* We should go! We're supposed to meet them in ten minutes.
  We're supposed to cheer for Dad.

LAURA: It's over.

HANNAH: What's over?

LAURA: The groundbreaking. It was over an hour ago.

HANNAH: Why didn't you take me there? We're gonna get into trouble! We
  were supposed to cheer for Dad.

LAURA: I kind of quit cheering. I'm gonna try to do something else.

HANNAH: What?

LAURA: *(Looking out to the ocean.)* I don't really know yet. *(Looking back to her
  sister.)* What else does Shoshana say?

HANNAH: She says . . . Wait! Here comes a wave.
  (They grab hands.)

LAURA: Here we go.

HANNAH: Here it comes!
  (Beat.)

LAURA: Ready?

HANNAH: OK!
  *(Hand in hand, giggling, they run back as the wave crashes. Lights fade on
  the sisters, laughing, and the sound of the Pacific Ocean.)*

END OF PLAY

PSYCH

By Evan Smith

PLAYWRIGHT'S BIOGRAPHY

Evan Smith's *Psych* and *The Uneasy Chair* have been produced by Playwrights Horizons. His play *Servicemen* was produced by The New Group; before that, it had been produced by New York Stage and Film at the Powerhouse Theater. His play *The Ecstasy of Lucy* was produced by the Home for Contemporary Theatre at HERE. Recently, Mr. Smith was named one of the ten recipients of the prestigious Giles Whiting Foundation Award.

INTRODUCTION

This play grew out of two separate but related phenomena I have observed lately — one, the almost universally horrendous time everyone I know has had in graduate school, and two, how an excess of goodness seems to bring down upon people nothing but misery. It is telling that one can use a phrase like "excess of goodness" and people will nod their heads in understanding, whereas in a proper world they would be flummoxed by the oxymoronic nature of the phrase. I have had several friends — mostly women, but some men, too — whose repeated, dogged attempts at doing good have brought only greater and greater enmity from the people they were dealing with. Why this should be, I don't know; anyone can offer several hypotheses, all are valid. I do not attempt to explain this behavior in *Psych*, merely describe it.

As for graduate school, I know several people — as it turns out, writers — who were all but destroyed by higher education. One acquaintance of mine, a very successful actress, having been told in graduate school that she should not hope to have a professional career, to this day can summon with alarming vividness the anger she felt at those short-sighted and ignorant teachers. Reports I have heard from other fields — law, medicine, the liberal arts — all repeat variations on the same story. It is a tale of sadism, mind games, and a poisonous strain of academic politics that everyone loathes but inevitably is drawn into. Most insidious, however, is the suffocating mentorship, in which a professor's attempt at molding a student's mind becomes a catastrophic battle of wills.

But graduate school is just a setting for this play and takes a backseat to the real story, which is of a friendship. The character of Molly may be the subject of the play, in that she talks directly to the audience, but Sunny is the object at the center. One of the peculiarities of working on this play has been seeing the dismaying varieties of opinions on the basic question of who Sunny is. Some audience members thought she was too sweet for anyone to have ill will toward her, and others thought she was incredibly annoying. One difficult conversation over drinks with an old friend culminated in my friend's admission that he would like to date Sunny.

This play has a number of melodramatic devices, which I hope will be taken in the spirit of theatrical fun. But most of all, I hope readers or viewers of this play will be able to position themselves to see both sides of Sunny (and both sides of Molly), the professional and the prostitute, the psycho and the psychologist, the passive-aggressive self-martyr, and the saint.

ORIGINAL PRODUCTION

Psych premiered at Playwrights Horizons, New York, in December 2001. It was directed by Jim Simpson. The cast was as follows:

BILL/MICHAEL/GAR/ADVOCATE . . . . Danny Burstein

DOMINIQUE/JANA/BARBARA STAFFORD/THERAPIST . . Marissa Copeland

SUNNY GOLDFARB . . . . Heather Goldenhersh

MOLLY SALTER. . . . . Enid Graham

DESIREE/KAREN/JENNIFER. . . . . Katie Kreisler

TODD COX/PROFOUND PSYCHOTIC . . . . Damian Young

TIME

Late 1990s.

PLACE

Various locations in Brooklyn and Manhattan.

PSYCH

There are several reception area chairs, a table/desk, on which sits a phone, and, against a wall, a trunk with a lock. There are many doors, the placement of which implies a maze. Molly stands down center with two suitcases.

MOLLY: The first thing I should say before I go into the whole sordid saga is I don't know how it all ends. For all I know it's still going on. If you're looking for closure, look someplace else. We're fresh out here. Second, I wasn't there for most of the pertinent conversations, so I'll try to stick to just the facts, the concrete deeds that are not open to interpretation, and reinterpretation, and analysis . . . And as I can't hope to fathom the depths of what these various people were thinking when they said what they said or did what they did, I will do my best to remain unemotional. Third, everything you are about to hear is true. It all happened to my dear, dear friend, Sunny Goldfarb —
(Sunny enters, dressed as a dominatrix.)
— who is not a composite, but an actual flesh-and-blood person. She lives in Brooklyn. We went to school together. I love her like a sister. She also happens to have a moderately peculiar part-time job, but please do not obsess over that. It is one of those random statistical anomalies that can distract you from the essential. Finally, to paraphrase someone, Satan is in the details. Pay close attention, and judge for yourself.

• • •

Sunny is reading a large psychology textbook. Molly turns, as though just entering.

SUNNY: Hey, cutie!
MOLLY: Hi! Wow.
SUNNY: How was your flight?
MOLLY: God, it was a nightmare. I'm sorry I'm so late.
(Molly puts down her luggage.)
SUNNY: No, it's fine. Let me give you the key to the apartment —
MOLLY: It is so great to see you!
SUNNY: I know, I can't believe it. You look great.
MOLLY: I do not. I've gotten so fat since Vassar.
SUNNY: Oh, shut up.

(Sunny fishes through her bag. Dominique, also dressed as a dominatrix, enters carrying a magazine.)

MOLLY: *(To Dominique.)* Hi.

SUNNY: Oh, Molly, this is Dominique. Dominique, this is Molly. We went to college together.

(Dominique fake-smiles and reads her magazine. Sunny produces a key on a ring.)

SUNNY: Here you go. One key opens all the locks. Feel free to stay as long as you want —

MOLLY: No, I'm going apartment hunting first thing tomorrow.

SUNNY: Please, stay, I'll be sooooo happy to have the company.

MOLLY: God, I can't believe I'm in New York!

SUNNY: Oh, Molly!

MOLLY: Oh, Sunny! *(They hug.)* I've missed you!

SUNNY: I've missed you, too!

MOLLY: So. Where are we? What is this mysterious job of yours, and why are you dressed like a dominatrix?

(Sunny is about to answer when the buzzer sounds again. Sunny goes to the intercom.)

SUNNY: Yes?

BILL: *(Offstage, through intercom.)* I'm looking for the House of O?

SUNNY: Second floor. *(She hits the door buzzer.)* *(To Molly:)* A client. Um, just go along with whatever I say. I'll explain later.

(Bill enters, pleasantly preppy.)

BILL: Um, Hi.

(Mistress Dominique looks up, then goes back to her magazine.)

SUNNY: Hi.

BILL: I've never been here before; I don't know exactly . . .

SUNNY: You want me to show you around?

BILL: Yeah.

SUNNY: Sure thing. Well, um, welcome to the House of O. Uh . . . We have three dungeons, a body cage, and a dog cage, and a sling, plus, um, various manacles on the wall, a mummification table . . . Oh, and antigravity boots, for upside-down suspension, and um . . . I'm Mistress Serena, this is Mistress Dominique — *(She gestures to Dominique — who glances up — then she gestures to Molly.)* — and this is Mistress, um . . .

MOLLY: *(On the spot and not liking it.)* Debbie. Hi.

(Molly waves sweetly.)

SUNNY: Mistress Debbie. OK. There is also Mistress Desiree, but she's running a little late. I guess she'll be here sometime. I hope. Do you have any questions?

BILL: How much does it . . . ?

SUNNY: We start at one hundred fifty dollars an hour, more if you want two mistresses, or anything highly unusual —

BILL: No, I wouldn't —

SUNNY: All we do here are fantasy scenarios. There is no sex between clients and Mistresses, and Mistresses are not allowed to take off their clothes. If you offer them money for any sexual service, you will be asked to leave, and there will be no refund. We accept cash and credit cards, but we do not accept checks.

BILL: OK.

SUNNY: So, what would you like? Would you like a session right now?

BILL: Uh, yeah.

SUNNY: OK, that's fine. I'm available, I'm Mistress Serena, and Mistress Dominique is available. Mistress Debbie, you're leaving now, aren't you?

MOLLY: That is correct.

SUNNY: Mistress Desiree is late. *(To Dominique.)* Do you know where Desiree is? Dominique?

DOMINIQUE: *(Shaking her head.)* Uh-uh.

SUNNY: I hope she's all right. Anyway, it's just me and Mistress Dominique tonight.

BILL: I guess you . . .

SUNNY: Sure. Of course. Do you want to tell me a little about what you'd like?

BILL: Oh, I don't know. Nothing too wild. The usual, I guess.

SUNNY: Well, you know, there really isn't anything that you could call "the usual."

BILL: Oh.

SUNNY: Everybody who comes here is pretty much unique.

BILL: Wow. I guess so.

SUNNY: So really, it's totally up to you.

BILL: Well, I've always been curious about . . . things like this . . .

SUNNY: S and M?

BILL: Yeah, but not just that.

SUNNY: Bondage?

BILL: Yeah, more that than the other.

SUNNY: You're not into pain?

BILL: No.

(Molly wanders the farthest point in the room, trying not to appear to be paying any attention.)

SUNNY: But you like the idea of bondage.

BILL: Yeah.

SUNNY: How do you see yourself?

BILL: I beg your pardon?

SUNNY: What kind of bondage do you fantasize about?

BILL: Nothing specific . . .

SUNNY: Rope? Chains? A cage?

BILL: Well . . .

SUNNY: You can talk about it. I mean, I do it all day. I don't think you're gonna shock me.

BILL: Yeah . . . No . . .

SUNNY: Would you like for me to make some suggestions?

BILL: Yeah.

SUNNY: Well, I'd start out really simple, just maybe a little rope to tie your hands behind your back, and then maybe I'd retie them over your head — *(He nods diffidently.)*

SUNNY: And maybe I'd put a black leather hood over your face. *(He nods.)*

SUNNY: Maybe I'd just do whatever I felt like. *(Pause.)* Is that what you'd like? For me to take control? Do you want to be a slave?

BILL: It's like . . .

SUNNY: What?

BILL: It's just — OK. I'm paying for it, right?

SUNNY: Right.

BILL: So you'll do what I want.

SUNNY: Right.

BILL: But you're in control.

SUNNY: Right.

BILL: And that's, you know, sort of how I pictured it, but . . .

SUNNY: Go on.

BILL: But if I change my mind, are you going to do what I want?

SUNNY: OK. Right. See, what we have here is a fantasy scenario. You know, in some part of your head, that you're paying to be here, and that if you want to go, you can go. But in the fantasy part of your head, you're tied up and you're my slave, and my word is your command. My job is to give you exactly the fantasy you want, and I'm pretty good at my job. I have to get to know you, but I can learn exactly what you want. *(He nods. Pause.)*

BILL: Are you reading that?

(He points to the large psychology textbook in Sunny's hand.)

SUNNY: Yeah. I'm applying to clinical psychology programs. I have an interview tomorrow.

BILL: I guess you learn a lot about psychology in a place like this.

SUNNY: Oh, you know it.

BILL: You have an interview tomorrow?

SUNNY: Yeah. I've been studying.

BILL: For an interview?

SUNNY: These interviewers ask you questions. Try to put you on the spot to see how you'll react.

BILL: Really?

SUNNY: Oh, yes. They're very tricky. I mean, I majored in psychology as an undergrad, but that was years ago. I've forgotten everything.

BILL: Where did you go to undergrad?

SUNNY: Vassar. So did Mistress Debbie.

(Bill looks to Molly.)

BILL: Really?

MOLLY: Yeah.

BILL: Are you in psychology, too?

MOLLY: No, no. Law. I just graduated from law school. I'm going to take the New York Bar exam.

BILL: You know, I used to date a Vassar girl.

SUNNY: Really? What was her name?

BILL: Well, I don't think I should — How did you happen to end up — ?
(He gestures, indicating the dungeon.)

SUNNY: Working as a dominatrix? It pays really, really well.
(Desiree enters, half dominatrix, half goth chick. She is crying.)

DESIREE: Help me!

SUNNY: Desiree, what's wrong?

DESIREE: Gar said he was going to kill me.

SUNNY: Oh, my God. Was he serious?

DESIREE: I don't know.

SUNNY: Where is he now?

DESIREE: He said he was coming here.

SUNNY: When?

DESIREE: Tonight.

DOMINIQUE: Look, Desiree, don't be bringing this shit here, OK? Leave your fucked-upness at home.

SUNNY: He's not coming here. There's no way.

DESIREE: Yes he is. He said he was. He had his bowie knife.

SUNNY: Do you have someplace else you can go?

DESIREE: No!

SUNNY: What about your sister's?

(Sunny begins stroking Desiree's arm to calm her down.)

DESIREE: No.

SUNNY: Why not?

DESIREE: You know why.

SUNNY: You can go one night without it.

DESIREE: What about tomorrow?

SUNNY: Worry about tomorrow tomorrow.

DOMINIQUE: Hey hey! I'm serious! Get your drug-infested little ass out of here before I throw you out!

SUNNY: Dominique, we're just talking.

DOMINIQUE: We have a client!

SUNNY: *(To Bill.)* I'm sorry, we'll be done in just a minute.

BILL: No problem.

SUNNY: Now Desiree. Calm down. You're going to go to your sister's. Don't call Gar. Don't go by the club. Don't call any of your connections and don't tell anybody where you're going. Are you listening to me? I want you to call me tomorrow morning, all right? Promise me. Promise me!

DESIREE: I promise.

SUNNY: Great. I'm very proud of you. You're very brave.

DESIREE: Let me stay here.

SUNNY: You can't stay here.

DOMINIQUE: Come on, Desiree.

(Dominique starts pushing Desiree to the door.)

DESIREE: Stop it!

DOMINIQUE: Get the fuck out, you fucked-up little junkie!

DESIREE: He's gonna kill me!

(Dominique shoves her out the door. Pause.)

SUNNY: Did you have to do that?

DOMINIQUE: You want to be next?

(Dominique returns to her magazine.)

BILL: *(To Molly.)* Some crazy place.

MOLLY: *(Cool.)* Oh, you know how it is.

SUNNY: *(To Bill.)* I'm sorry. Where were we?

BILL: Will that guy really try to kill her?

SUNNY: Oh absolutely. Last time, she needed seventeen pints of blood. She has a scar from her neck to her hip.

BILL: Why doesn't she call the police?

DOMINIQUE: She's an idiot.

SUNNY: It's really hard when you're an addict and your boyfriend-slash-supplier is threatening to kill you. You want to leave, but you need the drugs.

DOMINIQUE: She's a lying thieving bitch whore, and if she ever comes back here again, I'll kill her myself.

SUNNY: I'm really sorry you had to see all this. I promise it'll never happen again.

BILL: Well, it's an experience.

(Pause.)

SUNNY: So, where were we?

BILL: Oh yeah . . . You know, Mistress Serena, you're really nice, and smart, and I hope your interview goes well tomorrow. I think you'd be a great psychologist.

SUNNY: Thanks.

BILL: I was wondering if maybe Mistress Dominique was available?

SUNNY: Oh. Sure. No problem. Dominique?

DOMINIQUE: Shit. I've got to clean up. You'll have to wait.

BILL: No problem.

DOMINIQUE: And it comes out of your hour.

BILL: Yes, ma'am.

(Dominique and Bill exit. Pause.)

SUNNY: Well, let me give you directions to the apartment.

MOLLY: Great.

(Pause as Sunny starts to draw a little map.)

SUNNY: So. You're going to take the New York Bar Exam. That's so great.

MOLLY: Yeah.

SUNNY: As you can see, my life is a little crazy right now.

MOLLY: Oh . . . *(Molly makes a little deprecating gesture.)*

SUNNY: Anyway. I'm really happy you're going to be staying with me.

MOLLY: Oh, yeah. Me, too.

(Sunny smiles, happy. Molly smiles, terrified.)

• • •

Sunny changes from her dominatrix outfit into navy-blue pinstripe slacks, a crisp white blouse, a snug double breasted blazer, and sensible shoes. Todd enters, coming to a door.

TODD: Sunny Goldfarb?

SUNNY: Oh. Hi. That's me.

TODD: Please come with me.

(Sunny is struggling to get dressed. She ends up slightly disheveled and out of breath. They cross to Todd's desk and sit across from each other.)

SUNNY: Hi. Are you Dr. Cox?

TODD: Yes. Have a seat.

(She sits. He sits across from her, looking at some papers.)

I was just looking at your application, and it doesn't look like you're very qualified.

(A tense little pause while Sunny calculates her response.)

SUNNY: I'm sorry to hear you say that.

TODD: Why?

SUNNY: Because I want to go to school here.

TODD: You may be wasting your time.

SUNNY: Oh. *(Pause.)* I was hoping you might ask me some more questions. When I applied, I thought that I was pretty qualified. Enough to be, you know, in the running.

(He picks her résumé out of the papers.)

TODD: Like what are you talking about specifically?

SUNNY: I have a Masters in Developmental from Brown. I've been published in two respected psychology journals. I assisted on many trials at Brown. I interned at Cedars Sinai.

TODD: This is all pretty typical.

SUNNY: Really? Your applicant pool must be exceptional.

TODD: Well, what kind of questions do you want me to ask you?

SUNNY: Um . . . maybe, something like, why do you want to go to school here . . . what are my interests . . .

TODD: That's all here in your essay.

SUNNY: That's right. It is . . .

(Long pause as Todd observes Sunny.)

TODD: What drew you to psychology?

SUNNY: I've always been fascinated by psychology. Ever since I was a little kid, I've wanted to understand what makes people act the way they do. I think that if the field of psychology can help people to —

TODD: You've been interested in psychology since you were a little kid?

SUNNY: Yes.

TODD: What would draw a little kid to psychology?

SUNNY: Oh, the usual. I was interested in that kind of thing.

TODD: You must have had an interesting childhood.

SUNNY: Is analysis part of the application procedure?

TODD: Is there a reason you don't want to talk about it?

SUNNY: No, not at all. I love talking about my childhood. It's all I ever talk about. It was pretty normal. I fought with my parents a lot.

TODD: Is that normal?

SUNNY: I think so.

TODD: Really?

SUNNY: Yeah. I've talked with a lot of my friends, and they all seem to have gone through a phase of fighting with their parents. I know that means my evidence is just anecdotal, and my sample is not random, and my subjects were all drawn from a similar socioeconomic background, and they were all of a similar age, but . . .

TODD: Would it be abnormal, then, to not fight with one's parents?

SUNNY: Uh, that's an interesting idea. I don't know if I'm qualified to answer that.

TODD: That sounds like an evasion.

SUNNY: Yeah, I guess that's what it was.

TODD: So . . . ?

SUNNY: Well, my first instinct is to say, yes, it is abnormal to not fight with one's parents, but I don't know how generally that principle applies. Perhaps it only holds for people with exactly my demographic background.
(*Todd makes a note on a pad.*)

TODD: Tell me about your suit.

SUNNY: My suit?

TODD: Do you always dress so masculinely?

SUNNY: Uh, no. Is this masculine?

TODD: You don't think so?

SUNNY: I guess it is. I have to admit, though, that mainly I was trying to pick out something fashionable and stylish that also looked professional. I hadn't realized that it might also be read as masculine.

TODD: You don't think that a blue pinstripe suit is masculine?

SUNNY: Well, you know, when you put it like that . . . I suppose it is sort of androgynous, and yet that's the style being set these days for women. Society sends very mixed signals sometimes. One might almost say that for a woman to meet expectations of stylish femininity, she has to be masculine. She has to masculine to be feminine. But also, I think, deep down, I really do want to be a man.
(*He makes a note.*)

TODD: Tell me a little about your parents.

SUNNY: Well, I was adopted.

TODD: *(Perking up.)* Really?

SUNNY: Yes.

TODD: Do you have issues with that?

SUNNY: Oh, gosh. I guess so.

TODD: Like what?

SUNNY: Fear of abandonment, mainly.

TODD: You've thought about this much?

SUNNY: Oh, yes. I've thought about it. I mean, it cuts both ways, doesn't it? Yes, your birth parents abandoned you, but your adoptive parents sought you out and took you home and loved you and needed you. One makes you insecure, the other makes you secure. Yin and yang.

TODD: One, um, scenario is not more primal than the other?

SUNNY: Well, yes, abandonment is very primal, but nonadopted children experience abandonment anxiety in equal measure to adopted children.

TODD: Do you consider yourself secure or insecure?

SUNNY: I consider myself very secure.

(Pause. He makes a note.)

TODD: I think you're being easy on yourself.

SUNNY: Really?

TODD: I think so.

SUNNY: That could be true. Maybe I am being easy on myself. Insecurities are very hard to face on one's own. I'll work on that. Thank you.

TODD: Can you stay a minute?

SUNNY: Uh, sure.

(Todd exits through the upstage door. Sunny leans over to read his notepad. She turns it to face her, then turns it back. Todd enters.)

TODD: So tell my why you want to go to school here.

SUNNY: Well, I've been really impressed with the work of Barbara Stafford. I would consider it a privilege to study with her. I've done a lot of work in developmental and her name was everywhere. The Hartford Studies and all her Yale stuff. She's the one who drew me to clinical.

TODD: Ninety percent of your first year classes will be with me. Do you still want to go to school here?

SUNNY: Yes. Absolutely.

TODD: I think a lot of Barbara's work is overrated. *(Sunny nods.)* Where else are you applying?

SUNNY: I thought I would spread a wide net . . .

TODD: Where?

SUNNY: Um . . . Yale, Columbia, Berkeley, UNC, NYU . . .

TODD: Ambitious.

SUNNY: I figured, what have I got to lose? Except sixty-five dollars an application.

TODD: Do you honestly think you have a chance at Yale or Columbia or Berkeley?

SUNNY: I don't know. I just don't know.

TODD: So is this program your first choice, second choice, tenth choice?

SUNNY: I hadn't really ranked them like that. It all depends on where I get in.

TODD: You're telling me you don't have a first choice?

SUNNY: Well, each school has different selling points. Some have a great faculty, some have a beautiful campus, some have a convenient location . . .

TODD: All around. On average. If you could pick.

(She thinks.)

SUNNY: I guess I'd have to say here.

TODD: You don't sound too enthusiastic.

SUNNY: Well, I'm trying to hold something back here. I don't want to, you know, throw myself at you. Beg on my hands and knees. *(Pause.)* That wouldn't be fair to you.

TODD: We take so few students, we really want to make sure they all really want to be here.

SUNNY: Well, it's a great school.

(He stands and puts out his hand.)

TODD: Thank you for coming in.

(She stands and shakes.)

SUNNY: Thank you. *(She looks at him. He says nothing.)* OK. Good-bye.

TODD: Close the door behind you.

(She leaves the room, closing the door.)

• • •

Sunny exits. Karen and Michael enter, chic, with snap beans they snap and put on a plate.

KAREN: Oh. My. God. Sunny Goldfarb is a dominatrix. That is so perfect.

MOLLY: But she's a total failure. She's the least domineering person you've ever met. It's like watching Margaret O'Brien try to be a dominatrix.

MICHAEL: Why can't I remember her?

KAREN: You met her. She was at our table Spring Formal junior year. She was dressed like a medieval princess.

MICHAEL: And now she works in a brothel?

MOLLY: No! It's not a brothel. There's no sex. No nudity. It's like Disneyland. They walk around in elaborate character costumes and play mind games. And she's just doing it until she starts school. She just got accepted into a clinical psychology program.

KAREN: She's going to be a psychologist? Oh, God save us.

MOLLY: Why were all of you so mean to her?

KAREN: I wasn't mean to her.

MOLLY: Yes you were. You and Lise and Claire and Steph. You were total bitches.

KAREN: That is not true! I was always very nice to her.

MOLLY: Weren't you a part of that group that went to Steph's brother and said all those things?

KAREN: I had nothing to do with that.

MICHAEL: What happened?

MOLLY: Sunny was a part of this little set — Steph Cody and Lise Bundy and Claire what's-her-name —

KAREN: Minukin.

MOLLY: And Steph Cody's brother was visiting Vassar from Amherst.

KAREN: Chris.

MOLLY: And he fell instantly in love with Sunny.

KAREN: He did not.

MOLLY: Yes he did. See, you believe what happened later. Anyway, Lise and Claire and Steph all went to him and told him I-don't-know-what about Sunny and he immediately dropped her.

KAREN: He didn't drop her. You can't drop somebody over a long weekend. That's not time to pick somebody up.

MOLLY: The point is, these three girls who were supposed to be Sunny's friends all got together and stabbed her in the back.

KAREN: You didn't even know Sunny then. You weren't there.

MOLLY: I heard all about it.

KAREN: You heard Sunny's side.

MOLLY: I didn't *need* to hear their side. I've seen the way people take advantage of Sunny. She's very sweet and good and they were a pack of harpies who wanted to tear her down because Steph's brother liked her. Besides, if I had been there, it wouldn't have happened.

KAREN: Like you could have stopped it.

MOLLY: I know the difference between real friends and fake friends.

KAREN: Whatever. I was not a part of that.

MOLLY: Anyway. I get very protective when it comes to Sunny.

MICHAEL: Yes, you do.

MOLLY: Well. Enough about me. Have you two set a date yet? How long are you going to keep us all waiting?

(Karen looks at Michael.)

KAREN: Yes, Michael, how long are we going to keep them all waiting?

(He holds up the plate of beans.)

MICHAEL: Is this enough?

KAREN: More than.

(She takes the beans and exits.)

MOLLY: Did I just put my foot in it?

MICHAEL: No more than usual.

(Molly and Michael exit.)

• • •

Sunny and Todd Cox enter.

TODD: Have a seat.

(Sunny sits. He stands.)

Welcome to the first year class.

SUNNY: Oh, thank you.

TODD: Congratulations.

SUNNY: Thank you.

TODD: Are you excited?

SUNNY: Oh, yes.

TODD: I bet you are. How does it feel?

SUNNY: Great.

TODD: Yeah?

SUNNY: Really . . . great. I just wanted to ask you about this letter I got —

TODD: What letter is that?

SUNNY: This one. *(She produces a letter.)* It's from Columbia, where, it turns out, I was on the wait list.

TODD: Ah.

SUNNY: It says that my application was withdrawn because I enrolled in another program.

TODD: You did.

SUNNY: No, I made a deposit to hold my place in this program.

TODD: Same thing.

SUNNY: I don't think. so. I mean, if I wanted to withdraw my application to Columbia, I could have done it myself.

TODD: You did.

SUNNY: No, I did not. This letter says the Admissions Director of this program did. I never authorized that.

TODD: Oh, but you did. *(He produces the form she signed.)* Is that your signature? *(She looks at it.)*

"By my signature I agree that I have read, and will abide by, and be held to, all of the rules and by-laws of the program, stated or implied in the *Student Handbook of Academic Regulations.*" On page three of the Student Handbook, you will see that upon enrollment in the program, all degree candidates are required to withdraw all applications to other programs. *(He hands her the student handbook. She reads it carefully.)* Besides, you were at pretty much the bottom of the Columbia wait list. You wouldn't have gotten in.

SUNNY: They told you where I was on the wait list? *(He nods.)* What if I had been number one?

TODD: What difference does it make?

SUNNY: I don't remember you showing me this handbook when I signed this form.

TODD: I didn't. You didn't ask me to. *(Pause.)* Are you having second thoughts? *(Pause.)* After all, you did tell me this was your first choice.

SUNNY: It is my first choice, my only choice. I was just asking 'cause I got this in the mail, and I didn't know what it meant, and . . . *(She shrugs.)* But you know, I'm excited. *(She smiles.)*

• • •

Todd exits. Jana enters, carrying a book bag.

JANA: Yes! That's it!

SUNNY: And when he sits next to you in the student's lounge —

JANA: What is it he wears? That cologne?

SUNNY: I think it's Brut by Faberge.

JANA: God, it's like, "Please, Todd, sit someplace else!"

SUNNY: It wouldn't be so bad if he didn't get so close.

JANA: He thinks he's developing an interpersonal relationship.

SUNNY: And could his name be more phallic? Todd Cox?

JANA: Well, he's a Freudian.

(Jennifer enters, also with a book bag.)

JENNIFER: Hi, Jana.

JANA: Hi, Jennifer.

SUNNY: Hi, Jennifer.

JENNIFER: Finish that outline yet?

JANA: Not yet.

JENNIFER: Me either.

SUNNY: When is that due?

JENNIFER: Jana, I'll call you.

JANA: Sure.

JENNIFER: Bye.

JANA: Bye.

(Jennifer starts to exit.)

SUNNY: Bye, Jennifer! *(Jennifer exits.)* Why doesn't Jennifer like me?

JANA: Who says Jennifer doesn't like you?

SUNNY: Uh, Jennifer.

JANA: She said that?

SUNNY: She might as well have. She ignores me when I greet her, she won't look at me in class, she disagrees with everything I say . . .

JANA: You're exaggerating.

SUNNY: I'm not.

JANA: Well, she's shy. You have a dominant personality.

SUNNY: I do not. I'm totally field dependent.

JANA: Let's just say you're an ambiguous stimulus. To Jennifer.

SUNNY: What do you mean?

JANA: I don't mean anything. I'm sure she likes you fine. Or probably she doesn't think about you one way or the other.

SUNNY: She thinks about me.

JANA: You're being paranoid. Don't worry about it.

• • •

Jana exits. Molly enters.

SUNNY: Why do people hate me?

MOLLY: People don't hate you.

SUNNY: Yes they do. Some people do.

MOLLY: Well some people hate everybody.

SUNNY: But me especially. What is it? You would tell me wouldn't you? Is there something I don't know about that makes people dislike me?

MOLLY: Of course not! People like you! I like you. All your friends like you. You're pretty and smart and fun and funny, and you have an offbeat way of looking at the world that is very refreshing.

SUNNY: *(Fearful.)* Offbeat? How?

MOLLY: I don't know. Good offbeat. What is it? Why do you think people hate you?

SUNNY: You've never noticed it?

MOLLY: What?

SUNNY: People pulling away? Talking behind my back?

MOLLY: You're being paranoid.

SUNNY: That's what Jana said.

MOLLY: Who's Jana?

SUNNY: Someone at school. Do you really think I'm paranoid?

MOLLY: No! Sunny, look, don't think about it. It doesn't matter. You're wonderful. Everybody loves you. I love you. The whole world loves you. OK? *(Molly gives Sunny a big hug.)*

• • •

Molly exits. Jennifer enters.

SUNNY: Hey, Jennifer.

JENNIFER: Hey.

SUNNY: I bought a whole bag of bagels this morning. Want one?

JENNIFER: No, thanks.

SUNNY: I was really impressed with your comments in class yesterday. You must have a real gift for statistics.

JENNIFER: Thank you.

SUNNY: You want to have lunch sometime?

JENNIFER: Um, no thanks.

SUNNY: I don't mean today. Any time.

JENNIFER: I don't eat lunch usually.

SUNNY: Uh, dinner?

JENNIFER: Maybe. I have very strict dietary requirements. Probably not.

SUNNY: OK. Maybe we could go to a movie, or just have a drink.

JENNIFER: I have a boyfriend. I usually go to movies and have drinks with him.

SUNNY: No, no, I didn't mean a date. I have a boyfriend, too. I just meant, we could do something. We could double.

JENNIFER: I don't think so. He doesn't like that sort of thing.

SUNNY: OK . . .

JENNIFER: Sorry.

SUNNY: No, we've got plenty of time. It is a three-year program. Why don't I give you my number —

JENNIFER: Well, you know, I hardly ever call people.

SUNNY: Really.

JENNIFER: Yeah.

• • •

Jennifer exits. Todd enters. Sunny knocks on Todd's door.

TODD: Come in.

    (She goes in.)

SUNNY: Sorry I'm late.

TODD: What's the problem, Sunny? Why can't you be here on time?

SUNNY: I'm really sorry. I had trouble at work.

TODD: Sunny. I need to know how seriously you take this program.

SUNNY: I take it very seriously.

TODD: Do you? Sometimes it doesn't seem that way.

SUNNY: What do you mean?

TODD: It has been noticed that you often seem to be wearing inappropriate clothing.

SUNNY: In what way?

TODD: Revealing, clinging, provocative clothing. Is this what you wear in a session with a patient?

SUNNY: I never wear anything even slightly revealing with a patient. Do you think I'm trying to seduce my patients? I wear ankle-length dresses and sweaters.

TODD: And sometimes those sweaters stop at the midriff, and sometimes the dresses are made of clinging, silky, sheer fabrics.

SUNNY: I don't have any dresses in sheer fabrics. None that I wear by themselves.

TODD: You wear tights under them.

SUNNY: Yes.

TODD: And that's not provocative?

SUNNY: No.

    (Pause.)

TODD: There's been a complaint.

SUNNY: Someone complained about what I was wearing?

TODD: No, not about what you were wearing. How you were behaving.

SUNNY: Who?

TODD: One of your classmates claims you've been making unwanted advances.

SUNNY: That's crazy.

TODD: Do you know who made the complaint?

SUNNY: Who?

TODD: You don't know?

SUNNY: No. I can't imagine. These are supposed to be sexual advances?

TODD: Not necessarily.

SUNNY: Then what?

TODD: You don't know?

SUNNY: No! I said I didn't. I have not got the slightest idea who would accuse me of making inappropriate sexual, or perhaps not sexual, advances. Any behavior like that would be completely uncharacteristic for me. Ask anyone. And that I would do that here, at school, is just — It's insane. I don't even like anybody here. I only have one friend in my class.

TODD: You don't like anybody here? *(She slumps.)* Please don't get upset.

SUNNY: No, I'm not upset. I'm just . . . I'm sorry that I've inadvertently allowed some one to get this mistaken impression. That this person was misreading me so, um, so inaccurately.

TODD: What's your solution?

SUNNY: To what?

TODD: The problem.

SUNNY: And the problem is what?

TODD: See, I just don't get the impression you take this program very seriously.

• • •

Todd exits.

SUNNY: A *bagel.* I offered her a *bagel.*

MOLLY: And she files a formal complaint?

SUNNY: Can you believe that?

MOLLY: So, like, what did she accuse you of? Malicious bagel-offering?

SUNNY: Advances. I was making advances.

MOLLY: Sexual advances? Is she a lesbian, this girl?

SUNNY: No, she's obviously a homophobe.

MOLLY: So they think you're a lesbian?

SUNNY: I guess so. I don't know. Todd can't possibly believe her.

MOLLY: Can't you just explain your side of the story?

SUNNY: I did. He doesn't care. He's disciplining me. He wants me to fall in line. I mean, does this outfit look clinging and provocative to you?

(She's wearing a long cotton skirt and a tight top.)

MOLLY: Not at all.

SUNNY: I mean, this a normal outfit, right? Does this look like I'm trying to seduce my patients?

MOLLY: Not at all.

SUNNY: And why does he keep talking about my clothes? Doesn't that seem a little weird to you? My suit? My pinstripe suit? Remember, at my interview?

MOLLY: That's right.

SUNNY: My pinstripe suit that's so *masculine.* From the very first, he's had a thing about my clothes.

MOLLY: Creepy.

SUNNY: Obsessive. I'm not obsessive. He's the one that's obsessive. Jennifer is obsessive.

MOLLY: Yeah.

SUNNY: I mean, is this outfit sexy?

MOLLY: Sexy?

SUNNY: Is it seductive?

MOLLY: No, I mean . . .

SUNNY: What?

MOLLY: You look good . . .

SUNNY: Well, what am I supposed to do? Wear glasses and oxfords and, and —

MOLLY: No —

SUNNY: — whatever, *tents? That's* not normal. That's *ab*normal. I am very well socialized to my environment. They are the ones who are dissociated from reality. *(Little pause.)* So there.

MOLLY: *(Mock vehement.)* YEAH!!!

• • •

Jennifer enters. Sunny approaches a doorway.

SUNNY: Jennifer?

(Jennifer looks up.)

SUNNY: Hi, I was wondering if we could talk?

JENNIFER: I'm really busy.

SUNNY: It won't take any time.

JENNIFER: You know, I think I'd really rather not.

SUNNY: I just want to say that I think you've gotten a mistaken impression of me.

JENNIFER: I just said I don't want to talk.

SUNNY: All I want to do is apologize.

JENNIFER: That's not necessary.

SUNNY: I want to.

JENNIFER: I don't care.

SUNNY: What on earth did I do to make you hate me so much?!

JENNIFER: I don't hate you. I don't hate people.

SUNNY: Why did you file a complaint against me?

JENNIFER: Excuse me.

(She tries to move past Sunny through the door, but Sunny does not make room.)

SUNNY: Just tell me. I think we can work this out. I never meant to do anything to annoy you.

JENNIFER: What makes you think I filed a complaint against you? Did someone tell you that?

SUNNY: Come on, Jennifer. I need you to be honest with me.

JENNIFER: Are saying I'm a liar?

SUNNY: No! God, no. Just calm down and talk to me.

(Jennifer walks around the table in the other direction to get to the door. Sunny stands in the doorway.)

SUNNY: Why won't you talk to me?

JENNIFER: Are you going to let me out of this room?

SUNNY: What do you have against me? Why do you get this way?

JENNIFER: Can you even hear yourself? Everything you say is, "Why do you — " and "Why can't you — " Why is it always the other person?

SUNNY: All right. What have *I* done to make you so antagonistic?

JENNIFER: You haven't made me do anything. God! Are you going to let me out of this room, or do I have to scream for security?

(Sunny moves out of the doorway. Jennifer exits.)

• • •

MOLLY: What a psycho bitch from hell.

SUNNY: They know she's a lunatic. They know all about her history.

MOLLY: What history?

SUNNY: God, she's deeply troubled. All right, she's a Catholic — she was born a Catholic — but sometime in her twenties, she converted to Judaism. Then, she joined a *Hasidic* group and lived in Williamsburg for a few years, but then she quit that and became a *nun*. And then after a few years, she quit *that,* left the convent and married a *priest,* an ex-priest, and then got *divorced,* and that was when she decided to become a *psychologist.*

MOLLY: Jesus.

SUNNY: I weep for her patients.

MOLLY: Look. If she's accusing you of attacking her, what could it hurt to actually attack her, you know? Just grab her one day in the hall when no one is looking and say, "Listen, Jennifer, if you don't stop fucking with me, I will seriously fuck with you. I will fillet you like a mackerel."

SUNNY: Jennifer is not the problem. It's Todd. He's like a life form that's trying to crawl inside my brain and turn me into him. He's trying to colonize me. *(The phone rings. Molly answers it.)*

MOLLY: Hello? *(Molly freezes in terror/amusement. She puts her hand over the mouthpiece. Whispers.)* It's Todd Cox!

SUNNY: *(Whispers.)* I'm not here!

MOLLY: Um, she's not here right now. Would you like to leave a message? *(Pause. As if writing it down.)* Todd Cox called . . . call back right away . . . it's important. *(Pause. Molly walks over to the speaker phone and turns it on.)* OK. Um, can I tell her to what this is in reference?

TODD: *(On speaker phone.)* I'm calling from school. Tell her I'll be up late; she can call me when she gets in.

MOLLY: I will do that.

TODD: *(On speaker phone.)* And to whom am I speaking?

MOLLY: This her roommate, Molly.

TODD: *(On speaker phone.)* Thank you, Molly.

MOLLY: You're welcome, Todd. Bye.

TODD: *(On speaker phone.)* Bye.

(She hangs up the speaker phone.)

MOLLY: He'll be up late? You can call when you get in?

SUNNY: He's fucking with me. He wants me to confide in him. He wants me to depend on him.

(The phone rings. Sunny hits the speaker phone.)

SUNNY: Hello?

TODD: *(On speaker phone.)* Sunny?

(In a panic, Sunny gestures to Molly to talk.)

MOLLY: Uh, no, she's not here right now. Can I take a message?

TODD: Uh, no, I just called a second ago. I was just going to say, I'm out of the office, but she can reach me there after five.

MOLLY: After five. Okey-doke.

TODD: Thanks. Bye.

MOLLY: Bye.

(Sunny hangs up.)

SUNNY: He did that on purpose. He wanted to catch me in a lie.

MOLLY: Are you supposed to be at school?

SUNNY: No. He just doesn't trust me. He thinks I'm a liar.

MOLLY: Well, you are here.

SUNNY: Well, it's none of his business. I don't have to take his calls.

(The phone rings. They look at each other. Sunny hits the speaker phone.)

MOLLY: Hello? (Silence.) Hello? (Silence.) No one there?

(Silence. Molly hangs up the speaker phone.)

SUNNY: That was Todd. He is such a freak. He called again to see if I would answer.

MOLLY: Why would he?

SUNNY: He's a psychopath! I'm gonna star-six-nine his ass. (She picks up the phone and dials. Pause.) Gimme a pen!

(Molly grabs pen and paper and gives it to Sunny. Sunny writes down a number.)

MOLLY: Is that his number?

SUNNY: No. But he said he wasn't in his office.

(She starts to dial.)

MOLLY: What are you gonna say if he picks up?

SUNNY: I'm gonna hang up.

MOLLY: He can star-six-nine you right back.

(Sunny hangs up and thinks.)

SUNNY: Let me do it from your phone.

(Molly exits and comes back with another phone, stretching the cord to get it onstage.)

MOLLY: Here.

(Sunny dials. Pause.)

SUNNY: It's ringing.

MOLLY: *Hang up! Hang up!*

SUNNY: (Hanging up.) What?!

MOLLY: What if he has caller ID? I told him my name. Caller ID has your name.

SUNNY: He doesn't have caller ID.

MOLLY: How do you know?

SUNNY: I've never seen it.

MOLLY: He's not at his office.

(Molly's phone rings. They jump.)

SUNNY: He star-six-nined. Don't answer. He won't know it's your number.

MOLLY: Unless he has caller ID.

SUNNY: He doesn't have caller ID.

(The phone continues to ring.)

MOLLY: You don't know that.

SUNNY: Either way, he doesn't know your last name. Don't answer. If he star-six-nined, he won't know anything.

(Molly's answering machine suddenly picks up.)

MOLLY'S VOICE: This is Molly Salter, I can't —

MOLLY: Shit!

MOLLY'S VOICE: — come to phone right now, so leave a —

SUNNY: Turn it off!

MOLLY'S VOICE: — message, thank you, thank you, thank you.

MOLLY: Then he'll know we're home!

(Pause as they listen for a message. Silence. The machine turns off. Pause.)

MOLLY: Maybe it wasn't him.

SUNNY: It was him.

MOLLY: Go over his head. File a complaint with what's-her-name, the one you say is so brilliant.

SUNNY: Barbara Stafford.

MOLLY: She's the director of the program, right?

(Sunny nods.)

MOLLY: I mean Jennifer started it. Fight fire with fire.

SUNNY: Yeah. I should.

MOLLY: God, I wish I could be there.

SUNNY: You wanna be there?

MOLLY: I wanna be a fly on the wall.

SUNNY: I can arrange that.

• • •

Barbara Stafford enters. She is slim and pretty, and conservatively dressed, like a politician's wife. Sunny dials her tiny cell phone. The phone rings and Molly answers it.

MOLLY: Hello?

SUNNY: Hey. I'm just about to go in.

(Molly hits a button on the answering machine.)
MOLLY: OK. The tape is going.
(Barbara Stafford goes to the door.)
BARBARA STAFFORD: Sunny.
(Sunny turns.)
BARBARA STAFFORD: Come on back.
(Sunny places her still-open cell phone in her bag and goes through the door. Molly stays on the line, listening to the entire conversation.)
BARBARA STAFFORD: Hi. How are you?
SUNNY: Oh, I'm fine. How are you?
(They sit.)
BARBARA STAFFORD: I've always thought you have such a pretty name.
SUNNY: Oh, thank you.
BARBARA STAFFORD: I think of that song . . . Well. What can I do for you?
SUNNY: I just wanted to ask your advice on how to handle some things.
BARBARA STAFFORD: OK.
SUNNY: Well, for example, there's a student who always seems to misinterpret what I do, and what I say.
BARBARA STAFFORD: In what way?
SUNNY: Like I made an effort at the beginning of the semester to get to know her, so I tried to spend a little time with her, and she thought I was harassing her.
BARBARA STAFFORD: Why did she think that?
SUNNY: I don't know.
BARBARA STAFFORD: What did she say you had done?
SUNNY: I don't know. She filed a complaint.
BARBARA STAFFORD: Well, what do you think she said?
SUNNY: I think she said I was making unwanted, unspecified advances. Not necessarily sexual. I don't know. Todd told me about it.
BARBARA STAFFORD: And what did you really do?
SUNNY: Nothing. I just asked her to have lunch with me a couple of times, I invited her to a party, to a movie . . . I just tried to break through this wall of resistance I felt she had for me.
BARBARA STAFFORD: That doesn't sound like harassment. I had a student once, a male, who filed charge after charge of inappropriate behavior against me with the Dean. He charged me with everything, selling grades, sexual harassment, intimidation. He would not be placated.
SUNNY: What did you do?
BARBARA STAFFORD: I waited for him to graduate.

SUNNY: You think I should wait it out?

BARBARA STAFFORD: Well, this student is a classmate of yours. You're going to have all of your classes together. You'll be doing lab work together.

SUNNY: I know.

BARBARA STAFFORD: We all really need for the two of you to get along.

SUNNY: Yes, that's what I want, too.

BARBARA STAFFORD: I'm glad to hear you say that. The students who do the best here are the ones that can learn from their mistakes.

SUNNY: What exactly was my mistake?

BARBARA STAFFORD: You tell me.

SUNNY: Well, I can't think of anything that I should have done differently. I don't think it was my behavior that was inappropriate.

BARBARA STAFFORD: Well, I understand that it takes two to have a fight. And I've met the student in question here. She's very bright, but she has a lot of issues. I'm sure she was equally to blame.

(Sunny squirms.)

BARBARA STAFFORD: What?

SUNNY: From my perspective, the blame is not equal.

BARBARA STAFFORD: Are you aware she has filed a second complaint, with a request for disciplinary action?

SUNNY: No, I was not aware of that.

BARBARA STAFFORD: She says you attacked her.

(Molly is shocked.)

SUNNY: I see.

BARBARA STAFFORD: That you cornered her in a classroom, blocked her exit, became violently aggressive, and threatened her with bodily harm.

(Molly does a little mime/dance of frustration.)

SUNNY: Well.

BARBARA STAFFORD: Do you have a response?

SUNNY: Yes. My response is that that is a complete lie.

BARBARA STAFFORD: A complete lie?

SUNNY: Yes, Ma'am.

BARBARA STAFFORD: So you were never alone with this student in a classroom?

SUNNY: Yes, I was, very briefly, but none of what she says happened happened.

BARBARA STAFFORD: You didn't block the door?

SUNNY: No.

BARBARA STAFFORD: You didn't threaten her?

SUNNY: Absolutely not.

BARBARA STAFFORD: Why do you suppose she says you did?

SUNNY: I couldn't make a diagnosis, but . . . She is basically exaggerating the original event all out of proportion. All I did was go to apologize to her. I saw her walk into —

BARBARA STAFFORD: Apologize for what?

SUNNY: For nothing, really. I knew she had filed a complaint against me, and so I went to apologize for whatever, just to make her feel good, to make her . . .

BARBARA STAFFORD: To make her withdraw the complaint.

(Molly hangs her head.)

SUNNY: Yeah, I suppose. I just didn't want her to think I was against her in any way, because I'm not. I mean, I'm not dangerous. I wasn't harassing her. So anyway . . .

BARBARA STAFFORD: You followed her into the classroom . . .

SUNNY: And I said I wanted to apologize, and she got very defensive, very paranoid, and then she left. And I was standing in the doorway, because that's just how far I came into the room. I wasn't blocking her or anything. I certainly made no threats, and I did not become violent.

BARBARA STAFFORD: Is it at all possible that you are minimizing your aggressiveness, the same way that she is exaggerating it?

SUNNY: I wasn't at all aggressive. I was very passive. I went in there to apologize.

BARBARA STAFFORD: And how did you feel when she refused to accept your apology?

(Sunny shrugs.)

That didn't make you feel at all angry?

SUNNY: No. I was confused; her behavior confused me. It didn't seem rational.

BARBARA STAFFORD: I see.

SUNNY: You don't believe me.

BARBARA STAFFORD: I have no doubt that that's how you experienced it, with maybe a small amount of hedging, but that's natural. It's just — accusations like these, while often exaggerated, usually have some foundation in fact. Except when the accuser is suffering from a profound psychosis.

SUNNY: Have we ruled out that possibility?

(Barbara Stafford chuckles.)

BARBARA STAFFORD: I'm glad you came in today. I'm glad you came to me first. It shows you're willing to work with us on this.

SUNNY: Of course.

BARBARA STAFFORD: And we won't be getting any more of these complaints?

(Sunny shrugs.)

SUNNY: I hope not.

BARBARA STAFFORD: I'm asking you.
   (Barbara Stafford exits.)

· · ·

MOLLY: She's really good.
SUNNY: Well, I can be good. I'll be perfect.

· · ·

Jennifer enters with an open letter in her hand.

SUNNY: Dear Jennifer. Let me take this opportunity to xapologize for the way I treated you last semester. I've always been the kind of student who manages to get by on looks and charm, and it threw me for quite a loop when I started classes here. My old tricks didn't seem to work, and when I saw you, so confident, calm, and uncompromised, always succeeding on your own terms, I was both drawn to your efficiency and angered by it. Anyway, before I knew it, I was out of control. Thank you so much for intervening. I'll always "owe you one" for seeing to it I got the help I needed when I needed it most. Thanks again, Sunny Goldfarb.
   (Jennifer exits. Barbara Stafford enters.)
BARBARA STAFFORD: So, looking back on all those events, what have you learned?
SUNNY: I think the biggest problem I had was learning to put the needs of the group first — before my own, more selfish need for, I don't know, recognition, I guess. I wanted to stand out in some way, be a star, and I couldn't see how detrimental that was to my classmates.
   (Barbara Stafford nods.)
But you know, the funniest thing is, I'm so relieved. It seems so obvious now, but I just didn't understand that what's best for me is what's best for the program. I know that I'll come out of this a much more efficient team player.
BARBARA STAFFORD: Great. I'm really impressed with your progress. Thanks for coming in.
SUNNY: Thank you for seeing me. I know how busy you are.
   (Barbara Stafford exits. Todd enters.)
TODD: Hey, Sunny. I heard your evaluation went really well.
SUNNY: Really? I bet you put in a good word for me. You're always looking out for me.
TODD: I do what I can.
SUNNY: Well let me thank you now, 'cause, really, you've been invaluable. I

don't know if I would have made it through without your advice, and support, and acumen.

TODD: And you've been in therapy?

SUNNY: Yes, yes, with Robert Goldberg, who you recommended, thank you so much.

TODD: You like him?

SUNNY: Oh, he's wonderful! He reminds me so much of you.

TODD: Really?

SUNNY: Absolutely. And he's been so helpful. We've been talking a lot about my obsession with independence.

TODD: Yeah.

SUNNY: I don't know what it was, some feminist, valedictorian hang-up. I needed so much to be self-sufficient, I couldn't go to anyone and just say "Help me." Even when I was the most . . . vulnerable. And lost.

TODD: Yeah. I could see that.

SUNNY: Really? Sometimes I get the feeling you know me better than I know myself.

TODD: Hey, you never know. Look, I gotta run. I'll see you later.

(He exits.)

SUNNY: *(Calling after him.)* OK, and thank you so much! You fucking bastard.

• • •

Sunny exits. Molly enters with a tape player. Molly hits play. The tape plays back Sunny's meeting with Barbara Stafford. Molly listens.

BARBARA STAFFORD'S VOICE: Is it at all possible that you are minimizing your aggressiveness, the same way that she is exaggerating it?

SUNNY'S VOICE: I wasn't at all aggressive. I was very passive. I went in there to apologize.

BARBARA STAFFORD'S VOICE: And how did you feel when she refused to accept your apology? That didn't make you feel at all angry?

SUNNY'S VOICE: No. I was confused; her behavior confused me. It didn't seem rational.

BARBARA STAFFORD'S VOICE: I see.

SUNNY'S VOICE: You don't believe me.

BARBARA STAFFORD'S VOICE: I have no doubt that's how you experienced it

(Molly rewinds the tape and hits play.)

BARBARA STAFFORD'S VOICE: And how did you feel when she refused to accept your apology? That didn't make you feel at all angry?

(Molly hits fast-forward then play.)

BARBARA STAFFORD'S VOICE: It's just — accusations like these, while often exaggerated, usually have some foundation in fact.

(Sunny enters. Molly immediately turns off the tape.)

SUNNY: Hey. Watcha doin'?

MOLLY: *(Shifty.)* Nothing.

(The phone rings. They look at it.)

• • •

Todd enters. Sunny approaches a door and knocks.

TODD: Come in.

(She opens the door.)

SUNNY: You wanted to see me?

TODD: Yes, Sunny, have a seat.

(Sunny sits. He stands.)

TODD: It has come to our attention that you have in the past and may still work as a prostitute.

• • •

Todd exits. Jana enters.

SUNNY: Jana, did you tell anyone about where I work?

JANA: No. Why?

SUNNY: Because Todd just accused me of being a prostitute.

JANA: What?

SUNNY: I denied it, and they're making me sign a deposition saying I never performed sex for money.

JANA: Sunny, they can't do that.

SUNNY: They have. It's just, I did not tell a soul about Purgatory. Not a soul. Except you.

JANA: Sunny, I didn't tell anybody. I swear.

SUNNY: Then how did they find out?

JANA: I don't know. Are you sure you didn't tell anybody else?

SUNNY: Who would I tell?

JANA: I don't know, but it wasn't me, so please don't accuse me.

SUNNY: I'm not accusing you; I'm just asking.

JANA: And I said I don't know. What can they do to you, anyway?

SUNNY: They can throw me out, which is exactly what they want to do.

JANA: Sunny, if they want to throw you out, they can throw you out. They don't need an excuse.

(*Todd enters. Jana sees him.*)

JANA: I gotta go.

(*Jana exits.*)

TODD: Sunny.

(*She turns.*)

TODD: A letter from the director of the program.

(*He hands her a letter.*)

SUNNY: What is it?

TODD: The conditions of your continued enrollment.

• • •

Todd exits. Molly enters. She sits. She has been crying. Sunny knocks lightly on a half-open door.

SUNNY: Molly?

MOLLY: Hey! What's up?

SUNNY: Everything is just falling apart.

MOLLY: What?

SUNNY: I'm getting thrown out of school.

MOLLY: Oh, God.

SUNNY: I hate to walk into your room and just dump all this on you —

MOLLY: No, please. Tell me. What happened?

SUNNY: Somehow, they found out about the House of O, and Todd called me into the office, and basically said they thought I was a prostitute and that they want to kick me out of the program.

MOLLY: Can they?

SUNNY: Sure. Why not? They can do whatever they want.

MOLLY: What did you say?

SUNNY: I denied it. I mean, I'm not a prostitute. I don't take off my clothes. I don't have sex. I pretend, is what I do. I put on a show.

MOLLY: What do you mean you denied it?

SUNNY: Total denial. I said I had no idea what they were talking about.

MOLLY: What did they say?

SUNNY: They want me to sign a deposition.

MOLLY: So fine. You sign a deposition.

SUNNY: What I want to know is, how did they find out?

MOLLY: Did you tell anyone?

SUNNY: I only told one person, and she says she didn't tell anyone.

MOLLY: Well obviously she's lying.

SUNNY: Why would she tell anyone? It doesn't make any sense.

MOLLY: Well, if she's the only person you told —

SUNNY: I don't know, I mean . . . Why is this happening? Why do people attack me this way?

MOLLY: They're not attacking you, they're just . . .

SUNNY: What?

MOLLY: I don't know . . . God.

SUNNY: What's wrong? Have you been crying?

MOLLY: No.

    (She turns away.)

SUNNY: Your eyes are all red.

MOLLY: Don't worry about it.

SUNNY: What's wrong? Why won't you tell me?

MOLLY: Because I don't want to.

SUNNY: Why not?

MOLLY: Sunny — I just don't like talking about my problems as much as you do.

    (Pause.)

SUNNY: Do I talk about them too much?

MOLLY: No, you just like to talk about yours and I don't.

SUNNY: You've got to sometime.

MOLLY: Look — So what makes you think they're going to throw you out of school?

SUNNY: They gave me a list of demands. I have to sit out next semester; I have to get reevaluated; and then I have to reapply for admission next fall. I can't believe you won't tell me why you've been crying. You know you can tell me anything. I won't judge you. You know I think you're the smartest, most together, prettiest —

MOLLY: Please don't start that, Sunny. I'm not in the mood.

SUNNY: Start what?

MOLLY: Your sensitive, in control, get-their-confidence speech. It sounds like you're trying to talk a jumper off a ledge.

SUNNY: I mean it.

MOLLY: I know you do, but it still sounds false. You're just trying to get me to talk.

SUNNY: I want you to tell me what's bothering you.

MOLLY: OK. I'll tell you what's bothering me. Did you know that being a prostitute was grounds for being kicked out of a clinical psychology program?

SUNNY: I'm not a prostitute.

MOLLY: That's not what I asked you. I said, did you know —

SUNNY: Yes, I knew, that's why I didn't tell anyone.

MOLLY: Yes, you did tell someone; you told one person.

SUNNY: I trusted her. She betrayed me.

MOLLY: Sunny. You shouldn't have told anyone. You should have quit that job the minute you got accepted into a clinical psychology program. I mean, realistically, do you really think anyone is going to listen to your explanation of why being a dominatrix is not the same thing as being a prostitute? It's not that people don't understand the special circumstances of your job; they understand. Yes, it's legal and licensed; no, you don't take off your clothes; and no, you don't have sex. They understand all that. They also understand that you tie men up and they get off and then you get paid. Boom. You're a prostitute. They understand, and to them, you are a prostitute. None of which matters, because YOU TOLD SOME-ONE! You knew this could get you thrown out of school, and A, you did not quit, and B, you told someone. Why?! What on earth were you thinking?

SUNNY: Yes, it's all my fault. Jennifer hates me because I am a prostitute. Todd Cox is a jerk because I am a prostitute —

MOLLY: OK. OK. Let's move on. Todd Cox. He's an arrogant, self-centered, patronizing, pompous idiot. Have we established that?

SUNNY: Yes.

MOLLY: So, we have this information at our disposal, what do we do with it? Do we keep him happy because he holds our life in his hands? No, we show up late to his class every week.

SUNNY: It wasn't class! It was advisement and it was at 8:30 in the morning.

MOLLY: So?

SUNNY: I can't get up at 8:30 every Monday — No, 6:30, 'cause that's when I have to get up to make it to his office by 8:30.

MOLLY: Of course you can get up at 6:30. You just do it. Don't go into therapy over it. Just do it. You made a choice. You made a choice to be late, and you made an enemy of one of your faculty members.

SUNNY: So I was late a few times.

MOLLY: Now tell me this. Who is smarter, you or Todd Cox?

SUNNY: Me.

MOLLY: And Sunny, if there is one thing you cannot do, even with all your

amazing accomplishments, you cannot hide what you think about someone. You absolutely cannot. He knows you think you're smarter than he
is. I guarantee you he knows that. And I can also guarantee you that he
does not agree.

SUNNY: That's not my fault.

MOLLY: No, but it is your problem. As for Jennifer, from all accounts, she is
a cold heartless bitch and a devious bureaucratic infighter. Why did you
put so much effort into being her friend?

SUNNY: I was just trying to be nice.

MOLLY: Nice?

SUNNY: I didn't want her to hate me.

MOLLY: What you wanted to do was break her. You wanted your kindness and
charm to conquer her coldness and bitchiness, but it is a truth universally acknowledged that coldness and bitchiness are stronger than kindness and charm. Why can't you stand to have someone dislike you?

SUNNY: So then, what? It's wrong to try to make friends?

MOLLY: Sunny! You can't be friends with everyone! There are people who are
just inimical to each other. Jennifer is a bitch. You should just walk up
to her and say, "Jennifer, you're a bitch, and if you don't stop fucking with
me, I will destroy you." That she will understand. You try to make nice
with her, and she will get very confused and frightened, and then she'll
destroy you. You let people like that walk all over you. I've seen it a hundred times. You just keep trying. What is the point of pursuing friendship with someone you don't like? But that's beside the point. What this
all really boils down to is, you didn't get accepted at any of the Ivy League
schools you were hoping to get into, and you've been miserable where
you are, and I'm sure everyone there can tell, whether you mean for them
to or not. Maybe it's all for the best. Maybe you're subconsciously trying
to get yourself thrown out of a situation that is making you unhappy.

SUNNY: I am not trying to get thrown out of school.

MOLLY: Then I don't know what to say. You have bad luck. But I will say this,
if you go around telling everyone your problems, people will start thinking of you as a person with problems.

SUNNY: You mean that's what you think.

MOLLY: It doesn't matter what I think. I'm just a friend. I don't have any power
over your life. Sit out next semester, let them evaluate you, and hope for
the best.

SUNNY: I wish you would tell me what's got you so upset tonight.

MOLLY: Well, I'm not gonna, you know why? Because I've got it under control. I'm OK. I know what you want me to do. You want me to tell you all my problems so you can say everything will be all right and none of it's my fault, and then you can tell me all your problems, so I will say everything will be all right and none of it's your fault. You want me to say you're not a loser. That this all a run of bad luck, a strange coincidence, and despite striking similarities to events in the past, it is in no way predictive of events in the future. Well, Sunny, I just can't do that. Maybe you are a loser, maybe it is your fault, and there's a good chance nothing will be all right.

(Pause.)

SUNNY: I guess you must be right. I must do something to make people attack me. 'Cause now you're doing it.

(Light change as Molly steps forward.)

MOLLY: All right. From here on out, things get slightly more complicated, so let me, um, just let me put some stuff on the table for the sake of clarity. First, I was feeling a certain level of frustration at what was happening to Sunny, as you might well imagine. And second . . . um . . . OK. Second, I had my own shit to deal with. I don't mean to be crude, but . . . things were happening in my life, too, things I'm not particularly proud of, so I don't necessarily want to go into the details of that whole . . . *(She gestures, searching for the word.)* That's a whole other morass, so let's just stick to the morass at hand. Although, I suppose, they are related . . . But, um, you know, you reach a point at which all attempts at further clarification merely have the opposite effect. So, um . . .

(Molly returns to where she was before. The phone rings. Pause. Sunny answers it.)

SUNNY: Hello?

(Desiree appears.)

DESIREE: Hey, it's me.

SUNNY: Desiree?

DESIREE: Yeah, but don't call me that.

SUNNY: How are you? I've been so worried.

DESIREE: I'm fine. I'm great. But call me by my real name.

SUNNY: Carmen?

DESIREE: No, my real real name. Annie.

SUNNY: Annie. That's right. You told me that was your name. Am I on speaker phone?

DESIREE: Yeah.

SUNNY: Look, Annie, I'm in the middle of something right now —

DESIREE: I just wanted to know, do you want some CDs?

SUNNY: CDs?

DESIREE: Yeah, I'm giving away a bunch of CDs. I'm getting rid of all this shit that's cluttering up my life.

SUNNY: Honey, why are you giving away your music?

DESIREE: God, I don't know, I'm sick of it all, you know?

SUNNY: Well, where are you? Do you want me to come by?

DESIREE: No, I didn't mean right now. Just come by sometime and tell Gar I said you could take as many CDs as you want.

SUNNY: Are you at Gar's? I thought you weren't seeing him anymore.

DESIREE: Well, you know . . .

SUNNY: It's just that, sometimes Gar is a little dangerous, don't you think?

DESIREE: *(Suddenly crying.)* Sunny? You're the only one who's ever been nice to me. I really, really . . . I just want to say thank you, you know?

SUNNY: Hey, we're friends, right? Where are you? Tell me where you are, I'll come by and look through the CDs.

DESIREE: The CDs are at Gar's.

SUNNY: Where are you?

DESIREE: Hey, look, you're a really good person, Sunny, and I love you, OK? Just remember that.

(Desiree produces a small handgun.)

SUNNY: Desiree? Annie, I mean, what are you doing? How do you feel? You're doing good now, aren't you? You're OK?

DESIREE: Yeah, I'm fine. Just don't hang up, OK?

SUNNY: No, I won't hang up. What are you doing? Annie?

(Desiree tries to muffle her sobs.)

SUNNY: Are you crying? Why don't we have lunch today? Tell me where you are and we can pick a place near you.

DESIREE: I have to go to the bathroom. Don't hang up!

(Desiree exits.)

SUNNY: What? I can't hear you! Annie! *(Pause.)* Annie, say something! Where are you? Desiree?! Shit. Answer me right now! What are you doing? Don't do anything stupid, Annie! *(There is a deafening gunshot.)* Oh, God.

MOLLY: What is it?

• • •

Sunny exits. Michael and Karen enter.

MICHAEL: What happened?

MOLLY: She shot herself! We went to her apartment! I saw the body. She left the front door unlocked. She was in the bathroom.

MICHAEL: Oh, my God.

KAREN: Look, you have got to get out of that apartment. You can't live like this.

MOLLY: It's not my life. It's her life.

KAREN: It is your life! You are living your life there! It is where you live. You live with her. You share your life with her.

MICHAEL: Stay here for a few weeks. You can look for another place.

KAREN: You shouldn't be way out in Brooklyn, anyway.

MOLLY: I can't afford Manhattan.

KAREN: Well Queens, then! Staten Island. Newark. Whatever. Just get out of there.

MOLLY: Oh God! I can't.

KAREN: Yes you can. Why can't you?

MOLLY: She needs my part of the rent.

KAREN: The rent is the lessee's problem, not yours.

MOLLY: She's not my landlord! She's my friend!

MICHAEL: Molly, if you want to move out, just move out.

(Molly shakes her head no.)

MICHAEL: Why not?

MOLLY: I'm worried about her.

MICHAEL: More than usual?

(Molly nods.)

MICHAEL: Why?

MOLLY: She's been dropping hints. Little things about being sick of everything, wishing it would all end, wishing she could end it all.

KAREN: Christ.

MICHAEL: You think she's going to kill herself?

MOLLY: I don't know.

KAREN: It's not your problem.

MOLLY: What does that mean?

KAREN: If she's suicidal, you're not gonna stop her. You can't watch her every minute of every day.

MOLLY: No, but I can not abandon her.

KAREN: She's your roommate! Not your child!

MICHAEL: Karen, please, you're not helping.

KAREN: What would help? What possible remedy is there to this situation?

MOLLY: And if I were in trouble?

KAREN: You wouldn't be in this trouble.

MOLLY: But if I were, you'd be like, "So long! My friends don't get in trouble, so if you're in trouble, you must not be my friend."

KAREN: No, Molly, that's not what I'm saying. What I'm saying is it seems to me like this girl is in constant trouble. Her life is a perpetual crisis. You cannot help people like that. As soon as you help them out of one crisis they create another, and another. And you spend all your time rescuing them. When was the last time you studied for the bar exam? She's dragging you into her life. You're a wreck. Look at your hair.

MOLLY: My hair?

MICHAEL: Karen, stop it. Molly, I agree with Karen. I don't think this situation is good for you. And think of it this way. You've been living with this girl for how many months? How much have you helped her? From what you say, things have gone from bad to worse since you got there. Maybe you'd be doing her a favor by leaving. You certainly won't be harming her.

MOLLY: You think it's my fault? That I'm causing her problems?

MICHAEL: No, no. I didn't — I'm just saying if you can't help I'd say the same thing if you were spending all your time with someone who just played video games all day, or a drug addict, or, I don't know, some loser musician.

KAREN: Just tell me this. When did this girl kill herself?

MOLLY: Last week.

KAREN: Why did you wait a week to come tell us about it?

MOLLY: Because I'm worried about Sunny.

KAREN: No. You're not worried about Sunny. You're worried about yourself. You came here to get an objective opinion because you no longer have any objectivity.

MOLLY: I have objectivity.

KAREN: Did you ever consider that she's talking suicide as a way of keeping you around? Of prolonging the crisis?

MICHAEL: If you're asking us whether or not we'll think you're a bad person if you move out of Sunny's apartment, then the answer is no.

KAREN: Molly, you are not a bad person. You said yourself that you thought she was bringing it all on herself.

MOLLY: I never said that.

KAREN: Have you *met* any of the people at this school who are supposedly so evil? How do you know she's not making it all up?

MOLLY: She's not making it up.

KAREN: How do you know that?

MOLLY: Look, I'm not gonna sit here and defend Sunny's sanity to two people who won't even go out to goddamned Brooklyn to have dinner with her, OK?

(Pause.)

KAREN: So, why did you come here tonight? If you don't want our advice?

(Pause. Molly sighs.)

MOLLY: Because I need a place to stay for a few weeks.

KAREN: I'll get some sheets. We can make up the sofa.

(Karen exits.)

MOLLY: I'm sorry about all of this.

MICHAEL: Don't apologize.

MOLLY: I just . . .

(She goes to put her arms around Michael. He immediately pulls away.)

MICHAEL: I think Karen is starting to suspect.

(She steps away from him.)

• • •

Michael and Molly exit. Sunny enters and throws a huge pile of papers up into the air, which drift to the floor. Bill enters, in full slave gear, including a hood that leaves only his mouth free. Sunny sits down and opens her psychology text book.

SUNNY: Bill?

BILL: Yes, ma'am?

SUNNY: Why did you suddenly start coming to me?

(Slight pause.)

BILL: My mistress doesn't understand me.

SUNNY: How do you mean?

BILL: Well . . . When Mistress Dominique hurts me, it's because she just likes to hurt me. When you hurt me, I know it's because you love me.

SUNNY: Thank you. That means a lot to me. *(The intercom buzzes. Sunny goes to it.)* Yes?

MOLLY: *(On intercom.)* I'm looking for Mistress Serena?

SUNNY: Come on up. *(She buzzes the door.)* Hey, Bill, it's time to get in the trunk.

BILL: Yes, ma'am.

(She unclamps his wrists and opens the trunk. Bill climbs in. She shuts the lid. Molly enters.)

MOLLY: Hey.

SUNNY: Hey.

MOLLY: Whatcha doin'?

SUNNY: Organizing my files.

MOLLY: At work?

SUNNY: Well, I have a client in the trunk. It's downtime.

MOLLY: Ah.

SUNNY: I'm gonna quit. As soon as I get a little money together.

MOLLY: No, it's —

SUNNY: I am. I should have quit a long time ago. I've been thinking about what you said, and I think you're right about everything. I've been loading you with my troubles, and that's not fair.

MOLLY: I shouldn't have ranted at you like that —

SUNNY: You were right. I haven't been a good friend to you. But I'm working on it. I'll get better.

MOLLY: Sunny, the other day, what did you mean when you said you wished it would all end?

SUNNY: Wished what would all end?

MOLLY: After Desiree's funeral. You said how you wished it would all end, and then the other night you said you might end it all.

SUNNY: School.

MOLLY: Just school?

SUNNY: I wish I could just quit. But I can't.

MOLLY: That's all?

SUNNY: You think I'm going to kill myself?

MOLLY: No, it's just . . . I know you've been depressed.

SUNNY: And people are twenty-eight percent more likely to kill themselves within a year after someone they know kills themself.

MOLLY: Yeah.

SUNNY: I'm not going to kill myself.

MOLLY: I worry about you.

SUNNY: I know. Thanks. But you don't have to. I'm OK.

MOLLY: Good.

SUNNY: I've been taking Buspar.

(Molly looks questioningly at her.)

SUNNY: Sort of like Prozac with half the calories. Want one? Some good shit.

MOLLY: Maybe later.

SUNNY: I need a favor.

MOLLY: What?

SUNNY: I need you to be my mediation advocate. I'm suing my school.

MOLLY: Oh, Sunny. Don't.

SUNNY: I have to.

MOLLY: No you don't.

SUNNY: Yes, I do.

MOLLY: You don't! What are you going to accomplish except make more enemies and waste a lot of money?

SUNNY: Just listen to my plan.

MOLLY: No, I can't help you.

SUNNY: It's not that much work.

MOLLY: Sunny, Sunny, I'm saying no. I want you to hear me and respect that. I'm saying No. Look, here's the thing. You know I love you. You're one of my closest friends, *the* closest. But I don't think I'm doing you any good living with you. It's bringing out a side of me that I don't like.

SUNNY: What side?

MOLLY: You know.

SUNNY: No, what?

MOLLY: Bossy, mean, scolding.

SUNNY: I don't mind.

MOLLY: I do.

SUNNY: No, it's good for me. I like having you here.

MOLLY: Even when I bitch at you?

SUNNY: That's the way you are.

MOLLY: No, that's not the way I am! I'm not a bitch. You make me a bitch.

SUNNY: I make you a bitch?

MOLLY: No, you don't make me a bitch. But around you sometimes I get bitchy. It's a side of myself that I don't like.

SUNNY: Well, I'll stop.

MOLLY: Stop what?

SUNNY: Doing whatever it is that makes you . . . whatever.

MOLLY: It's not that simple.

SUNNY: What do you want me to do? You want me to clean up the papers? You want me to stop talking about school?

MOLLY: Sunny, no, just, forget about it. It's not something you can fix.

SUNNY: I can try. Just tell me what I do.

MOLLY: It's not something you do, it's who you are.

(Pause.)

SUNNY: Who am I?

MOLLY: Look, forget I even brought it up. It doesn't matter and I'm not expressing myself well. All I'm saying is, I'm going to live with Michael and

Karen while I look for a new apartment, so I can't help you with your lawsuit or whatever it is. So good luck and . . .

SUNNY: Why not?

MOLLY: Because I just can't.

SUNNY: You're too busy?

MOLLY: I can't because I don't want to.

(Sunny nods.)

MOLLY: I don't think it would be in the best interest of our friendship for me to get involved in anything like, um . . . Look, my stuff is in the stairwell. This neighborhood is not . . .

(Molly exits.)

SUNNY: What do you mean, it's "who I am"?

MOLLY: *(Off.)* Nothing.

SUNNY: You mean something.

MOLLY: *(Off.)* Just let it drop.

SUNNY: I think it might be important.

MOLLY: *(Off.)* Important how?

SUNNY: I seem to be provoking some sort of negative response in you, and you say it's not my behavior but my essential being.

(Molly enters with three pieces of luggage.)

MOLLY: That is not what I said.

SUNNY: You're leaving now?!

MOLLY: Yeah.

SUNNY: You can't just drop this on me and then walk out!

MOLLY: I don't mean to be abrupt, but I don't feel like this is the best time to go into it. Perhaps at a later date —

SUNNY: Stop it! Why won't you tell me?

MOLLY: Don't worry about it! It's not your problem. It's my problem.

SUNNY: It is my problem. Obviously I have a big problem.

MOLLY: Well, you know what? Just say, "Fuck you, Molly. Get out of my life."

SUNNY: I don't want you to get out of my life.

MOLLY: Right. Well, sorry. I'd like to be able to help you there, but I just can't.

SUNNY: You're supposed to be my friend.

MOLLY: Well, I'm not, OK? I haven't been your friend in a long time. Are you happy? That's what I didn't want to tell you. I no longer enjoy your company. I'm leaving. It's over. The End.

SUNNY: You just said you'll always love me.

MOLLY: I lied.

SUNNY: I don't believe you.

MOLLY: *(Dumbfounded.)* You don't believe me? *(She shrugs.)* OK.
   (Molly takes the key to Sunny's apartment out of her bag and holds it out. Sunny refuses to take it. Molly puts it on the table then exits with two of her bags. Sunny picks up the remaining suitcase and carries it offstage and re-enters. Molly re-enters.)
   Where's my suitcase?

SUNNY: You're not leaving 'til you tell me what's going on.

MOLLY: Sunny, give me my suitcase.

SUNNY: No.

   (Molly starts looking for the suitcase, exits, then returns.)

MOLLY: Sunny. Where is it?

SUNNY: Why don't you like me?

MOLLY: Give me my stuff!

SUNNY: Why don't you like me?

MOLLY: Give me my stuff!

SUNNY: Why don't you like me?

MOLLY: I don't have to tell you! What are you going to do, force me to be friends with you? It won't work.

SUNNY: I need to know! Why does this happen to me?

MOLLY: Stop it! Why —? It's like picking at a scab. You are forcing me to say things that will be hurtful.

SUNNY: You're the one who said you didn't like me. That's what you're saying.

MOLLY: OK. Fine. That's what I'm saying. I don't like you. So. What do you say back?

SUNNY: Why not?

MOLLY: NO! Say, "Well, I hate you, you fucking bitch, eat shit and die!" *(Pause.)* Say it.

SUNNY: I hate you, you fucking bitch, eat shit and die.

MOLLY: There.

SUNNY: And that is supposed to make us friends again?

MOLLY: No.

SUNNY: Then what's the point?

MOLLY: Give me my suitcase.

SUNNY: No.

MOLLY: I'm leaving, Sunny, I need my suitcase.

SUNNY: OK, OK, you want me to be more aggressive. You want me to be a hard-ass bitch. Fine. I'm not giving you your suitcase — I'm not letting you go.

MOLLY: You're not letting me go?

SUNNY: No. You want me to be a hard-ass, I can be a hard-ass.

MOLLY: I'll come get my suitcase later.

(Molly picks up her other bag and moves toward the door. Sunny blocks the way.)

MOLLY: This is what you did to Jennifer!

SUNNY: Bullshit! Jennifer was a classmate who was causing me problems at school. I was just trying to get her off my back. You're my best friend for the last ten years. I'm trying to — This my life! You want me to not care?

MOLLY: The more you beg, the more I —

(Molly tries to force her way past Sunny. Sunny pushes her back. Molly tries to shove her aside, but Sunny grabs her bag and pulls her back. They struggle for the bag. Molly grabs papers from the floor.)

MOLLY: I will destroy all of your work.

(Sunny gently returns Molly's bag.)

SUNNY: Please just tell me! What am I doing?! Why does everybody hate me?! What am I supposed to do?!

MOLLY: I don't know. Just please stop asking, OK?

(Molly moves to go out the door. Sunny moves to block her exit, standing defiantly in front of the door.)

MOLLY: You know, if I want to get through that door, I'm gonna get through that door. *(Pause. Molly approaches the door and stands in front of Sunny.)* I'm stronger than you are.

SUNNY: No, you're not.

(Molly slowly but with great force shoves Sunny out of the way and opens the door. Sunny slips on the papers and falls.)

SUNNY: I hate you, you fucking bitch. Eat shit and die.

(Molly turns to look at Sunny.)

MOLLY: Too late.

(Before Molly can exit, Gar enters. He carries CDs in plastic grocery bags.)

GAR: Hey.

SUNNY: Gar.

GAR: Desiree wanted you to have these.

(He throws the bags of CDs down next to Sunny.)

SUNNY: What is it?

(He squats and tries to untie the knots in the plastic bags, but they won't come undone. He becomes frustrated.)

GAR: Rrrr!

(He takes a huge bowie knife out from his boot and cuts one of them open. CDs spill out.)

GAR: CDs.

SUNNY: Oh. Thanks.

GAR: You know, you bitches really fucked her up.

SUNNY: You hurt her more than anyone.

GAR: I loved her more than anyone.

SUNNY: If you loved her so much, why did you hurt her?

GAR: I never meant to hurt her. I wanted to help her.

(Gar exits. Molly looks to Sunny, then away, and exits. A polite knocking comes from the trunk.)

• • •

Sunny exits. Molly and Karen enter.

MOLLY: And then she said, "Why does everybody hate me? What am I supposed to do?"

KAREN: You did the right thing.

MOLLY: And I just pushed her aside and walked out the door.

KAREN: You did the right thing.

MOLLY: Karen, I was so mean to her! I was so vicious! But she just kept — pushing it.

KAREN: She was manipulating you. It's passive aggressive self-martyrdom.

MOLLY: All she wanted was help and I shoved her out of my way.

KAREN: You did what you had to do.

MOLLY: What if I was wrong? You can't take something like that back.

KAREN: Something like what?

MOLLY: Denial. Desertion. Betrayal.

KAREN: Oh, God. I can't do this.

MOLLY: Do what?

KAREN: Shit. Fuck. All right. I'm just going to ask you.

MOLLY: Ask me what?

KAREN: Have you ever slept with Michael?

(Molly is stunned for a moment.)

MOLLY: No.

KAREN: Oh, God. That is such a relief. Because now that I know you're a liar, I can hate you without feeling guilty. I think you should get out of my house now.

(Molly starts to talk.)

KAREN: Don't start talking! I don't want to hear your side of the story. I don't want to know what's going on inside of your head. The only side of any

story that interests me right now is my side of my story. No. Actually, that's not true. You know whose story I'd like to hear right now? Sunny's. To think I *believed* you all those times you sat here and . . . I mean, is this how you operate? You move into somebody's house and find ways to destroy their life?

MOLLY: He said it was over between you.

KAREN: I said get out. *(Hysterical rage.)* GET OUT!

(Molly exits.)

• • •

Karen exits. Todd and Barbara Stafford enter, then Sunny and Sunny's Advocate.

TODD: Sunny, this really isn't necessary.

ADVOCATE: Nonetheless, Ms. Goldfarb would like to proceed.

TODD: Why? What do you think you're going to accomplish?

ADVOCATE: Ms. Goldfarb's goals are stated clearly in the brief.

TODD: Yes, well, I'll be sure to read this as soon as I get a chance.

ADVOCATE: Thank you. Do you have any other questions?

TODD: How are you going to afford a lawsuit?

ADVOCATE: One of the things you'll find in the brief, Dr. Cox, should you find the time to read it, is that it is Borough University's standing procedure to attempt to resolve all student complaints of faculty misconduct with binding arbitration. It substantially limits the expense of such disputes.

TODD: And what exactly is the alleged faculty misconduct?

ADVOCATE: Again, that is all outlined in the brief, if you care to glance through it —

TODD: *(Cutting him off.)* Sunny, why are making this so difficult? Why didn't you just come to me?

BARBARA STAFFORD: I think what Todd is asking, Sunny, is why have you taken such an adversarial stance? I've had the feeling from the beginning that you've been trying to wage an all-out war against the program. And this isn't about prostitution, or Jennifer. We all feel that you have a variety of issues to work through before you can successfully complete the program.

ADVOCATE: I think I should point out here, that the substance of Ms. Goldfarb's complaint has nothing to do with the unsubstantiated charges of prostitution, or the unresolved complaints filed by her classmate. The action being filed here is in reference to the violation of Ms. Goldfarb's civil rights.

TODD: Civil rights? Exactly how were her civil rights violated?

ADVOCATE: In the Americans with Disabilities Act of 1992, it was made a violation of federal law to deny equal access to public or private institutions of learning to Americans with disabilities, and the definition of disability was in 1995 expanded to include clinical depression, with which Ms. Goldfarb was diagnosed by a psychologist recommended by yourself, Dr. Cox. And it seems odd that the faculty of a program in clinical psychology could be so insensitive to the needs of one of their own students with this disability.

(Pause.)

BARBARA STAFFORD: What do you want, Sunny?

ADVOCATE: Miss Goldfarb is asking for very little, considering the circumstances. She wants to be reinstated in the program, her record expunged of academic probation, any complaints brought by fellow students removed from her file, and she would like an apology.

(Pause.)

BARBARA STAFFORD: I'm sure we can work something out.

TODD: Aren't you going to say anything, Sunny?

(Pause. She considers.)

SUNNY: No.

• • •

Todd, Barbara Stafford, Sunny, and the Advocate exit.

MOLLY: I moved out that weekend and went to stay with my brother in Hartford. I haven't heard from Sunny since. But when I turned on my computer for the first time after unpacking, I found all of Sunny's school papers, in a little folder she put on my hard drive when she was thinking Todd might break into the apartment and erase all her work. We were a little paranoid, I know, but at the time it seemed plausible.

(Sunny enters with a Slave. She puts him into a straitjacket and pajama bottoms. She puts on a white doctor's coat.)

MOLLY: So I started looking through them, and she had recommendations from her old professors, from every place she went to school or interned. And there was one from this guy who ran the violent ward at a psychiatric hospital-slash-prison. Where, apparently, Sunny was an intern, and where they had her giving routine psychiatric evaluations to what the man writing the recommendation called, and I quote, "Profound Psychotics." This is what he wrote about Sunny: *(She reads from a piece of paper.)* "Sunny

Goldfarb surpassed many previous interns when she showed up for the second day. The violent ward is at best bleak, and can at times be literally life-threatening. There are patients on the ward who have for years known nothing but the grim alternatives of psychotic hysteria and drug-induced torpor. Given the dispiriting job of administering batteries of evaluations to patients who are often incapable of responding in even an instinctual way, Ms. Goldfarb showed a remarkable perseverance with even the most dissociative of schizophrenics. The patience and compassion with which she struggled to establish contact with a mind so distant, with a rationale so foreign, was inspiring. Never have I met a psychiatric professional more determined to find some tangential point between herself and the mind of a profound psychotic, no matter how askew from the geometry of her own perception." *(Sunny sits with the Slave, who is now the Profound Psychotic.)* So anyway, I came back to L.A., which I hate, and a year went by, and the first time I tried to call her, the number was disconnected, and I have no idea where she is. I'm afraid to call her school. I know I treated her like shit.

(Molly's therapist enters.)

MOLLY: And I think, maybe I should just let her go. Just forget about her.

THERAPIST: Is that what you want?

MOLLY: I don't know. She was my best friend.

SUNNY: Hey, Steve. You ready to take some tests today?

PROFOUND PSYCHOTIC: It's there. It's there.

SUNNY: Is it there? What's there?

THERAPIST: Are you afraid of her?

MOLLY: No, I'm afraid of me, of what I'll do to her. Maybe it's better for her that I keep away.

THERAPIST: How would you hurt her?

MOLLY: Just trying to make her more like me.

SUNNY: What's your name?

THERAPIST: Do you miss her?

MOLLY: I think about her. Often.

SUNNY: Who are you?

(She marks something on a chart.)

MOLLY: I talk to her in my head. Give her advice. Ask advice. I wouldn't say I miss her. She's with me all the time. She's up here. She's in my head.

SUNNY: Do you know who I am?

MOLLY: But should I try to find her? Can I help her? Should I apologize?

THERAPIST: Would she forgive you?

MOLLY: Oh, yes, she would forgive me. She already has.

SUNNY: Who am I?

THERAPIST: And how do you feel about that?

MOLLY: Guilty. Who can live under the weight of all that forgiveness? All that love coming at you, *relentlessly.*

PROFOUND PSYCHOTIC: It's there. It's right there.

MOLLY: What should I do?

SUNNY: Who am I? Hey, look here. Who am I?

MOLLY: Doctor, what should I do?

THERAPIST: I'm afraid our time is up.

(Blackout.)

END OF PLAY

COPYRIGHT AND CONTACT INFORMATION

36 Views by Naomi Iizuka. © 2001 by Naomi Iizuka. Reprinted by permission of The Overlook Press. All performance rights are controlled by Morgan Jenness, Helen Merrill, Inc., 295 Layfayette Street, Suite 915, New York, NY 10012.

Be Aggressive by Annie Weisman. © 2001 by Annie Weisman. Reprinted by permission of the author. All inquiries should be addressed to John Buzzetti, The Gersh Agency, 130 West 42nd Street, New York, NY 10036.

Chagrin Falls by Mia McCullough. © 2001 by Mia McCullough. Reprinted by permission of the author. All inquiries should be addressed to Stage Left Theatre, 3408 N. Sheffield Avenue, Chicago, IL 60657.

Diva by Howard M. Gould. © 2001 Howard M. Gould. Reprinted by permission of Samuel French, Inc. All inquiries should be addressed to Linda Kirland, Samuel French, 45 West 25th Street, New York, NY 10010.

Music from a Sparking Planet by Douglas Carter Beane. © 2001 by Douglas Carter Beane. Caution: *Music from a Sparking Planet*, being duly copyrighted is subject to a royalty. All performance rights are controlled by Beth Blickers c/o The Helen Merrill Agency. No professional or nonprofessional performance of the play may be given without obtaining in advance the written permission of Beth Blickers, c/o The Helen Merrill Agency, and paying the requisite fee. Inquiries concerning all rights should be addressed to Beth Blickers, c/o Helen Merrill Agency, 295 Lafayette Street, Suite 915, New York, NY 10012; (212) 226-5015.

Psych by Evan Smith. Copyright © 2001 by Evan Smith. Caution: *Psych,* being duly copyrighted, is subject to a royalty. All performance rights are controlled by Sarah Jane Leigh, c/o ICM. No professional or nonprofessional performance of the play may be given without obtaining in advance the written permission of Sarah Jane Leigh, c/o ICM, and paying the requisite fee. Inquiries concerning all rights should be addressed to Sarah Jane Leigh, c/o ICM, 40 West 57th Street, New York, NY 10019.